Blackface Nation

Blackface Nation

Race, Reform, and Identity
in American Popular Music, 1812–1925

BRIAN ROBERTS

The University of Chicago Press
Chicago and London

The University of Chicago Press, Chicago 60637
The University of Chicago Press, Ltd., London
© 2017 by The University of Chicago
Published 2017

26 25 24 23 22 21 20 19 18 17   1 2 3 4 5

ISBN-13: 978-0-226-45150-3 (cloth)
ISBN-13: 978-0-226-45164-0 (paper)
ISBN-13: 978-0-226-45178-7 (e-book)
DOI: 10.7208/chicago/9780226451787.001.0001

Library of Congress Cataloging-in-Publication Data

Names: Roberts, Brian, 1957– author.
Title: Blackface nation : race, reform, and identity in American popular music, 1812–1925 / Brian Roberts.
Description: Chicago : The University of Chicago Press, 2017. | Includes bibliographical references and index.
Identifiers: LCCN 2016041541 | ISBN 9780226451503 (cloth : alk. paper) | ISBN 9780226451640 (pbk. : alk. paper) | ISBN 9780226451787 (e-book)
Subjects: LCSH: African Americans—Music—History and criticism. | Popular music—United States—19th century—History and criticism. | Popular music—United States—20th century—History and criticism. | Minstrel music—United States—History and criticism. | Music and race—United States—History.
Classification: LCC ML3479.R63 2017 | DDC 781.64089/96073—dc23 LC record available at https://lccn.loc.gov/2016041541

To Barbara
From northern peaks to prairie wastelands to academic forests prime-evil,
my partner on the trail of life.

Contents

Acknowledgments

Someone once told me that writing a second book would be easier than writing a first. That may be true for most people. Indeed, it seems many academics can get started on their research sometime midmorning, wrap up "data" collection by noon, and whip out the book in time for a quiet aperitif with friends. It has never worked this way for me.

This project started a long time ago, so long ago that many of the people I have to thank are retired. By retired, I mean dead. Or maybe they are living out in the woods someplace. I'm pretty sure they will not remember me. First there is the staff from the American Antiquarian Society—the staff, that is, from way back in 1999. The AAS got me started on this monster by granting me a yearlong residency, a fellowship supported by the National Endowment for the Humanities and the Charlotte Newcombe Foundation. While I was at the AAS, I benefited enormously from research suggestions and source-finding aid from Gigi Barnhill, Joanne Chaison, Tom Knoles, Marie Lamoureux, Sara Hagenbuch, and Laura Wasowicz. The legendary Caroline Sloat kept me on track and helped me make the transition from doing research on music to writing history. More recently at the AAS, Jacklyn Penny and Lauren Hewes provided much-needed assistance with illustrations.

I also need to thank the staff at the Lynn [Massachusetts] Historical Society; Wadleigh Library in Milford, New Hampshire; the Milford Historical Society; the G. W. Blunt Library at Mystic Seaport Museum; the Peabody Essex Museum in Salem, Massachusetts; the Haverhill [Massachusetts] Public Library Special Collections; the New Hampshire State Archives; and the New Hampshire Historical Society.

I benefited from several grants from my home institutions. Back when this research was a pile of notes, California State University–Sacramento gave me a couple semesters of reduced course load. They probably expected this book to be the result of the largesse, about fifteen years ago. More recently, but still back when few people carried phones, the University of Northern Iowa granted me a Summer Research Fellowship and a Professional Development Assignment, a summer of supported research, and a one-semester leave to write. I researched and wrote all I could but was still ten years away from getting it done. Over the years, I had a few graduate assistants at UNI who went out and retrieved sources: Patrick Parker, Tasha Fristo, Ray Werner, and Mindy Stump. My undergraduates were helpful in ways they probably never realized, for I tried out many of my craziest ideas on them.

Tim Mennel, my editor at the University of Chicago Press, has been all that a great editor can be, doling out equal parts comfort, hectoring threats, praise, whip-crackings, and pep talks. He guided this book through some stormy seas and helped me identify all the leaky places for patchwork and re-timbering. I also need to thank the press's excellent readers for giving so much of their time to the manuscript. All were indispensable in forcing me to clarify my thinking and hone my arguments. As with all readers' reports, I have come to appreciate them more as I look back on the experience of revisions. Finally, Marianne Tatom's copyediting helped me avoid a numberless array of wording issues and punctuation pitfalls. Any remaining errors are mine.

In the end, I have to say that writing this book was a pretty solitary experience. I needed two dogs to get through it: my beautiful Bolivian mountain dog Geraldine (aka Jelly) and the crazy border collie Moss (aka Mossy Glen of Randolph). The vast majority of help came from one source and one colleague. This was of course Barbara Cutter. She listened to me talk about this book, ad nauseam, I'm sure; she dealt with my flights of fancy, my sense of discovery, my fevers of purchase when we found ourselves in the music sections of local historical society gift shops. She kept me going; and there were times when I really, really felt like giving up. She even listened to quite a bit of the music I refer to here, including not only reenactments of the Hutchinson Family Singers and the Virginia Minstrels but the weird stuff: sea chanteys, ballads about false young rakes, the Nightmares. I can truly say this book would have been impossible without her.

Introduction

It was the dawn of a new millennium, and according to their cherished ideal of progress, Americans should have been leaving the old modes of expression behind. Yet there it was: in the fall of 2001, several all-white fraternities at major universities decided the best way to celebrate Halloween was by holding blackface parties.

The idea was not original. According to a spokesperson with the Southern Poverty Law Center, such festivities were on the rise, having become "a more regular occurrence than we would like to think." At the end of October, the brothers held their parties: drinks were drunk, fun was had, and mistakes were made. They had a good time, so good they *had* to post the party pictures to a social media site. This was one of the evening's mistakes. Offended visitors to the site forwarded the images to officials at the students' schools and on to civil rights organizations. The parties became "the incidents."[1]

What did the pictures show? Most, it seems, featured young white males in blackface make-up, decked out in backwards ball caps, "afro" wigs, fake gold jewelry, and T-shirts emblazoned with Greek letters. A typical example centers on two jaunty junior-achiever types. Their darkened faces do little to mask their identities; they are clearly white, privileged, middle-class college kids. Yet they have adopted poses in self-conscious rebellion against this identity, making "gang-related" hand gestures while sneering good-naturedly at the camera. Their shirts, innocent enough at first glance, are marked with the letters of one of the school's black fraternities.

Two of the images stand out. The first focuses on a pair of students in front of a Confederate battle flag. One, outfitted in Ku Klux Klan regalia, is holding a rope; the other, wearing the party attire of backwards cap and black make-up, has the end of the rope around his neck, tied in a hangman's noose. The second features a student dressed as a policeman—without black make-up—standing above one of his brothers in blackface. The "black" student is on his knees, cringing beside a bucket of cotton; the "cop" is holding a pistol, aiming it directly at the kneeling student's head.[2]

For a short time the schools became sites for a conversation about diversity. Administrators had several students hauled before investigative boards. Student associations, alumni groups, and concerned citizens all expressed outrage at the images. One reporter explained the controversy with reference to history. Citing the fact that the schools were in the southern United States, he summed up the parties as a product of Confederate culture: down there, he declared knowingly, blackface was an "ugly tradition." Several of the involved students procured lawyers who made predictable arguments: certain aspects of the parties may have been offensive, but they were protected as free speech; the fraternity high jinks may have been vulgar and irresponsible, but they were almost patriotic in style, as American as illegal fireworks.

The conversation did not last long. For school officials this was clearly not a "teachable moment." Following a hurried investigation, administrators revoked the charters of two fraternities and placed a third on probation. They suspended some twenty-five students and quickly announced that it was time to move on, assuring observers that their campuses were not "bastions of hate." The involved students continued with their own explanations. They "did not intend to be racially offensive," stated one of their lawyers. They were guilty of bad taste, admitted a fraternity-chapter president; yet, he added, they were "in no way racist or against diversity." The whole thing, declared several, reflected an attempt to emulate their heroes in the world of popular music. They had blacked up not because they were racists but "because it's cool."[3]

This book is about American culture and popular song during the nineteenth century. It is also about these blackface incidents. The starting point here is the War of 1812, which was about the time Americans witnessed a transition from vernacular traditions of music to printed songs and marketed ballads. The ending point is somewhere in the first two decades of the twentieth century, about the time of the first commercial music recordings. Of course this is all long before the relatively recent blackface parties. Yet the point here is that this period witnessed the development of many of the ways of thinking evidenced in the incidents. The period established many of the general patterns of American popular music, from its style and content to the way it reflected and perhaps even generated categories of ethnicity and identity. The argument here is that an exploration of popular song during this time—along with, of course, the people who created songs, listened to them, and derived meaning from them—provides insight into many of the most powerful cultural ideals in American history.

Some of the expressions from the blackface incidents are more easily discerned than others. Yet all raise questions. Nearly lost in the controversy, for example, is the issue of the white students' identity as patriotic Americans. What are we to make of the idea raised by their lawyers—and probably not coincidentally in one of the best-known cultural statements on college shenanigans, the 1978 film *Animal House*—of an essential connection between fraternity high jinks and patriotic Americanism? Next there is the easily overlooked fact that the incidents were the products of college fraternities. What are the meanings of such communal traditions at the heart of what is supposedly a deeply capitalist culture? Here, after all, were groups of future risk-takers and competitors that, for a moment at least, were "brothers," bonded in patterns of inclusion and exclusion, brought into utopian harmony by alcohol, loud music, and a shared sense that they were offending every decent person in the world.

What stand out in the images are the examples of racial thought. For these white college kids, black people were helpless victims; they were also rebellious, unashamedly materialist, and definitely "cool." These images were clearly rooted in stereotypes and thus offensive; but were they, as the college officials implied, simply about "hate"? There were also versions of ethnic whiteness in the images. On one hand, the pictures portrayed whiteness as a kind of imperialist non-ethnicity, an identity with the power to colonize the perceived selfhood of any and all ethnic others. On the other, they implied whiteness as a banal blankness from which these students want only to escape. These young men were middle class and white. While this position conferred power and privilege, they also seemed hostile to their own imagined identities.[4]

The direct examples of whiteness in the photographs may be stranger still. Here were the images that produced much of the outrage: the Klan member performing a lynching and the white cop threatening to shoot an unarmed black man. What does it mean that the only explicit portrayal of white ethnicity in the images was that of the standard racist? Finally, there was the reference to popular music as a motive for the parties in the first place. This reference, too, raises a host of questions. Why, for example, do these sorts of expressions frequently come up in music? How can something that appeared to observers as a racist act against black people be explained as an homage to black heroes in the world of popular song?

There may be myriad ways to go about finding the answers to these questions. For the historian, however, the search requires going back to some of the roots of popular song in America, back to a period when music may have been the dominant form of media in the United States. An example can be seen in 1844, a year in which many of the nation's most heated political, social, and cultural issues would be communicated and debated in song. In the summer of this year, two of the most popular songs in the northeastern United States were twinned in conflict: they shared the same tune, yet their messages reflected tensions that would produce a civil war.

The first, perhaps not surprisingly, was a blackface song, "Old Dan Tucker." The number's writer was Dan Decatur Emmett, an Ohio-born musician and former circus clown who would become one of the greatest performers on the blackface stage. A couple of years earlier, Emmett founded the Virginia Minstrels, the legendary blackface group that made the song famous. Later, in 1859, he would be credited with writing the best-known blackface song of all time, "Dixie" or "Dixie's Land," the anthem of the Confederate lost cause. The South's signature tune, in other words, came from a Northerner. "Dixie" would have a relaxed tempo, a light melody, and a comforting image—to many white people—of an ex-slave singing a nostalgic ode to the old plantation.

"Old Dan Tucker" was something else. According to contemporary critics, the song represented the stylistic peak of early blackface. Musically it was catchy, a blend of plucked banjo, fiddle scratching out an Irish-inflected jig, and a tambourine-and-bones–driven rhythm that grew stronger and more irresistible as the tune went on. The lyrics—timed so every consonant fell on a beat—contained many of the standards of minstrelsy: black dialect, nonsense couplets, and an ambiguous message:

> I come to town de udder night,
> I hear de noise den saw de fight;
> De watchman was a'runnin' roun',
>> Cryin' Old Dan Tucker's come to town!
>> So get out de way! Get out de way!
>> Get out de way, Old Dan Tucker,
>> You're too late to get your supper.[5]

The song's main character was a Northern free black; a poor barber, as the lyrics had it, unable to count past ten. He also wielded a straight razor. The lyrics expressed an admonishment or a warning: the free African American male of 1844 was either being denied supper after arriving late or, having barged into a boardinghouse after hours, was fighting his way to a late-night meal. Old Dan Tucker was comic, energetic, irresponsible, and a bit dangerous. White audiences loved him.

The second song is more surprising. This was an abolitionist anthem, the Hutchinson Family Singers' "Get Off the Track!" The song was the product of Jesse Hutchinson Jr., the merchant, poet, and manager of the quartet consisting of his sister and three brothers. The Hutchinsons have been referred to as the period's "anti-minstrels." They were involved in several middle-class reforms. Their concerts were characterized by proper manners and the careful enunciation of lyrics. They were no fans of blackface. Yet Jesse Hutchinson clearly enjoyed Emmett's tune. Indeed, he liked it enough to lift it, to borrow or even steal it for the abolition cause. Originally, he intended it for the 1844 national elections, as a campaign anthem for the antislavery Liberty Party. The Liberty Party came and went, but the song stuck around, spreading through abolitionist circles. The goal, as its lyrics suggest, was to link antislavery to the era's prime symbol of progress:

> Ho! the car emancipation,
> Rides majestic through our nation.
> Bearing on its train the story,
> LIBERTY! a nation's glory.
>   Roll it along! Roll it along!
>   Roll it along through the nation,
>   Freedom's car, Emancipation.[6]

In the song, at least, the abolitionist movement of the early 1840s was like a railroad train leaving the station: it was picking up steam, and anyone lingering on the tracks was going to be run over. Musically, the Hutchinson version was toned down: "Get Off the Track!" was set more to the tinkling of piano than the pounding beat of tambourine and stomped feet; it was more middle-class parlor than Irish jig.

Yet it was enough for its audiences. Debuted at an antislavery convention in Salem during the spring of 1844, the song became one of the best-known anthems in the abolitionist cause, a regular sing-along at antislavery meetings, and a centerpiece in Hutchinson concerts. Did audiences note the irony of a blackface tune in the abolition cause? More likely, they separated the song from its roots. In 1847, the Hutchinsons' *Granite Songster* listed "Get Off the Track!" as a "Railway Song," with lyrics "adopted to a slave melody."[7]

It made sense to think this way. After all, the two forms of expression—blackface minstrelsy and abolitionist reform—would seem at opposite extremes. Blackface has been depicted as at the very center of America's nineteenth-century popular culture. Abolitionism has been portrayed as a radical cause, a movement that before the 1850s, at least, seems far removed from any type of popularity at all. Blackface has been associated with the common folk, with the earthy masculinity of America's early working class. Nineteenth-century reform has been associated with the middle class. Often, as in depictions of the temperance movement, it has been connected to women's groups. It has been linked to social control, to the feminization of culture, to prudish efforts to contain and control the pleasures of a "free market."[8]

The energy of blackface, its militant vulgarity, even its humor-based racism, all give it an air of something quintessentially American. Reforms like abolition, on the other hand, have rarely crested into the American mainstream. Here, reform might be taken to refer to any effort on behalf of democratic inclusion or communal well-being over capitalist profit-seeking; it might refer to any protest of colonialism or ideology of social and racial hierarchy.

Looking backward, this type of reform appears to have made it into the nation's popular culture only a few times: in the sixties or the Vietnam War era, during the New Deal of the 1930s, and during the period just before and after the American Civil War. According to the common view of things, blackface may have been disturbing in its racial imagery but it was democratic in style, beloved by the masses, and a key texture in the rich fabric of popular Americana. Reform, particularly progressive, liberal, or leftist reform, has almost always been interpreted as at odds with American popular culture. Usually tagged with the term "radical," it has been depicted as marginal to the mainstream of history, outside American tradition.[9]

The narrative here challenges these assumptions. The chapters forming this narrative focus on a broad variety of musical genres, from parlor ballads to sea chanteys, from hymns to country dances, from alehouse glees to political anthems. My overall goal, however, is not to provide coverage of the broad history of popular music in the United States. Others have tried this, and though the task may be impossible given the nation's multiplicity of cultures, some have done so with a degree of success.[10] My goal, as it has emerged in the research and writing for this narrative, is to explore relationships between certain examples of early popular music in the United States and dominant American attitudes about tradition, community, patriotism, race, and ethnic identity.

Why music? First, musical sources are particularly rich when it comes to getting at American popular culture. More to the point, popular music is a different type of evidence altogether. Music offers an entrance into what the social critic and historian Johan Huizinga referred to as the "play space" of culture. The act of singing something—rather than saying it or writing it—is a conscious departure from everyday life. Singing is play, a form of expression that does not have to be taken seriously. It can thus express practically anything, including the most serious issues. Historically, song has allowed alternative ways of thinking to take shape, to enter the public sphere and become popular. Music has a special place in culture, according to the theorist Jacques Attali, for its ability to express change in the social or political order long before the changes are popular. Thus, popular song can be prophetic. It can also be revelatory, revealing subversions of the norm, sub-narratives to dominant history.[11]

Early America, in other words, looks and sounds different as a musical. For one thing, the musical version is more tied to vernacular tradition. The popular songs of the early part of the nineteenth century contain a host of oral traditions, from old English folk music to songs sailors heard in what they called "Senegambia," the slaving-station ports along the west coast of Africa. Thus, a musical version of America is global in heritage. As well, it provides a counter-narrative to neat stories of progress, for songs allowed many of the old, vernacular traditions to survive.

For another thing, the musical America is a much more communal place than might be seen using other lenses. In part, this may be due to the communal elements of song. Yet it may also be that communal traditions are more central to the United States than many imagine. Finally, the musical version of America offers key insights into issues of race and ethnic identity. For in music, we clearly see and hear that conceptions of blackness and whiteness developed side by side, that abolition and blackface were twinned in conflict, and that racial thinking framed and formed not only the oppressed but also the culture of the oppressors.

One of the main arguments in this narrative is that popular song was a key form of media in nineteenth-century America. Indeed, it is hard to imagine a medium less elite and more inclusive, one better able to express and communicate information, values, and beliefs to the broadest mass of people. Music was central to the creation of what the historian Benedict Anderson refers to as an "imagined community," the creation, that is, of a shared sense of American identity. Popular songs brought people together; they encouraged individuals to think of themselves as members of communities; they framed ideologies of how Americans looked, thought, and behaved.[12]

This book focuses on several communities that were imagined partly or largely through popular music. The first two chapters focus on the origin of ideals associated with American identities along with the development of national ideals of patriotism. Much of the source material for these chapters comes from a Boston printer at the time of the War of 1812, a man by the name of Nathaniel Coverly. From a musicology perspective, Coverly would not merit much attention. He was not a musician. He cannot be credited with the many songs he printed between 1812 and 1815. What Coverly did was delve into the past, find songs he thought might sell, and print them in the form of broadside ballads.[13] He found and printed drinking songs, alehouse revels that included roared-out toasts to rum, ale, and women. He printed bawdy ballads, songs filled with handsome swains, lusty widows, and sexually available farmers' daughters.

He printed trickster songs. In these ballads, merrymaking country girls thumbed their noses at clucking church elders, lowly tenant farmers stood up to landed aristocrats, and apprentices turned the tables on artisan masters. Often descended from ancient carnivals and seasonal revels, these songs offered singers and listeners a carnivalesque version of the world, a world upside down, an imagined play space in which, for a moment at least, the downtrodden and the disempowered might be on top.[14]

The ballads Coverly printed brought older traditions into modern popular culture. Ancient ballads from village festivals survived being uprooted from English soil; communal songs and dances made the passage to American settings. Carnival expressions lived on despite church and civic clampdowns, despite efforts to crush them as pagan, backward, common, or criminal. Expressions of the body and its yearnings remained central to the culture, persisting in the face of efforts to make certain acts private or forbidden, efforts to link the body with filth and sin. Such attempts to control traditional expressions did not, of course, banish them from the culture. Instead, they changed their meanings. Some communal traditions would become increasingly subversive, viewed as challenges to authorities. Many traditions of bodily expression would be increasingly depicted as "dirty" or forbidden in decent society. Yet both lived on, returning again and again to central places in American culture.

One of these places would be in the most popular type of song Coverly printed, the patriotic broadside ballad. Like other printers of the time, Coverly churned out a seemingly endless stream of patriotic ballads, from songs about the "founding fathers" to anthems on the American Revolution, the military exploits of the US Navy, and what made Yankees different from the English. Some of this effort came from timing. Coverly happened to be a printer at the time of the War of 1812, the United States' first conflict as a nation. Some of it reflected clear efforts to generate patriotic feeling, to create a shared sense of an American national identity.

Outlines of this identity may be seen in two ballads from Coverly's time, the songs "Yankee Doodle" and "The Star-Spangled Banner." Both are antique, both curiosities. Though often associated with the American Revolution, "Yankee Doodle" probably reached the height of its popularity during the War of 1812. Nowadays the thing sounds like child's play, a string of notes best suited to a toy piano, a set of lyrics that make little sense. Why would someone want to stick a feather in their hat and call it macaroni? What is the point of being a dandy?

Despite the reverence it is supposed to foster as a sacred object, "The Defense of Fort McHenry" or "The Star-Spangled Banner," as it came to be called, strikes many honest listeners as equally strange. The tune is nearly impossible to sing, and the lyrics seem designed as a tongue-twister. It is best enjoyed as a ritual of humiliation. Nearly everyone has witnessed the scene: while performing it at an event, some hapless singer gets lost in the lyrics or cracks on the high notes. Most brazen through. A few—the entertaining ones—collapse in tearful convulsions. Outside of the pleasure of watching such meltdowns, the song is a formality, an endured chore before a car race.

Would a bit of history improve these songs? One of the points of this book is that it would. Within its historical contexts, "Yankee Doodle" was a trickster song. According to lore, British soldiers came up with the ballad sometime between 1755 and 1763, during the conflict that came to be called the War for Empire (in North America), the French and Indian War, or the Seven Years' War. They invented it to mock the American militia, jeering the Yankees as provincial cowards and backwoods hicks. During the Revolutionary War, Americans adopted the song. They sang it without changing the lyrics, dismissive imagery and all, as if being a country bumpkin were a source of unmitigated pride. Over time, writers added new images: feathers in caps, "macaroni"— which everyone knew was slang for the gold braid English officers wore on their dress uniforms—and the Yankee dandy's mockery of aristocratic officers in the British Army.

The song reveals why early Americans liked dandies. To be a dandy was to be the most common and vulgar of individuals. Indeed, to be a dandy was to be proud of this position, to strut one's mediocrity in the face of excellence, to put on airs in front of one's traditional superiors. The point was to flout tradition by declaring the commoner's social equality with the aristocrat. By the War of 1812, the message would have been clear: in America, any backward idiot could be a dandy; the common American, no matter how lowly, vulgar, or stupid, was on proud and equal footing with the English gentleman.[15] In its context, the childlike "Yankee Doodle" was a trickster song, a carnivalesque reversal of order, a statement of radical, democratic egalitarianism.

Meanwhile, there is an explanation for the weirdness of "The Star-Spangled Banner." It turns out that Francis Scott Key, the poet who wrote the anthem's lyrics, was no tunesmith. Once he penned his weighty ode to a flag, he slapped it to someone else's music. In this case, he took the tune from the official song of an eighteenth-century social club, London's Anacreontic Society, a song called "To Anacreon in Heaven." Anacreon was the club's muse, a "jolly old Grecian" with a penchant for the joys of Bacchus, Venus, and wine. The members of the society belted out the song at each meeting:

> To Anacreon in Heav'n, where he sat in full Glee,
> A few Sons of Harmony sent a Petition,
> That he their Inspirer and Patron would be;
> When this Answer arriv'd from the Jolly Old Grecian
>   "Voice, Fiddle, and Flute,
>   No longer be mute,
>   I'll lend you my Name and inspire you to boot,
> And besides, I'll instruct you like me, to intwine,
> The Myrtle of Venus with Bacchus's Vine."

The Anacreontic Society was a gentlemen's drinking club. Here is the reason why the tune is so strange: it was meant to accompany wine, ale, and rum; it was designed to produce good drinking, bad singing, and great hilarity.[16] In its context, "The Star-Spangled Banner" expressed American patriotism as a balance between traditions. The song is both a drinking ballad and a statement of republican duty, a nearly seamless blending of patriotism with returned communal tradition and bodily desire.

Nathaniel Coverly's patriotic ballads suggest the emergence of competing variants of patriotism. Two are well known. One was the simple patriotism of following great men, the extolling of symbols like George Washington as national rallying points. Another was the patriotism of republican duty, the stress on the ideal that a republic depended on the virtues of citizens, that these virtues included self-sacrifice for the good of the nation, the intellectual act of keeping informed about current events, and the idea that the duty of the elite was to keep a lid on the passions of the American unwashed.

A third variant of patriotism might only be visible by looking at the most inclusive of popular-culture sources, documents like Coverly's broadsides and sources like popular music. This was a patriotism that offered a communal celebration of common behaviors. According to this ideal, the primary characteristic of Americans—what brought them together in communion—was their complete lack of sophistication, good manners, or refinement. What made them American was their vulgarity. Thus, the musical broadsides of Coverly's era reveal a type of patriotism that would increasingly split away from republican traditions and go its own way in American culture. It may have also become the most popular. This would be a variant of patriotism marked by a liking for violence, loud noise, and bodily expression, a patriotism of fireworks, drunken celebrations, and assaults on a culture of uplift.

This narrative's focus on Nathaniel Coverly and the popular music of his time offers several revelations about American popular culture. First, it reveals why so much of this culture would be devoted to sex and the body. Often these subjects are introduced as examples of a break with the past, as evidence for a decline from decency or a progressive liberation from oppression.[17] Here, they appear as returned traditions. The meanings of traditions like carnival and bawdy song would change over time; they would be altered by attempts to control or police them, by instances of repression. Yet they would remain at the center of popular culture. Second, this focus reveals a communal tradition at the heart of American popular culture, a deep tradition that produced continuous yearnings for community or even "communism" on American soil.

While popular song continued to express communities of interest, shared values, and cultural styles through much of the nineteenth century, it also expressed conflict. Many of these conflicts centered on the morality of the market-based capitalism that emerged in the United States after 1815. Many focused on the ethics of profiteering and exploitation, on moral questions raised by merchants who enflamed desires or industrialists who reorganized labor from the artisan model of production toward factory employment and wage work. The central conflict of the time was over the issue of slavery, along with questions about the place of African Americans in the United States.

Nearly the rest of this narrative, the greater part of the book from chapter 3 through chapter 8, focuses on struggles between two different communities of taste, style, political belief, and popular music. On one side of this conflict was the genre of music and theatrics known as "blackface," or later as "blackface minstrelsy." On the other side was the music of popular reform. The narrative in these chapters can be read as a double biography. Much of it focuses on the original Hutchinson Family Singers. Much of the rest centers on the blackface characters Jim Crow and Zip Coon, a few of their countless descendants, and the actual people who found themselves in the position of ignoring these characters, working against them, or using them to gain a voice in a nation that offered few alternatives.

Three chapters of this narrative focus wholly or partly on the Hutchinson Family Singers. The Hutchinsons were exemplars of the forming American middle class. According to the argument here, they belonged to the first generation of Americans who became middle class; and they may have belonged to the last generation who actually took middle-class values seriously enough to try to live by them. These values included giving a positive meaning to repression, propriety, and self-control. Middle-class types adhered to a vision of the world as split between public and private spheres, between what they imagined as a public and "male space" of competition, business, and politics and the private home, the female-run domestic refuge.

Middle-class Americans had faith in institutions like schools and government. They extolled the sanctity of motherhood and the innocence of children. They believed in vernacular gentility, a democratic ideal that the codes of politeness and proper behavior that were the markers of middle-class status did not come from birth or riches but from learning; they could be acquired through cheap etiquette guides. At times their values seemed contradictory: they were committed to material success and getting ahead; and they knew that striving to succeed in a capitalist economy might require lying, cheating, and taking advantage of people for profit. At the same time, their etiquette guides extolled the golden rule, politeness in social exchange, and responsibility for the well-being of strangers at a distance.[18]

In the first half of the nineteenth century, these values had a number of dramatic results. They produced religious awakenings, outdoor revivals, and scenes at the guilty bench, the seating area at the front of the camp meeting, to which merchants and their wives went to weep, wail, and confess the sins they committed on their way to middle-class success. They produced humanitarianism, a massive increase in the awareness of suffering at a distance, and the formation of reform groups to alleviate the pain of strangers. They produced waves of popular reform: mass movements to better the condition of poor people, to end drunkenness, and to abolish slavery.[19]

They produced the wild popularity of the Hutchinson Family Singers. Between 1843 and 1850, the quartet of three brothers and a sister from the same New Hampshire family sang in protest of capitalists who profited by selling alcohol, plantation owners whose wealth derived from slaves, sweatshop owners who exploited their laborers, and politicians who blithely supported an imperialist war. They sang in favor of temperance and government aid to immigrants. They promoted the immediate abolition of slavery and supported black civil rights, singing antislavery songs and demanding that their concerts be open to integrated audiences. They had personal ties and cultural affinities with individuals they referred to as "communists."

During this time, they were one of the most popular singing groups in the nation, at least to the north of the Potomac River and among groups who did not perform in black make-up. They probably seemed everywhere. Sheet music of their songs was a staple of middle-class parlors; their concerts sold out the largest halls; newspaper writers—both adoring and critical—followed their every movement.

The Hutchinsons might fit with dominant narratives of US history, except for one thing: if these were their issues, they should have been ignored or at least universally disliked. Their popularity seems puzzling. Indeed, this may explain why they have remained largely hidden from historical review. Much of the early work on the singers is antiquarian and anecdotal. They come across in this literature as a kind of American Von Trapp Family, charming but without much political or social significance. When musicologists discovered their existence, they seemed unsure what to make of them. For two of the best of these scholars, Charles Hamm and Dale Cockrell, the Hutchinsons could only be analyzed as people out of time, as distant forerunners of the protest singers of the sixties—the *nineteen*-sixties. Recently another musicologist, Scott Gac, has produced the most nuanced interpretation of the singers. Yet even this analysis struggles with their popularity. It made sense, according to this work, that the Hutchinsons would be popular with reformers and abolitionists; yet this should have been a narrow milieu. Thus, it argues, the Hutchinsons' wider popularity may have come from audiences who paid no attention to their messages or took the singers *à la carte*, relishing the songs while rejecting the politics.[20]

The argument here is that the Hutchinsons were popular to a large extent precisely because of the politics. Much of the evidence makes it clear that audiences did pay attention to their messages. They probably had little choice, for the singers were enormously controversial. Given the militancy of their critics and enemies, it would have been odd to be unaware of their political stances. Well before Harriet Beecher Stowe's *Uncle Tom's Cabin*, the Hutchinsons took abolition into the mainstream of American culture. They also suggest that other issues and causes were in the American mainstream: issues such as the criticism of amoral consumption, protests to wars of aggression, and the treatment of immigrants and laborers; causes like American communism or experiments with alternatives to capitalism.

The contention here is that the Hutchinsons were not ahead of their time. The high point of their success came in a period one scholar has called a "communitarian moment" in American history. It may just as well be called a "middle-class moment." The period, from about 1833 to around 1850, constitutes perhaps the single period that members of an American middle class took their own values seriously, the moment the mass of the bourgeoisie actually tried to follow ideals such as politeness, respectability, and humanitarianism. This was a time many middle-class Americans took a close look at the market system they were creating and tried to picture alternatives. It was a time of communal experiments: from Brook Farm to the Amana Colonies to the archipelago of Shaker villages that ran from Massachusetts to Kentucky.[21] One of the main vehicles for expressing these alternatives was popular song.

This narrative focuses on popular images—often expressed in music and song—of Brook Farmers, Shakers, Native Americans, and domestic women, communists all in the American imagination. The Brook Farmers expressed communal values in what they understood as the uplifting and unselfish spirit of the music later known as "classical." In the mid-nineteenth century, more than a few Americans went to villages established by the "United Society of Believers in Christ's Second Coming." They went to watch the members of this society—the Shakers—perform songs and dances, to engage in their musical "labors," as they called them. Some went to mock and scorn; many came away entranced by one of the nation's most vibrant forms of folk art. At about the same time, many Americans became interested in an even less visible manifestation of the nation's communal yearnings, the "parlor Indian." Here, middle-class Victorians sang "Indian songs" in the parlors of well-appointed houses; ballads that pictured Native Americans as communal, closer to nature, and incapable of deception.

Finally, this was the time of the Jenny Lind–mania, the historical moment in 1850 when a Swedish opera singer performing classical arias represented the summit of popular music. Called the Swedish Nightingale by an adoring American press, Lind represented the absolute of domesticity. She was the perfect woman. When she began closing her concerts with the song "Home, Sweet Home," she brought thousands of Americans to tears. The home would be a hallmark obsession of the American middle class; an object of nostalgia, a haven in a heartless world, a stark alternative to the market culture of competition and deception. It became both America's greatest communist utopia and the base for a gender system that balanced market-based manhood with a concept of moral womanhood. In many accounts of the middle class, these expressions are dismissed as examples of repression or silliness. They are less repressive when they are connected to abolition, less silly in the form of the Hutchinsons' songs.

Part of the argument here is that the Hutchinsons reveal the deep history of liberal idealism and progressive activism in America. Nineteenth-century reformers have often been depicted as joyless prudes or wild-eyed crazies from beyond the mainstream of politics or culture. Yet they were almost always talented individuals, often celebrated as representing the best qualities of the age. The Hutchinsons, like other reformers, railed against the "bad habits" of a nation committed to a philosophy of amoral consumption. They sang against habits like drinking alcohol and smoking cigarettes. For this reason, the temptation is to see them as prudish and fussy, as stuck-up members of an outdated and stiffly Victorian middle class.[22]

At the same time, the Hutchinsons also sang out against national bad habits of bigotry, prejudice, and exploitation, the bad habits of slavery, Indian removal, and the denial of equality to women, African Americans, and immigrants. They reveal a history of causes that were popular in the mid-nineteenth century and that today would be called radical, perhaps even "anti-American."

To understand why they would be seen that way, we turn to blackface minstrelsy. A simple definition for blackface is that it was a musical genre in which actors and singers blackened their faces and hands with make-up and performed what were nearly always spurious versions of African American song, dance, and expression. The easy explanation is that it involved the creation of bygone racial stereotypes, "black" characters from "Jim Crow" to various "Uncles," "Aunts," and "Mammies" of song, stage, and product package.

The problem is that the genre resists simple definition or easy explanation. According to lore and quite a bit of historical scholarship, blackface developed in the 1830s in the northeastern United States. Things get fuzzier on when it came to an end, or if it ended at all. It began as a Northern and not a Southern phenomenon, emerging in the urban theaters of northeastern cities like New York, Boston, and Philadelphia. Many of its songs were energetic and raucous, much of its comedy consciously vulgar.

Part of the problem of defining blackface is that it was always fluid, always morphing into new acts and flowing into new areas of popular culture. In the 1840s, performers like Dan Emmett added better musicianship to the genre, refining away its harsh edges and turning it from a focus on single acts to full shows. Blackface became blackface minstrelsy; single songs and acts—such as "Jim Crow" or "Zip Coon"—became bits in a larger theatrical. By the 1850s, the standard minstrel show had three parts: an "Intro," in which the performers displayed their musical talent; an "Olio" composed of songs, skits, and jokes; and a finale, composed of some characteristically "black" behavior, such as a plantation scene or a cakewalk.

The historical scholarship on blackface minstrelsy has undergone a number of rounds of interpretation and revision. According to an early approach rooted in folklore studies and musicology—an approach very much still around—blackface was an act of cultural ventriloquism. In playing minstrel characters, white performers from the 1830s through the Civil War were doing black songs and dances. They were performing songs they had stolen in their travels through the slave South. Blackface, according to this interpretation, was comprised of actual African American expression.

Later scholars challenged this finding. Blackface tunes, they argued, derived more from Scots-Irish tradition and the songs of English music halls. The genre's imagery and lyrical content reflected racist inventions. For these scholars, blackface remained the favorite music of common-class Americans. It allowed poor white American males to lift themselves up by punching down, striking at a powerless ethnic other with a host of dismissive and cruel stereotypes.[23]

More recent historians have turned away from the genre's racial messages and toward its working-class origins. Focusing for the most part on early blackface, these historians have returned to the idea that blackface performers stole or borrowed black song for their acts. Performers, they point out, did not need to travel to plantations for their material, for they had ample opportunities to hear black song in the Northeast. Blackface, these scholars argue, was largely a mode of masked class conflict.

According to this analysis, white performers and blackface audiences did not necessarily intend to demean black people. They chose to focus on black characters because they offered the widest possibilities for the expression of controversial political criticisms. Black characters, because they were understood to be poor and authentically unrefined, could say anything; they provided, in other words, the best cover for assaults on the politics and culture of the elite and the middle class. The music and style of blackface, according to these scholars, was raucous, energetic, and just plain fun. Combining black rhythm, Scots-Irish jig, and a dash of white supremacy, blackface appealed to Irish immigrants and served Yankees as a recruiting tool for what was then the proslavery and white-supremacist Democratic Party. The whole thing, as one of these historians has put it, was "about race without necessarily being racist."[24]

The interpretation here is partly an effort to build on these arguments. At the same time, it challenges and complicates them in several ways. First, unlike just about every other book on American popular song in the nineteenth century, this narrative seeks to move beyond the assumption of essential categories of "white" or "black" music. And unlike many treatments, this one does not assume that minstrelsy was black music. Some of the focus here is on the songs of African American slaves before the Civil War. Some is on sailors and sea chanteys, an apparent case of "white" people singing "black" songs. The argument in this section is this: if someone wanted to hear black song in nineteenth-century America, it might not have been a good idea to go to a Southern plantation, for slavery may not have been conducive to singing. And if they wanted to hear white men singing black songs, they would have been better off joining the crew of a whaling ship than going to a minstrel show.[25]

This narrative includes a population typically left out of discussions of black music, the antebellum-era, black middle class. Here, the focus is on abolitionist leaders, writers, and editors, individuals like David Walker, Samuel Cornish, and Frederick Douglass. While these individuals had to deal with issues of slavery and civil rights, the record shows that they also spent time thinking about relationships between popular music and perceptions of black people in America. Early civil rights leaders had their own examples of black music, from the antislavery songs collected by the black abolitionist William Wells Brown to the performances of Elizabeth Greenfield, the African American opera singer known as "The Black Swan." They also had their own version of a black identity, an identity that was educated, proper, and refined; an identity in sharp contrast to blackface and that may have been a response to it.

Later, the focus turns to a post–Civil War generation of African American performers. This includes the "coon song" star James Bland, the gospel choir from Tennessee's Fisk College, the Fisk Jubilee Singers, and some of the artists and writers of the Harlem Renaissance. The argument here is that in a nation committed by this time to white supremacy, the oppression of black people, and the musical pleasures of blackface style, these individuals faced difficult choices. They could reject stereotypes, assert themselves, and risk a lynch mob. Or they could play the minstrel, turn blackface stereotypes to their advantage, and risk strengthening them to the point of erasing the difference between racist image and black identity.

The individuals in these chapters were a diverse group. Some were committed to ideals of equality and the creation of a black community; others were out for themselves. Some fought against blackface imagery; others embraced it in order to be heard. What they all show, however, is that the idea of what constituted "black music" in America was very much up for grabs through and beyond the nineteenth century. None suggest the validity of using blackface—or anything else, for that matter—to stand for black music.

A second area of divergence between this narrative and others is on the association between blackface and the American working class. The working class of this assumption was composed almost solely of artisan laborers: young, often former apprentices and journeymen associated with skilled trades. The category excluded women, slaves, and unskilled workers. In fact, the "working class" who generated the first blackface craze of the 1830s consisted of a subset of workers, a population comprised almost entirely of young white males, many who saw their status falling as the old artisan system became replaced by factory labor.[26]

Considered in this context, blackface can be seen as something of a last-ditch effort on the part of these individuals to maintain their status. Blackface style, according to this argument, represented a shift in the identity of the worker, from a skilled artisan to a character rooted in authentic masculinity. Blackface re-masculinized the American "worker" at the precise moment the factory threatened to turn "him" into an operative. The genre's imagery continued the cultural exclusion of blacks and women from the category of worker.

Meanwhile, there is evidence that audiences and supporters of early blackface consisted of more than a collection of white junior artisans who were becoming factory workers. As conflicts between blackface fans and reformers suggest, the blackface community included successful merchants, newspaper editors, proslavery politicians, and former master artisans who were on their way to becoming the owners of small factories and sweatshops. In other words, at the time some historians have claimed blackface was a working-class entertainment, there is evidence that its audience included members of the nation's economic and cultural elite: powerful entrepreneurs who owned factories, exploited sweated labor, and wanted to direct worker anger away from themselves; gentlemen of property and standing who ran for office, defended slavery, and wanted things to stay as they were; newspaper editors who drank rum, chewed cigars, and spat invective at what they saw as the feminized idealism of bourgeois reformers.

The idea that blackface represented working-class exuberance versus middle-class repression does not match the cultural fluidity of the genre. It fails, that is, to take into account the changes the genre underwent through the nineteenth century. In the 1830s and 1840s, blackface audiences had several major clashes with middle-class reformers. By the 1850s, the American middle class embraced blackface. The embrace, in turn, added another layer to the genre's style. Along with the older, vibrant, and consciously vulgar style of numbers like "Jim Crow" and "Old Dan Tucker," there appeared the deeply emotional and sentimental songs of Stephen Foster. Along with the effervescent, free Northern black of many early acts there emerged the happy and loyal slave.

With the appearance of this character, blackface could penetrate the South and "Dixie" could become the Confederate anthem. In the second half of the century, increasing numbers of African Americans moved into the genre. By the turn of the century, blackface was everywhere in American culture, from stage to product packaging to the very term—"Jim Crow"—associated with the nation's system of racial hierarchy. By this time, blackface was well on its way to becoming America's gift to the world.

Finally, the narrative here reflects an effort to place blackface at the center of American race and class ideologies. This is not, however, a return to the idea that the genre was an example of punching down, that it reflected the racial cruelties of bygone days, or that it offered a racially tinged vehicle for members of the working class to mock the "respectables" among the middle class.

Here, this narrative is informed by several warnings from recent scholars on the relationship between culture and ideologies of oppression in America. First, for racism to work as a set of ideas or a culture, it must operate within a complex system of events, institutions, laws, and practices that also create and support racial hierarchy. Second, a culture of racism must be analyzed in a way that conveys its scope: any analysis that depicts the racist as marginal, deviant, or evil does not get at the scale of culture. Third, any approach that takes racism seriously must analyze its effects on both the oppressors and the oppressed.[27]

Blackface clearly emerged within a much larger framework of racial hierarchy in America. This included, of course, the slave trade, the creation of slave markets, and the development of government systems for putting down slave insurrections. In Boston at the time of the American Revolution, it included a warning: a rusty cage at the old city gate, occupied by the desiccated corpse of an unnamed leader of a slave revolt. In South Carolina, it included police surveillance: a tradition founded on the professional slave patrol. Once drawn from local volunteer militias, by the early nineteenth century, patrols in the Carolinas, Virginia, and elsewhere in the Cotton Belt were forerunners of the modern police force: their members were paid; they rode a specific area called a "beat"; and they had the power to stop, search, and punish any black person they encountered. The state-sponsored system of racial hierarchy would include the dispossession of perceptually non-white populations, the use of racial profiling in police work, the resort to double standards in jail sentencing, and the expulsion of free African Americans from certain counties, neighborhoods, and public spaces. Elsewhere, scholars have referred to this system as the "racial state"; a system, that is, in which racial oppression was built into the structures of society and government.[28]

Blackface would provide support for this system. It would not do so by being easily identified as "racist." One of the problems with studies of racist "cultures" or "attitudes" in America, as critics have pointed out, is that they often depict racism as pathology. Racism, in other words, is typically characterized as arising from ignorance and prejudice; it is marked by cruelty, hostility, and hatred. Thus, it lies dormant in the culture until the wrong people take charge; or it exists at the margins, with the hate-mongers and the crazies. One of the points of this narrative is that blackface did not work this way at all. Few among the genre's early audiences, and practically none of its early performers, would fit the standard mold of the racist. As they were likely to put it, they loved "their" black people.

Far from producing marginal ways of thinking, blackface expressed and produced a form of racism that meshed well with the modern racial state. It did so by linking racism with pleasure. In blackface performance, the black character became a vessel for a host of desires: for authentic masculinity, for sexual potency, for violent self-assertion, for liberation from culture itself, along with an embrace of guilt-free consumption. Blackface performance depicted black characters as bodies without minds. They were uneducated, but they had a type of street smarts. They got drunk, sang, danced, and gambled away all their money; they were free to fight, have sex, and eat anything they wanted. There may be places in the world where these characteristics could be interpreted as hostile or dismissive. But blackface emerged in America.

What made blackface a part of the American racial state was the way it maintained hierarchies. The genre's versions of black behaviors, while they may have been beloved by its audiences, were always low; they always existed on a level beneath what was acceptable in an imagined culture of whiteness and moral respectability. In part, this is what made the minstrel show's humor and spark, for blackface was nothing if not an all-out celebration of the low and disreputable. Elsewhere, scholars would refer to this as "vitalist racism," a type of racism characterized by a powerful white attraction to certain supposed black characteristics, a white desire for black style, dance, song, and modes of expression.[29]

Here, it is referred to as "love-crime" racism. The "love" in the term should be obvious: then, as now, many white Americans loved their version of black people. James Stirling, one of a number of roving abolitionists who toured the South in the antebellum era, captured the characteristic almost perfectly in his report on the attitudes of slaveholders in 1857:

> They feel affection for the negro as a dependent and protected race, but they cannot brook the idea of equality with those whom they have so long regarded as inferiors. A drunken Kentuckian expressed the feeling coarsely but pithily, in my hearing: "I like a nigger," said he, "but I hate a damned free nigger."[30]

Substitute the word "free" with "educated" or "uppity," and you have a way of seeing that would last into and through the twentieth century.

The crimes would be directed against African Americans who refused to stay low, who failed to "act properly," in the words of Harlem Renaissance writer George Schuyler, who gave offense "by being intelligent."[31] They would also arise from blackface stereotypes. Some of the most beloved elements of black-face—the blackface character's physicality, his love of violence, his dangerous masculinity—would become rationales for many of America's worst crimes of racial oppression. Blackface would have the power to arm unarmed black men, transforming any and all white crimes against them into perceived acts of self-defense.

Finally, blackface would define both the oppressed and the oppressors. The argument here is that blackface would work to create and strengthen at least three ideological identities: the authentic and masculine working class; the expressive, musical, and lowly African American; and the stiffly white and repressed middle class. Blackface generated some of the most cherished ideals in American culture. It helped create the idea that all forms of etiquette or up-lift lead directly to the corruption of one's true self. It promoted the belief that the pragmatic authenticity of "street smarts" will always trump the pretentions of institutional book-learning. It contributed to the idea that the American middle class was homogeneous and lily-white. It gave strength to the con-cept that self-improvement goes against the "nature" of blackness, that black people were incapable of learned thought, that their expressions would always be spontaneous and natural.

In the end, blackface was not just about black people: it was about au-thenticity and shocking the prude; it offered both a depiction of fun-loving blackness and a rebellion against whiteness. After the 1840s, it became a revolt against certain values that stood in the way of a growing culture of consump-tion, a rebellion by young entrepreneurial types against stiffness, ethics, and uplift. This rebellion codified whiteness as the better part of culture. It made an imagined blackness an entry to the desires of the marketplace.

All of this may sound a bit like a return to the idea that blackface offered a masked way for its audiences to mock the middle class. It is, and it is not. As the narrative suggests, blackface may have originated with a white subset of the American working class, but it quickly spread. Meanwhile, the context for blackface was not just class conflict but also the struggle between forces that defended slavery and the abolition movement.

Here, we return to the Hutchinson Family Singers. For, as this narrative has it, this was also a conflict between music-based communities: a conflict be-tween the blackface community and the community of reformers that coalesced around the Hutchinson Family Singers. It is one thing to say that blackface was about shocking the prude, to celebrate it for offering a comedic takedown of middle-class affectation. It is quite another if the prudes in question had as their issues not only temperance but the seeking of alternatives to capitalist exploitation, the promotion of the equal rights, and the abolition of slavery.

This narrative's focus on the Hutchinsons and blackface minstrelsy during the middle decades of the nineteenth century reveals the development of conflicting values. On one side was a value system stressing social responsibility, communal ideals, and human perfectibility. On the other side was a promotion of vulgarity, spontaneity, and a version of human nature rooted in desires and appetites.

When it came to these values, at least, one side won and the other lost. By the end of the Civil War, blackface was on its way to reigning supreme as the basis of American style. Increasingly, this style merged with a culture of consumption. By the turn of the century, many of the Hutchinsons' songs and expressions would strike American listeners as strange: they lacked any rhythm that might lead to pelvic thrusting, and they had few elements that would make a person want to spend, buy, eat, have sex, or get drunk.

The "blackness" at the heart of American popular music had the power to produce all of these desires. This blackness promoted racial slumming, the liberating act of white people getting in touch with their "dark sides," the momentary release from reticence that allowed white people to sing lovingly of "gamblin' men," dance the "Black Bottom," or buy cigarettes with Rastus on the package.[32]

As the modern culture of consumerism gained strength, white people had to be able to lose a sense of social responsibility. Through blackface, they imagined this as letting go of their whiteness, abandoning themselves to dark desires, becoming black. In the second half of the nineteenth century, blackface characters became symbols of consumption, to the point that they moved from the stage to the market shelf, from minstrel show to product package. In a culture that stressed white stiffness and ethical respectability, along with a host of blackface characters who constantly gave in to appetites and passions, blackface would be one of the main engines of modern capitalism.[33]

This book deals with some of the most powerful ideals in American popular culture. American patriotism to this day tends to be articulated as militant vulgarity, as a celebration of ignorance and a love for loud noise. The American working class still tends to be associated with authentic masculinity. The middle class remains pictured as white, stiff, and prudish. Blackness continues to be tied to unfettered desire and fear-inspiring potency, to the ability to freely consume without responsibility, and to a natural propensity for violence that can always be met with justified deadly force.

The question may arise: how could something as apparently benign as popular music have generated such powerful ideals? What must be remembered is this: when it came to the transmission of ideas, music predated all other types of media. It may also be a particularly powerful media form. Its ubiquity, its existence as popular amusement and background noise, its very banality, all contributed to its enormous power. The point of this book is that as much as America exists in history, it is also a musical.

Carnival

Arriving in Boston by sea in 1815, you pass several islands as your ship sails the channel to the inner harbor. At last a view of the city appears, first as hills rising from the water: Beacon Hill, known in earlier and earthier times as Mount Whoredom; Negro Hill, now the city's most exotic neighborhood and a center for sailors' delights. Closer in, the landscape changes to a warren of piers, wharves, and warehouses, all reaching for the trade of Europe, the West Indies, and the American Coast. Chances are, your ship will land at Long Wharf. Extending some two thousand feet into the harbor, with its south side open for ships and the length of its north side lined with storehouses and shops, the largest vessels in the world can tie up at it, even at low tide.

Two years earlier, the city's docks would have been quiet, the result of war and blockade. Now peace has returned, along with the chaos of commerce. Disembarking, you make the walk toward land, weaving through sailors loading cargo, past shops and hawkers, at last to the end of the wharf. A right turn will take you to old Dock Square, once a landing for small vessels, now high and dry as a result of landfill and construction, the site of Faneuil Hall and the city's main marketplace. Along the way would be streets, smells, and sounds evoking the city's commercial energy: Market Street and Merchants' Row, the smell of tar, baking bread, and distilling rum; a soundscape of drums and hand-bells attracting buyers to shops and merchant stalls, the cries of mongers singing the virtues of meat and fish; the cobblestone-rumble of wagons and carts.[1]

Instead of turning right, you turn left, where walking past India Wharf toward the Custom House, you turn up Milk Street. Running from the harbor's waterline to the Old South Meetinghouse, the street is primarily residential. Yet there, about three-fourths its length, at the corner of Theatre Alley and next to Samuel Shed's grocery, is a small shop. You might easily overlook it. Indeed, it seems city officials did just this. According to the *Boston Directory*, the street has several businesses, Shed's grocery along with a hairdresser, an apothecary, and a goldsmith. Each is marked as a shop with the letter S. The directory includes no such designation for this place.[2] Here, at this tiny shop, you are standing before one of the centers of a nascent American popular culture.

This is the print shop of Nathaniel Coverly Jr. Like other Boston printers, Coverly produced pamphlets, handbills, and announcements for meetings. He would be best remembered for printing broadside ballads, single-page songs for the common tastes. Sold for six cents a sheet, the rag-paper ballads were meant to be enjoyed as keepsakes as well as lyric sheets for popular songs. Many had artwork above the lyrics. None included musical notation. Perhaps they were meant to be sung to a variety of tunes; more likely, the tunes were so well known that notation was unnecessary. They took their themes from a variety of sources, from history to politics to news of the day. The majority originated from traditional expressions and practices of common folk.

Coverly's broadsides represent Boston's street culture of the period. They are meeting points: between oral traditions and a modernizing technology of print; between vernacular expression and mass culture. Among their traditions and folk expressions, perhaps the most numerous would revolve around images of sex and carnality. This might seem hardly surprising. American popular culture would be fixated on themes of bodily expression. Yet Coverly's broadsides indicate that such expressions are not the result of progress or an escape from the repressive past. Instead, they are reflections of the past. They are expressions of one of the main dynamics of popular culture: the repression of vernacular traditions by an official culture, the persistence of these traditions along with their continual return in new forms. At Nathaniel Coverly's print shop and in the broadsides he printed between 1812 and 1815, you see the past and future of American popular culture.[3]

The Containment of Carnival

For Nathaniel Hawthorne, American culture began with a carnival, a song, and a clampdown on free expression. His story "The Maypole of Merry Mount" placed these origins in the struggle between two New England colonies: the gloomy Puritan settlement at Plymouth and the more fun-loving village of Merry Mount. Hawthorne's Merry Mount was a place of colorful traditions:

> All the hereditary pastimes of Old England were transplanted hither. The King
> of Christmas was duly crowned, and the Lord of Misrule bore potent sway. On
> the eve of Saint John they felled whole acres of the forest to make bonfires, and

danced by the blaze all night, crowned with garlands, and throwing flowers into the flame. At harvest time, though their crop was of the smallest, they made an image with the sheaves of Indian corn, and wreathed it with autumnal garlands, and bore it home triumphantly. But what chiefly characterized the colonists of Merry Mount was their veneration for the Maypole.[4]

In the colony's first spring, the villagers gathered to celebrate around this maypole, to dance, sing, and hold a wedding ceremony. Anyone could take part in the revels, including the local Indians, including a dancing bear.

This was the tradition of carnival. Literally the celebration of the flesh, of bodily expression and desire, the tradition was central to folk cultures throughout the world. Its origins predate recorded history. For generations, carnivals took the form of harvest festivals, springtime revels, or midsummer night-fests. In England, they appeared in songs and dances around maypoles or giant bonfires, in raucous celebrations overseen by the "Lord of Misrule." Or they took place in the more formal ceremonies to mark the winter solstice, appearing in ancient rituals centered on pines, firs, and holly. Symbols of summer's inevitable return, these evergreens harkened back to the pre-Christian old religion, to vernacular beliefs in elves, sprites, and forest people.

By the time of the English colonization of North America, traditions of carnival had long existed in a dynamic relationship with the official culture. The Church waged war on the old beliefs and pagan ceremonies. Church leaders coopted the ancient rituals, overlaying seasonal festivals with a calendar of saints' days and fasting times, folding the winter and spring revels into the holy days of Christmas and Easter. They contained the carnival, sponsoring their own versions of the festivals: with various special masses, thanksgivings, and even the old "feast of fools."[5]

Through this dynamic, the carnival took its modern form. It became a brief period of licensed transgression, sanctioned by authorities as long as it did not get out of hand. During the time and place of carnival, normal hierarchies could be ignored or reversed: passion could be raised above reason; magistrates could be burned in effigy; common fishermen might be crowned kings and lords. Carnival was a world upside down, a place of "carnivalesque" expressions, a time of playful and chaotic alternatives to the seriousness of day-to-day life. In time, the tradition took on ambivalent meanings. To be sure, carnival allowed common people to vent frustrations against the forces of order. It also remained dangerous. Even sanctioned carnivals could get out of control.[6]

According to Hawthorne, leaders at nearby Plymouth saw the revels at Merry Mount in just this latter way, as a subversive threat to their Christian order. "Unfortunately," he wrote, "there were men of a sterner faith than those maypole worshippers." These were the Puritans, "dismal wretches" whose "festivals were fast days," whose maypole was the "whipping post." Toward the end of the story, the zealots arrived to put an end to the revels. Their leader, Governor Endicott, ordered the maypole chopped down and the revelers whipped. He had the dancing bear shot, suspecting "witchcraft in the beast." For Hawthorne, the scene was the wellspring of a culture rooted in a struggle between "jollity" and "gloom." In his version of events, gloom came out the winner: the nation's Puritan past would be dark and bleak.[7]

Hawthorne based his story on a real event from New England's earliest colonial period. In 1627, at an English "plantation" or colony near Plymouth that had recently changed its name from Mount Wollaston to Merry Mount, there was a carnival to mark the coming of spring. The colony's members set up a maypole, a white-pine staff some eighty feet in length, decked with ribbons and flowers and topped with a set of buck's horns. They promised "good cheer" for "all comers." By all comers, they meant Indians.

According to the colony's official account, the event was a raucous affair, with drinking, much beating on drums, and the rhythmic firing of "guns, pistols and other fitting instruments." It also featured a song written for the occasion, which the revelers sang while dancing around the maypole:

> Drink and be merry, merry, merry boyes,
> Let all your delight be in Hymens joyes,
> So to Hymen now the day is come,
> About the merry Maypole take a roome.

Elsewhere, the song honored the "sweet nectar" of drink and the joys of Hymen, the pagan goddess of sexual fertility. One verse toward the end invited the Indian women in attendance to join the dance, declaring that the "nymphes free from scorn" would be "welcome to us night and day."[8]

Just as in Hawthorne's story, the Puritans were not amused. According to Plymouth Governor William Bradford, the rival colony's leader Thomas Morton had declared himself a "Lord of Misrule." Merry Mount had become a place of "beastly practices" and "mad bacchinalians." Most disturbing was the maypole, the way it seemed to dissolve all order and hierarchy. "They also set up a May-pole," Bradford wrote, "drinking and dancing about it many days together, inviting the Indian women for their consorts, dancing and frisking together (like so many fairies, or furies, rather) and worse practises."[9] Not long after the maypole incident, the leaders at Plymouth had Morton arrested and charged with several crimes. Ultimately they banished the prisoner, primarily for trading weapons to the local Indians but also for the treasonous act of daring to break down the hierarchy between white colonists and the Indian

subjects they needed to control and remove. They dispersed the colony at
Merry Mount, burning its buildings, taking the time and care to obliterate all
evidence of its existence.

Yet the repressed, as it is wont to do, returned in new form. First, Morton
did not go away. In 1637 he published a book titled *New English Canaan*, a
narrative that was half description of the natural beauty of New England and
half scathing parody of the Puritans. The response of New England's magistrates was predictable: they made the screed the first banned book in American history.[10] Still, references to Morton and Merry Mount kept cropping up
in novels and stories, in the itching recognition that the conquest of America
might have gone differently.

Meanwhile, gloom did not settle on England's American colonies. At its
foundation, the carnival was an overturning of hierarchy and a celebration
of the flesh. Undoubtedly, this was what made it such a threat. The institution of hierarchy, often and particularly in the form of racial hierarchy, along
with the suppression of the body, would be perhaps the main characteristic
of modern order.[11] Yet even in Puritan New England, disorders and fleshy desires had a way of returning.

And the results could go to the brink of carnival. In 1642, magistrates at
Plymouth indicted a teenager named Thomas Granger for the crime of bes-
tiality. The boy, it seems, had committed buggery with a veritable ark of domestic creatures: a mare, a cow, two goats, five sheep, two calves, and a turkey.
Witnesses testified that they had seen the boy buggering the horse. Granger
confessed he had done so—several times. Were onlookers laughing at this
point? Most likely they were properly somber when, according to the laws of
Leviticus, Granger was put to death and the animals were slaughtered.[12]

Elsewhere, there were efforts to police society for more mundane examples of "fornication" and "lewd behavior." Town records at the colony of New
Haven reveal that fornication was an elastic charge. In 1662 the New Haven
court called a man and wife "to answer for their going together in such a
sinful way of fornication as they had done before marriage." The court ruled
the husband whipped and the wife fined four pounds. Lewd behavior was
an equally capacious category of misconduct. In another case, magistrates
charged a man with putting his arms around a woman in an "adulterous and
filthy" manner. The court ordered him to stand in the pillory for an hour.[13]
There were no scarlet letters in such cases, and—officially, at least—no as-
persions cast on the character of the accused. That, most Puritans believed,
would be left to the mysterious judgment of their god. Instead, court members hurried through the cases and hoped the punishments would put an end
to the episodes.

Some hoped the magistrates would look the other way. The problem was simple: to go looking for cases of carnival misconduct was to find them. By far the most common were the complaints against individuals for "disorderly night meetings." In February 1662, the New Haven court called a man and wife to answer charges that they had held a festival at their house marked by "playing at cards & singing & dancing." The court fined the couple five shillings each. In January 1665, magistrates charged a group of young men with "gross disorderly carriage" and the singing of "corrupt songs." This time the court judged their actions to be of "such a haynous nature" that it fined the men twenty-shillings each and sentenced them to sit in the stocks.[14]

In these cases official power worked simply. The arrests for lewd behavior, the clampdowns on disorder, and the rules against corrupt songs all operated as oppressive forces. They could be directly felt and struggled against. The problem was that such power only worked to a limited extent. In 1687, Puritan minister Samuel Sewell reported that a maypole had been cut down by authorities in Charles Town, Massachusetts. Just as quickly, he noted, local fishermen erected a larger one in its place. In some places, local officials suppressed the theater. Yet everywhere groups kept alive the old winter revels, caroling raucous wassailing songs as they moved from house to house, staying warm through handouts of grog and cider. At Christmastime, others maintained the tradition of mumming plays and carnival processions, drunkenly performing old fables in costumed masquerade.[15]

Where the crackdown worked best was where its power was more lightly felt. Consider, for example, the disciplining of dance. Long associated with carnival and the awakening of sexual passion, traditional dances could be wild affairs. They were the stuff of street festivals and village competitions, the lively hornpipes of sailors, the improvised jigs and reels of Scots-Irish peasants. In British North America, attitudes toward the pastime depended on region. In the Quaker colonies of Pennsylvania and West Jersey, dancing was forbidden altogether. In Virginia, the gentleman class encouraged it. Puritan leaders considered certain types of dance "lewd" and an "incitement to adultery." They forbade dancing on the Sabbath, or at places such as taverns or weddings, where it was likely to be associated with drunken excess.[16]

Or they banned it when it challenged the official order. In 1684, a dancing master named Francis Stepney opened a school in Boston. He announced that he would teach dances for couples, or "mixt dancing," and proclaimed his classes would be held on Thursdays, the traditional day of sermons and public punishments. He also issued a shocking statement: in one dance lesson, he could teach "more Divinity" than could be found in the Old Testament. The Puritan response was swift and severe. Increase Mather wrote a screed against mixed dancing. The town's court shut down the school and issued a warrant for its founder's arrest. Stepney had no choice but to flee Boston.[17]

Still, the dancing master may have been on to something. By the time he skipped town, many had begun to encourage dancing. What they had in mind was the practice that came to be known as "English country dance," or "contradance." Country dances took their names from the tunes they employed, and many, as their titles suggest, had decidedly earthy origins. There was "Piss Upon the Grass," "Cuckholds All A Row," and "Johnny Cock Thy Beaver."[18] With the appearance of publications like John Playford's *The English Dancing Master* in 1651, dancing masters reworked the old folk tunes into social dances for mixed-gender sets of participants. They designed "minor sets" for two couples, "major sets" for at least a dozen people, and "longways sets" for "as many as will." The dances began, typically, with lines of men facing lines of women in the sets.

The result was hardly a carnival of self-expression. This was dance as self-discipline, social movement set to the etiquette of intricate steps. The directions for the country dance "Excuse Me" provide a typical example:

> First Man and first Woman Cross over and pass into the 2d Couple's Place, then take Hands and turn round 'till the first Man is in the 2d Man's Place; then the 2d Couple do this over as the first Couple did, the rest doing the same. Then the first Man and 2d Woman meet and fall back, and turn S. And the first Woman and 2d Man meet and fall back, and turn S. Then the first Couple cast off and go down on the Outside of the 2d Couple and go the whole Figure, 'till the first Woman comes to the 2d Woman's place, and the first Man into the 2d Man's place, then the 2d Couple cast off and go the whole Figure of 8 between the first Couple 'till they come into the 3d Couple's place, and flip up the Middle, 'till they come to their own places again, the rest doing the like.[19]

Following these instructions required concentration. A wrong move or missed cue could be a social disaster. Masters urged dancers to "listen to the music," let their steps "fall with the beat," and above all pay attention. "You are still part of the dance," one warned, "even when it is not your turn to be active."[20]

English country dance tamed the carnivalesque elements of its earlier tunes. Soon the dance "Piss Upon the Grass" became the more refined "Nancy Dawson," removed from its earthy origins and renamed after the popular English dancer known for her performances in "The Beggar's Opera." Social dance, meanwhile, could be envisioned as a key to the acquisition of bodily control. As one instruction book from 1698 had it, if "civilly used," the art of dancing was "excellent for Recreation" and made the body "graceful in Deportment." Knowledge of how to dance was therefore "a Quality very much beseeming a Gentleman."[21]

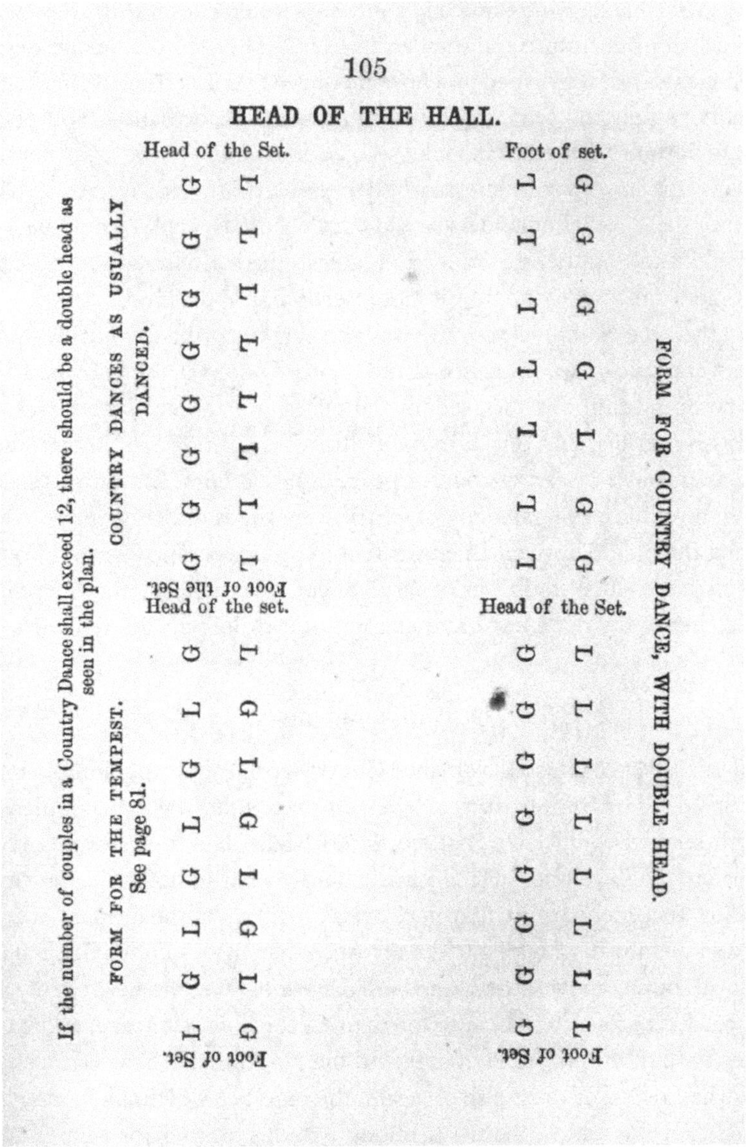

HEAD OF THE HALL.

Head of the Set.   Foot of set.

If the number of couples in a Country Dance shall exceed 12, there should be a double head as seen in the plan.

COUNTRY DANCES AS USUALLY DANCED.

FORM FOR COUNTRY DANCE, WITH DOUBLE HEAD.

FORM FOR THE TEMPEST. See page 81.

Foot of the Set.
Head of the set.

Head of the Set.

Foot of Set.   Foot of Set.

FIGURE 1.1. Dance as self-discipline. Despite the common notion that dancing is a form of liberation against authority, the country dance or contradance reflected a positive repression of musically inspired bodily expressions. This form for the starting positions of dancers, with its arrangement of ladies and gentlemen into rigid sets, suggests how Puritans could go from opposing "mixt dancing" to supporting contradance as a mode of healthy exercise and bodily control. "Form For Country Dance, With Double Head," in Elias Howe, *American Dancing Master and Ball-Room Prompter.* Cambridge: Miles & Dillingham Printers, 1862, 105. Courtesy of American Antiquarian Society.

The wild dancing of untamed jigs and reels would continue in areas beyond the reach of print culture and standardization. Yet by 1800 the linkage of dance to self-control was confirmed by a host of etiquette books. These warned against "laughing loudly in company," "drumming with feet or hands," and perhaps most important, "contempt in looks, words, or actions" for one's partner in the dance.[22] This lapse in manners may have been hard to avoid given the intricacy of dance steps. New Englanders would continue to dance. So would people in the middle and southern colonies and later in the nation's states. At the same time, more dancing did not mean more freedom of expression.

By the time Nathaniel Coverly was running his print shop in Boston, efforts to crack down on the carnival and on expressions of the body had a long history. Both traditions survived, in alehouses, private revels, and backwater Christian revivals. Ensconced in the culture of common folk, they returned in spontaneous folk expressions, in processions, at fairs, and during election days and militia musters, many of which were times of drunkenness, revels, and masquerade. They remained a threat to order. As officials would repeatedly discover, while traditions of carnival could be policed, and the policing would change their content and meanings, they would always return.

Irish Charivaris and Smutty Staves

If officials in Boston missed Nathaniel Coverly's print shop and omitted it from the city's directory of 1815, such an oversight was understandable. Little about Coverly seemed significant or noteworthy. His father had been a printer in Boston before the Revolution. He too made hardly a stir in his trade. During the rebellion, the elder Coverly may have been caught up in the ferment and published something disparaging to the British. When troops under General Gage occupied the city in 1775, the old man fled Boston. Over the next twenty years he moved his press from town to town: to Chelmsford, Concord, and back to Boston for a short time; to Plymouth and then to Amherst, New Hampshire.

He had two sons during these years, the oldest of which, born in 1775, he named after himself. Nathaniel Jr., along with his brother John, apprenticed with his father. The Coverlys printed whatever gave promise of selling: broadsides, pamphlets, and primers; captivity narratives, *The Poor Man's Companion*, and Henry Fielding's salacious novel *Tom Jones*.[23]

Around 1795, Nathaniel Jr. became a partner with his father and together they published a small newspaper, the *Amherst Journal*. The journal did not last long. Within a few years they were back in Massachusetts, this time in Salem. In 1802 they were declared bankrupt and forced to sell their press. Somehow, most likely with help from family members, Nathaniel Jr. was soon back in business. In 1805, he opened his shop on Milk Street in Boston. In the next few years, his father would retire, and by 1815 the old man would be listed as living in a back alley on High Street. His brother, apparently, went into business elsewhere. By 1812, Coverly Jr. was a married artisan with a small family of unknown size. Despite the apparent insignificance of his shop, he was one of Boston's well-known printers, known at least by a common clientele.[24]

Coverly and his shop were typical of the artisan system of labor, a system that had persevered in its basic organization since the Middle Ages. He was a printer and a printer's son, a man with a calling rather than a profession. He started as an apprentice, learning the rudiments of the trade for a number of years. He moved on to become a journeyman, in his case a junior partner with a share of profits. Finally, he became a master printer, inheriting the tools of the trade and opening his own shop.[25]

His shop was small and crowded. This too was typical, for Coverly lived and worked according to artisan traditions of household production. Home and work were not separate spaces; and his shop had to double as living space and place of production. Within its narrow confines, his family's daily activities—cooking, eating, socializing, and sleeping—had to share space with the tools and products of his trade: with type, rag paper, and ink; with lye for cleaning type and strung ropes for the hanging and drying of freshly printed pages; with the printer's punch and the hand press. Had he been more successful, his "family" might have included an apprentice or two, for the traditional concept of family included co-resident employees along with blood relatives. He was not successful. In the words of one historian, the Coverlys were little more than "itinerant printers" who "lived and died in obscurity."[26]

Yet if Coverly was poor in means, his product was rich in tradition. Ballads and balladeers had been around for centuries. Their origins lay at ancient meeting places, at public squares where city-dwellers came for social or ceremonial gatherings, at urban or rural markets, where farmers and vendors brought goods to crossroads, where actors, jugglers, and musicians gathered to perform for commerce-drawn crowds. In these ballads, one would hear fables, histories, and news of the day, all of which could be altered on the spot according to the whims of the singer—the storyteller, or *griot*—and the needs or desires of the gathered audience.

Broadsides were a more recent phenomenon. A prominent form of the print culture that emerged and spread after about the year 1500, they were also more controlled, offering audiences a genre of fixed text and stable content. Coverly did not write his broadsides. For topical and contemporary pieces, he employed a local poet by the name of Nathaniel Hill Wright. For the most part, his calling was to set in type the words of long-dead *griots* and singers, contemporary poets and ministers, politicians and common people off the street, to print expressions that promised to sell at six cents per broadside sheet. Most of his trade was probably to peddlers. He sold his sheets whole-sale, as his ballads declared, offering discounts for the dozen or gross. As well, his cramped shop and living quarters almost certainly contained shelves of broadsides for ready sale to passersby from the streets.[27]

Among these was a ballad inviting buyers to experience, in song and im-age at least, a returned tradition of carnival. Called "Tid Re I," the ballad was a comic narration of an Irish wedding, a celebration of the "marriage of Miss Kitty O'Donavan to Mr. Paddy O'Raffety." Undoubtedly the ballad's music was lively, for its lyrics were an attempt to capture the spirit of a roaring good time:

> Sure won't you hear what roaring cheer,
> Was had at Paddy's wedding—O;
> And how so gay they spent the day,
> From the Churching to the bedding—O.

According to the ballad's lyrics, the wedding party included a collection of stock Irish characters and behaviors: from "Sturdy Pat" to "Morgan Murphy," from "jigging" and the playing of "merry pipes" to the eating of a large num-ber of "pratoes." The song's narrative ended with an equally stock outcome: a drunken brawl caused by a "flowing mudder of whiskey," along with a capering serenade for the bride and groom as they made their way to the wedding bed.[28]

"Tid Re I" pictured the wedding ceremony as a ritual of fertility and unre-strained appetite. In its reference to the serenade for the bride and groom, it included the old peasant tradition of the charivari, a practice whereby groups accompanied wedded couples to their bedchamber then stayed outside through the night drinking, singing, banging pots and pans, and generally making as much noise as imagination and stamina allowed. Once common throughout Europe, the "shivaree," as it became known in the backwaters of America, was in decline as acceptable practice by 1815.[29] In "Tid Re I," it survived, in print, in song, and in the imagined practices of a less civilized Irish.

If a spirit of carnival persisted in these broadsides, so did examples of bodily expression. Coverly printed more than a few ballads of love and lust. In fact, judging from their numbers, these must have been among his most popular. His shelves contained double-entendre songs, ballads like "Hunting the Hare" and "The Valley Below." They included songs of sexual exploits, examples such as "Will the Weaver" and "The Reformed Rake." They were stocked with a colorful collection of traditional carnal characters: cuckolded husbands, lonely young wives, randy rakes, and a multitude of sexually avail-able farmers' daughters.

Among the most popular of these images was that of the sexually potent woman. The ballad "The Female Drummer" focused on the common motif of masquerade, along with a standard double-entendre reference to certain sexual practice. Here, a young maiden runs away from her parents, dons men's clothing, and becomes a regiment drummer, where, as she sings it, she learns to "beat upon my rub-a-dub-a-dum." Discovered and discharged when an officer's wife falls in love with her, she later marries. "And now I have a husband, a drummer he's become," she sings at the song's conclusion, "And I learn him for to beat upon my rub-a-dub-a-dum." In "The Old Man and the Young Wife," a servant maid marries her master. She is scarcely twenty years old. He is "four-score-and-two," or eighty-two, cold as stone and so jealous of rival young sparks that he imprisons her in his home. For years she prays he will die. At last her prayers are answered. And having been "left a widow with youth and beauty bright, after a scene of sorrow she reap'd her heart's delight."[30]

In "The Vintner Outwitted," another young maid agrees to "lie with" a vintner for five pounds. Afterward, he refuses to pay. She calls the local magistrate. The vintner explains, saying he never planned to pay this "rent," for all he "put in her cellar" was "one poor pipe of wine." At song's end, the magistrate decides for the maiden and the sexually aggressive woman is triumphant:

> And when she had got her money all,
>   She jingled it in her purse,
> She clap'd her hand on her cellar door,
>   And swore it was never the worse.[31]

These expressions were not limited to common folk. From the early colonial period through Coverly's time, among the foremost sites of bodily expression were places of bachelor culture, the theaters, alehouses, and men's clubs that were gathering places for gentlemen and "middling sorts" from merchants to artisans. In England, much of this culture centered in clubs and theaters, in Oddfellows Lodges, and in the male crowds gathered at London's Covent Garden, the New Royal Circus, or Drury Lane. This culture thrived in America, in some places at theaters, in others at fraternal lodges, and everywhere at taverns and "publick houses" like Boston's "Bunch of Grapes," the "King's Arms," and the "Blue Anchor."[32]

These were places of meetings and sociability, providing food and drink along with alehouse songs, games, and political discussion. Within them was a culture of masculine expression perhaps best captured by popular toasts. During the late colonial period, gentlemen at London's Bon Vivant Club roared out toasts to "Our Beloved Sovereign, the King, and success to his arms by Land and Sea!" Tavern crowds in America raised bowls to "The Constitution of England

and its bulwarks—her wooden walls!," celebrating their rights as Englishmen along with the British Navy. Other toasts attested to carnal sources of affection. These included the punning: "May we sometimes *do a-miss* that we may reflect on *doing well*"; the blandly droll: "Happiness to our wives and comfort to our sweethearts"; and the riddling and often failing (especially when the assembled were in their cups): "What we all like, what we all love, and what every one dislikes being called, comprised in a word of five letters, G-L-A-S-S!"[33]

At some point during the evening came the alehouse sing-alongs, the roared-out series of gentlemen's catches, cantatas, and glees. Men sang raucous ballads like "The Nymph's Reply" or "I Whoop'd Among the Lasses."[34] Later in the evening and after quite a bit of "fat ale," the crowd might belt out "The Charms of the Bottle," or "Friendship and Wine." Once fully in their cups, its members might also get mellow, harmonizing tearful expressions of male sentiment and yearning in songs like "Woman for Man" or "The Charms of Lovely Peggy."[35]

The songs were all in good fun, part of a gentlemen's culture blending carnal expression with male conviviality. Published in songbooks, they were almost sure to carry imprimaturs of moral approval. "There has been complaints," declared the preface of one songster published in 1782, "that publications of this kind frequently abound with ribaldry and indecency." In *this* case, its writers enjoined, the "greatest care" had been taken in selecting the songs, "to exclude every thing that would have the smallest tendency to corrupt the morals or offend the ear of the most delicate reader."[36]

Some songs were proudly indecent. These were the bawdy ballads transported from English taverns and music halls, places such as "The Coal Hole" in Fountain Court and "Fielding's Head" at Covent Garden. In these masculine locales, gentlemen could rub elbows with a more common crowd, and the songs might be decidedly earthier. They could also be older. Some of the earthiest ballads date back to the Middle Ages, to Chaucer and Rabelais, and later to Thomas D'Urfey's collection of bawdy songs in his 1719 publication *Pills to Purge Melancholy*. In 1604, William Shakespeare had Ophelia sing one in *Hamlet* to signify her madness:

> By Gis and by Saint Charity,
>> Alack, and fie for shame!
> Young men will do't, if they come to't;
>> By Cock they are to blame.
> Quoth she, before you tumbled me,
>> You promis'd me to wed.
> So would I ha' done, by yonder sun,
>> An thou hadst not come to my bed.[37]

Bawdy ballads appeared in a variety of gentlemen's songsters: *The Cock-hold's Nest*, *The Frisky Vocalist*, and *The Cockchafer*. They were rife with images of male and female carnality. And they were pointedly dirty or "smutty." One typical "smutty stave," for example, concerned a lass named "Ellen Love-cock" who had her "am'rous desires" awakened during a walk with "Young Lubin":

> Young Ellen blushed like any rose, / But O, she couldn't resist him.
> His fingers wandered 'neath her clothes, / And, filled with joy, she
> kissed him.
> While pressed unto her belly tight, / His roger left its station,
> And stood revealed before her sight. / While she felt such a queer sensation.
>
> Four times they played their amorous sport, / Till nature could no longer.
> Then Ellen sighed, "O would, my dear, / That roger was but stronger!"
> But, after all, indeed it's true, / Whate'er our rank and station,
> Young Roger is the only thing / To cure a queer sensation.
> Tooral, &c.[38]

Ballads like these could also be found in the drawers of Coverly's shop. In some of these songs of desire, the erotic content was masked. Many expressed a then-traditional theme: a gentleman's power to exploit the maidenhood of common peasant girls. In the ballad "Ranordine," a young rake meets a maiden on a mountain trail and whips out his "gun," promising to protect her virginity from sexual rogues. He then forces himself upon her, abandons her, and warns her not to tell her parents. In the song "Bunch of Rushes," another maid agrees to "lie down" with a swain, provided he promises not to "tease" her "nor break my bunch of rushes." "Kind sir," she sings, "you make too free, / Do you mean to ill use me, / Because that I am poor and low?" He does proceed to "break her rushes," though in this case he agrees to marry her.[39]

Others among Coverly's ballads were more straightforward in content. The ballad "Corydon and Phillis," which appeared in D'Urfey's ribald collection of 1719, fit more with standards of bawdy song. Here was a narrative marked by double entendre and mounting erotic tension. In the song, a young couple meets in a "lonely grove" to talk about their affection; and, as the ballad's refrain has it, "something else, what I do know but dare not tell." The rest of the stanzas have an element of the striptease, as the couple kiss, and a "pretty leg was seen." Then came Corydon's hand, which "wander'd o'er her breast." And of course there was "something else." The ballad continues in this teasing fashion for several more verses, until it is clear that the young couple have reached the point where there is "nothing else," that what began with a kiss has ended with full consummation. At this point Corydon falls asleep. Phillis, meanwhile, takes the role of the sexually aggressive female:

> But Phillis did recover / Much sooner than the Swain,
>   And blushing ask'd her lover, / Shall we not kiss again?
>   And something else, &c.[40]

These expressions suggest a near-complete failure to repress the body, perhaps even an imagined "healthy sexuality" of a pre-Victorian age. Yet Coverly's broadsides also reflected increasingly stringent efforts to impose standards of shame and sexual control. Capital as they may have been, these songs suggest the way the body would return in a culture devoted to its repression. It would return as an object of desire filtered through shame, as a subject of pleasure and disgust, as something dirty.

Many of these ballads prefigured a style of expression that would become a fixture in America: a framework of moral didacticism surrounding a colorful and detailed picture of carnal pleasure, a warning from an official culture, yet a warning awash in the very pleasures it warned against. A typical example appears in "The Farmer's Daughter." The ballad begins with a "jovial plough-boy," who takes a break from his work and sings a song. His singing attracts a farmer's daughter. Soon enough, the young rake is "ploughing and sowing in her land" while she sings, "I think I see the world, it does turn round." After they finish, she sings, "I fain would see the world turn round again." And so the song proceeds:

> Then John began ploughing and sowing as he had done before,
> Till he had sowed the last grain that he had left in store;
> She said my dearest jewell one word I'll speak to thee,
> If I should chance to prove with child consent to marry me.
>   *Whack, fol de rol, de rol, de rol, rol da, whack.*[41]

In later verses, the abandoned maid does have a child. At last, the ballad comes to its warning: be careful, "all you farmer's daughters." There would be no such warning for the jovial ploughboy. And even here, the moral might be lost amid the pleasures of all the ploughing and sowing.

Within a few decades, the moral framework for this sort of thing would become thicker and more threatening. The carnal pleasures such morals warned against would also become more detailed and varied. Soon enough, this combination of moral warning and detailed carnal pleasure would produce a literary style, a type of writing some scholars would refer to as "dark reform" or "immoral didacticism." In this style, writer after writer would delve into the foul moral sewers of various places and times, supposedly to scour

CORYDON AND PHILLIS.

YOUNG Corydon and Phillis,
  Sat in a lonely grove;
Contriving crowns of Lillies,
  Repeating tales of Love.

Chorus.

And fomething elfe,
  And fomething elfe,
What I do know
  But dare not tell.

But as they were a playing.
  She ogled to the Swain;
It fav'd her plainly faying,
  Let's kifs to eafe our pain.
    And fomething elfe, &c.

Ten thoufand times he kifs'd her
  While fporting on the green;
And as he fondly prefs'd her,
  Her pretty leg was feen.
    And fomething elfe, &c.

So many beauties viewing,
  His ardour did increafe;
And greater joys purfuing,
  He wander'd o'er her breaft.
    And fomething elfe, &c.

This Nymph feem'd almoft dying,
  Diffolv'd in am'rous heat;
She whifper'd faintly fighing,
  My dear, your love is great!
    And fomething elfe, &c.

At length one effort trying,
  His preffing to withftand;
She faid, the while complying,
  O! take away your hand!
    And fomething elfe, &c.

Young Corydon grew bolder,
  This moment did improve;
This was the time he told her,
  To fhow how he could love.
    And fomething elfe, &c.

But Phillis did recover
  Much fooner than the Swain,
And blufhing afk'd her lover,
  Shall we not kifs again?
    And fomething elfe, &c.

Thus love his revels keeping,
  Till Nature made a' ftand;
From talk they fell a fleeping,
  Holding each other's hand.
    And fomething elfe, &c.

FIGURE 1.2. The return of repressed desires in a "smutty stave." The ballad "Corydon and Phillis," which appeared in a 1719 collection of ribald songs and which Nathaniel Coverly printed in 1812, shows that sexual imagery in popular song is hardly new. Though the crackdown on the body and on sexual expression would be a hallmark of modernization, both would continually return to popular culture and in popular song. *Corydon and Phillis*, printed by Nathaniel Coverly, Boston, 1812–1814; Isaiah Thomas Broadside Ballad Collection, AAS. Courtesy of American Antiquarian Society.

them clean. Reader after reader would overlook the cleaning to enjoy the sewage.[42] Others would refer to this as pornography.

Generations of Americans would discover that every attempt to crack down on the body, to suppress its functions, urges, and appetites, would result in its return. Sometimes it would return according to patterns of old traditions. Often it would return surrounded by a discourse of control, as something smutty or forbidden, as a source of pleasure saturated with shame, the shame heightening the pleasure. Nowhere would the body return more often than in popular song.

Official Power and the Trickster

As a printer, Nathaniel Coverly was part of a culture moving in the direction of increased control and standardization. His broadsides themselves were taming mechanisms, transforming dynamic oral ballads into static text, subjecting them to the control of fixed type and stable meanings. Some of his ballads, such as the many he printed on criminal behavior and public punishments, were expressly designed to confirm official power. One of these, "God's Judgement on Murder," offered a standard example of the genre. The broadside invited the public to "Go view the execution of Tully and Dalton!" "They mount the scaffold," declared the text in an effort to capture the scene. "The awful moment arrives!" it continued. "The catastrophe is finished! O! God!" Finally, the ballad concluded with a lesson: "Go then, ye votaries of guilt, / Ere virtue, fame and life be lost, / Go purchase wisdom, cheaply, at their cost."[43]

In Coverly's culture, as in his broadsides, power was manifested in a number of ways. The ballad "Captain James" offered an oral-culture primer on the Whig theory of politics, the idea that power without question could lead to corruption without limit. The supposedly true story took place on a ship sailing from Carolina to England. At some point in the voyage, the ship's captain of the title received a slight offense from a young cabin boy. According to the song, he had the boy tied to the mainmast. For three days, he refused to feed him, whipping him each time he cried out in hunger. The lyrics then moved into details that would rivet the most jaded listener:

> When seven days I thus had kept him, / He now to languish did begin,
> Begging for a little water, / I some urine gave to him,
> He poor soul refus'd to drink it, / What I prepar'd, when I'd done
> I made him drink the purple gore / That from his bleeding wounds did run.
> His excrements I then him gave. / Excrements which he had voided,
> Forcing him the same to eat, / And because he did refuse it,
> Eighteen stripes I gave him strait. / With that the distressed creature,

To his savior loud did cry, / In this wretched situation,
   This poor creature now did *die*.[44]

By the song's end, the captain had submitted to a higher power. Having confessed his crime and provided balladeers with a song and a moral lesson, he awaited hanging and gibbeting by British authorities.

Sometimes power worked mysteriously. Examples of the news-of-the-day function of many broadsides, ballads such as "Thomas Moorhead" and "Shocking Earthquakes!" were statements on the arbitrary power of an often-cruel Christian god. The first focused on a sailor found at sea clinging to the wreckage of a capsized ship, a young man who survived by eating his crewmates:

> Moorhead surviv'd—what awful sight! / See all his shipmates dead—
> And to preserve his wretched life, / He on their bodies fed;
> Be thankful Moorhead, to the Lord, / For his protecting care,
> That you was sav'd while others dy'd, / And still His mercy share.
> Myster'ous are the ways of GOD, / Which all his works declare,
> Let all in him then firmly trust, / And beg his tender care.[45]

The second, which told of the earthquake that struck Charleston, South Carolina, in February 1812, featured an angry deity who might target the innocent and guilty alike. Witnesses to the quake were "transfix'd with horror" as they heard the mingled screams of sinners and "frantic mothers," dying with babies clutched to their breasts. The ballad's message called for complete submission: "Then mortals, bow beneath th'Almighty's rod, / Prepare, O! man, to meet an injur'd God.[46]

Then as now, people loved gore, violence, and a good disaster. Along with them they often received lessons on power relations. According to these popular images, the working of power was nearly beyond question. Power came from the top—from magistrates, judges, and sheriffs—and it worked its way down the social ladder. Many at the time pictured society as a strict hierarchy, moving from an imagined God through official authorities and the elite (or, before the Revolution, through the king and government placeholders), through the "middling sort" of merchants, artisans, and freeholder farmers, and finally through the ranks of laborers, servants, and slaves. In America, one of the most important distinctions, especially before the Revolution, was between gentlemen and commoners.

On the high side of this relationship were the members of the elite who could claim a gentlemen's status by birth, property, leisure, or learning. On the low side were the common masses of everyone else. Relations between these two orders of beings were marked by a traditional etiquette of condescension and deference. Commoners were expected to make a show of deference to their superiors, bowing or cringing in their presence. At times a gentleman could rub shoulders with the common sort, deigning to speak to them, perhaps joining them for a drink on Election Day. On these occasions his "condescension" carried no pejorative meanings. At other times he pulled rank. A gentleman could horsewhip a commoner for refusing to move from a walkway; he could give one a caning for "putting on airs" or trying to rise above his natural station.[47]

Another distinction was between men and women. By tradition, law, and practice, this was a patriarchal culture. In Coverly's time, official records continued to list women in proprietary terms, as generic daughters or wives of named fathers and husbands. Women could own property only if they were unmarried or widows. Under the ancient law of couverture, marriage equaled a kind of legal death for women, and all they owned would pass to their husbands. According to the ballad "A Song for a Wedding," the woman's place was defined by submission; or, as the song had it, she "must be subjected, / Unto her husband's will, / That nothing be neglected, / Her duty to fulfill."[48]

Traditional ballads like "The Frog and the Mouse" rooted these ideals in nature, locating social hierarchies in conceptions of a great chain of being that ran from human to animal, from higher to lower orders, from the strong to the weak. In the song, a frog meets a rat and together they go to the home of a mouse to drink some ale. Suddenly a cat and kittens enter: the cat eats the rat, the kittens eat the mouse. The frog escapes, only to be gobbled up by a duck. "So there was an end of one, two and three," the song concluded, "The Rat, the Mouse, and Billy Froggy."[49] For lowly cabin boys and frogs alike, this was a cruel world.

As a printer, Nathaniel Coverly often found himself working to confirm power as top-down, legitimate, and rooted in nature. As a printer of broadsides for a common clientele, he frequently found himself subverting this order. In other words, while his broadsides represented official culture, they also had to appeal to plebian tastes. As a result, his ballads blended official culture with vernacular tradition. One example can be seen in Coverly's publication of "A New Bundling Song," a reprint of a late eighteenth-century ballad smack in the middle of arguments over the place of tradition within a modernizing culture.

At the time few topics were more evocative of tradition than bundling. In 1811, "Captain Grose's" *Dictionary of the Vulgar Tongue* defined bundling as "a man and a women lying on the same bed with their clothes on." In America, according to the Captain, "husbands and parents frequently permitted travelers to *bundle* with their wives and daughters." Having developed in Europe long before a modern culture of privatization, the practice was in part a necessity, a result of cold winters and simple poverty. During the colonial period and later in some areas, the sharing of beds was common, for it maximized body heat and saved firewood. Entire families might share a straw-tick mattress in a one-room cottage, while individual homes offered shared beds for peddlers and schoolteachers. Well into the nineteenth century, travelers slept with strangers in low-cost inns and taverns, while young clerks thought nothing of partnering up in the single-bed rooms of cheap boardinghouses.

Bundling was also a courtship ritual, a traditional practice that allowed young couples a night of intimacy before marriage. And here, with the rise of modern sensibilities of bodily repression, it ran into critics. While it allowed couples to share a bed for a night, its standards dictated that they were to remain fully clothed or securely wrapped in bundling sheets and separated from each other by a bundling board. Yet as critics pointed out, everyone knew the tradition led to sexual behavior. By the second half of the seventeenth century, ministers began to sermonize against the practice: it was rustic, outdated, and worse, it was a source of carnal temptation. As Washington Irving would later put it, wherever it existed there were "an amazing number of sturdy brats" produced "without the license of law, or the benefit of clergy."[50]

Balladeers and printers of broadsides came down on both sides of the issue, oscillating between a defense of folk traditions and efforts to police bodily temptations. As one ballad, "In Favor of Courting," had it:

> Since in a bed a man and maid, / May bundle and be chaste,
> It does no good to burn out wood, / It is a needless waste.
> Let coats and gowns be laid aside, / And breeches take their flight,
> An honest man and woman can, / Lay quiet all the night.

The practice was safe, concluded the song, or at least as safe as any contact between courting couples. During bundling, "Bastards are not at all times got," and non-bundling couples could find plenty of opportunity to give in to carnal passions before marriage.[51]

Nathaniel Coverly may have printed a version of this song. But his more successful effort took the side of a modernizing culture. Much like the anti-bundling ministers and writers, "A New Bundling Song" linked the practice to the rustics of America's rural backwaters. The song's main focus, however, was on women. They were the primary defenders of the practice:

> Some maidens say, if through the nation,
> Bundling should quite go out of fashion,
> Courtship would lose its sweets; and they
> Could have no fun till wedding day.

It shant be so, they rage and storm,
 And country girls in clusters swarm,
And fly and buzz, like angry bees,
 And vow they'll bundle when they please,
Some mothers too, will plead their cause,
 And give their daughters great applause,
And tell them, 'tis no sin nor shame,
 For we, your mother, did the same[.][52]

In the song, it was the country girl who complained of the chafing gown, the young maid who wriggled her way out of the bundling sheet. The male "spark" profited from the opportunity, as he "nought feels but naked skin." In the popular imagination, at least, bundling embodied women, allowing them to express sexual appetite. So the song set out to kill the tradition. "Probably no single thing tended so much to break up the practice," claimed a later historian of the ballad. "We have found many persons who distinctly remember the publication of this song, and the effect it had on the public mind." The song resulted in "such a general storm of banter and ridicule that no girl had the courage to stand against it, and continue to admit her lovers to her bed."[53]

Considered as a whole, these types of expressions reveal a culture in which traditions of carnival and bodily expression were increasingly yoked to official control, in which elite power and plebian taste were twinned. The result cannot be seen as simply contributing to the power of official culture. Carnivalesque elements remained in the common folks' enjoyment of a good execution. They survived in plebian tastes for lurid details of crimes, in the pleasure of hearing about Captain James forcing a poor cabin boy to eat his own urine, blood, and excrement. "A New Bundling Song" may have railed against lascivious country maids, but at mid-narrative the ballad still contained common tastes for the carnival tradition of the sexually aggressive woman.

Elsewhere, Coverly's ballads were more directly subversive. In these ballads, one element of the carnival escaped containment more often than any other: this was the standard imagery of the weak turning the tables on the strong. Typical of the genre was "The Farmer's Daughter, or, The Barley Maid." In the ballad's narrative, a married gentleman goes out riding and meets a farmer's daughter on horseback, carrying barley to the market. He makes her an offer: in exchange for some "delight," he will buy her a silk gown, a fan, and a pair of gloves. This is too much for the maid to resist. After a trip to the market, where he buys her the gifts, together the two ride into the countryside, looking for a place to engage in their delights. They come to a swift stream. Because the maid has the larger horse, she offers to carry everything across: her gifts, the gentleman's belongings, and his heavy bag of gold coins. Then comes the reversal: as the maid crosses, the gentleman suddenly realizes his horse is too small to follow. He can only watch helplessly as she rides off with the loot.

On one hand, the ballad was a morality tale, another effort to discipline sexual behavior. To be sure, it ended with a warning:

> Take my advice each marry'd man,
> Be constant to your partner,
> Lest you be serv'd as I have been,
> By this sly farmer's daughter.[54]

On the other, it had a standard characteristic of the carnivalesque. As the farmer's daughter rode off with her gifts and the married man's gold, what listeners heard was a trickster tale, a ritual of reversal in which the weak were able to outwit the strong.

These tales were among the most common of Coverly's ballads. They were also among the longest, their length taxing the printer's necessity of fitting them to a single page. From this, one might assume they were among the oldest, their oral-tradition origins, in which length was not a problem and ballad-eers could add as much detail or side story as they wanted, predating the rise of print culture. Many focused on female characters. Others focused on the character of the double trickster, female and dead. The rise of the dead would be a hallmark of common traditions of carnival. After all, no group could match the dead's claims to being so often oppressed, put down, or trodden underfoot. And so they would continually rise up, in Day of the Dead festivals, in tales of horror, in gothic stories of restless spirits.

And in Coverly's broadsides, as wronged and vengeful women. Two examples are the ballads "Handsome Harry, or, The Deceitful Young Man" and "Rosanna." In the first, Handsome Harry seduces and abandons a "fair maiden," escaping to sea and leaving her "with child." She hangs herself in the woods. A few days later, hunters discover her body, her flesh partly eaten by ravenous crows. Her ghost then appears on Harry's ship, causing a storm and threatening to drown the crew. The ship's captain responds by having Harry thrown overboard. As the deceitful young man drowns, the trickster takes her revenge. In the second ballad, a young rake seduces Rosanna, a "lady fair" and "daughter to a worthy knight." Worried she might expose him to her noble parents, he then murders her and buries her body. Roses grow upon the unmarked grave, roses that never wilt or die, even in winter. When local villagers gather to see the miracle, the young rake cannot resist joining them. He touches one of the flowers; it wilts; and the villagers—who know precisely what this portent means—proceed to dig up Rosanna's rotting corpse. Though dead and a woman, Rosanna is not powerless: at ballad's end, her seducer is in jail, awaiting his public execution.[55]

These trickster-tale ballads did not need to be old. Consider one of the most popular ballads of the period, "Yankee Doodle." While the origins of the ballad are somewhat mysterious, there is some agreement that British troops developed it sometime between 1755 and 1763, during the Seven Years' War, singing it in mock Yankee dialect as a commentary on the poor showing of colonial militias. The words to one version were openly derisive toward the colonials:

> Brother Ephraim sold his cow, / And bought him a Commission,
> And then he went to Canada, / To fight for the Nation;
> But when Ephraim he came home, / He proved an arrant Coward,
> He wou'd'n't fight the Frenchmen there, / For fear of being devour'd.[56]

As it appeared in the broadsides in Coverly's shop, the song offered a commentary on American provincialism. Its focus was on the young son of a country farmer and his visit to George Washington's camp during the Revolution. There, the rube sees a host of overwhelming sights: large cannons, soldiers who enjoy the luxury of eating molasses every day, and a "tarnal proud" George Washington acting the "dandy," seated in his "meeting-clothes" upon a "slapping stallion." Overwhelmed, the farmer's son runs back to his country home.[57]

Despite the apparently dismissive images of "Yankee Doodle," Americans embraced the song, making it an anthem of the Revolution. Quite likely, the embrace was a result of the image. The song's imagery portrayed Americans as rustics and provincials, as common rabble. Yet this rabble had dared to rise up against the most powerful nation on earth. Common Americans could see themselves in the song's depiction of George Washington, as Yankees decked out in meeting clothes and feathered hats, as dandies who could put on airs without being horsewhipped or caned, as tricksters who had reversed the order of things and pronounced themselves the equals of British gentlemen.

As one of Coverly's ballads declared, the result of the Revolution was a "world upside down," a world in which the lords of "Old England" were laid low while America rose.[58] According to this imagery, the promise of America lay in its radical reversal of order and its elevation of the common folk. Within this returned tradition, the ultimate trickster would be the American common folk themselves. In the ballad "Yankee Doodle," we see the birth of a trickster nation.

2

The Vulgar Republic

On June 1, 1812, President James Madison delivered a message to Congress asking for a declaration of war against Great Britain. Following two weeks of heated debate, Congress approved the message, barely, in the closest war vote in American history. For the next two years, the conflict was on. Along the American coast, the British Royal Navy would run a blockade and cripple much of the country's economy. In Washington, British troops would march in, take the capital, and burn many of its public buildings. In Boston, Nathaniel Coverly would print ballads to rally the public spirit:

> BRITANNIA'S arm'd, *Marauders* come,
> The cannons' roar, the beating drum,
> Increase the WAR'S alarms;
> Her fleets *Blockade* and line our coasts,
> Of vict'ries won, *Great Britain* boasts,
> *To arms! To arms! To arms!*[1]

It would be a difficult task. The War of 1812 has been termed America's "Forgotten War." For many, it might best be forgotten. After all, the conflict was not a bright hour in the nation's military history. There were at least two large-scale invasions of Canada. The fighting Canadians repulsed both and made it look easy. Early on, a fledgling US Navy had a few good moments. But the British Navy was the best in the world; and as it tightened its blockade, the Yankee exploits all but disappeared. The performance of American troops was an embarrassment, little more than a record of forced retreats, the refusal of militias to cross state lines, and in the conflict's darkest days the surrender of an entire army. The nation's lone undeniable success on land, Andrew Jackson's victory at New Orleans, came only after the treaty ending the war.[2]

For many observers, the conflict lacked a clear cause; and so, even from the outset, it spawned a broad and popular antiwar movement. One of the most often-cited causes was the British government's passage of the "Orders in Council," a set of rules developed in 1806 to blunt Napoleon's plans for European dominance. The Orders declared that foreign ships bound for the continent had to first call at a British port, where they would be assessed duties before being cleared for continued sailing. Yankee merchants howled over this denial of "free trade." Farmers in the interior were less concerned, and the issue proved a hard sell for a war drive.

Another spark came in June 1807, when the captain of the British ship-of-the-line *Leopard* stopped and boarded the American frigate *Chesapeake*, taking four of her crew members as deserters from the British Navy. This time many more Americans cried their outrage at the denial of "sailors' rights." Yet the event preceded the fighting by five years. Finally, there was a sense that the talk about Orders in Council, revenge for the *Chesapeake*, and even the motto "Free Trade and Sailor's Rights" was little more than window dressing. According to the war's many critics, the real motive for the conflict was conquest: a band of American War Hawks wanted Canada.[3]

For Nathaniel Coverly, the coming of war promised an increase in trade. He could expect commissions for the printing of military recruitment songs. He would have anticipated a ready audience for ballads providing news of the day, reports of the most recent victories, and if they happened, the setbacks of the nation's military forces. With the help of his hired lyricist Nathaniel Hill Wright, he would have the task of providing a steady stream of pro-American ballads to be sung in Boston's public squares and alehouses. Like other printers, his role in the war would be to stir up patriotism. Then, as now, the issue raised a question: just what was patriotism?[4]

Roots of Patriotism I: The Communal Tradition

A couple of weeks after Madison's war message to Congress, two events happened at almost the same time. First, after a lengthy debate, Congress came back with a declaration of war against Great Britain; second, news arrived that the British Parliament had rescinded the Orders in Council. The United States was at war. Yet one of the reasons for the war had evaporated. Still, Yankee printers trundled out calls for patriotic duty. In Boston, Nathaniel Coverly issued "A New Patriotic Song":

> COLUMBIANS, arouse! and attend to the call,
>   Of heaven-born freedom, and act with decision;
> No longer let tyrants your birth-right enthrall,

> But form in bright union, a firm coalition.
> In a brotherly band,
> United we'll stand,
> No despot shall lord it, o'er this our dear land,
> And long shall our nation with gladness proclaim,
> The ardor which kindles at liberty's name.[5]

The ballad had many of the hallmarks of early American patriotism. It contained the standard references to liberty and freedom. It offered a call for unity in the face of British tyranny. Above all, it featured images of a people defined by brotherhood and self-sacrifice. Here, as elsewhere, American patriotism would be characterized by returned traditions of community.

Many would have dated these traditions back to New England's "Pilgrim fathers." In 1630, shortly after the landing of the Massachusetts Bay Company, the Company's leader John Winthrop delivered the most celebrated statement of these values in his sermon "A Modell of Christian Charity." In Winthrop's phrasing, the Puritan colony would be a "City upon a Hill," a beacon for the reform of the world. There were, he noted, many threats to this mission, foremost among them the colonists' "carnall intencions." To "avoyde shipwracke," he prescribed a communal ethos:

> Wee must be knitt together in this worke as one man, wee must entertaine each other in brotherly Affeccion, wee must be willing to abridge our selves of our superfluities, for the supply of others necessities, we must uphold a familiar Commerce together in all meekness, gentlenes, patience and liberallity, wee must delight in eache other, . . . mourne together, labour, and suffer together, allways having before our eyes our Commission and Community in the worke, our Community as members of the same body.[6]

This communal ethos would be central to the settlement of New England. Five years later, an anonymously authored pamphlet called *The Ordering of Towns* provided a model for "ideal plantations" as waves of colonists spread out from Boston. According to the pamphlet, each town would be organized around a meetinghouse. Around this center point would be a village green and a cluster of houses, "orderly placed to enjoy comfortable communion." Beyond the houses, in widening concentric rings, would be communal pasturelands and woodlots.[7]

For the English common folk who made up the majority of early and willing immigrants to the colonies, nothing would have been more familiar or rooted in tradition. Most were descended from generations who lived in communal villages. Many could trace their families to clusters of houses located on a squire's estate. At the center of these settlements was typically a marker, perhaps a marked birch, a wooden post, or a shaft of cut stone. Most likely the object had as many names as there were dialects and regional references. Cultural geographers have called it a "roland." The roland oriented traditional settlements. It provided a central point around which tenant farmers and craftspeople built cottages and buildings, some of which contained commonly held livestock and tools for farming, around which they developed rings of common fields.[8]

From the Middle Ages through the seventeenth century, church and civic authorities cracked down on the roland as a symbol of the pagan past. Officials removed the ancient staffs, replacing them with stone crosses or village fountains. Beginning in the sixteenth century, the enclosure movement scattered other communal settlements. Members of the land-owning aristocracy "enclosed" or privatized their estates, evicting the clusters of tenants who worked and lived on them according to the old ways. The displaced made their way to burgeoning cities, to places like London, Manchester, and Liverpool. Many became cheap labor for maritime trades and industrial factories. Some became willing immigrants to the North American colonies.[9]

Still, the old traditions remained inscribed on the land. In backwater towns in England and elsewhere in Europe, ancient center staffs may have been replaced by crosses or fountains, but the new markers remained rolands in function and practice. They still focused the community toward its center; they still stood as material reminders of the communal ways of the past. In colonial New England, the tradition thrived for a time. In many towns the village green and the steepled meetinghouse stood as vestigial rolands. The maypole was the roland in carnival colors. Eventually, however, villages turned to trade, common lands were divided and sold, and Puritans became Yankee mercantilists, their commitments to individual success outpacing communal ideals.[10]

None of this should be taken as imbuing these early settlements with nostalgia. Small, tight-knit villages with a shared communal ethos were not free of social problems. In old-country villages, the days and nights of local festivals around the roland could also be times of large-scale fights, as groups from surrounding settlements tried to break in on the ceremonies and locals defended themselves from "outsiders." In the villages of New England, fear of outsiders often took the form of atrocities against Quakers, Shakers, and others viewed as having beliefs outside the norm.

The very tightness of center-oriented village life could generate unhealthy tensions. These tensions may have erupted in the Salem witchcraft outbreak of 1692–1693. One of the problems in Salem, as a number of historians have argued or implied, was the fact that people paid attention to one another— maybe too much attention. They looked for neighbors who were strange, or different, or more successful than the norm. When they found them, they accused some of witchery.[11]

The point here is that a communal ethos exists at the heart of American history. The existence of this ethos along with the transitions within it can be traced out in song. Indeed, echoes of the old values may be especially evident in America's most communal of song genres, the hymn and the psalm. In the early years of colonization, official Puritan culture objected to the singing of "corrupt songs." Yet few had problems with the singing of assorted catches, rounds, and riddle-songs to pass time at work or in homes. All would have admitted that singing—particularly the singing of psalms—held a central place in Puritan culture. Through the eighteenth century, the most popular book in British North America was the Bible. The second most popular was the *Bay Psalm Book* or *Whole Book of Psalms*. In fact, with its initial printing in America in 1640, the *Bay Psalm Book* may have been the first book published in the colonies.

The book contained several hints about the culture's approaches to psalm-singing. Originally it included no musical notation. The point was simple: the biblical verses of the psalms were more important than the tunes. The text did include arguments about the propriety of singing. As the book's preface had it, psalm-singing raised several questions:

> First, what psalms are to be sung in churches? whether David's and other scripture psalms, or the psalms invented by the gifts of godly men in every age of the church. Secondly, if scripture psalms, whether in their own words, or in such meter as English poetry is wont to run in? Thirdly, by whom are they to be sung? whether by the whole churches together with their voices or by one man singing alone and the rest joyning in silence, & in the close saying amen.[12]

The hefty tome's preface provided a set of answers. Its writers averred that along with biblical psalms, others by "godly men" could be sung in churches and included in the *Psalm Book*. They held that psalms could be translated into English meter and set to popular melodies, "as the Lord hath hid from us the Hebrew tunes." Finally they maintained that since one of the reasons for singing was to foster communion, congregations should sing psalms together, "with one heart and one voice."[13]

The doctrinal statements gave early psalmody many of its characteristics. To facilitate singing, the psalms had a simple rhyme scheme from their translation into English meter. To produce the communal effect of meeting-goers singing with "one heart and one voice," ministers followed the practice of "lining out." The minister or choirmaster would sing each line of verse separately so listeners could catch the words and melody. The entire congregation would then roar out the line. The result was a folk survival, a call-and-response pattern of song associated with oral cultures.

Puritan congregations enjoyed the style of lining out, the back-and-forth sociability of call and response. They took pleasure in the psalm tunes, for many were borrowed from popular songs. Their critics called them "Geneva jigs," a reference to the vivacity of the tunes along with the Swiss origins of Calvinist thought. "Make yee a joyfull sounding noyse," sang the minister from the *Bay Psalm Book*'s 100th Psalm. His flock would repeat the line joyfully, making the meetinghouse rafters shake. So went the Puritan version of the Doxology, "Old Hundred":

> Make yee a joyfull sounding noyse / unto Jehovah, all the earth:
> Serve yee Jehovah with gladness: / before his presence come with mirth.
> Know, that Jehovah he is God, / who hath us formed it is he,
> & not ourselves: his own people / & sheepe of his pasture are wee.[14]

The singing of psalms in the old way, declared a defender of the style, was a "savourie sauce" to the experience of the meeting. "Yea I may say this," he added, "this spiritual sauce is meat it self. In singing we pray, we praise, we confesse, we petition, we exhort, we meditate, we believe, we joy, we mourne."[15]

The results, according to one historian, were "artistically dreadful." Early observers of American ways were "astounded by the noise," adds another, "which carried miles across the quiet countryside." The communal style of psalmody provided a forgetfulness of self, a seamless bond with others. The "rude and primitive singing in our old meeting house always excited me powerfully," wrote Harriet Beecher Stowe years later, adding that it "brought over me, like a presence, the sense of the infinite and eternal."[16] It also, declared critics of the style, produced a lack of consciousness of one's own bad singing. For many, the issue was an overly free expression of emotion in the form of "quavering." Since no two members of any congregation "quaver alike or together," wrote one in the 1690s, the typical psalm sounded "like five hundred different tunes roared out at the same time." The effect, declared another, was a "horrid medley" that "may no more be called *Singing* than *Hollowing*."[17]

For decades the debates raged, between supporters of "natural singing" or singing by ear and lining out, and "reformed" singing or singing by musical notation. Slowly, region by region, the reformed-singing advocates won the day. The first edition of the *Bay Psalm Book* with musical notation appeared in 1698. From this date, the shift was on from psalmody to hymnody. The greatest English hymnist, Isaac Watts, placed the style in the service of controlling young people. Watts's Sunday-school hymns introduced children to self-discipline, picturing a deity who witnessed every secret sin. Elsewhere he resorted to the controlling mechanism of terror. Children, according to one Watts hymn, should never tease old, bald men; unless, of course, like the biblical story of the rotten kids who made fun of the prophet Elisha's dome, they wanted an angry god to send a couple of bears to tear them to pieces:

> When children in their wanton play, / Serv'd old Elisha so;
> And bid the prophet go his way, / "Go up, thou bald-head, go."
> God quickly stopt their wicked breath, / And sent two raging bears,
> That tore them limb from limb to death, / With blood, and groans, and tears.[18]

This kind of thing was probably more enjoyable for bald men than it was for children. Yet it was enjoyable. Along with composers like John Newton and William Billings, Watts would set hundreds of biblical verses to standardized musical arrangements. Hostile to the vernacular style of lining out, the movement stressed making psalms and hymns more pleasing, with easier rhyme schemes and catchier melodies. Eventually its members moved from biblical verse to more topical lyrics, from Watts's hymns for children to Newton's confessional "New Britain" or "Amazing Grace," to Billings's hymns promoting the cause of the American Revolution.[19]

One result was better singing. Another was the taming of meetinghouse song. Soon, congregations began identifying their best singers for membership in the choir. In doing so, they silenced the former shouters of lined-out psalms, relegating them to positions of passive spectatorship. By the American Revolution and into the early decades of the nineteenth century, the "horrid medley" of traditional psalmody survived for the most part only in the backwaters. By this time church choirs were holding rehearsals. Some went on concert tours, subjecting sacred song to the marketplace. The style was undoubtedly more pleasing. "And yet," declared one singer in a reminiscence, "when I remember how little we kept in view the main and real object of sacred music—when I think how much we sang to the praise and honor and glory of our inflated selves alone . . . I am inclined to feel more shame and regret than pleasure at those youthful recollections."[20] Here was a shift from tradition to modernity, a transition in values from the communal to the individual.

Echoes of the old traditions remained. In many New England towns, the meetinghouse continued to represent a vestigial roland. Villagers still looked suspiciously upon outsiders; farmers still collected stray livestock from the community pound. The traditions would survive in common-folk conceptions of a moral economy, in the belief that profit must be subservient to community well-being. They would take form in bread riots and anti-rent riots when merchants and landlords ignored the ideal. They would appear in town

meetings, voluntary associations, and nostalgia for the kinship of rural settlements. In Nathaniel Coverly's Boston, they remained inscribed on the landscape, a short walk from his shop to Washington Street, then to Tremont, then
past the burial grounds to the old Boston Common. They would reappear in
moments of national crisis, in the trying times of the Revolution and the War
of 1812.

Roots of Patriotism II: The Revolution

When war broke out, Nathaniel Coverly had a ready stock of patriotic ballads,
some lifted from fellow printers, many inherited from his father. Most dated
from the period of the American Revolution. These ballads suggest the ped-
dling of two myths. One portrayed the Revolution as a tax revolt, a coherent rebellion by a mass of Americans all engaged in mercantile trade, all outraged at
British taxes. Another held that the Revolution and its fruits were attributable
to a few great leaders; it never would have happened without men like John
Adams, Ben Franklin, and George Washington. During the Revolution, these
ideals failed to explain the event. By the outbreak of the War of 1812, enough
time had passed that many believed American patriotism was a specific ideal,
a predictable way of thinking that could be controlled and managed.

The first of these myths was at the center of the ballad "American Taxation."
Reprinted by Coverly at the time of the War of 1812, the ballad began with
Britain's reasons for taxing the colonies, the belief that America was a land of
"milk and honey." And so, according to the song's version of the British minister Lord North, it was time for the colonials to pay up. The lyrics followed a
soon-to-be standard chain of events: a sugar tax followed by the Stamp Act;
an outraged response by a people who naturally hate taxes, a series of harsher
acts from the "Coercive" to the "Intolerable," and a war fought under the motto
"what kind heaven gave us, who then shall take away."[21]

At the time the picture was not this neat. In the 1760s and early 1770s,
the merchants who objected to British taxation and made up most of the
membership in the Sons of Liberty faced an enormous challenge of building
popular support for rebellion. One problem was that common people cared
little about taxes. The taxes were light and soon rescinded; many colonials
either did not pay them or failed to recognize them when they did. Another
problem was that common folk had their own agendas. Slaves and Indians
were not polled, of course, but African American slaves wanted freedom, and
Native Americans wanted protection against white expansion. White farmers
wanted land opened for planting and settlement, which meant more slaves to

do the work and the forcible removal of Indians. Tenant farmers in the Hudson River Valley of New York wanted revenge against the region's hated landowners, the families like the De Lanceys and Van Rensselears who charged exorbitant rents and ran their massive estates like feudal lords. Among common people there was anger enough for a rebellion. The problem for the Sons of Liberty was that the resentments were often directed not at taxes but at the privilege of the colonial elite.[22]

In the buildup to war, many pamphleteers continued to flog the taxation issue. Others turned to communal traditions, attempting to create shared characteristics that could be called "American." Focusing on the "Coercive Acts" and the British occupation of Boston, the hymnist William Billings rooted his 1778 publication of "Lamentation Over Boston" in the language of the psalms. His people of Boston sat down by the "Rivers of Watertown" (not Babylon), where "We wept, we wept, we wept, / When we remembered thee, O Boston." The hymn offered a consoling vision of American exceptionalism, the tribulations of a chosen people awaiting their imagined god to preserve and defend them and restore the land "unto us."[23]

Elsewhere, a host of "Liberty Songs" pictured American characteristics in terms of a devotion to freedom and the rights of common people. Freedom had any number of meanings. Leaders of the rebellion tended to have something very specific in mind. For many it was the lifting of the English laws restricting American shipping and trade to British ports. For others it was gaining recognition for land claims in the Ohio Valley, land that according to the British Proclamation Act was beyond colonial claim and reserved for Indians. To achieve their ends, they had a twofold task: they had to foment a rebellion while keeping a lid on plebeian anger. The taxation issue may have been their preferred tactic. Yet they were willing to adopt a more heated rhetoric, a language of common people with the "natural right" to rise against their oppressors.[24]

They were playing with fire. One gauge of what common people did with their freedom was Boston's annual celebration of "Guy Fawkes Day," or "Pope's Day," as it was called in the colonies. This anti-Catholic festival centered on a giant wagon called a "Pope's Carriage." The wagon had to be large enough for effigies and costumed celebrants: typically a mimic Pope along with an assemblage of bishops, monks, and the devil, complete with horns, tail, and pitchfork. In some years the wagon held an enormous paper lantern lit from within by torches. Small boys, or "devil's imps," danced inside the glowing contraption, their movements casting macabre silhouettes. Mobs of men pushed and pulled the carriage through the town, some beating on "Pope's drums" or blowing whistles, many in license-giving disguises of mummer's costume and

face paint. At several points they stopped at houses or merchant shops to collect money for liquor and food. At each stop they roared out the carnival's
traditional song:

> The Fifth of November, / As you well remember,
>   Was gunpowder, treason and plot;
> I know of no reason, / Why the gunpowder treason,
>   Should ever be forgot.

To a point the festival was harmless, little more than an annual blowing-
off of plebeian steam. But in Boston a tradition developed of having not one
but two Pope's Carriages, one from the poorer North End and another from
the more well-off neighborhoods to the south. By day the wagons passed in
friendly camaraderie. By night the North Enders began taking advantage of
the carnival to get in a few strikes at their neighbors. Soon a new tradition developed: the two mobs would fight over the possession of their carriages. The
resultant battles became wild affairs, characterized by massive fistfights along
with the use of clubs and paving stones as weapons. The ceremony ended in
a giant bonfire; the mobs burned the wagons along with barrels, fence posts,
and whatever else they could collect during the day.[25]

Whipping up outrage at official order was one thing; controlling this sort
of effervescence was another. Still, as Coverly's broadsides indicate, balladeers
were willing to ramp up the anger. Some ballads focused on safe targets: individuals like King George and Lord North who were an ocean away. Others
took a more dangerous tack, directing plebeian anger toward "domestic enemies." They heaped epithets on the loyalist Tories, calling them "cut throats"
and "tyrants," referring to them as a host of "minions, placemen, pimps and
pensioners."[26]

The rhetoric had its effect. In the spring of 1764, a group of frontier farmers from western Pennsylvania made their way to Philadelphia to see what
the talk was about. Going by the name the "Paxton Boys," they asserted their
freedom along the way by massacring twenty Indians, "Christianized" Indians, according to the stories of the event. While the killing of mere Indians
may have raised little notice, this massacre of Christian Indians suggested the
problem of riling up the crowd. To Ben Franklin, the Paxton Boys were little
more than "white savages." A year later, in August 1765, the common participants in Boston's annual Pope's Day carnival met near the old town gates. They
renamed a nearby elm a "liberty tree," and from it lynched an effigy of the recently appointed stamp man, Andrew Oliver.

For the local Sons of Liberty, this was well and good. They were less pleased
when later in the day the mob engaged in the old custom of pulling down

Oliver's house. Two weeks later the same mob ransacked and set fire to the house of Governor Thomas Hutchinson. That night, as the Sons of Liberty worried about their own property, the angry crowd watched the flames with carnival delight and chanted an alarming refrain: "Let it burn, Let it burn, Let it burn."[27]

After the shooting started, it became easier for propagandists to fan the flames of revolution. One common ballad theme was British pride and presumed scorn toward colonials. According to "The Battle of Bunker Hill," British Regulars marched off believing the Yankees would surrender at their sight. They would then stroll into Boston, capture the "rebel kings" John Hancock and Samuel Adams, execute them, and stake their heads on Beacon Hill. The song "General Burgoyne's Lamentation" had the notoriously foppish British general singing of his contempt for "rebels" and asking his troops: "What say you my lads, must we yield unto men, / That we have so long held in such great disdain?"[28]

The point was irony: both the British Regulars and "Gentleman Johnny" would get their comeuppance. At "Bunker Hill," the Regulars took the hill but paid a terrible price in killed and wounded. The ballad "British Lamentation" was an attempt to convey the tone of the shocked troops. "I wish," the ballad had the Regulars singing, "I'd ne'er come to America." As for Burgoyne, his army's vaunted invasion from Canada would be slowed by an overabundance of camp followers, the rugged topography of the Green Mountains, and the fact that he launched it in early summer, at the height of black fly season. By the time the invasion reached western New York, the general was looking for a place to fall. He found it at Saratoga, where he surrendered his entire army. Broadside ballads would again picture Saratoga as an ironic reversal. At the outset of the invasion, Burgoyne had seen the Americans as a "cowardly crew." According to the song, his defeat taught him a hard lesson: "To my woeful experience, I find it was false, / For I find that the Yankees are equal to us."[29]

Even during the conflict, these ballads failed to completely funnel plebeian anger against the British. At the beginning of the war, the breakdown in attitudes was most likely by thirds, with a third of colonials supporting rebellion, a third loyal to the crown, and a third—probably the largest third—uncaring, neutral, or on the fence, waiting to see what happened. The main cause of the war was often the conflict itself. Between 1775 and 1780, armies trampled fields, forcibly requisitioned farm animals for food, and burned villages that presumably harbored weapons or rebels. The fence-sitters were brought down from their perches by the daily atrocities of an occupying force and a mass conflict.

Like all wars, the thing was a mess. In the spring of 1775, the acting governor of Virginia, John Murray, Lord Dunmore, issued a declaration that slaves who fought for the British would be freed at the war's end. In the war's early days, nearly a thousand flocked to his banner. In the Hudson River Valley, tenant farmers waited to see which side the region's landlords would join. When they sided with the rebellion, the farmers went the opposite direction, joining the loyalists for a chance to fire a musket at the hated squires. Here as elsewhere—in the Green Mountains, along the Pennsylvania frontier and into the Ohio Valley, in Virginia and the Carolinas—the conflict descended into civil war, bloody clashes between militias and Indians, and payback for personal grudges.[30]

In the end, the best the rebellion's leaders could say was that it worked out, despite the bloody chaos. It worked out, that is, for Northern merchants, Southern planters, and those with land claims in the West. Lord Dunmore's proclamation had the unintended effect of uniting the colonial elite. Faced with this "black deed," the South's planter class aligned with New England merchants against the terrifying prospect of a slave revolt. Underfunded and overmatched, continental armies managed to stay in the field. Militia and regular troops performed their function, making camp, making noise with drum and fife, and making their presence known to the British.[31]

In Britain, opposition to the war grew through the course of the conflict. In the fall of 1781, the English general Lord Cornwallis surrendered his army at Yorktown in Virginia. He had his military band mark the occasion by playing the ballad "The World Turned Upside Down." The lyrics to one version of the song caught the tone of radical change:

> This world is like a whirligig, and swiftly spins about,
> And nations like great statesmen are sometimes in and out,
> To Britain, France was forc'd to yield, and lay her banners down,
> Now Britain to America must cringe and fear her frown.[32]

In the following years, a nascent American popular culture would create and frame the event, particularly the idea of an ordered revolution of "Americans" against a tyrannical and foreign "British." The Revolution would have enormous effects on American society and culture. One, of course, would be the forming of a nation out of thirteen colonies, first in a loose confederation of states, later in the form of a constitutional republic, still later in the rise of a distinct national politics in the administrations of Washington, Adams, and Jefferson. Another would be a rhetorical tone surrounding much of the nation's politics, a "scurrilous" language of slander that the rebellion's young leaders engaged in and decried.

Still another of the Revolution's effects was the change it wrought on American slavery. In the post-Revolutionary ferment and amid all the talk about rights and liberty, a number of slaveholders from Philadelphia down through Virginia freed their slaves. The states of Vermont, New Hampshire, and Massachusetts passed legislation declaring immediate emancipation and putting an end to the institution. Meanwhile, balladeers penned a first generation of abolition songs, songs like the *Patriotic Gazette*'s publication of "The Negro's Lamentation":

> ALMIGHTY GOD, why mad'st thou me,
> Servant to sin and misery?
> Dids't thou not make of flesh and blood,
> My mortal frame, ALMIGHTY GOD?
> Did't thou not form my frame of clay—
> Am I not made as pure as they?[33]

Northern states with higher numbers of slaves—Connecticut, New York, New Jersey, and Pennsylvania—passed laws that called for a gradual phasing out of slavery.

These changes did not put an end to slavery. Nor for that matter did they do much to improve the condition of the vast majority of Americans who were in bondage. The new constitution included three articles with sections relating to slavery: one that counted slaves as "three-fifths" of a person, another laying out a fugitive slave law, and a third that guaranteed the international slave trade until the end of 1807 and imposed a duty of up to $10 for each imported slave. Meanwhile, the phaseout of slavery in the North led to a shift in the nation's black population to the South. After this time, with the rise of Northern textile factories, the development of the Deep South Cotton Belt, and the massive growth of an internal slave trade, the region's slave population exploded. By about 1830, some ninety percent of the nation's black people were in the South and in bondage. Within a generation of the Revolution, observers of the United States could speak somewhat accurately of a free North and a slave South. The change did not spell an end to the racial state. What it did do was create the conditions for the Civil War, along with an American tendency to equate slavery with blackness.[34]

Elsewhere the rebellion produced a language of rights for common citizens along with hatred toward aristocrats or "aristos," the elite gentlemen of the former order. Suddenly, old-style gentlemen all but disappeared from the new republic. Merchants like Ben Franklin and Paul Revere became artisan printers and smiths; planters like Thomas Jefferson became yeoman farmers. Above all, the Revolution—in popular song and rhetoric at least—produced an imagined community of Americans.

At the center of this community was the early republic's roland-in-human-form, George Washington. From the Revolution through the War of 1812, the imagery of Washington as a patriotic icon would appear in poem, painting, and perhaps most often in song. At his death in 1799, the *Patriotic Gazette* devoted its entire "Repository of the Muses" to ballads of remembrance for the fallen hero, from songs like "Ode to Washington" to "George, the War-Torn Soldier." In these ballads, the general was a beacon to the world:

> *European* kingdoms caught the strain,
>   From mount to vale—from hill to plain
> *All hail to Freedom's, Virtue's, Glory's Son!*
>   Ye worlds repeat, repeat! 'Tis WASHINGTON![35]

In later years, publications like the *Gazette* continued to offer collections of "Dirges, Hymns, and Anthems, composed on the death of GENERAL WASHINGTON," all having been "carefully selected from the numerous effusions of ingenious grief, which have flowed spontaneously from various quarters of our country."[36] The rebellion, according to the focus on Washington, was controlled from the top; it was the product of great leaders, even one great man. In Boston, Nathaniel Coverly published several broadside ballads extolling the "father" of the nation, from "The American Union and the Birth of George Washington" to "Saw Ye My Hero George," to "The Death of Washington" and "Lady Washington's Lamentation for the Death of Her Husband."[37]

By 1800 this creation of Washington as a national roland would culminate in perhaps its most well-known expression, the book *The Life of Washington* by Mason Weems. An itinerant bookseller who peddled everything from Bibles to his own semi-pornographic tales of alcohol and murder, "Parson" Weems created a serviceable icon for a young nation's values. To begin with, the national symbol was a paragon of honesty. Man and boy, Washington could not tell a lie. To demonstrate the claim, Weems invented a story involving young George, a hatchet, and his father's favorite cherry tree.

Washington's youth was marked by industry and incremental success; his manhood by temperance and friendly condescension toward his slaves; his war service by military genius and love for his troops. His old age was characterized by wisdom gained with learning and time. Europe, he learned, was a cesspool of corruption; a representative government run by men of merit was something to be respected; and taxes, while "more or less inconvenient and unpleasant," needed to be levied, raised, and paid. His life was characterized by self-sacrifice, duty, and benevolence; in his will, he even promised at his wife's future death to free his slaves.[38] In all things, according to Weems and the generations of Americans who would read the parson's book, Washington was a roland for an American community.

Patriotism I: Republicanism

Between 1812 and 1815, Nathaniel Coverly was far from alone in his attempts to whip up patriotism. Writers and printers everywhere rushed pro-war effusions into print. The "British Lyon" needed a good knocking-down again, claimed a New York pamphleteer. "Americans will in this important crisis, acquit themselves like men," he declared confidently, adding that a "fervid zeal of patriotism" would fill "the heart of every true citizen."[39] Patriotic zeal materialized, though perhaps not in the way writers like these anticipated. During the war one version of patriotism would be composed of a set of high ideals. Gathered under the name "republicanism," it would become known as the "true" patriotism of the enlightened. It would also propel many Americans toward an antiwar stance.

Republicanism has been depicted as America's dominant ideology of patriotism in the years following the American Revolution. Its meanings were as varied as its adherents. During the period of the early republic, Federalists and Jeffersonian Democrats, Southern planters and Northern merchants, wealthy politicians, common farmers, and artisan laborers all would have been likely to call themselves republicans. At its base the ideology was simple: it held that a republic, a government based on the will of the people through representatives, could survive only if its citizens were committed to virtues of independence, civic involvement, and self-sacrifice.[40]

The ideology contained elements of radical thought. Its originators spoke of the natural rights of common citizens. Many of its proponents were hostile to "aristos." Yet its radical promise was tempered. During the early republic, its adherents thought of citizenship as limited to property holders, to individuals with a "stake in society." Women were largely excluded from its rhetoric, except in their roles as republican wives or mothers, as helpmates to husbands and bearers of future male citizens. Slaves, along with people who owned no property, were completely excluded.[41] To many, the ideology seemed based in social leveling, in pulling down the elite to a level with the common masses. To its critics, its leveling promises were a fraud. "All Republicans," claimed the Dean of Gloucester during the Revolution, "suggest no other Schemes but those of pulling down and leveling all Distinctions above them, and of tyrannizing over those miserable Beings, who are unfortunately placed below them."[42]

Above all else, republicanism was an ideal of duty. Parson Weems's George Washington was both modeled on the theory and a model for Americans. The good republican was expected to take an active part in public life; to do so, he needed to make himself aware of current issues and politics; to learn, question, and criticize, to value enlightened thought and cool debate. The function of this duty was twofold: the first was to restrain the power of government, to defend the republic against potential abuses and corrupt policies; the second was to counteract the passions of democracy, the tendency of masses and majorities to be motivated by bigotry, ill-informed prejudice, and plain stupidity.[43]

Nathaniel Coverly almost certainly thought of himself as a republican. As the war broke out and even as he trotted out his father's broadsides from the Revolution, his other productions raised a host of criticisms of the nation's war policies. One question was simple: why had war been declared on Britain? In the years before the war, trade had been brisk with England. In fact, it had been so good that France, under Napoleon, had seen it as a direct threat, and had attacked American shipping. The result was a conflict known as the "Quasi War," a period of tensions and clashes between the United States and France that ran from 1798 to 1801. As well, France was led by a clear despot. Coverly's shop contained a number of broadsides depicting Napoleon as a comic figure and corrupt tyrant, a "*parlez-vous*," as one ballad put it, bent on "slaughter, rape and plunder."[44] Why had the nation not declared war on France?

Coverly's ballads also contained republican critiques of other national policies in the years before the war. One was "The Sedition Act," a ballad responding to the Adams administration's effort to criminalize dissent and criticism of the government. From its first lines, the ballad took the voice of republican reason, even to the point of debunking one of the myths of the Revolution. The enlightened, as the ballad's lyrics declared, had known all along that the Revolution-as-tax-revolt idea was a myth. They had supported the rebellion anyway, in the name of the citizens' right to overthrow oppression, to create a republic, and to speak freely against tyranny and corruption. In fact, they had joined the rebellion for the very rights the Sedition Act denied. Freedom, the song concluded, meant the rights of free speech and free press. It certainly meant more than the right of merchants to enjoy profits without taxes:

> The bill of sedition, and alien law,
>   Are aimed at the vitals of freedom;
> Contriv'd by a party, the people at awe
>   The good of our states did not need them.
> But it is in our bless'd constitution declar'd,
>   From printing our thoughts, we should not be debar'd
> Nor the freedom of speech should remain unimprov'd,
>   Now what do you think of sedition?[45]

Another of Coverly's prewar efforts, "The Embargo," suggested the more tempered elements of republican ideology. These too led to criticisms of the war. For Boston's merchants and sailors, the 1807 *Chesapeake* affair produced widespread outrage. In response they invoked ideals of "free trade," "sailors' rights," and national honor as reasons for war against Britain. When, instead of declaring war, Congress at President Thomas Jefferson's urging passed the "Embargo Act," they were equally outraged at the response. "Jefferson's embargo" effectively barred American trade with England. The policy, as Coverly's ballad made clear to listeners, was a disaster for New England's maritime industries:

> Our ships all in motion, / Once whiten'd the ocean,
> They sail'd and return'd with a cargo;
> Now doom'd to decay, / They have fallen a prey,
> To Jefferson, worms and Embargo.[46]

When it came to the function of government, the radical republican was in accord with the conservative Tory. Government existed to facilitate trade; it was created to protect profit and property. From a republican standpoint, the conclusion was simple: any act that damaged the nation's financial health was suspect.

Five years later, the same criticism would be leveled against the war itself. According to one of Coverly's republican broadsides, the "best trump" to play against Britain was not war but the power of "American manufactures," the many "fabricks" that "patriotic zeal began" and the British depended upon. The trump had been wasted by the despised embargo. "Do you hate WAR," asked another of Coverly's broadsides before continuing in this voice:

> Think, think, upon those *blissful days*,
> When COMMERCE Spread her flowing sails,
> And wafted to our *then* bless'd shore,
> The choicest fruits of India's vales!
> 'Twas then the *"Golden Age"* of PEACE,
> The age when PATRIOTS reign'd–
> When WASHINGTON stood at the helm,
> And *Democratic power restrain'd!*[47]

The song offered a pantheon of republican references: blissful commerce and profit, true patriots and their enlightened age of peace, and Washington himself, the national roland strong enough to stand against the unreasoning passions of the democratic mass.

By the end of 1812, a full-scale antiwar movement had sprung up in New England, a popular movement rooted in republican principles and patriotic duty. Critics assailed the causes of the conflict, particularly the motives of the Western and Southern "War Hawks." To be sure, since the *Leopard-Chesapeake* affair there had been a lot of talk about sailors' rights and freedom of the seas. But as far as its detractors could tell, the war drive focused on more material issues. The real prize, critics claimed, was Canada. The real goal of the War Hawks, they declared, was a northward expansion of American empire.

In 1813, a Massachusetts branch of the "Washington Benevolent Society" published a July Fourth sermon delivered by the minister Jacob Catlin, a screed called *The Horrors of War*. The pamphlet offered readers the nearest thing to a primer on a republican response to the War of 1812. The war, according to Catlin, would cause enormous harm to trade and commerce. It would elevate prejudice and violence into "absurd notions of virtue and honor." It would lead to the outlawing of dissent. The nation, he declared, would have to "*amend*, and *amend*, and *amend*, the constitution." Ultimately, the war, and especially the War Hawk goal of invading Canada, would "consume republican principles." Catlin concluded with a dire prediction:

> The liberty and independence which we celebrate this day, will be very short-lived blessings, if we persist, like the angry nations of Europe, in a state of perpetual war. Be the flames of war ever so pure and just, yet they will gradually consume republican principles. War measures, as you cannot but observe, are greatly embarrassed by the long debates and tardy operations of a republican government. Nothing but *despotism*, or *enthusiasm*, can ever keep pace with the exigencies of war.[48]

For the minister's listeners and readers, the criticism was an example of "true" patriotism, a patriotism unmarred by "absurd notions of virtue and honor."

Despite being surrounded by these statements, despite producing more than a few himself, Nathaniel Coverly would print a larger number of broadsides celebrating the war. The reasons may be rooted in his context. To begin with, Coverly could not afford to turn down commissioned recruitment ballads. Nor could he afford to print many antiwar pamphlets with complicated republican arguments. From Coverly's shop, the city jail was only a few blocks away. The harbor end of Milk Street had once been "Hallowell's Shipyard," and the remains of planking, spars, and ironwork still littered the area. Several of the city's earthier taverns dotted the neighborhood: the "Sign of the Punch Bowl," "The Roebuck," and "The Bite." Shipyards, jails, and taverns were places likely to be frequented by the nearly one-quarter of Boston's inhabitants who made their living through a connection to its maritime industries.[49] They were also places frequented by buyers of Coverly's broadsides. These common folk would push his broadsides in their own directions.

Patriotism II: Drinking, Whoring, and Making Noise

Coverly had been marketing to these salty types since he opened his shop. His shelves included numerous ballads focused on common sailors, from "The Jolly Sailor" to "The Sailor's Farewell," "Tom Starboard," "Tom Halliard," "Meg of Wapping," and "Heaving the Lead." Elsewhere, observers who bothered to pay any attention to sailors saw them as the lowliest of workers, as drunken louts and tar-stained brutes. At sea, according to the standard view, they were numbed by physical labor, whippings, and grog; on shore, they were sure to spend their money on whiskey and whores.

In Coverly's ballads, they were at the center of the culture. Ballads like "The Sailor Boy" pictured them as representative American youth, as boys who yearned for adventure, went to sea, and were missed by their doting mothers. Others portrayed them as models of masculinity, as men who would always return to their "sweet Polly" or "dearest Nancy," as romantic heroes who though "they love and feel like other folks" were ready to "seize the capstan bar," and manfully face the perils of the sea.[50]

Whatever his stance on the war, Coverly's acceptance of commissioned recruitment ballads meant he would have to appeal directly to these maritime workers. An example might be seen in the simply titled "Naval Recruitment Song." The ballad began with the announcement that the forty-four-gun frigate, the *President*, was ready for sailing, that genuine "tars" would be welcomed to the crew and "swabs" would be rejected. It went on to make a typical appeal: "Yes we have room for a true-hearted sailor, / Who knows what to do in a ship, / Who never was known for a flincher, / When seamen were wanted on deck."[51]

In the early period of the war, these appeals to the common sort were helped by naval victories. None was more shocking than the victory of the USS *Constitution*, under Captain Isaac Hull, over the British ship-of-the-line, the HMS *Guerrière*. Word of the engagement reached Boston in September 1812. Immediately, Coverly printed "Hull's Victory, or, Huzza for the Constitution." The ballad offered a toast to the exploit that undoubtedly made the city's alehouses rattle:

> Ye true sons of freedom, give ear to my song,
> While the praise of brave HULL I attempt to prolong,
> Let each bold hearted hero now fill up his glass,
> And our favorite sentiment rapidly pass.
> *With our brave noble Captain, we'll still plow the main,*
> *We'll fight and we'll conquer, again and again.*[52]

In this song, as in many others on the engagement, much of the focus was at the top, on "brave Hull" and his cool gallantry under fire. Like the post-Revolutionary focus on Washington, the ballad offered an ideal of patriotic expression rooted in hierarchy and the heroic leadership of great men. Indeed, for a long time in New England, Isaac Hull came about as close as a mortal could to rivaling Washington.[53]

A longer legacy would be established by an alternate version of the event: a narrative that focused on the *Constitution* itself and its crew of common tars. A key to this story may have been in the facts of the engagement. The *Constitution* overmatched the *Guerrière*. The American vessel was more recently built, larger, and constructed of better material; she had an advantage in sail space, speed, guns, and broadside metal weight. These advantages would tell in the battle, which lasted little more than twenty-five minutes and left the *Guerrière* so damaged that she had to be destroyed rather than taken as a prize. On paper, however, the ships were evenly matched. Both were frigates. According to British and American perspectives, being evenly matched, or even having an advantage in size and guns for the *Constitution*, meant the Americans were the decided underdogs. After all, the British Navy was far and away the best in the world.[54]

For people in England, news of the *Constitution*'s victory came as a shock. For common New Englanders, it produced a giddy celebration that would be unrivaled during the war. Here, in literature, poem, and song, the rumor that solid shot from British cannons had bounced off the *Constitution*'s sides became a fact; the fact became evidence for the ship's magical qualities. Writers dubbed her "Old Ironsides," and she became a symbol of national strength, another roland for patriotic orientation. Much of the attention also fell on her crew. The exploit resurrected the old trickster theme, the rhetoric of a common rabble overcoming the haughty British. Little wonder, then, that another of Coverly's broadsides set the exploit to the tune of "Yankee Doodle."[55]

Little wonder too that among Coverly's broadsides celebrating the victory, one would be a ballad by an actual sailor. The balladeer was James Campbell, listed on the broadside as a "Boatswain's Mate on board the Constitution." A sailor himself, Campbell knew what Coverly's clientele wanted in a ballad. They wanted detail. His version offered listeners by far the most elaborate account of the fight. They wanted battle action and plenty of gore. Campbell gave them hot lead and sailors' blood, which "from the scuppers in a scarlet stream did pour." Finally, sailors wanted to hear about sailors. Campbell gave them the example of himself, shifting the heroic focus from the officers at the top to the common seaman.[56]

To be sure, Coverly printed recruiting broadsides for infantry as well as sailors; and his shop provided ballads and broadsides covering news from the war's inland operations. But this involved a series of disasters, at least during the first

HULL'S VICTORY,

OR, HUZZA FOR THE

CONSTITUTION.

Ye true sons of freedom, give ear to my song,
While the praise of brave HULL I attempt to prolong,
Let each bold hearted hero now fill up his glass,
And our favorite sentiment rapidly pass.
    With our brave noble captain, we'll still plow the
CHORUS.   main;
    We'll fight and we'll conquer, again and again.

With a fine springing breeze, our sails they were bent,
And with hearts full of joy to the ocean we went,
In the fam'd Constitution a taught and staunch boat,
As ever was seen on the water afloat.
    With our brave noble Captain, we plow'd the deep main,
    And when he commands, we are ready again.

On the twentieth of August, a sail we espied,
We hove too, and soon we came up along side ;
The drum beat to quarters, to quarters we run,
And each tar bravely swore to stand fast to his gun.
    Our Captain so brave, as we sail'd on the main,
    Now bids us a harvest of glory to gain.

A broadside the foe quickly into us pour'd,
We return'd 'em the favor direct on the word,
Each heart was undaunted, no bosom knew fear,
And we car'd not a snap for the saucy Guerriere.
    With our noble commander we fought on the main,
    And we'll conquer with him when he bids us again.

The balls now flew thick, and quite warm was the play,
Their masts and their rigging was soon shot away,
We shatter'd their hull with all possible speed,
With our good spunky bull-dogs, of true Yankee breed.
    'Twas thus with our captain we fought on the main,
    With him a rich harvest of glory to gain.

The blood from the enemy's scuppers ran fast,
All hopes of subduing us now were quite past :
So they wisely concluded, by hob or by nob,

That 'twas best to give o'er what they thought a bad job,
    With our true noble Captain, we'll fight on the main,
    And we hope that with him, we'll soon conquer again.

The Britons had seldom before seen the like,
For we rak'd 'em so clean, they'd no colours to strike ;
So a gun on their lee they were forc'd to let fly,
To inform us they didn't quite all wish to die.
    'Twas thus with our captain we fought on the main,
    And we're ready brave boys, to fight with him again.

In twenty-five minutes, the business was done,
For they didn't quite relish such true Yankee fun ;
So we kindly receiv'd 'em on board our good ship,
Many cursing the day when they took their last trip.
    With our brave noble captain we'll still plow the main.
    We'll fight and we'll conquer again and again.

Now homeward we're bound, with a favoring breeze,
As full of good humor and mirth as you please,
Each true-hearted sailor partakes of the glass,
And drinks off a health to his favorite lass.
    With our brave noble captain we've plow'd the deep main,
    With him we the laurels of glory did gain.

Now success to the good Constitution, a boat
Which her crew will defend while a plank is afloat,
Who never will flinch, or in duty e'er lag,
But will stick to the last by the American flag.
    So true to our colors we'll ever remain,
    And we'll conquer for freedom again and again.

When again we shall plow old Neptune's blue wave,
May honors still circle the brows of the brave,
And should our bold foes wish to give us a pull
We'll show 'em the good Constitution and HULL.
    And now with three cheers ere we sail to the main,
    We will greet our brave Captain again and again.

FIGURE 2.1. The *Constitution* as national symbol; the vulgar tar as true son of freedom. Printed by Nathaniel Coverly immediately after the American frigate's sinking of the HMS *Guerriere* in 1812, the lyrics to this ballad were most likely written by Coverly's ready-poet Nathaniel Hill Wright. The ballad offered a celebration of the victory, a sing-along to make alehouses rattle, and a hint of a coming shift in the focus of American identity. In addition to an older focus on great men like George Washington as representative Americans, popular ballads would increasingly focus on the exploits of seamen and tars, creating a linkage between patriotism and the most vulgar or common behaviors. *Hull's Victory, or, Huzza for the Constitution*, printed by Nathaniel Coverly, Boston, 1812–1814; Isaiah Thomas Broadside Ballad Collection, AAS. Courtesy of American Antiquarian Society.

two years of the war. In June 1812, the Yankee invasion of Canada got underway. The plan involved a three-pronged attack: a western advance from Fort Detroit, a second across the Niagara River, and a third across the Saint Lawrence toward Montreal. In early July, some two thousand American troops under Brigadier General William Hull crossed from Detroit into Canadian territory.

Hull shared the confidence of the War Hawks. "Inhabitants of Canada," he stated in a proclamation timed to the invasion, "You will be emancipated from tyranny and oppression, and restored to the dignified station of freemen. Had I any doubt of eventual success, I might ask your assistance, but I do not. I come prepared for every contingency." Within a month, the general had lost two outposts, overextended his supply lines, and found himself surrounded. On August 16, he surrendered Fort Detroit and his entire army.[57] Coverly printed a ballad recounting the invasion, but it was hardly heroic. As the ballad "Hull's Surrender" had it, the defeat could be explained only with reference to treason. With a "brave, gallant army," Hull had gone to Detroit, where he swore to "accomplish a noble exploit." But then came a mysterious reversal:

> Ah! Quickly alas! defeat and disgrace,
> Star'd our brave noble soldiers quite full in the face,
> When they thought that the victory was sure to be won,
> Their general gave up, *without firing a gun.*
> *Then do traitors still dwell on Columbia's fair shore,*
> *IF THEY DO, let them dwell in her borders no more!*[58]

The two other prongs of the invasion also went badly, and by the beginning of 1813 all was quiet on the Canadian front. There would be other attempts to invade Canada during the war. A few would see limited success. Yet these actions received far less attention than the naval war. In part, this reflected attitudes in New England. Throughout the region, the antiwar movement remained popular, and much of its criticism fell on the imperialist designs toward Canada.[59]

Coverly's naval broadsides, on the other hand, found a ready audience. A few months after her engagement with the *Guerrière*, in late December 1812, the *Constitution* met and took another British frigate, the HMS *Java*. Again, the enemy's ship's "scuppers ran with British blood." Again, the common boatswain's-mate James Campbell wrote a ballad of the engagement. Yet this time the *Constitution* was under the command of Captain William Bainbridge. Thus, it may have become even more apparent that the exploit's real hero was "Old Ironsides," along with her collection of "Yankee Tricks" and "true Yankee boys."[60]

Following this action, the American fighting fleet would find itself in-creasingly port-bound, bottled up by the tightening British blockade. Still, between this second of the *Constitution's* exploits and Captain Oliver Hazard Perry's victory on Lake Erie in the fall of 1813, Coverly continued to print bal-lads of naval exploits, no matter how small. These included the pyrrhic vic-tory of the "sloop of war" the *Wasp*, which took the British sloop the *Frolick* before being taken herself by a giant seventy-four-gun British man-of-war. It included the actions of Yankee privateers like the *Saratoga* and especially the USS *President*, which did their part for the war effort by plundering British merchant ships.[61]

In these ballads, the war aims were clear: it was "Free Trade and Sailor's Rights!" Meanwhile, whether sloop, privateer, or frigate, the guns spoke for the rights and status of common people: the lowly sailor had become a "jolly seaman bold," a "noble tar," a "dandy," a "hero" brilliantly lit by "rays of fam'd glory."[62]

These ballads contained little of the language of republicanism, nothing of the rhetoric of thoughtful analysis or cool debate. Instead, they focused on the imagery of common men engaged in common behaviors. They favored im-ages of sailors returned from sea battles and headed for the alehouse, waiting women, and whores on shore. They were the stuff of drunken celebrations, full rum cups, and groggy sing-alongs. In these ballads, traditions of commu-nity returned in a common version of patriotism. What made it common was its appeal to sailors, to people who had not learned the value of repressing folk behaviors. From a gentlemanly standpoint, such expressions would no doubt look vulgar. In the ballad "Cash in Hand," for example, the crew of the USS *President*, under the command of John Rodgers, celebrated the taking of a British packet with "260,000 dollars in gold and silver on board." The song offered a tone of militant vulgarity:

> The British sure, did not well like,
> This mode of our proceeding,
> And swore the taking of their cash,
> Was no mark of good breeding.[63]

Americans, according to these broadsides, were "Yankee Tars," proudly vulgar sorts rooted in a common culture of taverns, drink, and sexual grati-fication. By the end of the war, these sailors were "Columbia's sons," repre-sentative Americans who were "proud, rough, undaunted and free." They had "touch'd up John Bull" and "humbled haughty Britain's pride." Old tradi-tions would return in these ballads. They returned in the trickster imagery

of "Yankee Doodle," in a culture of wild dancing and drink, in ballads celebrating another privateering exploit of Captain John Rodgers and the USS
President:

> Now toast our Commodore so brave, / In toddy, flip, or brandy.
> And strike aloud the merry stave, / Of Yankee Doodle Dandy.
>
> Yankee Doodle join the tune, / To every freeman handy,
> Let's shake the foot and rigadoon, / To Yankee Doodle Dandy.[64]

In this more common version of patriotism, traditions of community
would return along with an old culture of carnival and bodily expression. The
vulgarity was not the result of a capture of patriotic imagery by lower-order
Americans. It was not the result of the ignorance of common sorts, their failure
to understand patriotism's true meanings. To the contrary, Coverly's broadsides
demonstrate that one form of American patriotism would be vulgar and common because it was devoted to people who were widely recognized as vulgar
and common. In 1812, an English observer would describe the common sailor's
"trio of pleasures" as a bawdy song, a rum-filled bumper, and a "street-pacing
harlot." This type of man, the observer added, "rarely thinks, seldom reads, and
never prays."[65]

According to the most popular variant of patriotism during the War of
1812, this was also the representative American. In 1815, American patriotism
had a number of meanings: it could mean support for a war, going along with
heroes, questioning government corruption, and protesting a war. It could
also mean a celebration of older traditions of behavior that bound common
folk together in an imagined community. It could be expressed by drinking,
whoring, and ending up in the gutter, by getting drunk and singing at the top
of one's lungs, by drunkenly celebrating the nation, a military victory, or one's
own vulgar self. In this variant of patriotism, love of country was twinned with
love of self, provided one's self was common enough, vulgar enough, and even
disgusting enough to represent an ideal of absolute democracy.

The War of 1812 would end with an ironic twist. Finally, under the command of Andrew Jackson, a ragtag collection of infantry, militiamen, and pirates would win a clear victory at the Battle of New Orleans. What happened
in the engagement suggests that Americans had no monopoly when it came
to poor military performance. Or perhaps it suggests that battles are always
subject to luck, that the best tactics are always invented after the fact.

Charged with the defense of New Orleans, Jackson entrenched his motley
assemblage to the south of the city, on the Plains of Chalmette. The British,
under the command of the heavily decorated Lord Edward Packenham, had a

much larger force. They also had low-lying ground to cover in their assault on Jackson's line, including a ditch just under the American guns filled with the Louisiana delta's notoriously thick mud. Two weeks after Christmas, on January 8, 1815, the British force launched its main attack. Soon the assault slowed in the mud. Then several of Packenham's officers broke into argument. As the mass of redcoats waited in the glue-like bog, there was heated talk about retreating, continuing forward, or waiting for reinforcements.

On the British side, it was the worst mistake of the war, for the argument brought the advance to a halt directly in the American line of fire. Within minutes, it seemed, Packenham's force suffered more than two thousand men killed, wounded, and missing. Jackson's force had just eight men killed and thirteen wounded. The exploit would come nearly a month after the war officially ended. It would also produce, a few years later, what became the most popular song of the war, "The Hunters of Kentucky." Penned by Samuel Woodworth and made famous by Noah Ludlow, a stage actor and manager of a theatrical troupe that traveled through the nation's far west, the song affirmed the patriotic ideal of the United States as a nation of common types.

The "Hunters of Kentucky" made Ludlow, who performed it everywhere dressed in a fringed buckskin costume, into one of the country's best-known theatrical stars. It made the British out as foreign plunderers, raised the idea of New Orleans as a multicultural city stocked with the "booty" of wealth and "beauty" of girls of "every hue," and hailed Jackson as the city's defender. Two verses conveyed the tone:

> You've heard, I 'spose, how New Orleans
>   Is famed for wealth and beauty;
> There's girls of every hue, it seems,
>   From snowy white to sooty.
> So Packenham he made his brags,
>   If he in fight was lucky,
> He'd have their girls and cotton bags,
>   In spite of old Kentucky.
>
> But Jackson he was wide awake,
>   And was'nt [sic] scar'd at trifles
> For well he know what aim we take
>   With our Kentucky rifles.[66]

In later years Jackson would be "Old Kentucky" as well as "Old Hickory," and the song's refrain, a repeated "Oh, Kentucky, The Hunters of Kentucky," would be shouted out by voters in several elections, three of which would be for the presidency. Finally, while the song reaffirmed an ideal of patriotism as rooted in the imagery of common Americans, it would also herald another shift in focus. In New England during the War of 1812, this character was represented by the sailor. The "Hunters of Kentucky" brought up what would become an even more popular image: the sharpshooting westerner, the rugged backwoodsman, the sometimes plainspoken, sometimes crowing character represented by Daniel Boone, Davy Crockett, and Andrew Jackson himself. The song marked a shift toward the frontier as the wellspring of the American character: for later generations, the sailor would become the frontiersman.

At Coverly's shop, the broadside marking Jackson's victory offered his customers an early example of this shift. The broadside included a short prose narrative of the engagement, which featured England's "self-styled invincibles biting the dust before the green back-woodsmen of America," along with a snippet of Jackson's official report of the battle. To this, Coverly attached a ballad that he either lifted from another printer or commissioned from a poet, a song devoted to the "glorious achievement" of Jackson and his "sons of the soil." Still, it seems New Englanders were not quite ready to embrace the frontiersman and leave the sailor behind. Coverly's ballad had a note of internal tension and irony, as the songwriter set Jackson's tribute to the well-known sailors' anthem "Ye Hearts of Oak."[67]

Coverly's broadsides on the peace treaty would be more effusive. "HAIL heav'n born Goddess! lovely PEACE," sang out the first line of one. With peace, the nation could return to commerce and trade:

> Descend sweet Peace,—and on thy wing,
> The halcyon days of plenty bring;
> From Albion's tyrant monarch free,
> Our sails shall whiten ev'ry sea.[68]

For a while, Coverly cashed in on the good times. In the fall of 1815, he began printing his best-selling production, a pamphlet that would eventually go under the name *The Female Marine, or, Adventures of Miss Lucy Brewer*. A lurid blend of urban vice, pirate tale, and redemption narrative, the pamphlet, most likely written by Nathaniel Hill Wright but possibly by Coverly himself, again reflected a meeting point between tradition and modernity. In telling the story of Lucy Brewer, it focused on the old character of the female trickster, a young woman who disguises herself as a sailor, goes to sea, and for a time becomes a pirate before settling down and getting married.

The story's modern elements may have been the key to its success. For Lucy Brewer also represented the dangers of Boston's return to commerce. Born in the country, she comes to the city for opportunity. Once there, however, she finds herself in a growing economy of urban vice: seduced, abandoned, and forced to become a prostitute in a Boston brothel.[69] Her resort to piracy was not a decline into lawlessness but part of a competitive climb back to respectability. The end of the war would eventually be seen as the beginning of a great transformation, a market revolution, a shift to the competitive culture of modern capitalism. From his tiny shop, Coverly continued to print trickster tales, old traditions in a culture increasingly bent on progress. As might be expected, he would be supplanted as a leading printer for Boston's common folks, by changing styles, by other, more modern printers. He would die, "in obscurity," in 1824.

Jim Crow's Genuine Audience

In the fall of 1825, New Yorkers gathered to celebrate the triumph of art over nature. The occasion was a milestone in both the nation's infrastructure and the workers' culture of the period: the opening of the "Grand Western Canal." Soon to be better known as the Erie Canal, the artificial waterway ran from Albany to Buffalo, connecting the Hudson River to Lake Erie. From there one could get to Lake Michigan; and from there—or from a swampy place on the lake soon to be called Chicago—one could cross an easy height of land and arrive at the Mississippi River. The canal's opening, in other words, promised to link an entire continent. The project had employed thousands of laborers and taken seven long years to complete. There seemed much to celebrate, and so the ceremony promised to be among the largest the city had seen. It would include speeches honoring the canal's builders, orations from political dignitaries, and testimonials from leaders of the city's largest artisan organization, the General Society of Mechanics and Tradesmen. It would feature songs and theatrical performances, many created for the occasion.

On the day of the event, a parade rolled along Broadway, a grand procession meant to honor the nation's workers and demonstrate the importance of labor to the republic. Though the record is silent on this, quite likely all of the "workers" who marched in the parade would have been skilled or semi-skilled laborers. Most likely there were no slaves among the marchers, though the canal's completion occurred two years before slavery was legally ended in the state and African American slaves would have helped dig the enormous ditch. Still, some of the marchers may have been African American. At the beginning of the nineteenth century, cities like Philadelphia, Boston, and New York had small but visible populations of black bricklayers, coopers, and carpenters.

If some of these black artisans worked on the canal project, and if they marched in the opening parade, they might have blended in almost to the point of invisibility. For, as the period's ideals had it, the artisans marched not by ethnicity or rank but massed beneath and behind the emblems of their guilds, organized by the banners or symbols of the carters, the smiths, the wrights, and a host of other trades. On this day the parade's centerpiece was a platform on wheels pulled by junior artisans. Positioned on this moving stage were the city's printers, the artisans who always seemed to grab the center of attention. This time they were leading the parade's onlookers in song, for they had arranged themselves around a large placard with lyrics to mark the occasion.

> 'Tis done! 'tis done!—The mighty chain
> Which joins bright ERIE to the MAIN, . . .
> 'Tis done!—Proud ART o'er NATURE has prevailed!
> GENIUS and PERSEVERANCE have succeeded!
> Though selfish PREJUDICE assailed,
> And honest PRUDENCE pleaded.
> Then hail to ART which unshackles the soul,
> And fires it with love of glory,
> And causes the victor who reaches the goal,
> To live in deathless story.[1]

Five years later, a very different example of the period's workers' culture occurred at the port of Charleston, South Carolina. By this time, the General Societies of the North, along with other nascent artisan trade organizations called "Brotherhoods" or "Workingmen's Parties," were hard at work excluding African Americans from the ranks of skilled laborers. For the leaders of these organizations, the point was clear: black people were slaves; they were not to be recognized as workers or as equals. Some white workers, it seems, had not yet received this message. During the summer of 1830, the authorities at Charleston arrested a white sailor named Edward Smith, charging him with smuggling an illegal pamphlet into the South.

During his trial, Smith testified that he received the pamphlet in Boston. While he was working at the docks, he claimed, a "coloured man" had approached him, a man who was "genteely dressed" and of "decent appearance." Rather than treating this well-dressed figure as an equal, Smith seems to have seen him as a superior. According to his testimony, he figured him for a man of learning, perhaps "a bookseller." The man, said Smith, asked him to carry copies of a pamphlet to Charleston. Once in the port, his task was simple: he only had to "give them secretly to the black people."

Smith agreed to the favor. The pamphlet was *David Walker's Appeal to the Colored Citizens of the World*, a screed that called for black people to become educated, arm themselves, and forcibly put an end to slavery. The well-dressed man was most likely David Walker himself, the small-time Boston merchant who in addition to writing the pamphlet was one of the most active leaders of the Northeast's small cadre of black abolitionists. He was perhaps the only one of this group, to this point at least, to make a public call for an immediate end to slavery by whatever means necessary. A common white worker had agreed to do a favor for the most militant black abolitionist in the nation. As a result of this favor, he had smuggled into the South the period's most radical piece of antislavery literature.[2]

These two examples suggest much about the culture of young white American workers in 1820s. The first, which came at a time when African Americans still existed within the nation's pre–Civil War artisan trades, reveals a culture characterized by widespread beliefs in the dignity of labor or "art," in the phrasing of the time. The second occurred at the historical moment labor organizations actively began to exclude blacks from the ranks of the "worker." At the same time, this example suggests that for some, the older hierarchies of class and social rank still took precedence over a newer ideal that any white man was better than any black man. Edward Smith's experience suggests the survival of leftover traditions of social deference, the social code by which common men like him were expected to make shows of respect to their social superiors. In this case, a white worker was willing to show deference to a black intellectual.[3]

Within a decade or so, both examples would seem antiquated to observers of the cultural style of American workers. Fewer Americans would celebrate work as art. It would become increasingly difficult to find a young white worker likely to defer to a gentleman, much less to an African American gentleman who appeared to be a man of learning. Two developments heralded these changes: one was the transformation of America known as the market revolution; the other was the emergence of a more masculine and aggressive working-class style, a style expressed in the songs and images of blackface minstrelsy.[4]

Artisan Republicanism and the Market Revolution

By the time the Erie Canal parade rolled down Broadway, processions and festivals had been part of urban life as long as anyone could remember. Ceremonials marked the passing of years: winter had the old solstice traditions repackaged as Christmas; spring and summer had May Day celebrations along with the newer "Independence Day" rituals of July Fourth. Autumn was a time of harvest festivals and thanksgivings, with local holidays in nearly every city, town, and village. In New York, there was Evacuation Day, the November 25 celebration of the withdrawal of British troops from Manhattan during the Revolution. In 1830, city-dwellers used the same day to celebrate the French Revolution along with the worldwide spread of republican virtues, the expansion of citizenship, and freedom of the press.[5]

For early labor organizations like New York City's General Society of Mechanics and Tradesmen, these holidays offered a chance to promote the status of artisan labor. The General Society stressed two central tenets of artisan culture: the dignity of the arts and the unity of American workers. To demonstrate their skills, craftsmen occupied pulled wagons during processions, moving stages on which they theatrically made their products for all to see. Here, coopers worked on barrels, wrights spoked wagon wheels, and tinsmiths made lanterns. Young apprentices marched alongside, carrying signs with product-related mottos: for the city's chair makers, "Rest for the Weary"; for the shoemakers, "United We Stand."[6] Artisans marched not by order of masters, journeymen, and apprentices but together, unified beneath the emblems of their crafts. The point was hard to miss: America's workers were marked by a spirit of community and contentment. Three verses of one procession song, ostensibly penned by Benjamin Franklin, the nation's patron saint of artisan labor, provided an example of the ideal:

> Each tradesman turn out, with his tools in his hand,
>   To cherish the arts and keep peace thro' the land;
> Each apprentice and journeyman join in my song,
>   And let your full chorus come bounding along.
>
> Ye Shoe-makers nobly, from ages long past,
>   Have defended your rights with the awl to your last;
> And Cobblers, all merry, not only stop holes,
>   But work night and day for the good of our soles.

The song would have taken marchers a good length of a procession route. Its punning verses covered a host of trades. Its chorus was catchy: "Happy and free, happy and free, all are united, happy and free."[7]

At the head of the processions was likely to be the banner of the General Society: an image of a muscled arm and gripped hammer along with the Society's motto, "By the Hammer and Hand All Arts Do Stand." The motto represented the sacred place of the artisan's craft in the workers' culture. A type of intellectual property, the worker's art was an intricate set of rules and methods for countless crafts: the building of a boat, the molding of bricks, the milling of wheat. Acquired and perfected over time, a man's art gave him a sense of self; it made him a contributor to the republic, an entitled citizen, the equal of any other man.[8]

Together, these symbols and images expressed an ideology of artisan republicanism. At the ideology's base were the standard republican principles: faith in the idea of representative government; belief that such a government could survive only through the virtues of its citizens. Like the larger concept of republicanism, the artisan's version defined good citizenship in terms of public involvement; it too stressed civic virtues of duty, honesty, and the willing sacrifice of self-interest. Where it differed was in the expansion of virtue to include skilled labor. From the standpoint of artisan republicanism, all workers contributed to the wealth of the nation. Yet only a skilled trade could give the worker the independence necessary for unselfish citizenship. Thus, labor, as long as it was skilled labor, *was* a republican virtue.

The ideology was not inclusive. In the eighteenth century and into the nineteenth century, there were numbers of African Americans in artisan trades; and some, no doubt, would have shared these ideals of worker virtue. One well-known example was James Forten, a successful master sailmaker in Philadelphia who employed at least a dozen journeymen and apprentices at his shop and who seemed to be always involved in the Quaker City's post-Revolutionary celebrations of the republic. Slaves, on the other hand, appear to have been completely excluded from status as workers; they were also left out of the ideal of artisan republicanism. What this meant was both simple and difficult to get one's mind around: in the United States, the definition of "worker" had the effect of rendering a very large percentage of actual workers unseen, uncounted, and invisible. This way of seeing created difficulties at the time and ever since. Decades later, it meant that many historians of labor in the mid-nineteenth century would either omit or overlook slaves from the category of the early American "working class." At the time, it meant that buildings like the US Capitol, in Washington, DC, a structure built largely by artisan slaves who were paid but had to remit most of their salaries back to their masters, had to be conceived as springing up by magic.[9]

So slaves, according to the logic of artisan republicanism, were not workers at all. Neither were servants, unskilled wage-workers, or the large number of mostly female outworkers who took sewing or stitching piecework into their homes. These were "hirelings," people who, much like prostitutes, sold their bodies to anyone who would pay an hourly wage. The labor of hirelings and slaves was degrading. It offered no hope of the pride, upward movement, and independence that came with the acquisition of a presumably true skill. As the abolitionist leader Frederick Douglass recalled, the mere fact that some black artisans had once been slaves seemed to taint their labor, even after they became free. Having trained as a ship's caulker in the Baltimore shipyards, and having again remitted his salary to his master, the escaping Douglass was told shortly after arriving in New York that any attempt to get a job at his old trade would result in violence. Artisan caulkers, it seems, might have been willing to work with a black man in their trade, but not with a "slave."[10]

Furthermore, the artisan system did have its hierarchies and conflicts. In many shops journeymen, who were paid a piece rate for completed products, found themselves shading the line into wage work. At the bottom of the system were apprentices, typically young boys in their early teens who were contractually bound to masters until their legal majority at age twenty-one. Apprentices sometimes ran off. Masters could resort to the law and the posting of runaway announcements in their effort to retrieve them.

Artisans may have marched as one during parade days, but in actual shops, the master artisan was in charge. Though not marked by the discipline of the time clock, the workweek ran from Monday through Saturday, and the length and pace of the workday were subject to the master's whims. Apprentices commonly lived with masters, where according to ideas of the time they were part of his family. By tradition they were not paid. Instead, they received room, board, and the promise of learning a skill in exchange for the standard seven-year apprenticeship. Masters were not only expected to train them in their craft but to see to their proper upbringing. Literature on the topic advised them to watch over their apprentice's "natural appetites," to teach them "principals of religion and practices of virtue."[11]

For some masters, this meant using force. In early popular literature and song, masters were notorious for beating their apprentices. Apprentices were equally renowned for playing tricks on the old men, for sneaking off at night or during work hours. One example of the master–apprentice relationship can be seen in the well-known ballad "Sally in Our Alley," a song that appeared everywhere in early American culture, from theatricals to country dances to satires of Thomas Jefferson's notorious affair with his slave Sally Hemings. In this version of the song, an apprentice sings of sneaking off to rendezvous with his girl along with his master's harsh reaction:

> When she is by I leave my work, / I love her so sincerely,
> My master comes like any Turk, / And bangs me most severely;
> But let him bang his belly full, / I'll bear it all for Sally,
> For she's the darling of my heart, / And she lives in our Alley.
>
> My master and the neighbors all, / Make game of me and Sally;
> Wer't not for her I'd better be, / A slave and row a galley.

For when my seven long years are out, / Why then I'll marry Sally:
Then we'll wed, and then we'll bed, / But not in our Alley.[12]

Though meant as a comic piece, the song suggests that physical punishment
was hardly unexpected within artisan culture. Journeymen, for their part,
were less subject to this type of control. As paid workers, they typically lived
on their own, sharing rooms in urban tenements or boardinghouses. Their
positions as unregulated youth made them a constant threat, and magistrates
often urged masters to exert greater discipline over their former charges.

If the ideals of artisan republicanism did not always reflect the realities of
artisan shops, they did structure conceptions of identity. Family names inherited from the middle ages—the many Smiths, Masons, and Wrights—provide
evidence of the age-old connection between craft and identity. Master artisans and journeymen in skilled trades had social status. In the terminology of
the time, they were "middling sorts," members of a social group beneath merchants and landowners yet clearly above unskilled laborers or the common
rabble. Even lowly apprentices believed they had this status, or would one day
acquire it. As one apprentice blacksmith recalled, the promise solaced countless hours of work. "Worked another day at blacksmithing," the young man
happily noted to himself, adding, "although I can't see my way through my
apprenticeship yet I can see that I have fairly begun."[13]

For others, the artisan system allowed for camaraderie and pride in work-
manship. In some workshops, according to recollections, masters let literate
journeymen read aloud from books and newspapers while their fellows worked.
Many remembered taking breaks and sharing a social dram of whiskey. Others
recalled the groggy tradition of "Saint Monday," in which after a weekend of
revels the master allowed junior artisans to come in late and take it easy for the
day, working at a hangover pace. What set the system apart, according to these
recollections, was the human pace of production. As one hatter in New Jersey
put it, the pace allowed him "to contemplate the work" and created a sense of
connection to the craft: "I felt real satisfaction in being able to make a hat."[14]

Artisan republicanism would have enormous staying power. It would provide impetus for worker self-identification through the nineteenth and much
of the twentieth centuries. Expressed in ritual and song, it would serve as
the foundation for labor fraternities, workers' brotherhoods, and unions. Its
ideals of self-improvement would place artisans at the heart of early reform.
By the middle decades of the nineteenth century, there would be countless
Mechanics Associations for charity and temperance. And, in rhetoric at least,
it raised the status of labor. By the late 1820s, claimed the editor of a mechanics magazine, the time was coming when the mechanic arts would take their

proper place in American society, "and we shall see each individual of our labouring community taking a higher stand."[15]

Things did not work out this way. Signs of coming threats to the artisan system were difficult to see in the years of the early republic. But they were there. In 1790, a mill owner named Samuel Slater constructed one of the nation's first textile mills along the Pawtucket River in Rhode Island. Ten years later, Slater's factory employed more than a hundred workers. In the next decade, over sixty textile mills would spring up in the United States. Most would be centered along rivers and canals in eastern Massachusetts, central New Jersey, and around Philadelphia; all would contain hundreds of mechanized looms, whirling spindles, and wage-paid machine-tenders. These were the early signs of what would be called a market revolution. Other signs appeared with the explosion of economic energy after the War of 1812. Suddenly, new roads, turnpikes, and canals were everywhere, part of an emerging "American Plan" of government support for transportation projects, nearly all devoted to the movement of goods.[16]

Most junior artisans would have believed in something akin to progress as they saw it, in their own climb up a ladder of competency and independence that they believed would come with the acquisition of a skill. They were not so sure about the progress of technological change. In the English Midlands, improvements in textile production produced the factory and the power loom by the closing years of the eighteenth century. They also produced the Luddites. Here, bands of workers proclaimed themselves followers of "Ned Ludd," an eighteenth-century English weaver who, according to myth and mumming play, had smashed his loom in a fit of anger. They then organized into armies and declared war on machines. In Nottingham and Yorkshire, they broke into factories, smashed looms, and marched to the strains of Luddite songs:

> These Engines of mischief were sentenced to die,
>   By unanimous vote of the Trade,
> And Ludd who can all opposition defy,
>   Was the Grand executioner made.[17]

In America, threats of technological change produced voices like that of Thomas Skidmore. A Connecticut-born schoolteacher, inventor, and free-thinking republican, Skidmore would be one of the founders of the Workingmen's Party of New York. In 1829, he published a long tract, *The Rights of Man to Property!* Many of the tract's ideas were standards of artisan thought: factory labor and wage work were degrading; both reduced the worker to a state of dependency. As for the newfangled factory machines, Skidmore admitted they might increase production. Yet they could also lower wages. Indeed, they might do away with the need for workers at all. Finally, the Connecticut Yankee proposed several responses to the market revolution: one was the equitable redistribution of all wealth; another was that America's workers should rise up, take the factories, and regain control over production.[18]

Other observers had been raising doubts about capitalist relations for at least a generation. For common Americans, it seems, the immoderate pursuit of profit could be defined in simple terms. It was cheating. The result was a number of ballads aimed at popular tastes that might be called cheating songs. In Nathaniel Coverly's time, the cheaters of these songs were the elite: they included lawyers, merchants, and landlords, who "with hearts as hard as flint, though their tenants are starving they still raise the rent."[19] By the mid-1820s, the focus of these songs turned to the master-artisan-turned-profiteer. Comic ballads featured the corner-cutting techniques of carpenters; the miller's use of the "toll dish" to skim grain from farmers; the merchant's promise of easy credit to lure his customers into crippling debt. In verse after verse, the songs described the sly practices of a "country of late, become all a cheat":

> The Blacksmith will cry out his stock is so dear,
> He cannot trust out his work but a year;
> He'll set a few shoes and he'll mend your old plow,
> And by the next fall he must have your best cow.
> The Tinker he'll tell you he'll mend all your ware,
> For little or nothing, but cider and beer;
> But in a small patch he'll put nails a full score,
> And in stopping one hole, he makes twenty more.[20]

The songs heralded a coming crisis. In their procession to mark the opening of the Erie Canal in 1825, New York's artisans were celebrating the beginning of the end for the artisan system of labor. By the early 1830s, manifestations of a great transformation were everywhere in the Northeast: in the expansion of trade facilitated by canals and other improvements in transportation, in an increase in the number of "brain workers," in the many clerks, bookkeepers, and managers needed to oversee the flow of goods from producers to markets to consumers. Most disturbing for junior artisans, they would be evident in the development of large-scale factories and the rise of factory towns, places like Albany, Utica, Troy, and Rochester along the length of the Erie Canal.[21]

By the late 1820s, master artisans were doing their best to compete with the factories. Often this meant expelling journeymen and apprentices from their shops and hiring wage-workers in their place. Many of the old shops became small factories, places of sweated labor and temporary hirelings, with modern machines replacing the tools and skills of the old trades. Many artisan–merchants moved to new quarters, to private homes in better neighborhoods, as work became increasingly separated from home, as the traditional model of the extended family based on kinship relations and live-in laborers was replaced by values of privatization and the new ideal of the nuclear family.

Expelled from their former households and increasingly forced to work for falling wages, apprentices and journeymen went an opposite direction. They gravitated toward cheap boardinghouses in poorer city wards or on the bad side of town. In Boston, this meant the North End. In New York, it meant the Sixth Ward, the site of the Bowery and the Five Points, neighborhoods that would become known as America's worst slums. They would be joined by immigrants and migrants to the city, surrounded by overcrowded tenements and teeming streets.[22] And as they found themselves on the way to becoming a permanent, degraded, and angry working class, by the early 1830s they would see images of labor that would leave them angrier still.

The Mill Girl and Working-Class Culture

In popular culture and song, a new image of the worker emerged in the 1830s. Two verses from one of the many songs focused on the image provide an outline and context for the character:

> While Fact'ry wheels roll slow or whirl,
>   And bell doth toll or ring,
> And New-Year comes—the factory girl
>   May meditate and sing:
>
> Sing—how Time's wheels unceasing roll,
>   To spin her Life's short thread;
> And think—how soon Death's bell will toll
>   To call her to the dead.[23]

The imagined worker of this song was not a craftsman but an "operative," the operator of a machine containing the artisan's skills in its mechanical design. The new worker's labor was neither art nor means to independence. It was a dull routine, a daily shift marked by factory bells, a grinding trudge toward death. Most alarming for artisans, the image was feminized. The new worker was a "factory girl."

What produced this alternative image of labor? The answer lies in widespread American attitudes about the nation's transition to modern capitalism. Americans had known what happened with this transformation for some time. They had the example of England. According to many observers, English

industrialization produced a number of distressing results: the rise of a permanent working-class population; the concentration of this population around factories; the appearance of factory cities that were dirty, crowded, and dangerous.

Northern critics compared the English factory system to slavery. The "manufacturing districts of England," declared one labor spokesman in 1833, had
produced workers whose degradation made them "precisely like Southern
slaves." Southern observers claimed England's factories made slavery look
good by comparison. They presented, declared a writer for the *Southern Literary Messenger*, "scenes of physical suffering, and mental degradation, and
moral pollution, to which the annals of African slavery, in its harshest and
most unmitigated forms, furnish no parallel." Even the most ardent supporters of industrialization fretted over the issue. Having been warned by England,
wrote one, "great anxiety has been naturally felt about the experiment, yet
novel, of building up a manufacturing population."[24]

The factory girl would be a product of this anxiety. Early on, the image
would be most associated with the factory city of Lowell, Massachusetts. In
1822, the first mill opened at Lowell's site along a falls on the Merrimac River,
the Merrimac Manufacturing Company. Others soon followed: Hamilton Mill,
Appleton, Boott, and Tremont Mills. To avoid the degradation of workers, textile companies built dormitories, communal dining halls, libraries, and lecture
halls, all with the goal of making their factories into centers for social uplift.
To avoid a permanent working class, they instituted a policy of hiring young
women. According to theory, these New England farm girls would work a few
years, earn enough for a dowry, and then leave to get married. By 1830, Lowell
and its downriver "sister city," Lawrence, had some 100,000 textile spindles in
operation. Nearly each was tended by a female operative, who along with female
doffers and carders made up some seventy percent of the Lowell workforce.[25]

These mill girls quickly became a popular-culture fixation, a focus of essay, poem, and song. For the Lowell system's boosters, the operative's main
task was to demonstrate "that corporations should have souls," that factory
work was "not degrading," and that factory workers were "capable of virtue."
Lucy Larcom, a mill girl herself, would catch the tone: the operatives were
"girls who loved everybody, and were loved by everybody."[26] They were "girls
from the country," claimed the *Handbook for the Visitor to Lowell*, with a "true
Yankee spirit of independence." And, as the guide's author made sure to add,
while they "pass a few years here," they were not "on this account, less good
wives, mothers, or educators of families." The poet John Greenleaf Whittier
summed up public perceptions in a magazine article: they were "Nuns of Industry," representing "acres of girlhood, beauty reckoned by the square rod."
They were "flowers gathered from a thousand hillsides and green valleys of

New England." "Who shall sneer at your calling?" asked the poet. "Who shall count your vocation otherwise than noble and ennobling?"[27]

The experiment did have its doubters. As one Virginian wrote in an issue of the *Southern Literary Messenger* from 1835, it was the Southern opinion that the factories would have a "demoralizing tendency." The factory girl might arrest the trend, he noted, for "the females watch each other's deportment with the most jealous vigilance." But, he averred, "the *natural* course of these establishments seems to be *down the stream of vice.*" For other critics, the innocence of the mill girl raised more specific fears. "Many are far removed, at a critical point of life, from parental oversight," intoned one minister on the subject, adding that with no "permanent inhabitancy" in their factory cities, "they must meet the moral privations and perils incident to a transient residence, and a populous city."[28]

Such fears lent themselves to images of country girls being seduced and abandoned—even murdered—by urban rakes. In 1833, a ballad called "The Factory Maid" followed this script. Set to the tune of "The Star-Spangled Banner," the song told the sad tale of "Sarah M. Cornell, who left the factory and was murdered near Fall River, Rhode Island."

> OH! list the sad tale of the poor factory maid,
>> How cheerful she went when the day's work was over,
> In cloak and in bonnet all simply arrayed,
>> To meet a dark Fiend in the shape of a lover.
> How gladsome and gay she tripped on her way,
>> But alas! on her path the foul murderer lay.
> Oh! weep for Maria, the poor factory maid,
> So charming, so fair, and so basely betrayed.[29]

Mill girls themselves also had doubts about the system. They were especially dubious when it came to the Lowell boosters' imagery of the uplifting qualities of factory work. While boosters extolled Lowell's "temples of industry," the girls faced fourteen-hour shifts, the miserable air and deafening noise of the mills, and the daily discipline of incessant factory bells. They had "turn outs" or strikes in 1834 and 1836, the results of wage cuts and raised rents for increasingly privatized boardinghouses. During the strikes, they sang their own songs:

> Oh! isn't it a pity, such a pretty girl as I—
> Should be sent to the factory to pine away and die?
>> Oh! I cannot be a slave,
>> I will not be a slave,
>> For I'm so fond of liberty
>> That I cannot be a slave.[30]

The strikes failed, the wage cuts remained, and boardinghouse owners raised their rates. According to one mill worker, many of the first wave of factory girls left Lowell. The mills replaced them with immigrants, and "the *status* of the factory population of New England gradually became what we know it to be to-day."[31]

Still, the girls remained a cultural fixation. Within a few years of the rise of the Lowell system, according to one guidebook for the Boston area, a visit to Lowell was as necessary as a day trip to the Lexington Battlefield or the garden wonders of Mount Auburn Cemetery. The guidebook invited visitors to "sit down by this machine, from which is flowing a rivulet of whitest carded wool, soft as a snow flake, and gaze on those factory girls!" All would have "pretty faces," it promised, along with "nicely shaped feet and neatly turned ankles." The images continued to proliferate with the appearance of the *Lowell Offering* in 1840, the company-sponsored magazine featuring poems, songs, and stories from the mill girls themselves. With its cover art featuring a young girl, a book in one hand, a modest shawl in the other, surrounded by symbols of virtuous industry—a church, a beehive, and a factory—the magazine, which had a publication run from 1840 to 1845, offered "ideal mill girls, full of hopes, desires, [and] aspirations." In imagery, at least, factory girls remained "poets of the loom, spinners of verse, artists of factory life."[32]

For the boosters at Lowell, the image accomplished its purpose. According to statements like "The Song of the Factory Girl," Lowell and Lawrence were places of "happy industry":

> Let us list to the song of the factory girl.
> As she sings 'mid the hum, and the clack, and the whirl;
> Tho' her task it be hard, yet her heart it is light;
> And she sings at her "loom," from the morn till the night.
>
> Then if healthy, and merry, the factory girl be,
> Who this life can enjoy, any better than she?
> And to you let us whisper a word ere you go;
> If we have a good offer, we marry you know.[33]

They were also places where labor had been feminized. "Why it is nothing but fun," wrote one mill girl in a published letter on tending spinning-frames, adding that the girls were "not occupied half the time." They were never tired after their day's toil, declared a writer for the *Boston Atlas*. And so they were able to "sally forth" every evening, "all well-dressed and lady-like," to partake of a church meeting or a lyceum lecture. Occasionally, noted a guidebook, one or two of the looms might snap a thread, "just so they can be touched by delicate fingers, and peer into pretty faces!"[34]

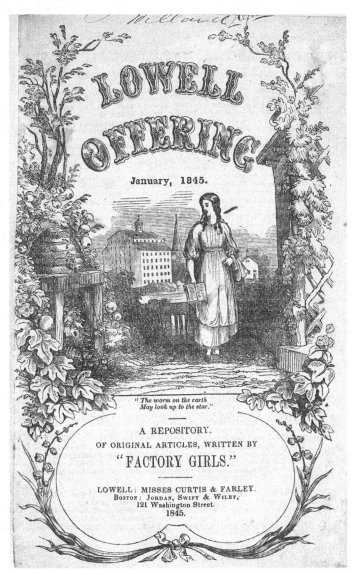

FIGURE 3.1. The new face of labor, circa 1830. The 1845 cover of the *Lowell Offering*, the magazine published by a consortium of cotton-mill companies, offered a depiction of a new model of laborer, the "female operative" that had been in place since the early 1830s. With the rise of factory work, labor could be reconceived as lacking in meaningful skill, dependent, and as this image clearly suggests, very feminized. In the 1830s, songs by, about, and sung by "factory girls" became a popular phenomenon in the Northeast. One result was a crisis for an older ideal of the independent and masculine artisan. *Lowell Offering, January, 1845. A Repository of Original Articles, Written by "Factory Girls."* Boston: Jordan, Swift & Wiley, 1845. Courtesy of American Antiquarian Society.

Charming as they were for many Americans, these images heralded a fearful future for young men in the artisan system of labor. By the early 1830s, many journeymen and apprentices faced a crisis, a crisis in the meanings of work and the identity of the worker. For many, artisan republicanism no longer described their lives or the realities of work. The future lay in the factory. It also lay in declining status, lower pay, shoddy tenements, and overcrowded neighborhoods, in their supplanting as middling sorts by an increasing population of jobbers and clerks, the brain workers who would become a new middle class.

Artisan festivals continued to mark the holidays. Processions of tradesmen continued to roll down the main streets of New York, Boston, and Philadelphia. Displaced journeymen and apprentices tried to maintain ideals equating work with art, to hang on to the old traditions of democratic uplift in workers' hymns. As one festival hymn had it, even as late as 1845, the mechanic's art was still divine:

> God of our Being! We / In love would raise to Thee
> > Our songs of Praise:
> Thou mad'st the HAND! whose skill, / Controll'd by Thought and Will,
> > Makes Art divine![35]

Yet the old rhetoric was changing. In the 1830s, labor organizations turned increasingly to the desperate move of trying to redefine factory labor as "white man's work." The General Trades Societies and Workingmen's Parties were already making efforts to banish African Americans from artisan trades. Now they, along with other workers' groups, moved to exclude black workers from factories. Meanwhile, in festival speeches and in song, the master artisans who dominated the General Society increasingly stressed a more entrepreneurial brand of republicanism. One writer for a mechanics' magazine offered a defense of artisan labor in the name of higher productivity, claiming that in the future the "intelligent handicraftsman" would outdo the "senseless machine," that he would constantly "shorten the processes of his labor."[36] Others stressed an artisan version of uplift and reform, emphasizing workers' involvement in temperance associations and charitable societies. As one artisan-based "cold water melody" had it:

> The laboring men they want more work, / And higher wages too;
> They'll help to roll the temp'rance ball, / With better times in view;
> They'll saw, and chop, and grub, and dig, / And spade and shovel away,
> Without a drop of alcohol, / By night or yet by day.[37]

These moves and statements contained a whiff of desperation. Here was an effort to make factory labor the domain of white workers, but the labor itself remained degraded and perceptually feminized. For many, it may have been hard to see a difference between the factory laborer and the old concept of the hireling. Here was a vow that hanging on to the old ways would lead to a speedup; a promise of sobriety in exchange for higher wages and a chance to "grub and dig."

Former junior artisans had a number of outlets for the expression of this crisis. Some joined Workingmen's Parties. Others joined neighborhood gangs and secret societies, organizations from which they could express frustrations according to the old tradition of vandalism and a good street riot. Still others may have thought of the Luddites. But the Luddite movement was dead, crushed with 12,000 troops of the English Army in the summer of 1812. Besides, the growth-boosters in America knew all about the example of England; and again they sought to avoid the Old World's mistakes. They provided more funding for the early police patrol known as "The Watch." They outfitted hired minions with copper badges and charged the "coppers" with patrolling the boundaries of worker neighborhoods, with defending the wealth and property of those benefiting from the market revolution.

Most junior artisans continued to align their interests with their old masters and the General Trades Societies. On election days, they lined up with Tammany Hall and the Democrats. They seemed willing to go along with the new rhetoric tying factory labor to race privilege, language that pictured wage work as white work. They seemed to accept an emerging coalition that increasingly defined the pre–Civil War Democrat Party, a political unity, that is, between factory owners, the old master artisans who ran the General Trades Societies, and the slaveholding class of the South. In accepting this coalition, they found themselves providing political cover for the elite owners of large Southern plantations. With the Northern "workers"—an increasingly all-white group in the North—on their side, these slave owners could speak of themselves as men of the people, as defenders of the common folk.[38]

They would defend these folk by excoriating an early abolitionist movement. Part of the anti-abolitionist rhetoric of slaveholders and Northern white workers would be represented in twisted logic: in decrying the condition of Southern slaves, abolitionists were ignoring the wage slaves of the North. Following this logic, white workers in the North continued to express their political identity as Andrew Jackson men, committed to progress, to western expansion, and increasingly to an ideology of white supremacy. They still attended labor festivals and listened to speeches. Sometimes they made catcalls to their old masters from the back rows. More often, it seems, they applauded the shop-worn statements on the dignity of art, the unity of artisans, and the privileges of white labor. Even as they applauded, however, they still had a problem: factory labor may have increasingly been seen as white labor, but it was still demeaning. It was still, according to this logic, a form of wage slavery; it was still, as songs about the mill girl too often reminded them, work that was unskilled, dependent, and feminized. Denied other outlets to express frustrations, many turned to cultural expressions.

In doing so, they laid claim to the cultural space of the urban theater. In 1827, there were six major theaters in New York City: the Park, Lafayette, Richmond Hill, and Bowery Theaters, along with Chatham Gardens and Niblo's Garden. The large structures—some of which were capable of holding audiences of up to two or even three thousand—offered a blend of elite control and democratic participation. Like theaters in Boston and Philadelphia, New York's theaters tended to be owned by elite stockholders. Nearly all had ideals of social hierarchy built into their architecture and design. At the front of the theater was the stage. Moving outward from the stage were the seating areas of pit, gallery, boxes, and third tier. Each of these areas were indicative of the social and economic status of their occupants. At the midpoint of this hierarchy was the pit, an open space directly before the stage, along with the gallery, a semicircle of bleachers elevated and set back some distance. These were the areas for the middling sorts, a mass of journeymen, master artisans, and small-time merchants.

At the high end of the theater's hierarchy were the rows of boxes, the second tier in most theaters. Here were the seats of the "better sorts," the large-scale merchants and the gentlemen of property. From their private boxes, they could look down on the action on the stage or at the crowd in the pit, their elevated positions attesting to their social dominance. Finally, ascending above and behind the boxes was the low end of the hierarchy. This was the third tier, the "notorious" third tier, in the language of the time. Here were the cheapest seats, places for the most common of theatergoers, wage-workers, apprentices, and in some theaters, African Americans. Here, too, gentlemen retired from the boxes for food or drink from third-tier bars, while prostitutes, among the few women in the theater, trolled for customers.[39]

To put it more simply: within these spaces, the elite sat above, the democratic masses milled below, and the prostitutes, rum sellers, and drinkers occupied the "guilty third tier." The action onstage tended to confirm this blend of hierarchy and somewhat controlled democratic participation. During the 1820s, much of this action followed elite and patriarchal tastes, with light musical dramas or comedies, both devoted to escapist themes and messages of moral uplift. There was quite a bit for the masses here, but there was also an aura of didactic improvement. For many, moral uplift provided the rationale for the theater; constant references to the ideal offered a defense against the old

puritanical prejudices associating actors with liars and actresses with prostitutes. New York mayor Philip Hone stated the defense during the 1826 celebration to mark the laying of the Bowery Theatre's cornerstone: the theater,
he declared, would "improve the taste, correct the morals, and soften the
manners of the people."[40]

Despite these elements of patriarchal control and moral didacticism, audiences were hardly passive. By current standards, the theater would have been
a terrifying space. The reasons had to do with technology and tradition. First,
theaters were lit by gaslights, which at this point could not be dimmed during
performances. This meant the action in the audience was just as visible—and
often just as interesting—as the action onstage. Second, the audience, particularly the members in the pit and gallery, had what was considered a "democratic right" to participate in the action onstage. According to this tradition,
actors had an obligation to play to the pit and gallery, to get their approval
with the large theatrical movements associated with a melodramatic style.
The "pittites and gallery gods" would respond according to tradition: cheering actors who met their approval, hissing those who did not, demanding
instant encores, throwing objects onstage, even rioting.[41]

Changes in the theater began appearing in the 1820s. Through the decade,
increasing numbers of former journeymen and apprentices began to appear
in the pit, gallery, and third tier. Theater managers in areas where workingmen congregated began catering to these audiences, lowering their ticket
prices, offering nightly spectacles more fitting with their needs. By the early
1830s, while the Park Theater and Niblo's Garden remained elite theaters, the
manager of the Bowery and Chatham Theaters, Thomas Hamblin, began courting the laboring men of the Sixth Ward and Lower East Side.[42]

Hamblin's audience represented the young, male culture of the Sixth Ward
and the Five Points. Its members included firemen, gang members, and thousands of junior artisans who could see their status slipping. Here, as elsewhere,
theaters continued to produce many of the same plays: fairy tales, Bowdler-
ized Shakespeare, and heroic melodramas. In their nightly fare, they offered a
pastiche of mixed genres. At Boston's Eagle Theater, a play like *Sam Patch in
France* might be followed by William Richards singing "his celebrated Welsh
song" the "Maid of Cllanglothnn," then by a snippet of the play *William Tell*
along with more entr'acts, a "Scotch Strathspey" performed by "Miss Caroline
Fox, and a "Comic Song" by "Mr. Merryfield."[43]

What changed was the audience. No longer subject to elite control, audiences at the Bowery Theater were increasingly boisterous, more vulgar in their
style. They had long been loud; now, at least for some middle-class observers,
they became terrifying. One observer described a typical night at the Bowery

Theater as consisting of little more than "loud and threatening noises" welling up from the pit, which "heaved" in "wild and sullen tumult." There was a "roaring crush" of tobacco chewing and spitting. And finally, there were "the yells and screams, the shuddering oaths and obscene songs, tumbling down from the third tier."[44] By 1832, this audience had to a large extent taken over the Bowery. The theater had become a space marked by an energetic interplay between performers and audiences, a space in which the members of an emerging working class could express frustrations and release pent-up anger. Faced with the factory's apparent feminization of labor, they were primed for a theatrics of remasculinization. What they were looking for was a new model of manhood, something real, something expressive and potent.

Jim Crow, Dandy Pat, Zip Coon

On the evening of November 12, 1832, the actor Thomas Dartmouth Rice went out on the boards of the Bowery's stage dressed in rags, his face and hands darkened with a paste of burnt cork. He performed as the character "Jim Crow," singing a song of the same name and doing a shuffling dance step between verses:

> My name is Daddy Rice, as you berry well do know.
> And none in de 'Nited States like me, can jump Jim Crow.
> Weel about an' turn about, and do jis' so,
> Ebery time I weel about, I jump Jim Crow.[45]

The next day, as a magazine writer later put it, "found the song of Jim Crow, in one style of delivery or another, on everybody's tongue." Within three years Rice would leave for England, where the song would again be a smash. "Nothing," claimed a writer for the sporting paper *Spirit of the Times*, "has equaled the popularity of this '*Virginia Nigger.*'"[46]

According to lore, Rice's performance of "Jim Crow" marked the first appearance of blackface in American popular culture. From the reaction, one might think Rice's audience had never seen anything like it. To the contrary, white performances of black songs and characters were popular on the stage from the second half of the eighteenth century. Theater records for New York City reveal that in 1767, an actor by the name of "Mr. Tea" regaled audiences with a "Negro dance in character." A 1793 play, *The Irishman in London, or, the Happy African*, featured the character of "Cubba," a black female servant played by a white actor as a happy and witty slave. Another play, *Laugh While You Can*, introduced a similar character in 1799, a comic musician who went by the name "Sambo."

MR T. RICE

AS

THE ORIGINAL JIM CROW

New York Pub. by E. RILEY N.29 Chatham St.

FIGURE 3.2. Jim Crow, the standard of authentic identity. Thomas Dartmouth Rice's performance of the blackface character Jim Crow at New York's Bowery Theatre in 1832 has been depicted as America's first blackface act. In fact, Rice developed the character over time, picking up parts of the act from other performers and basing it on other characters. Interestingly, one of these characters was the stage Irishman, and thus not "black" at all. Jim Crow represented the authentic, free African American of the North, a character uncorrupted by manners, affectation, education, or any type of self-control. He became a model for a rising version of working-class masculinity. "Mr. T. Rice as The Original Jim Crow" (New York, E. Riley No. 29 Chatham St., n.d.). Courtesy of American Antiquarian Society.

The phenomenon continued into the years of the early republic. As the theater fully blossomed in the Northeast after years of suppression, Americans flocked to see versions of Shakespeare's *Othello*, with its lead role played by white actors in various shades of blackface. Many understood the play as a parable on the dangers of interracial sex. In the 1820s, Charles Matthews, an English comic singer, performed several black characters on the American stage, supposedly going so far as to study black dialect in order to improve his act. He became known for a dialect version of Hamlet's famous soliloquy: "To be or not to be, dat is him question, whether him nobler in de mind to suffer or lift up him arms against one sea of hubble bubble and by opossum end 'em." At the word "opossum," Matthews's audiences went wild, shouting for him to sing his signature song. Matthews complied with "Opossum Up a Gum Tree," a ditty later performers would introduce as a "South Carolina Negro Air."[47]

Still, no previous act made anything like the stir of Rice's "Jim Crow." While blackface had been around, suddenly the moment was right for an explosion in its popularity. One of the performers who would cash in on the craze was George Washington Dixon. As early as 1829, Dixon was known for what is widely considered the first "blackface" song in content and style. This was "Coal Black Rose," a song done in the voice of "Sambo," a free black from the South who expressed his longing for the character Coal Black Rose.[48] At about the same time as Rice's performance at the Bowery, Dixon became better known for his performance of the song and character "Zip Coon."

Jim Crow and Zip Coon would be the foundational acts of blackface. Through the 1830s, into the 1840s, and even down to the present, practically every blackface song and act would derive from the two characters. The songs, along with the characters and their performers, had a number of elements in common. First, Rice and Dixon probably were not the authors of the songs. Most likely, they picked up tune, lyric, and even the acts themselves in shards and pieces, borrowing parts from other performers, adding their own touches as time went on. Second, both performers had connections with the declining artisan culture of the American Northeast. Finally, both Jim Crow and Zip Coon expressed needs and desires of their emerging working-class audiences.

Thomas Rice was certainly in a position to understand these needs. Born in New York City in 1808, Rice came out of two cultures: that of the declining mass of junior artisans and that of the urban theater. As a young man, he apprenticed as a carpenter. Either he was dismissed from his apprenticeship or he failed to find work as a journeyman. By the 1820s, he had moved on to the theater. For a while, he appeared in minor roles in New York. Again, he failed to find steady work. In the late 1820s, he opted for the last move of the failing stage performer. He signed on with an itinerant theater troupe and headed west. Somewhere in his travels through Pittsburgh, Louisville, and Cincinnati, he developed the song-and-dance routine that came to be "Jim Crow." He was definitely performing the routine by the summer of 1830. He continued to hone the act for the next two years, performing it as an "entr'act" between plays on urban stages in Philadelphia, Baltimore, and Washington, DC, before returning to New York City.[49]

By the time of his famous performance at the Bowery Theatre, Rice's career had been marked by insecurity. Like his audience, he was looking for a point of resistance to the changes of the market revolution, a sense of self rooted in authenticity. He would find this sense in Jim Crow. The most popular account of the character's origins—taken from Rice himself—placed it in Cincinnati. Here, Rice, who was playing entr'acts as a drunken Irishman, found himself wandering the streets between performances, "alert for everything that might be turned to professional and profitable use." Suddenly, he heard a black stage driver, "lolling lazily," singing the song in "an unmistakable dialect." It occurred to him: "might not 'Jim Crow' and a black face tickle the fancy of pit and circle, as well as the 'Sprig of Shillalah' and a red nose?" That night, according to the story, Rice dressed in rags, blackened his face, and performed the song to wild applause.[50]

In later years, as they vied for the title of the genre's originator, blackface performers would make the same claim: the songs and acts were stolen, not invented. Edwin Christy, the founder of the wildly popular Christy's Minstrels, said he took his material from black riverboat workers and stevedores along the Mississippi. William Whitlock, later a member of the Virginia Minstrels, averred that during the 1830s, while touring the South with the circus, he would "steal off to some Negro hut to hear the darkies sing and see them dance." As a later historian would put it, blackface was "originally inspired by genuine slave songs," as white minstrels visited plantations, as they listened to African American songs in cotton and sugarcane fields, on steamboats, and at river docks, and as they took them for use on the stage.[51]

Rice's contexts suggest an alternate possibility. His background as a failed artisan would have given him an understanding of the anxieties of the Bowery audience. His time in the theater would have left him a sense of how to play to their needs, to give them a character resonant with their desires. In effect, blackface may have originated from context as much as contact. The giveaway lies in the story of Jim Crow's origins. According to the story, Rice was already performing songs in character, in a character marked by drunkenness, a red nose, and a "Sprig of Shillalah." Before he was Jim Crow, Rice was a stage Irishman.

The character had been around before blackface exploded in popularity. Wherever it appeared, it offered a popular commentary on authentic selfhood. "Oh, I'm the boy called Dandy Pat," sang one of the persona's many performers:

> I was born in the town of Ballinafat,
>   I'm Pat the Dandy, O!
> My leg and foot is nate and trim, nate and trim;
> The girls all cry "Jist look at him!"
>   That's Pat the Dandy, O!
>   I'm Dandy Pat! Heigho! I'm Dandy Pat! Ochone! Eigho!
>   From Magherafelt to Ballinafat, there's none comes up to Dandy Pat![52]

On the surface, songs of this style seem little more than a collection of stereotypes, their goal to demean an immigrant population many native-born Americans feared and hated. On a deeper level, their popularity with working audiences suggests equal measures of yearning.

To be sure, there was no shortage of anti-Irish prejudice in the American Northeast, particularly as directed against the waves of impoverished and Catholic immigrants who came as a result of enclosures and potato famines. According to estimates, more than a quarter-million Irish immigrants arrived between the years 1820 and 1840. With their status already slipping, native-born junior artisans feared them as rivals and accused them of driving down wages. For artists, they were simian-like creatures, all receding brow, beady eye, and jutting jaw. For pamphleteers and novelists, they were mired in Catholic superstition and bizarre ritual. For Americans everywhere, it seems, they were regarded though the lens of old Anglo hostilities, as uncivilized and undisciplined, as very close in essence to African Americans.[53]

Irish stereotypes had appeared in popular song and onstage for generations. One of Nathaniel Coverly's broadsides allowed his common clientele to enjoy a brogue-inflected soliloquy in the form of "Father O'Brian's Celebrated Sermon" to a group of freshly arrived immigrants:

> So there ye are now, ye slabber up wickedness as if it was butter milk or bunnaugh clapper, ye haven't a morsel of goodness in ye half so big as a scraugteen potatoe. You come here with your beads and avemaries in your claws, while perhaps, ye are thinking whose throat ye shall cut, . . . ye are a pack of such bloody minded bog trotters; for the devil burn me, but I dare say it was some one or t'other of ye who killed poor Teddy Ballin O'Graugh, upon the blind quay, where if it had not been for Jemmy M'Gee and myself the poor fellow had lost his life because of it.[54]

The soliloquy had the standard characteristics of Irish minstrelsy: its use of comic dialect and vernacular expression; its references to potatoes and rosaries as symbols of Irishness; and its resort to malapropism: O'Brian's charge that one of his listeners had killed Ballin O'Graugh, almost causing him to lose his life.

All these images would go into the character of the stage Irishman. The song and act, meanwhile, would be increasingly standardized. First there was the reference to the character's origin: he was a rube from rural Kilkinney, Killarney, or Kildare. Next there was his migration to America: for he was by nature a roving Irishman, waxing nostalgic over the green hills of his native land even as he affirmed his decision to leave them. His attraction to America lay in the fact that the United States was a democracy, a place as he understood it where he could raise his status through strenuous self-affirmation. The lyrics to one song provide a typical example:

> My name is Ned O'Manney, I was born in sweet Killarney;
>   I can fight, dance or sing, I can plough, reap or mow:
> And if I meet a pretty girl, I never practice blarney,
>   I've something more alluring, which perhaps you'd like to know:
>
> I'm none of your Bulgruderries, nor other shabby families,
>   But can unto my pedigree, a pretty title show:
> Oh! I'm of the O's and Mac's, and likewise the sturdy wacks,
>   That live and toil in Ireland, where the Apple Praties grow.[55]

In the America of the stage Irishman, the key democratic right was the right to boast. Accordingly, the songs nearly always had verses in which the character crowed his qualities: he was handsome; he was rich; he was a gentleman.

The joke, as performers made clear, was that none of the boasts were true. In fact, the character was unattractive and destitute. He was a poor Irishman putting on airs. His charm was that he would always give himself away. At some point in the act, in the song's verses, or in a soliloquy between verses, he would expose his true nature. Thus, in one line he might sing of his preference for "iligant pastry," or his fine "pedigree," only to reveal himself in another: proclaiming his love for a "noggin of poteen" and a good "donnybrook." He bragged of his estate only to reveal that for him a mansion was a hut of mud and thatch. His fancy cane was a club-like shillelagh, his highbrow monocle an empty whiskey bottle.[56] Despite his claim to respectability and refinement, at any moment he was likely to break into an energetic jig or a drunken reel, a rousing version of "Erin Go Braugh," or a refrain dominated by the standard stereotypes:

Fal lah lue ful lah lue whack fal de riddle,
Sing fal lah lue fal lah lue whack ful de ray,
With my sprig of shelalegh I'll sing to your fiddle,
To a small drop of whiskey I'll never say nay.[57]

With Rice's performance of Jim Crow, blackface characters began to supplant the stage Irishman as a symbol of authentic identity. For audiences who had seen this kind of thing before, particularly for Irish immigrants among the audiences, Jim Crow offered an improvement on the "Irish Gintleman." Rice played the character as the lowest of the low: barefoot, dressed in rags, and black, a uniform shade of deep black produced by a paste of burnt cork. The character had no fear of losing social status. He was free in a double sense: free as an ex-slave living in the North; freed by his poverty and race from affectation, anxiety, or worry about the future.

Jim Crow had no pretense of book learning. He sang in a broad "Negro" dialect. He seemed barely to know what he was saying or singing. Yet he could say anything: engaging in clever wordplay, improvising whole verses for different nights and audiences, mocking political figures, even condemning slavery. Rice played the character with a swagger, with a physical potency that, given the frequently cited racial fears of the time, should have been more than a little disturbing. His dance was marked by an athletic muscularity, by flexed legs, fast shuffle steps, and quick spins, by lively jumps and lusty pelvic thrusts. His audience was not disturbed. Lithographs of his Bowery performance suggest an audience in the throes of a spasmodic charge of energy. Many rushed the stage, joining the character in his dance or shoving one another in wild glee; others remained in the pit, stomping and churning in ecstatic delight.

To the audience at the Bowery Theatre, few characters could have been more therapeutic. At a time of rapid change, at a time in which their very identity—as workers, as true citizens of the republic, even as men—was under threat, Rice's act demonstrated that identity could be fixed, that there were alternative means to masculinity outside the acquisition of artisan skills. Jim Crow was the authentic Northern black, poor but free, uneducated but with a kind of native intelligence, potent, self-expressive, and always dancing. In this character, New York City's declining junior artisans discovered precisely what the time called for; in his free expressions, in his masculinity, in his blackness, they discovered a model of identity that reached to the very bedrock of authentic selfhood.

George Washington Dixon's Zip Coon played more to their anger. Dixon had a varied career: before appearing on the stage, he worked as a spiritualist and a hypnotist. Later he proclaimed himself a professional athlete, a champion walker in the sport of "pedestrianism." In the 1820s, he had closer ties to New York's artisans than Rice, for he was the editor of one of the city's small pro-worker newspapers. He also appeared on the stage, taking the name "Buffalo Dixon" or "Buffo" Dixon for his loud and masculine style. Just when he began performing as Zip Coon is unknown. He was among the earliest blackface performers to cash in on Rice's success, and by 1833 or 1834 at the latest, Zip Coon rivaled Jim Crow as blackface's most representative and well-known character.

In listening to the songs, one might easily assume that the difference between the characters was in style, not meaning. The music for Zip Coon was far catchier than that of Jim Crow. The lyrics were set in the same version of a soon-to-be-standardized black dialect. Both characters were meant to be free blacks with roots in slavery; "Zip" was a diminutive for "Scipio," a standard slave name derived from plantation owners' images of themselves as inheritors of Roman republicanism. Both had surnames indicative of their animal essences, crow and coon suggesting their less-than-human status.

Yet if Rice played his character as an expression of black authenticity, Dixon performed his as a vision of authenticity corrupted. Jim Crow dressed in rags; Zip Coon came onstage decked out in an exaggerated version of aristocratic frills and finery. He was, he claimed in the song, a very learned scholar:

> I went down to Sandy hook, toder arter-noon;
> I went down to Sandy hook, toder arter-noon;
> I went down to Sandy hook, toder arter-noon;
>   And de fust man I met dere was old Zip Coon.

> Old Zip Coon is a very larned scholar,
> Old Zip Coon is a very larned scholar,
> Old Zip Coon is a very larned scholar,
>   He plays on the Banjo Cooney in de hollar.[58]

As presented in sheet-music illustrations and onstage, Zip Coon was a character who had been corrupted by an embrace of uplift.

Zip Coon's main reference was to another of the workers' favorite characters, the upward-climbing urban dandy. The character appeared without the blackface in songs like "The Handsome Man," a song published in 1835. The song's sheet-music cover art portrayed the character much like song-and-dance men would have presented him onstage: decked head to toe in shiny top hat, flower-lapelled overcoat, tight pants, and delicate high-heeled shoes. The artist pictured the character in an overtly "feminine" pose before a

FIGURE 3.3. Zip Coon, the effect of uplift on black authenticity. George Washington Dixon's performance of Zip Coon represented the other side of the coin: the free black character corrupted and feminized by his attempted embrace of middle-class uplift. Much of blackface's comedy would come from the character's failed attempts to put on airs, sound educated, or "act white." Jim Crow as the authentic black and Zip Coon as the corruption of authenticity by uplift would constitute the seminal characters of blackface and blackface minstrelsy. Sheet-music cover: *Zip Coon, A Favorite Comic Song*, New York: published by J. Hewitt & Co., 1833–1835. Courtesy of American Antiquarian Society.

mirror, his lack of manly qualities pronounced by limp wrists, knock-knees, and protruding buttocks. Of course the character had the standard dandy's props: a top hat, a flaccid walking cane, and a useless monocle. As for his utterances, these were the height of narcissistic banality. "I am a very handsome man," announced performers in the song's refrain, "a very, very, very handsome man."[59]

Dandies had not always been this noxious. By tradition, the term "dandy" meant something akin to "fine," or "swell." In the colonial period, it found use as a colloquial epithet for privileged gentlemen, their privilege marked by their bearing and finery of dress. During the Revolution, the term took on positive and radical meanings, representing—in "Yankee Doodle"—the revolutionary ideal that commoners could challenge the old colonial hierarchies; they could stick feathers in their caps and declare themselves the equals of aristocratic gentlemen. Through the 1820s and beyond, Americans would continue to invoke this version of the dandy as a symbol of democracy.

Worker-inflected dandy songs stressed an alternative version of the character as the laboring man's opposite. According to one version, the character could be seen every day promenading Broadway, "dressed in the height of fashion" and admiring his reflection in the windows of passing shops. His object, according to another, was to flaunt his learning and bearing directly in the face of the common working man:

> See the Fops now in college striving to get knowledge,
> With their Virgil, Greek and Latin, 'tis so handy-O;
> With their narrow dandy coats, & their fancy high-heel boots,
> While their father's purse of specie is the dandy-O.[60]

Here was a persona calculated to produce howls of rage and scornful laughter from working-class audiences. This version of the dandy was a stage representation of the thousands of educated young men who made the transition from the country to the city in the 1820s and 1830s. In their minds, they came for the new opportunities created by the market revolution. They were looking for employment as clerks, jobbers, scriveners, and merchants. For the laborers of the Five Points, they were hated figures, little more than opportunists looking to profit from the very changes—the rise of factories, the declining demand for artisan skills—that threatened former artisans with degradation as hireling workers. In effect, the dandy would be a target against which urban workingmen could turn their frustrations and hatreds. By placing the character in blackface, by grafting the dandy on to a blackface character, George Washington Dixon provided a racial cover for this expression of rage. He also heightened the anger, exaggerating the distance between authentic selfhood and dandy pretense, giving it a specific target.

Blackface would focus the anger of an emerging working class. The target of this anger would not be the people directly responsible for worker degradation, the former masters who expelled junior artisans from their shops, rehired them as waged employees, and were now working them as sweated labor. Within a short time, this target was largely standardized; whether it appeared as "The Handsome Man," as "Zip Coon," or later as the corked-up "Dandy Jim from Caroline," the character was practically the same.[61] In sheet-music covers, he was standardized to the point of exact sameness: pictured as feminized, usually in close proximity to a mirror, always imbued with a heavy dose of narcissistic pride. The result would be a hilarious debunking of the artifice of uplift, an exposure of it as "putting on false airs," as a movement that led to the corruption of one's authentic self. The foundation for Jim Crow and Zip Coon would be the nature of blackness, the idea that the representative black male—poor, uneducated, and always singing or dancing—was the bedrock of authentic identity. The main target would be the representatives of a culture of uplift, the members of a rising middle class.

4

Black Song

To Frederick Douglass, black song meant the arias of Elizabeth Greenfield, the opera singer known as "The Black Swan." Greenfield's singing, claimed a review from an 1851 issue of *Frederick Douglass' Paper*, reflected the "divinest of arts." The Swan could "charm and delight the most refined audience," declared another reviewer. To members of the antebellum era's Colored Female Reform Societies, black song meant an anthem such as "Am I Not a Sister," from the abolitionist songster *The Liberty Minstrel*:

> Am I not a sister, say? / Shall I then be bought and sold?
> In the mart and by the way, / For the white man's lust and gold?
> Save me then from this foul snare, / Leave me not to perish there.[1]

To William Wells Brown, black song meant ballads like "The Lament of the Fugitive Slave," from his own collection of antislavery ballads. Or it meant whatever he liked, including the "sublime melodies of Handel, Hayden, and Mozart."[2]

In mid-nineteenth-century America, black song might have had a number of meanings and references. Yet for a majority of Americans, none of these examples would fall under the category. According to dominant perspectives, the African American music of the time may be found nowhere else but in the songs of slaves. Black culture in nineteenth-century America is understood as slave culture. Reform, popular opera, and any art referred to as divine would fall under the category of elite or middle-class culture. And middle-class culture, as everyone knows, is "white culture."

To the historian and civil rights leader W. E. B. DuBois, the equation between black song and slave song reflected a paradox of black expression: if, that is, the origins of African American song lay in the hated condition of slavery, the songs themselves, whatever their beauty, would be at best "half despised." Still, the equation has remained one of the best-loved assumptions in American history. It follows from a set of assertions: before the Civil War, the black experience in America was that of slavery; black culture originated in slavery, and black song originated as slave song. Both harkened back to an "African musical heritage."[3]

This "blackness" or "Africanness" is primarily characterized by a freedom of self-expression, by uninhibited songs and shameless yearnings. The result of this way of seeing would create an image of black culture all but indistinguishable from the blackface stage. The standard approach to exploring black song in America has been to start with essentialist assumptions. According to this idea, there have always been categories of black song and white song; there are songs that express the essence of ethnic identity, songs purely European or African, black or white, slave or free.[4]

A better starting point may be the recognition that ethnic or national cultures did not develop in vacuums but through contacts and exchanges. As the evidence here suggests, the boundaries of a culture are never fixed or solid. "Anglo-American" or "white" sea chanteys could contain picked-up elements of "African" or "black" song and style; in fact, they probably contained elements of style from around the world. One might find "white" songs issuing from black slaves; songs collected as examples of "natural" black expression. Finally, black people could make contributions to a perceptually "white" middle-class culture. Indeed, it would be nearly impossible for any culture to develop without these exchanges.[5] A more accurate approach may be to explore the origins and contexts of "black" song and "black" culture in America, to take a close look at what became included in this category along with what would be excluded, to examine the musical expressions that would become known as white as well as black.

Work Songs

In 1832, Fanny Kemble, the most celebrated actress in England, came to the United States to try performing in the American theater. She soon gained widespread acclaim. Then, just as quickly, Pierce Butler took her from the stage. One of the nation's most eligible bachelors, Butler was a Philadelphia gentleman who stood to inherit a cotton plantation on Georgia's Sea Islands. In 1834, Kemble and Butler were married. Two years later, Butler inherited his plantation and the couple sailed for "Butler's Island," to a plantation with some five hundred slaves. "I knew nothing of these dreadful possessions of his," Kemble recalled. During the next year she would get to know these slaves, their songs, and their music.[6]

It would not be easy. As a foreign ingénue in the American theater, Kemble would have almost certainly heard examples of blackface songs. What she heard on Butler's Island was something else. "I thought," she wrote to a friend, "I could trace distinctly some popular national melody with which I was familiar in almost all their songs; but I have been quite at a loss to discover any such foundation for many that I have heard lately, and which have appeared to me extraordinarily wild and unaccountable." Most of these songs she heard when her husband's slaves rowed her between Butler's Island and the mainland. She tried a description: a "single voice" chanted a melody; the rowers repeated the chant, their "voices all in unison" as they used the "rhythm of the rowlocks for accompaniment." It was all "very curious."[7]

Kemble's account came near a dead-on description of a call-and-response work song, a pattern associated with West African traditions. Hearing songs in this pattern was a common experience for travelers in the tidewater regions of Georgia and South Carolina. In 1808, Englishman John Lambert heard a rowing song on the Savannah River, one in which a singer chanted a line followed by a response of alternating "aye, ayes" or "yoe yoes" from the chorus of rowers. Years later, another traveler described songs he heard while being rowed on rivers in South Carolina, writing that they consisted of one line sung by a "chief performer," which was then repeated by "the rest as a chorus." The singer, he added, "worked into his rude strain" any subject that came his way: work, the river, even the boat's white passengers. The folklorist George Cable recognized the same pattern in rowing songs he heard on the Mississippi River and the bayous of Louisiana. One had a chorus shout of "Bamboula!" He traced the word and found it was a West African term for a type of drum.[8]

These songs often baffled white listeners. During the Civil War, the abolitionist Harriet Ware was nonplussed by a song she heard from the boatmen who rowed her from Port Royal to Saint Helena Island. "The Negroes," she wrote a friend, "sang to us in their wild way as they rowed us across—I cannot give you the least idea of it." The English visitor W. H. Russell tried a description of a rowing song for the readers of the London Times. He called it a "barbaric sort of madrigal in which one singer beginning was followed by the others in unison, repeating the refrain in chorus, and full of quaint expression and melancholy." Fresh from the urban North, he compared the song to the expressions of a blackface group he had recently seen. The slave song was "as unlike the works of the Ethiopian Serenaders as anything in song could be."[9]

Described by white onlookers as "curious," "unaccountable," and completely unlike blackface, these songs fit characteristics historians and musicologists have attributed to African traditions. They also describe the "Anglo-American" sea chantey. In the mid-nineteenth century, the songs of sailors and workers in maritime industries provide evidence that African or African American culture found expression among white people. They suggest that the lines between white and black song are not as well defined as many musicologists have drawn them.

African Americans in the South certainly picked up "white" songs. Slave musicians like Henry McGaffrey, who served on a plantation in Louisiana, were expected to play the fiddle for white dances and learn a number of popular songs. McGaffrey's repertoire included the tunes "Sally Goodin," "The Cacklin' Hen," and the blackface tune "Arkansas Traveler."[10] Another "slave song" supposedly found in various Southern locales had these verses:

> One morning in May, / I spies a beautiful dandy,
> A-rakin' way of de hay / I asks her to marry,
> She say scornful, "No."
> But befo' six months roll by / Her apron strings wouldn't tie.
> She wrote me a letter, / She marry me then,
> I say, no, no, my gal, not I.

The song has been presented by musicologists as indicative of African attitudes toward sexuality, attitudes less inhibited than those of whites, more expressive and free. Yet its origins lay elsewhere. The lyrics are an almost word-for-word version of "The Female Hay-Makers," a ballad of seduction and abandonment printed by Nathaniel Coverly and sold at his Boston shop between 1812 and 1815.[11]

Whites also picked up music associated with black style. Working within standard assumptions, one historian of black culture has declared that African American slaves found European dances "too sedate and formalized."[12] So did white folks. In his travels through the South in the 1850s, the reformer and future landscape architect Frederick Law Olmstead ran into a Mississippi slave owner who went by the name "Old Yazoo." Asked if "his Negroes" danced much, Old Yazoo roared out a definitive yes. Indeed, he encouraged them to dance several times a week and "all night" on Saturdays. The outburst left the abolitionist Olmstead somewhat confused; this did not fit his model of the racist white Southerner. "I like to hear Negroes sing," he replied, lamely moving to the next topic. So did the slave master: "Niggers is allers good singers nat'rally," he replied, adding, "I reckon they got better lungs than white folks." At this point the subject reminded Old Yazoo of a pastime called "plank dancing":

You stand face to face with your partner on a plank and keep a dancin'. Put the plank up on two barrel heads, so it'll kind o' spring. At some of our parties— that's among common kind o' people, you know—it's great fun. They dance as fast as they can, and the folks all stand round and holler, "*Keep it up, John!*" "*Go it Nance!*" "*Don't give it up so!*" "*Old Virginny never tire!*" "*Heel and toe, ketch a fire!*" and such kind of observations, and clap and stamp 'em.[13]

If white dance was stiff and formal and black dance, as one historian has put it, "involved wild gyrations to a furious rhythm," then plank dancing was certainly black dance. Old Yazoo, a white man and a slave owner, liked nothing better than getting on a plank and doing an energetic "black" dance.

Perhaps nowhere was this cultural exchange more pronounced than in the sailor's chantey. There may have been good reasons for this phenomenon. Common sailors and African American slaves had several similarities in culture. Both were in the lowest ranks of society. Through the antebellum era, sailors represented a kind of "human flotsam," writes one historian, a motley crew of deserting soldiers, bail jumpers, thieves, and runaway apprentices.[14] Neither held this station by choice. Into the nineteenth century, press gangs from the British Royal Navy reserved the right to go ashore and take poor men into custody, literally kidnapping them into a life at sea.

Both occupied a world of strict hierarchy. For slaves, the order descended from the "big house" or plantation manor to the thatched huts of the quarters, moving down from master to overseer to slave drivers and slaves. For common sailors, the shipboard hierarchy ran from stern to bow or back to front, from the captain in his cabin astern, to the lower officers in their quarters amidship to the lowly foremast men in the forecastle, the tight quarters beneath the forward deck. Both sailors and slaves navigated a world of arbitrary power; both could be punished for running away; both were subject to ritualized floggings.[15]

Of course, slaves were slaves and sailors were nominally free. This did not mean sailors were white. The proportion of African American workers in the maritime trades was higher than in any free-labor-based industry in the United States. According to one count, on the eve of the Civil War there were some six thousand black men serving on American merchant vessels, another three thousand on whaling ships.[16] Finally, the lives of both were dominated by isolation and work. Sailors' tasks had a mundane regularity: there was the daily swabbing of decks, the endless painting of ships, the loading of goods at various ports of trade. Sailors, like slaves, were called "hands," as if the laboring parts of their bodies were the whole of their beings. At sea there was the constant work of sailing the vessel, the pulling on lines and turning of wenches, the countless times when, as one put it, "all hands" were busy "setting up the riggin'." There was the manning of pumps. Sailors expected vessels to leak; some barely stayed afloat without constant effort below-decks. One captured the experience: "Pump, pump, pump all the time. My Country! I suffer for you."[17]

Both developed songs to deal with the tedium and ease the completion of mind-numbing tasks. For African Americans in bondage, these have been called slave songs. For sailors, they were "chanteys." The term is often used to cover two types of songs. One was the forecastle song, or "forebiter." These were songs for passing away the time while not working, the tedious hours of the evening, bad weather, or becalmings. Common themes included the sailor's ship and the officers on board, along with grog shops, brothels, and food. Many recounted tales of the good treatment of Jack Tar when he was ashore with money, the turning him outdoors when his money was spent. Others stressed the primacy of fortune in the sailor's life, the belief, as one whaleman put it, that luck was always "the best man on board."[18]

The other type of chantey, the work chantey, followed the same call-and-response pattern that scholars have identified as coming from Africa or slavery. One singer—the chanteyman—sang the verse, and the rest of the crew sang a response or refrain. The chanteyman was expected to have an array of songs for different tasks: halyard chanteys and pump chanteys with a fast rhythm to coordinate the hauling on lines, the raising of sails, or the working of pumps; rowing chanteys timed to assure that oars would rise, dip, and pull simultaneously; and finally the slower capstan or windlass chanteys, the songs sung by full crews to coordinate the pushing or heaving of mechanical winches, the heavy work such as raising an anchor that required concerted exertion and more time to recover between the bursts of effort during the refrain.[19]

The call-and-response pattern of these songs may be seen and heard in a typical halyard chantey. The song most likely dates from the 1830s and appeared in Richard Henry Dana's account of his 1841 voyage to California, *Two Years Before the Mast*:

> Around the corner we will go, / 'Round the corner Sally
> Around Cape Horn we all must go, / 'Round the corner Sally
> If I had a little gal in tow, / 'Round the corner Sally
> I would tow her off to Callaio. / 'Round the corner Sally.[20]

As this song suggests, sailors picked up material for chanteys from a number of diverse sources. Indeed, if common seamen were among the lowliest workers in America, they were also among the most worldly. In the early decades of the nineteenth century, whaling and merchant vessels expanded their voyages into the far reaches of the Pacific Ocean. Meanwhile, the China trade generated stores of crockery at custom houses from Salem to Charleston.[21] Yankee sailors had opportunity to borrow songs from African American populations along the Atlantic seaboard, in Caribbean islands, and at various South American ports of call. In the most isolated of these places, such as the Sea Islands off South Carolina and Georgia, or in Antilles ports of Saint Vincent, Grenada, and Tobago, local black populations retained pronounced traits of African culture. In these ports, songs identified as chanteys survived into the twentieth century.[22]

Sailors also made contact with parts of Africa. The American slave trade continued through 1807, as ships picked up human cargo at West African slaving stations on the coasts of Gabon, Sierra Leone, and Gambia.[23] Even after the suppression of the trade, American ships continued to make contact with the African coast. They stopped for provisions and water at Monrovia, at Santa Cruz Island off Teneriffe, and at the Dutch fortress of "El Mina." They picked up crewmen at "Cape Messurado," an anchorage one American officer referred to in 1846 as "our largest Color'd Colony." Some joined British vessels in patrolling for illegal slavers, stopping and boarding vessels off the coast to check papers and cargo manifests.[24]

A few took part in the illegal slave trade. This activity may have been particularly enticing for some whaleship owners. By the early 1840s, Nantucket's whaling industry had gone into decline, a result of longer voyages, diminishing returns, and the silting-in of the island's harbor. According to later interviews with several among the island's old salts, the Quaker merchants who dominated the industry survived the down years, but only by entering a very literal black market. "No sir," declared one former sailor, "it don't do to go too deeply into how money was made here by our Quakers." Registered whalers survived by carrying "medicines" (most likely opium) from India and China or, as one put it, by "blackbirding," by working the African Coast and "running cargoes of slaves to Cuba and Brazil."[25]

Whether made through illegal slaving or engaging in patrols to suppress the trade, such contacts had an effect on the lyrical content of sea chanteys. Consider one of the best known of these songs, the topsail-halyard chantey "Blow, Boys Blow." With its earthy language and references to patrolling packets, the early nineteenth-century chantey attests to both the survival of slave-running and the disgust many sailors felt for it:

> Was you ever on the Congo River / Blow, Boys Blow
> Where fever makes the white man shiver / Blow, Me Bully Boys Blow
> A Yankee ship comes down the river / Blow, Boys Blow
> Her masts and yards they shone like silver / Blow, Me Bully Boys Blow

What do you think she's got for cargo? / Blow, Boys Blow
Why black sheep that've run the embargo. / Blow, Me Bully Boys Blow
What do ye think they got for dinner? / Blow, Boys Blow
Why monkey ass and donkey liver. / Blow, Me Bully Boys Blow

Yonder comes the Arrow packet, / Blow, Boys Blow
She fires a gun can't ye hear the racket. / Blow, Me Bully Boys Blow
Blow me boys and blow forever, / Blow, Boys Blow
O Blow me down the Congo River. / Blow, Me Bully Boys Blow.[26]

By the middle decades of the nineteenth century, points of contact between slave songs and "Anglo-American" sea chanteys were everywhere. Sailors during these decades sang a halyard chantey called "Whiskey Johnny." In 1862, the Union officer Thomas Higginson recorded ex-slaves in his black regiment singing a marching song with a similar cadence called "Hangman Johnny." In the 1850s, slaves in several areas of the South sang work songs with the refrain of "Hilo." The refrain has been interpreted as a dialect version of "holler" or "hollow," a term common in the rural South for a small valley or mountain ravine. This might have been the case, for in 1843, the Northern poet William Cullen Bryant heard one such song on a South Carolina plantation. Bryant, perhaps with a poet's keener ear, distinctly heard the refrain as "hollow."[27]

At the same time, sailors often used "Hilo" as a chantey refrain. The term had two references. One was the island of Hilo in the Hawaiian chain. The other was the town of Hilo, Peru, an important South American whaling station and, as many sailors had it, a great place for rum and whores.[28] Whatever their references, the similarities between "hilo" and "hollow," the appearance of the term "hilo" in slave songs, and the structural commonalities of the songs themselves provide strong evidence for cultural formation through constant exchange. Examples such as these suggest that both the Anglo-American sea chantey and the slave work song reflect music that cannot be categorized as slave, black, Anglo, or even American. Instead, they reflect a broad synthesis of cultures, cultures that can be called transatlantic or even global in origin, cultures that clearly developed across lines of ethnicity.

Parlor Songs

Frederick Douglass half-despised these songs. Before his escape from slavery in Maryland in 1838, he often heard examples. There were the shouted chanteys at the Baltimore shipyards where he worked as a caulker; there were the outbursts of slaves at the "Great House Farm," singing in exultant joy as they went to receive their monthly rations. "The hearing of these wild notes always depressed my spirit," wrote Douglass in his autobiography. Many, he admitted, were beautiful. Still, he could never remove them from their context: for him, they recalled the "dehumanizing character" of slavery.[29] Against these songs of forced labor and joyful submission to the master's power, he offered the contrast of his new home in the whaling port of New Bedford, Massachusetts. The port's black sailors sang no "loud songs," he noted; they worked "noiselessly," with "dignity." The town was a place of "wealth, comfort, taste, and refinement," he wrote, "such as I had never seen in any part of slaveholding Maryland."[30]

From the publication of his classic narrative in 1845 to the present, Frederick Douglass has existed in the American imagination as one of the nation's two or three representatives of "the slave experience." His preference for "taste and refinement" has occasionally threatened this status. The problem, as a number of historians have argued, was that after 1845 Douglass ceased to speak as a slave. He became a promoter of schools, literary societies, and reform associations, an almost militant proponent of uplift and respectability. He became middle class.[31]

He was far from alone. One of his predecessors was David Walker. Born around 1796 along the Cape Fear River in Wilmington, North Carolina, Walker was the son of a free black woman and a male slave, an accident of birth that made him free and isolated. At the time Wilmington's population included well over a thousand African Americans. Only nineteen were free. Walker spent his youth and early adulthood in rootless wandering. He lived for a time in Charleston, South Carolina. He later claimed to have passed through Georgia, Alabama, Kentucky, and Mississippi. In 1825, he settled in Boston. There, he opened a clothing and rag shop in the city's North End.

He also became a community activist. He joined Boston's African Methodist Episcopal Church and the local black Masonic Lodge. In 1826, he helped found the Massachusetts General Colored Association. He became a regular at the Association's ceremonies, hosting its annual Abolition Day Dinner, a celebration of the abolition of slavery in Massachusetts in 1800 and the British West Indies in 1804. Finally, he spent some of his time writing *David Walker's Appeal to the Coloured Citizens of the World*. When the pamphlet turned up in 1830, observers immediately characterized it as the most inflammatory abolition publication of the time. Any number of its themes outraged readers: from its criticisms of the hypocrisy of Christians who owned slaves to its hints at the need for a nationwide slave rebellion. The English abolitionist Harriet Martineau found it "perfectly appalling." She castigated Walker for calling his "colored brethren to drown their injuries in the blood of their oppressors."[32]

Among the pamphlet's overlooked themes was a call for a more uplifting revolution. According to Walker, slavery had reduced African Americans

to the *"most wretched, degraded* and *abject* set of beings."* And so he set out
to fight the institution with uplift. In his appeal, he portrayed himself as a
stern teacher, stalking the streets of Boston with a copy of *Murray's English
Grammar* tucked beneath one arm, examining black schoolboys on rules of
speech. "Not more than one in thirty was able to give a correct answer to my
interrogations," he wrote, adding that only five out of one hundred were "able
to correct the false grammar of their language." Arguing that ignorance kept
slavery alive, he concluded with a call for enlightenment. "Men of colour,"
he declared in the appeal, "I call upon you . . . to cast your eyes upon the
wretchedness of your brethren, and to do your utmost to enlighten them—*go
to work and enlighten your brethren!"*[33]

In the following decades, a large number of African Americans would
heed Walker's call. They would form associations of uplift and self-help.
They would counter the arguments of proslavery forces by making themselves models of dignified respectability. Their names appeared regularly in
the abolitionist press: the Forten and Purvis families of Philadelphia; the Remond and Douglass families of Salem and Boston; the New York City ministers Peter Williams, Charles B. Ray, and Henry Highland Garnet. They would
include merchants and professionals: William Whipper and Stephen Smith,
partners in a lumberyard in Washington; Macon Allen, a lawyer in Portland,
Maine; William Allen, a "Professor of Belles Lettres" at Central College in
New York. Their ranks would be swelled by individuals providing services
to black populations that only African Americans would or could supply:
by undertakers and dentists; by barbers and hairdressers like John Vashon,
Pierre Toussaint, and John Peck; by doctors such as John Degrasse and J. Mc-
Cune Smith.[34]

According to observers then, as now, they should not have existed. As one
foreign observer of American habits wrote in 1836, any American, North or
South, whether "rich or poor," "ignorant or learned," "avoids contact with the
Negro as if he were infected with the plague." A currently accepted historian
puts the matter simply: racism and prejudice were "rampant throughout antebellum America."[35] In the "free North" perhaps even more than in the slave
South, African Americans were shut out of the larger society. City directories
had separate sections for "coloreds." They were restricted to neighborhoods
known as "blacktown" or "bucktown." They were barred from militia duty and
from carrying the mail. They had the right to vote only in certain states, and
then only when they met property-holding requirements and paid their poll
taxes.[36]

Here again was the racial state, an apparatus built on government, law,
and social practice that justified racial hierarchy in the past and would try

to maintain it for the future. Yet many individuals found loopholes in the system. Their numbers were few, relative to the white population. Still, they were enough to support schools for black students, providing the students themselves along with salaries for their teachers. Free African Americans who could vote were not plentiful, but they made up one of the most solid voting blocs in the early republic, even to the point of worrying the old white-supremacist Democrats of Tammany Hall. Meanwhile, they swelled the ranks of early antislavery societies. The site for the original drafting of the American Antislavery Society's "Declaration of Sentiments" was the home of James McCrummell, a black dentist in Philadelphia. Always present at such meetings, they contributed to the movement's statements on black uplift, its dedication to "the right and duty of every human being to improve his mind."[37]

Finally, free blacks supported some seventeen African American newspapers published before the Civil War, contributing to them as subscribers, agents, editors, and writers.[38] One of the earliest was published in New York City by Samuel Cornish. The paper began as a typical abolitionist sheet, the *Rights of All*. In the early 1830s, Cornish changed the name to the *Colored American*. Like other black newspapers of the time, the *Colored American* was short on funds and thin on length, its pages devoted to antislavery articles, editorials, and reports of abolition meetings. Like others, too, it had plenty of filler: lifted material, articles taken from other sources, bits of fiction, and assorted anecdotes. Here, readers would find the stuff of black middle-class culture.

Cornish chose his filler carefully. Often, what he looked for was material that would expose the illogic of racial essentialism. Some of his examples consisted of conundrums, one or two lines in the spaces between longer articles. "If a colored man is brown enough to be called a Spaniard," read one, "it matters not that every body knows to the contrary—he can be respected and well treated." Others were short anecdotes. One told the story of a female slave in Kentucky who claimed she was white, sued her master for her freedom, and despite evidence that her mother was black, won the case when the jury decided she lacked "the characteristics of the African." Another recounted the case of two black men who applied to a medical school in New York. The first declared he was from Connecticut and received a rejection. The second claimed he was from India, got in, and took classes with other "white" students.[39]

A number of these anecdotes stressed the importance of education in confusing race prejudice. One, sent in by an agent for "the Schools for Colored Children," recounted the tale of a young man who went to New Orleans as a servant to a white gentleman. In short order, according to the article, the man found himself dismissed from his situation, arrested as a vagrant, and taken to the city's slave market. Mounting the auction block, he appealed to the gathered bidders "in a manner that gave evidence of a mind cultivated by instruction." The appeal sent "the gentlemen of the fetters" into confusion, causing them to doubt if such an educated young man could really be a slave. It also had its "desired effect." The man "was set at liberty, his shackles unriveted, and he is now free as he was born."[40]

Cornish also either looked for or produced articles that provided examples of the middle-class ethos of self-improvement. "It is a privilege to live in our day," he wrote in an editorial, when "powerful, combined efforts are making throughout the land, in behalf of temperance [and] moral reform." Much of this content followed William Lloyd Garrison's admonition in his standard speech to African American audiences. "Remember, the eyes of the whole nation, are fixed on you," declared the editor of the *Liberator* in a speech dating to 1831. "If you are temperate, industrious, peaceable and pious," he added, "you will show to the world, that the slaves can be emancipated without danger; but if you are turbulent, idle and vicious, you will put arguments into the mouths of tyrants." In 1837, an antislavery convention report echoed the refrain: "Nothing will contribute more to break the bondman's fetters than an example of high moral worth, intellectual culture and religious attainments among the free people of color."[41]

In the *Colored American*, the result was an emphasis on temperance, female domesticity, charitable associations, and literary clubs. As one letter to the paper had it, the decade of the 1830s produced a "number of associations, male and female, devoted to the mental and literary improvement of our people." Another explained the point:

> [These associations] will tend to clear us from the charge of indolence, or indifference to our own welfare, which has been heaped upon us; and also, from that foul aspersion, as to the inferiority of our intellectual capacities, with which many have been pleased to brand us. . . . They show too that we are not a people, wholly given up to revelry and licentiousness, as we have been basely misrepresented, but that the leisure hours of many are devoted to thought and literary improvement.[42]

To be sure, the paper's writers were not averse to criticizing members of the white middle class. One told the story of a black businessman who accepted a dinner invitation from a white philanthropist, only to be treated rudely by the man's wife. Another recounted the tale of several wealthy abolitionists who threatened to withdraw their daughters from female seminaries if they accepted African American girls.[43] One point of these stories is obvious: even the most philanthropic members of the white middle class could be mired in hypocrisy. Another was more subtle: according to the *Colored American*, these behaviors were marks of bad manners. For Cornish as for his writers, racially motivated rudeness was a sign of ill breeding, prejudice a result of ignorance. Neither could be squared with middle-class standards of education and etiquette.

Did these stories attest to the growth of a black middle class? The question was of paramount interest to the paper. The *Colored American* regularly updated its list of agents as indicators of such growth. It also reported on the circulation of antislavery petitions. According to the paper, in 1837 nearly a thousand black men and women signed a request to repeal laws authorizing slavery "yet found" on New York's statute books. Finally, the paper cited the latest population statistics, always making special note of the number of free blacks in the nation, states, counties, and cities. In 1820, the black population of New York City was 10,886, a majority of which were slaves. By 1835, the paper would report it at 15,120, nearly all of whom were free. The implication of this accounting was most likely clear to the paper's readers: as the population of free African Americans increased, so grew a black middle class.[44]

By the early 1840s, there were signs that such a thing might crest into visibility. In 1841, a pamphlet appeared under the title *Sketches of the Higher Classes of Colored Society in Philadelphia*. Using the ironic pen name "A Southerner," its writer claimed to be a strong advocate for social distinctions. He insisted, however, that these distinctions should be based on class rather than race: on a hierarchy of difference between the "virtuous and exemplary" and the "vicious and worthless." Philadelphia, he claimed, had countless whites who fit the lower category. It also had large numbers of African Americans whose values and behavior merited their placement in the higher designation.

The writer turned to his evidence. By the end of the 1830s, he claimed, Philadelphia was home to fifteen African American churches, four black temperance associations, three black literary societies, and three black debating clubs. Black civic associations like the "American Society of Free Persons of Color" were composed of the city's most refined inhabitants, with gentlemen like Richard Allen, James Pennington, and Robert Purvis, with exemplars of female benevolence like Amy Cassey and Sarah Douglass. The worth of the city's "colored higher classes," he maintained, was not marked by wealth but by culture, by their "ease and grace of manner" in society, by their "strict observance of all the nicer etiquettes, proprieties and observances that are characteristic of the well-bred." They were sober, industrious, and respectable:

"oppressed neither by the cares of the rich, nor assailed by the deprivation and suffering of the indigent." These qualities, the pamphlet concluded, made "their society agreeable and interesting to the most fastidious."[45]

Few Americans took these statements of uplift more seriously than Frederick Douglass. In the mid-1840s, Douglass would become one of America's main philosophers on the radical notion at the heart of middle-class culture; the ideal, that is, that anyone could join. The only requirement was a willingness to don the mantle of "respectability." According to Douglass's narrative, all one needed to achieve respectable status was a public-school reader (he found his in a Baltimore gutter), a bit of etiquette (which he picked up from the black bourgeoisie of New Bedford) and, if one were born into a degraded condition, a burning will to leave the condition behind. Few would be more often cited as a living manifestation of this radical promise. As one observer had it, Douglass was "*himself* an argument that cannot be refuted, in favor of the capability of the negro race for the highest degree of refinement and intellectuality."[46]

Along with his narrative and his personal appearances, Douglass's primary vehicle for his democratic ideal of uplift would be his newspapers. This literary effort would herald a transition away from his early association with William Lloyd Garrison. The idea seems to have taken material form in Britain, where Douglass traveled and lectured in 1845 and 1846. He returned to America with some $2,000 in funds raised by English supporters, ready to start the business. Garrison advised against it. There were too many black papers already in circulation, he warned his former protégé; one more would make little difference in the cause and would surely fail. Douglass refused to listen. After a move to Rochester, New York, he created the first crack in his widening break with Garrison by setting up a press in the basement of Rochester's African Methodist Episcopal Church.

Thus was born the *North Star*. The paper's original masthead listed Douglass and Martin Delany, a fellow black abolitionist, as co-editors, along with William Nell as publisher. Unlisted would be Julia Griffiths, a white Englishwoman Douglass met in Newcastle. She would serve the paper as editor, fund-raiser, and writer of literary notices and book reviews. A joint production, the paper reflected Douglass's vision. In its prospectus, he announced it would "attack slavery in all its forms and aspects." He also declared its mission: to "promote the moral and intellectual improvement of the colored people." In this respect, the paper would follow the tradition of Cornish's *Colored American*. Yet there was a major difference. Because of Douglass's reputation, the paper would have a large white audience. First as the *North Star*, and later after the summer of 1851 as *Frederick Douglass' Paper*, white subscribers would outnumber blacks by a ratio of five to one.[47] Like blackface minstrelsy, in other words, Douglass's paper provided a black voice to a white audience.

The message would be the direct opposite. One of Douglass's points was to promote African American schools, libraries, and reading rooms, to make visible institutions of black self-help, benevolence, and uplift. He devoted much of its space to reform, covering topics from school-board meetings to temperance to women's rights. "The Temperance cause, we are happy to learn, is making considerable progress among colored people in the East," claimed one of the paper's many articles on the subject. "Let us remember," declared the writer, "a poor white man can better afford to get drunk than a rich black man." The article concluded with a standard warning: "every impropriety committed by one of us, is charged to the account of our whole people."[48]

The paper also covered popular music. For the African American press, this was a touchy subject. Samuel Cornish at the *Colored American* stayed away from it for the most part. When he did mention the topic, he made sure to cite examples such as a children's concert at "Miss Paul's School" sent in by a "New England Correspondent." The children's "musical pieces," claimed the correspondent, were marked by a "distinct pronunciation," a "propriety of manners," and a style of "refined society."[49] In a similar manner, the writer of *Sketches of the Higher Classes of Colored Society in Philadelphia* depicted black music according to standards of polite culture. The pamphlet described music as a parlor diversion and a measure of refinement:

> It is rarely that the visitor in the different families where there are two or three ladies, will not find one or more of them competent to perform on the pianoforte, guitar, or some other appropriate musical instrument; and these, with singing and conversation on whatever suitable topics that may offer, constitute the amusements of their evenings at home. The love of music is universal; it is cultivated to some extent,—vocal or instrumental,—by all; so that it is almost impossible to enter a parlor where the ear of the visitor is not, in some sort or other, greeted there with.[50]

Douglass provided extended coverage of the subject. He spent little time on slave expressions. He did, however, note with irony the fact that by the end of the 1850s "slave songs" were becoming popular with white aficionados. "It is remarkable," he declared in one article, "that the only music which has been thought purely American in its origin, thus appears to have been brought over centuries ago from Africa, in the pestilential hold of the slave ship."[51] Instead, he focused on examples of musical uplift and the style of the middle-class parlor. He reprinted abolition hymns from George Clark's *The Liberty Minstrel* along with William Wells Brown's antislavery ballads. He included accounts of performances by Jenny Lind and the opera singer Adelina Patti. He lifted reviews of "sacred music" at African American churches, concerts that, as the reviewer put it, were marked "by a propriety of manners which was perfect," by songs that represented the "modesty" of their performers along with a "high level of musical talent."[52]

In the 1850s, he focused the paper's attention on Elizabeth Taylor Greenfield, the "Black Swan" of the opera stage. Born in Natchez, Mississippi, in or around 1809, Greenfield, according to her press clippings, was taken to Philadelphia as an infant. There, she was adopted by a Quaker family. When her singing talent became obvious, her adoptive family encouraged her to study music, to make a career for herself as a singing instructor. By the early 1850s, she was singing professionally, performing concerts of operatic pieces throughout the Northeast. Her audiences were relatively small. Yet the critics who saw her acclaimed her for her powerful and rich voice.[53]

During these years, Douglass and the contributors to *Frederick Douglass' Paper* sought to make her a representative example of black song. The first goal seems to have been to stress her blackness. "Miss Greenfield," declared a review of the Swan's 1851 performance at Rochester's Corinthian Hall, "is about medium height, square built, compact, and stoutly made. Her 'color,' (by no means unimportant in this country,) is that of a ripe chestnut, or a dark brown. She is evidently of complete African descent, and has the features which distinguish our variety of the human family." The paper's second goal was to establish the respectability of her audience. This audience, according to the reviewer, included a "large number" of the "refined and influential" among the black community, along with a strong presence of wealthy whites, the city's "upper ten." Finally, the reviewer turned to the effect of the concert itself, an effect framed by a culture of black uplift:

> The moral effect of that concert will not be lost on those who attended it. It cannot fail to raise our afflicted and much underrated people in popular estimation. Our white fellow-citizens had before them a colored woman—one of that race held in slavery, and deemed only worthy by this nation to toil under the lash, raise cotton, rice, sugar and tobacco; to be bought, sold and hunted like wild beasts; and yet this woman possesses musical powers, ability to charm and delight the most refined audience.[54]

Greenfield herself seems to have been less concerned about the politics of her performances. In 1854, she reached the height of her career when she toured England and sang for Queen Victoria. Touring in the 1850s, she often performed before segregated audiences, a fact Douglass declared an example of "wound-inflicting conduct." Still, his paper continued to print glowing accounts of her concerts. Greenfield, one declared, had taken to ending her concerts in the same manner as Jenny Lind, with an encore performance of "Home, Sweet Home." According to one correspondent, the Swan's version provoked the typical middle-class response: "a lady of fine musical taste and accomplishments, who sat near me, burst into tears." The correspondent concluded: "Having selected as her aim the divinest of Arts, that are requiring of the most arduous of culture, it was but a light thing for her to meet Prejudice face to face and crush it."[55]

For Douglass, it was precisely this uplifting quality of music that made it so central to middle-class culture. "Music," he would write, was a "delightful recreation," an "innocent amusement" with a power to dispel "the sourness and gloom which frequently arise from petty disputes," a power to prevent "evil thoughts and evil speaking."[56] For him, as for Samuel Cornish and members of a black middle class, "black song" expressed these qualities: in the singing of schoolchildren and church choirs, in the cold-water hymns of "colored temperance societies," in the antislavery ballads of abolition meetings, and in the arias of the Black Swan. As these individuals would have it, much of black song was an expression of middle-class culture. For them, black song expressed an ideal of inclusiveness in which all Americans might meet in the middle.

Slave Songs

Despite the efforts of individuals like Cornish and Douglass, increasing numbers of Americans would equate black song with slavery. Much of this equation would derive from blackface minstrelsy. Much would rest on the weight of sheer numbers. By the outbreak of the Civil War, there were some four million African Americans in bondage in the United States, about eighty-eight percent of the nation's total black population. Nearly all were in the South, in states that would join the Confederacy along with Southern border states. In states like South Carolina, Georgia, and Mississippi, with the largest numbers of slaves and highest ratios of slaves to the free population, slavery was almost without doubt the most visible characteristic of the society.[57]

In these places, particularly on Southern plantations, observers regularly claimed to see and hear slaves singing. As one expert on slave songs would put it in 1862, wherever slaves worked on a plantation, they kept time to their labors with music. Others recalled spirituals wafting up from plantation slave quarters.[58] Too much can be made of these claims. One ex-slave who worked on an Alabama cotton plantation did not recall singing in the fields. The master, he declared, "did not allow his slaves to idle." Another denied there was any singing on his tobacco plantation in North Carolina, saying simply "they worked them too close." Meanwhile, long hours of labor left little time for other types of song. Asked if her fellow laborers sang "spirituals" or "plantation songs" in the quarters, a former slave on a Georgia plantation said they "sang nothing." They were too tired, and besides, she added, "we were not allowed to make noise anyway."[59]

Still, the plantation seems to have produced its share of song. One of the main reasons seems to have been that plantations produced an enormous amount of work. Planters and overseers typically adhered to one of two ways of organizing labor on plantations: it was the "gang system" or the "task system." Many planters preferred the gang system, where slaves worked in gangs from sunup to sundown. Most slaves preferred the task system. Here, overseers and drivers assigned individuals specific tasks for the day, perhaps the weeding of a certain section of field, or the gathering of firewood. They based these assignments on the physical abilities of individuals: the hardest tasks went to "full hands," usually adult males; lesser tasks were given to "half hands" or "quarter hands," to women, children, and the aged. When the tasks were done, one's time was one's own. According to Orris Harris, his fellow slaves on a Mississippi plantation "always sang when in the field at work." Singing was an adjunct to labor, he recalled; it passed the time and made the tasks more endurable.[60]

The tasks went on year-round. During the off-season, planters ordered the clearing of lands to put more acreage in production. Field hands cut trees, removed stumps, drained swamps, and fertilized fields with manure, mud, and organic material. The planting season began early, usually in February on cotton plantations, with field hands furrowing the soil with hand hoes and planting seed. During the growing season they chopped cotton, hoeing the weeds between the rows. Much has been made of supposed distinctions between field slaves and house slaves. Indeed, plantation slaves might work as artisans, house servants, or at any number of tasks outside agricultural labor. Yet during the planting and harvesting seasons, masters expected to see everyone in the fields. On Alexandre De Clouet's cotton plantation in Saint Martin's Parish, Louisiana, servants performed at their regular stations between November and August. When the cotton bolls burst, the usual distinctions did not apply. From August through October, according to De Clouet's diary, "all hands picked cotton."[61]

As much as they would be rooted in African oral traditions, slave songs emerged out of the rhythms of this work and the discipline of labor. A single song could have a faster or slower rhythm depending on the task it accompanied. "On the water," one observer noted, "the oars dip 'Poor Rosy' to an even *adante*; [while] a stout boy and girl at the hominy mill will make the same 'Poor Rosy' fly, to keep up with the whirling stone."[62] Elsewhere, singing merged labor discipline with social pleasure. For corn-shucking, many slaves later remembered that planters tried to create an evening of social labor, offering the incentive of food and drink and encouraging the singing of songs.[63]

By such encouragement, masters and overseers hoped to turn forced labor into something that could be enjoyed. "Everybody loved to attend" these gatherings, one former slave from a plantation near Nashville, Tennessee, recalled, and "just so the corn got shucked, the white folks didn't care how much fun we had." A variation of the same approach applied to work in the fields. According to an ex-slave from Mississippi, workers in the field always "sung to keep time with the hoe, and that would make them work faster." Another recalled that the overseer expected everyone on the plantation to sing while they worked, for it "made them work better."[64]

If work structured slave song, so did white paternalism and paranoia. Frederick Law Olmstead found several fatherly slave masters during his Southern travels. "Oh, they are interesting creatures, sir," he quoted one as saying of his slaves, "and with all their faults, have many beautiful traits. I can't help being attached to them, and I am sure they love us." The sunny attitude applied to sunlight hours. "In the daytime it seemed impossible to associate suspicion with those familiar tawny or sable faces that surrounded us," recalled a young woman from Virginia years later. "We had seen them for so many years smiling or saddening with the family joys or sorrows; they were so guileless, so patient, so satisfied." Yet "when evening came again," she recalled, so returned the doubts and fears; and the "bolts were drawn and rusty firearms loaded."[65]

Throughout the South, this pathology would have a major effect on all forms of black expression. Simply put, there were few times or places slaves were not under the loving and fearful eyes of white folks. Among the most common sites for this dynamic between surveillance and expression were the holiday celebrations that broke up the plantation season. The frequency of celebrations depended on masters. Caroline Malloy, an ex-slave on a plantation in Sumter County, Georgia, recalled that there "were a few days when the slaves were given a holiday," generally at "Christmas time and on the Fourth of July." Joe McMormick claimed there were no such "frolics" on his nearby plantation, again citing "too much work" as the reason.[66]

Harriet Jacobs's recollection of Christmas festivities in North Carolina attests to surviving elements of African tradition. During an annual celebration that came to be known as the "Johnkannaus" or "John Canoes," slaves marched and danced from plantation to plantation, beating a drum called a "gumbo box," playing triangles and jawbones, and singing songs in return for money or rum. Others remembered more formal dances and dinners in which celebrants danced "the Cotillion" or the "Pigeon Wing," and feasted on "barbequed chicken, pork, coffee, cakes and pies." One former slave on a plantation near Edgefield, Georgia, recalled that her master encouraged frolics on a regular basis, despite the fact that he was a Baptist minister. Others recalled being allowed to dance within earshot of the white parties at the plantation big house.[67]

These expressions rarely proceeded without a white presence. Robert Laird recalled that it was his master himself, a plantation owner in Copiah County, Mississippi, and an accomplished fiddle player, who provided the music for the slaves' Christmas celebrations. According to Anna Peek, the fellow slaves on her plantation in Polk County, Georgia, would prepare all day for a holiday frolic, digging barbeque pits, baking ash cakes, and constructing tables and chairs. Just as all was ready, the event would come to a halt. Everyone had to wait until the white folks arrived. Only then, Peek recalled, could the feast begin. The rest of the day passed under seemingly benign surveillance, with singing and dancing contests judged by the white onlookers.[68]

The white audience was an expected part of the slave frolic. During holiday slave dances, one former slave recalled, "white people would come and watch the fun." Another remembered that "lots of times the white folks would give them something good to eat after they'd danced." James Lucas, a former slave on Jefferson Davis's Mississippi plantation, recalled that during the annual Christmas dances, "white folks would look on and see who danced the best." He added that the master and his wife "laughed fit to kill at the capers we cut."[69] Along with laughter, discerning eyes looked for confirmation of slave happiness; they kept watch for suspicious behavior, for individuals who held back, for slaves who did not sing and dance with self-forgetful abandon.

If examples of paternalism and surveillance were easy to find in the plantation South, so were signs of paranoia and cruelty. These included the ubiquitous slave patrols. First instituted in South Carolina in 1704, these police gangs were composed of small companies of men, usually five or six, who patrolled a "beat," a certain geographical area either in town or country. They took their members from the local militias, early on offering a release from regular militia duty as their only compensation. By the nineteenth century, nearly all who served in them were paid in money. The pay created an economic incentive for poor, non-slaveholding whites to defend the master class.

Patrol tasks depended on setting. For urban patrols, they involved enforcing the slave curfews that were on the law books of most towns, breaking up gatherings of three or more slaves, and watching for signs of insurrection or arson. In rural settings, their principal duty was to keep watch on the roads and pathways between plantations, checking slaves for the written passes or "tickets" that allowed them to travel from place to place. They also made visits to plantations with absentee owners and searched slave quarters, looking for runaways, weapons, or reading materials.[70]

As indicated by the ubiquity of the song "Run, Nigger Run," the patrols would have a major influence on slave culture and song. Versions of the song appeared in practically every region of the South. Sally Brown, an ex-slave on a plantation near Commerce, Georgia, recalled that the song originated with the patrols themselves. The patrols, she claimed, "were something like the Ku Klux [Klan]," and as they rode horseback on their beat, they would sing a "little ditty" that "went something" like this: "Run, nigger run, the patty rollers'll git you, / Run, nigger, run, you'd better get away." Slaves learned the song, sang it, and passed it on to their children. The result was a chilling effect: "we were afraid to go any place," Brown recalled.[71]

Signs of the system's cruelty were just as common. During the Civil War, reformer and Union officer Thomas Wentworth Higginson found a device designed to produce what later torture practitioners would blandly call "stress positions" on a plantation in South Carolina. The machine, he wrote, was "so contrived that a person once imprisoned in it could neither sit, stand, nor lie, but must support the body half raised, in a position scarcely endurable." Before the war, Northern abolitionists often charged slaveholders with cruelties, citing as evidence the anecdotes of former slaves. When defenders of the institution dismissed the stories as exaggerations, the reformers turned to printing advertisements for runaways clipped directly from Southern newspapers. In doing so, they turned the slave owner's words against him, for here was the stark language of a system that literally marked humans as property:

> Ran away, a negro woman and two children. A few days before she went off, I
>   burnt her with a hot iron on the left side of her face. I tried to make the letter M.
> One hundred dollars reward, for a negro fellow, Pompey, 40 years old. He is
>   branded on the left jaw.
> Ran away, a negro girl called Mary. Has a small scar over her eye, . . . the letter A
>   is branded on her cheek and forehead.
> Fifty dollars reward for the negro Jim Blake. Has a piece cut out of each ear, and
>   the middle finger of the left hand cut off to the second joint.
> Ran away, a negro man, named Ivory. Has a small piece cut out of the top of each
>   ear.[72]

Easter Jones declared that in her experience, slavery was "nothing but hard work and cruel treatment." Her overseer and master, she said, would "whip you so hard your back would bleed, then they would pour salt and water on it." Henry McGaffrey recalled that his "Old Marse was hard on his slaves" on his Louisiana plantation: "I saw him many times tie his slaves and strip them to the waist and beat them till the skin would break. Once I saw him whip my mammy and the blood ran down her bare back, and then he put salt on it. I cried and he said 'if I didn't shut up he would beat me,' then I went behind the kitchen to cry."[73]

W. B. Allen, a former slave on an Alabama plantation, recalled two common methods of whipping slaves, the "Buck" and the "Rolling Jim." "Throwing a Nigger into the 'Buck,'" he recalled, "consisted in first stripping him, . . . making him squat and tying his hands between his knees to a stout stick run behind the bend of his knees." He was then pushed over and whipped, each strike causing him to convulse in agony, or "buck." The "Rolling Jim" was equally brutal:

> In the "Rolling Jim" system, a Nigger was stretched on his stomach at full length on a large log, about eight feet long. Into holes bored in each end of this log, wooden pegs were driven. The feet were securely tied to one set of these pegs . . . and the hands to the pegs at the other end. The victim was then ready to be worked on. [As he was whipped the] muscular contortions of the Negro on the log caused it to sway—hence the name, "Rolling Jim."[74]

Surveillance, slave patrols, and punishment all exerted a force on slave expressions. Most often, they altered them by the threat of their universal presence. "White folks," according to former slave Edward Jones, often stationed themselves near the quarters of his Alabama plantation to "eaves drop." Accordingly, Jones recalled, "it was a habit for us to talk about white horses when we meant white folks, so if they heard us they wouldn't know we were talking about them." At other times, the force was more direct. Members of slave patrols often claimed they followed the sound of music in order to break up slave gatherings. "The only time I was ever whipped was for slipping off to dances," recalled one ex-slave from a Mississippi plantation. Patrols had sanction to whip slaves found without passes. Their members also used their power in other ways. In one example recalled by a former slave, the members of a patrol discovered a group of slaves at a dance, started to whip them, then ultimately let them go "if they would sing and dance some more."[75]

Within the slave system, it seems, white people had the power to force African Americans to be expressive, to sing and dance under coercion and the threat of punishment. One of the cruelest elements of the transatlantic slave trade was what a later historian would call the "joyless ceremony" of "dancing the slaves." The practice, according to the slavers and crews, was thought to be therapeutic. The forcing of captive Africans to the deck and making them dance in irons allowed the holds to be aired out and supposedly kept the slaves from submitting to suicidal melancholy. For this reason, slave-ship crews took the ceremony seriously. One white crew member was often tasked with circulating among the slaves with a whip, a "cat-o'-nine-tails" designed to make the human cargo jump, dance, and seem happy.[76]

Some former slaves recalled speculators forcing them to dance on the auction block. "I remember one gal that came from Africa," recalled one, "she said when they put her on the block to sell, they told her to dance for them." Orris Harris recollected no dances on his plantation in Amite County, Mississippi: "We never had dances in the quarters, and I don't remember any dances at the big house." He did recall that his master sometimes played the fiddle, and that on these occasions "he made" two of the household slaves "stand there and knock the back step." According to Harriet Miller, an ex-slave on a plantation in Magnolia, Mississippi, one of the slave's tasks was to provide entertainment for white onlookers. Occasionally, she remembered, there were white parties with "fine company" in the "big house." On those evenings, "they would call the niggers up and have them dance for fun."[77]

These recollections might be removed from their context of force; they might be depicted or even remembered as examples of an unquenchable penchant for self-expression, an innate ability to dance joyously in the direst of situations. Yet, as former slaves William Wells Brown and John Little pointed out at the time, when it came to slavery, context was everything. In many ways, Brown's period as a slave was typical in that nothing typified his experience. During his bondage in Missouri, his master hired him out as a hotel servant, carriage driver, printer's assistant, and steward on a Mississippi River steamboat. In the 1830s, he worked as a gang boss for a slave trader. Here, his master charged him with the responsibility of driving slaves from Saint Louis to New Orleans and, once there, preparing them for sale.[78]

The task involved all the elements of market hucksterism. "I was ordered," recalled Brown, "to have the old men's whiskers shaved off, and the grey hairs plucked out where they were not too numerous." When there was too much gray hair for plucking, the trader gave him "a preparation of blacking to color it." He also had to display the product, to herd his charges into the "negro pen." Brown's master was determined that potential buyers should see only examples of healthy self-expression. "Before the slaves were exhibited for sale," Brown wrote later, "they were dressed and driven out into the yard. Some were set to dancing, some to jumping, some to singing, and some to playing cards. This was done to make them appear cheerful and happy." As Brown recalled it, he "set them to dancing when their cheeks were wet with tears."[79]

According to John Little, an ex-slave from North Carolina who escaped to Canada in the 1840s, slaves did sing. They did dance. Observers of the institution along with these expressions might "think they know a great deal about it," he wrote. And yet, he added, "they are mistaken":

> They say slaves are happy, because they laugh, and are merry. I myself, and three or four others, have received two hundred lashes in the day, and had our feet in fetters: yet, at night, we would sing and dance, and make others laugh at the rattling of our chains. Happy men we must have been! We did it to keep down trouble, and to keep our hearts from being completely broken: that is as true as the gospel! Just look at it,—consider upon it,—must not we have been very happy? Yes I have done it myself—I have cut capers in chains![80]

Slavery would be characterized by paternalism and labor, by surveillance, cruelty, masking, and performance. Later recollections would be framed by all of these characteristics, by former slaves waxing nostalgic about the "good old days," reminiscing about plantation spirituals and happy work songs. As well, there would be voices like that of Charlie Moses, an ex-slave on a plantation in Marion County, Mississippi. "When I get to thinking back on those days," he would say later, "I feel like rising out of this here bed and telling everybody about the harsh treatment us colored folks were given." His master was cruel. The work was ceaseless. His recollections were bitter and vivid. They were vivid except, that is, when it came to songs. "Songs?" he would reply to a question on the subject. "I only recall one right now." His recollection could only have subverted the interview:

> Free at last,
> Free at last
> Thank God Almighty
> I'm free at last.[81]

5

Meet the Hutchinsons

Anna Thaxter of Dorchester, Massachusetts, was a sterling example of proper young womanhood. Left an orphan in 1841, she had an adequate inheritance, more than enough to pay for boarding school and piano lessons. By 1844, the eighteen-year-old was living with relatives in the town just outside Boston. Though she appeared a model of elegance and charm, she had secret doubts about her qualities. She threw away too many hours in "listless idleness." She wasted too many days socializing with friends. "I have lately been led to think much of my selfishness," she wrote in a new diary. "In looking back on my past life I see, comparatively, very few things done for the good of others." The criticism led to questions. "Whom have I benefited? Shall I spend my whole allowance upon myself?"[1] She promised to devote more time to self-improvement. She would donate to local charitable associations and join the temperance society. She would attend lectures at the lyceum and try to read serious literature.

Life would still have its pleasures. As her diary attested, there would be afternoon teas and interesting conversations. There would be the excitement of playing piano and singing "Love's Young Dream" to a parlor audience. And there would be the intense thrill of a serenade from a group of young gentlemen. On a summer's evening during a visit to Springfield, Anna and a few of her friends were about to retire to bed when they found themselves "aroused by the sound of music." Some men were singing outside the house. The serenaders went through their repertoire, starting with "Young Agnes," working their way through "The Gondolier," and ending with the flourish of "To Greece We Give Our Shining Blades." Still in their nightclothes, the young women "rose instantly." They went to a window of their room, leaned out, and listened with pleasure.[2]

FIGURE 5.1. Favorites of the northeastern middle class. Hailing from the "mountains" or rather the rolling hills of southern New Hampshire, the Hutchinson Family Singers represented the characteristics of a rising American middle class. Well mannered and respectable, connected to the uplifting qualities of a newly conceived benign nature, and increasingly involved in reform, they would become the most popular American singing group of the 1840s, at least among singers who did not perform in blackface. Sheet-music cover: *The Old Granite State, A Song, Composed, Arranged, and Sung by The Hutchinson Family*. New York: Firth and Hall, 1843. Courtesy of American Antiquarian Society.

For Thaxter, music had enormous power. Like others in her sphere, however, she was suspicious about the music of the popular stage. At age twenty
she would write in her diary of being invited to a play by "Mr. Swan." She
turned Swan down, saying she was "somewhat undecided about the theatre."
Soon she reported another invitation, this time to a concert by the Seguins,
a family of opera singers. Again she refused. She "was inclined to think" the
theater's "effect upon the actors and actresses cannot be very good." And so,
she wrote, "we ought not to give our countenance to the performance by attending." A few days later she enjoyed her first evening at a theater. "It was a
beautiful, warm, moonlight evening," she wrote, and "the music was delightful." She added what would become a standard postscript: "Abby Hutchinson"
was as "simple and natural as possible."[3] The performers who broke through
her barrier of propriety were the Hutchinson Family Singers.

The Hutchinsons had this effect on a lot of respectable people. By the time
Anna Thaxter opened her diary, they were famous. Their signature song, "The
Old Granite State," was a parlor staple. Their performances filled theaters from
Boston to Washington. According to one observer, word of a Hutchinson performance could cause entire communities to talk for weeks of "little else but
the coming concert." "Oh, it was beautiful," exclaimed one of their audience
members at the time, adding that the "three boys and one girl" of the group
were "all of them very pretty" and "quite young."[4] They were also proper and
well mannered. "They have become great favorites with the public," declared
another audience member, owing to their "fine voices," their "pleasant and
modest manners," and their "perfect sense of propriety."[5] At a time when the
American middle class was forming, the Hutchinsons would become the favorite performers of middle-class audiences.[6]

"Will You Come and Hear Native-Born Singers?"

A few years earlier, the singers could only dream of crowds attending their
concerts. They started out on their first serious tour in 1842, traveling in a
used four-wheeled carriage, a "carryall" pulled by two forty-dollar horses. The
term was apt, for the vehicle carried all they needed: with violins belonging
to Judson and John hung from inside stays, with Asa's cello lashed on top and
Abby's small hair trunk tied to a rear rack. They followed an itinerary laid out
by the few performers, traveling shows, and lecturers who toured before them,
promising themselves they would "concertize" as long as profits met expenses.
Starting from their hometown in New Hampshire, they went east to the shore,
then west to Vermont, then into upstate New York.

In the evenings, they sang in hamlets, towns, and cities along the way. They spent many days haggling over the price of horse feed, hall rentals, and printers' bills for programs. They spent more days on the road, creaking along in the carryall. Saving every penny, they avoided toll roads and sometimes sang to farmers for their suppers. The tour never quite broke even. In remote villages, where traveling performers were rare, they drew small audiences. In larger towns and cities with more worldly citizens, they did much worse.[7]

There were times they felt like giving up. They were looking for respectable audiences, people who could afford to pay twelve and a half cents for an evening's entertainment. They could not be sure these audiences existed. In fact, for would-be performers who lacked a reputation on the urban stage or the cachet of "success in Europe," a career as entertainers, particularly in the American interior, had become possible only with recent changes. Most of these changes would be products of the transitions of the 1820s through the 1850s, the period known as the market revolution in America. These included improvements in the means of travel and recreation, the building of roads, canals, and railroads along with the construction of hotels, restaurants, and legitimate sites for public performances. They included the rise of an American middle class, the mass increase of the number of people in towns and cities who had leisure time, disposable income, and appreciation for the arts.[8]

The early years of the singers corresponded with these developments, from the first stirrings of large-scale industry, to the abandonment of rural callings for urban professions, to the emergence of bourgeois audiences and the rise of a commercial popular culture. The Hutchinsons hailed from Milford, New Hampshire, a town of some 1,500 souls about forty miles northwest of Boston. In the 1820s, Milford was typical of medium-sized communities in the American interior. Situated on the banks of the Souhegan River, it had limited industry, a few sawmills that lined the river and were regularly washed away by springtime floods. Locally, it was known for its small farms and granite quarries. It was also known for its many people named Hutchinson. According to census figures for 1840, more than two-thirds of the state's households by the name lived in the area, some twenty-seven in the village proper.[9]

Most of these families were small farmers, and many were connected through blood or marriage. Among the largest was the "tribe," as its members called themselves, of Jesse Hutchinson and Mary (called Polly) Leavitt. Married in 1800, Jesse and Polly Hutchinson exceeded even the prolific child-producing patterns of the time. Between 1802 and 1829, Polly gave birth to sixteen children, thirteen of whom survived into adulthood. The future singers were among the youngest of these siblings, born on a 150-acre homestead two miles out of the village center.[10] In Milford, growing up Hutchinson conferred a deep sense of belonging. Father Jesse was a town selectman. A Hutchinson was the town constable. Blood relatives were everywhere, as were kin by marriage.[11]

The family dominated the town's Baptist church. Indeed, the church would give the singers their first voices. They learned to sing by singing hymns, led by their mother, who knew every verse of Isaac Watts "by heart." In 1829, the meetinghouse elders appointed one of the middle children, eighteen-year-old Joshua Hutchinson, to the position of choirmaster. According to one recollection, however, the family's faith came near to stifling their interest in song. John Hutchinson remembered later that sometime around 1830, the family patriarch attended a revival and suddenly discovered that his violin was the devil's tool. And so, John claimed, he took the thing to a woodshed and came back later with a fiddle-shaped tobacco box. He also banned secular music from the homestead. For a time, at least according to this story, the young Hutchinsons had to sing and play their own violins on the sly. While John Hutchinson's memory may have been faulty on this issue, the fact that he told such a story may reveal the psychic difficulties generated by an attraction to secular, commercial song.[12]

During this time the world broke in on Milford. To the generation of the Hutchinson parents, Milford was not an isolated town. Coming out of the War of 1812, it was connected by a decent road to Nashua and from there by a good turnpike to Boston. Yet in the mid-1820s, it seemed to one curmudgeonly town resident that a host of new "isms" suddenly hit the community, ideas imported from faraway places like Boston, Lowell, and Lynn. Young people, he noted, began acting alarmingly "independent," convinced they were "able to think and judge for themselves." Reform lecturers passed through the area, along with complete strangers bearing tales of opportunities elsewhere.[13] About this time, Jesse's third-oldest son, Andrew, left the homestead for Boston. He opened a dry-goods store on Purchase Street. A few years later, Jesse Hutchinson Jr. left for Lynn. News came back that he had opened a hardware store.

Soon the youngest Hutchinson brothers were making regular trips to Lynn and Boston. These visits to their city brothers would have several effects. They would be introduced to an emerging culture of the urban middle class. They would also make further contacts with the world of commercial music. By the 1830s, dozens of musical societies had appeared in the American Northeast. New York and Boston had their Handel and Hayden Societies, while nearly every city and town had its Mozart Society. Elsewhere there were local variations: the Alleghany Musical Society near Pittsburgh, upstate New York's Glens Falls Music Society, the Amherst Musical Society of inland Massachusetts.[14]

All had the purpose of introducing city folk to music that was refined, respectable, and middle class. As one musical scholar put it at the time, the point was to make music a "dignified and venerated subject" rather than a "plaything of the present." There were diverse opinions on just what constituted respectable music. For the officers of the New York Philharmonic Society, the style for the middle classes was "fashionable music": the fantasias, overtures, and operatic arias of Italian and German composers, the symphonies and concertos of Mozart and Beethoven. For Boston's Handel and Haydn Society, it was a well-trained chorus singing the old hymns along with choral arrangements of classical works. For P. T. Barnum and the management of his soon-to-be New York institution the "American Museum on Broadway," it was popular song and musical theater, all done in an atmosphere of family-friendly propriety.[15]

These institutions sought to educate public tastes and tame the theater, refining away its reputation for immorality and rough democracy. With the opening of his American Museum in 1839, Barnum took a direct route. He had his museum's theater designed without the "notorious third tier," thus getting rid of the section's bars, rowdies, and roaming prostitutes. He also ordered the pit filled with fixed seats; there would be no more milling before the stage. Having tamed his audience with interior design, the master showman could advertise his theater as free from vulgarity, as a space that was safe even for proper women. Within a few years, the old pit would all but disappear from better music halls and theaters. Meanwhile, the managers of the New York Philharmonic explained the proper use of fixed seating and intermissions. Audience members who wanted to move about could do so at the intermission, its programs declared; otherwise, they were "politely requested to remain in their seats."[16]

Elsewhere there was a boom in musical instruction. In Boston and New York, institutes and academies offered classes in proper singing as well as the playing of musical instruments. Many promised easy lessons in the "Italian" or "do-re-mi" style of musical notation. Others tied instruction to standards of feminine refinement, advertising training for female students in piano, singing, and "lady-like deportment."[17]

No one cashed in on the boom more than Lowell Mason. Originally from Massachusetts, by the early nineteenth century Mason was in Savannah, Georgia, running a dry-goods store and teaching music at a local Sunday school. In the mid-1820s, he returned to Boston. There, he began offering lessons in vocal music to children in the public schools, charging the modest rate of one dollar per term.[18] He also found backing for a two-part scheme: his first goal was to create a niche, to convince Boston's schools to make musical education part of the required curriculum; his second was to exploit it, to open a school for the training of music teachers.

The results were spectacular. Advocating the high-sounding "Pestalozzian method" of instruction, Mason managed to get the schools to go along with the scheme by the early 1830s. One result was that generations of hapless students would be forced to take music classes and, *à la* Pestalozzi, sing their multiplication tables. Another was that Mason, along with George Webb of the Handel and Haydn Society, would found the Boston Academy of Music. Within six months of its opening in 1834, the Academy enrolled some 1,500 prospective music teachers. Within a few more years, Mason would be New England's—and possibly the nation's—leading expert on musical instruction. He also became something of a brand, with money rolling in from a growing list of Lowell Mason–authored hymnals, songsters, and instruction manuals.[19]

The effects soon reached the American interior. In the early 1830s, a man by the name of Phineas Stimpson opened a singing school in Milford. Although several of the Hutchinson siblings showed up from time to time, the school was probably not very good. As they remembered it, Stimpson was the town cobbler, more a shoemaker with a passion for singing than a real music teacher. Clearly, the young choirmaster Joshua Hutchinson figured opportunities remained in the field. A few years later, Joshua went to Boston, took a ten-day course at Mason's Academy of Music, and returned to Milford to open his own singing school.[20] If music had ever been banned from the Hutchinson homestead, it clearly made a dramatic return by the late 1830s.

On Thanksgiving Day 1839, Joshua organized a "family concert" at the Baptist meetinghouse. The performance featured fifteen Hutchinsons, the parents along with all thirteen of their surviving sons and daughters. From this point, the youngest Hutchinson brothers knew what they wanted to do. "I wanted to go out in the world and see what it was made of," recalled John Hutchinson of his post-concert euphoria. He envisioned himself singing "to numerous audiences" and dreamed of a "gathering in of piles of money—gold, silver, and quantities of paper."[21]

By this time such a thing seemed imaginable. When it came to attracting respectable audiences, there even seemed to be a formula. In the 1830s, the English-born singer and actress Clara Fisher made a career out of singing "Home, Sweet Home!" Published in 1829, the song was perfect for young people in transition from country to city, from extended families to the new standards of urban privatization associated with the middle class. Hearing it, they could dream of home and gild it with nostalgia.[22] By this time, some towns in the interior could fill their various lyceum buildings and Mechanics Halls for what the fashionables called a "concert," an evening of music from an Italian "prima-donna" or an English music-hall virtuoso.

The standout in the last category was Henry Russell. By the late 1830s, the English singer had gained an American following as a master of musical theatrics, singing and acting out a list of songs that called forth his thespian abilities. In "The Ship on Fire," he made audiences feel the horrors of a burning vessel; in "Woodman Spare That Tree," he made them weep for a stately elm. Russell knew how to appeal to a Yankee crowd: he made sure to lighten his programs with a comic piece or two; he also took to singing a patriotic number called "England and America," a ballad extolling the bonds between the world's *two* greatest nations. Finally, the Englishman's success could be measured in material terms; even in the interior, he got away with charging the city rate of fifty cents per concert.[23]

Following their Thanksgiving performance, three and sometimes four of the Hutchinson brothers—Judson, John, and Asa, sometimes joined by Jesse Jr.— attempted to make a career as professional singers. They bought the latest songsters and sheet music Boston had to offer. They practiced their harmonies in a room above Andrew Hutchinson's store. Judson and John worked on their violin playing; Asa practiced on the cello. When they felt ready, they gave a number of concerts, mostly in or around Milford, performing as "The Aeolian Vocalists."

Of course, it all turned out to be much harder than someone like Henry Russell made it look. A later lithograph of one of these concerts at the village of East Wilton, New Hampshire, provides a suggestion of their ambitions and the pathetic results. Drawn from the brothers' recollections, the room was small, with barn-like floorboards, cracked walls, and peeling plaster. For their stage, the brothers laid a wide plank over three barrels. For their lighting, they placed candles atop the plank, enough to raise smoke and cast flickering shadows.

Yet the image indicates their anticipation of a good crowd. The brothers also laid planks across the room's chairs to create improvised bench seating, to maximize places for an expected audience. They need not have bothered. The lithograph presents a dismal scene, with Judson and Asa singing and sawing away on violin and cello, and John between them holding his sheet music before him like a newspaper and squinting at the lyrics through the candle smoke. The audience, if the lithograph is correct, consisted of twelve people, well spaced, with at least two empty benches for doffed coats and

FIGURE 5.2. Creating an audience for native-born, respectable singers. As the Hutchinsons, or "Aeolian Vocalists," as they were then calling themselves, discovered in the late 1830s, it was tough to muster up a crowd for respectable Yankee singers. This drawing of Judson, John, and Asa Hutchinson performing at East Wilton, New Hampshire, suggests the difficulties of their earliest tour. The small audience, the cracked plaster on the walls of the room, and the primitive barrel-and-plank stage are all indicative of the singers' early lack of success. "The East Wilton Concert," picture from John Wallace Hutchinson, *The Story of the Hutchinsons*, vol. 1. Boston: Lee and Shepard, 1896, 44. Courtesy of American Antiquarian Society.

shawls. As one of the brothers recalled, they usually passed a hat at the end of these concerts. Typically, it came back nearly empty.

For a time, they soldiered on. In Boston, they looked up Lowell Mason, hoping he might offer some advice on how to refine their style. The singing master showed them the door after suggesting they purchase one of his manuals. They tried out for Boston's Handel and Haydn Society and were immediately asked to join its large chorus. After thinking it over, they refused. The reason they cited suggests the power of their ambition: they were afraid their individual talents would be lost in the mass of singers.

By this time, the young Hutchinsons seemed closer to becoming bourgeois merchants than professional singers. In 1831 and again in 1835, Milford's Baptist Church held revivals, hoping for a return of its wayward sons and daughters. Most of the Hutchinson brothers renewed their church covenants. Even brother Andrew returned from his Boston shop to be re-baptized in the Souhegan River. Yet the revivals failed to stem the tide. Shortly after returning to his store, Andrew let it be known that he had converted to Unitarianism. Judson and another brother, Zephaniah, moved to Lynn, where they went into business as grocers. Near the end of 1840, John and Asa joined them. By 1841, the *Lynn Directory* listed six of the Hutchinson brothers as living in the town. Their businesses, from Jesse's hardware store to Zephaniah's grocery, lined one side of an entire block on Exchange Street.[24]

Late in 1841, the singing brothers made two decisions that would affect their fortunes. First, they decided that Jesse Jr. should drop out of the group to become its part-time manager. Judson, John, and Asa made the wise choice of replacing him with their thirteen-year-old sister, Abigail. Second, they made a vow to get more serious. They declared they would go on a real tour in 1842, visiting towns and cities at a distance. They would rent substantial halls. They would print broadside advertisements for their performances along with programs, and if they had money to spare, they would pay a crier to walk through towns shouting out their appearance. They bought two horses, rigged the family carryall, and headed east.

On February 9, 1842, broadsides for "The Aeolian Vocalists" went up in Portsmouth, New Hampshire. The posted program, which also listed the singers as "The Hutchinson Family—Three Brothers and a sister," suggested their continued search for an audience. For the local rustics, they offered a gimmick: "not the least interesting of the Evening's entertainment will be the performance of 3 men on two instruments, and the playing on the Violin and Violincello with their Feet!" The broadside also appealed to patriotism and respectability:

> It is with some degree of confidence that this family appeal to the patron-age of the citizens of Portsmouth, being themselves NATIVES of the GRAN-ITE STATE, and only claiming a PORTION of that patronage which is often lavished upon foreigners of inferior merit. . . . [T]heir Concerts have been highly approved by all classes, being patronized by the best judges and most respected citizens.

The program attested to the singers' artistic ambitions. Rather than fol-lowing the popular formula of listing a collection of patriotic standards, they loaded it with instrumental pieces, four-part glees, and individual songs, some comic, many sentimental, nearly all of recent minting and popular with the more sophisticated types of eastern cities. Finally, after listing the ticket price of twelve and a half cents, the broadside asked the all-important question: "Now, Citizens of Portsmouth, will you come and hear the Native Born Yan-kee Singers?"[25] Through much of their 1842 tour, the Hutchinsons would find no answer to this question. They would, however, learn to present themselves as middle-class performers.

Merchants, Artists, and Girlish Innocence

Sometime in 1844, ten of the Hutchinson brothers gathered in a studio for a photographic portrait. The resultant image suggests the transitions of the time. At center frame sit the two oldest brothers: David, his gaunt and harsh face resembling that of his father; and Noah, his softer, handsome features inherited from the Leavitt side. Aside from the difference in their features, they appear as similar types, models of respectable New England farmers, exemplars of the early republic's "middling sort." Their poses are stiff, their faces set in hardworking severity, their senses of self rooted in inner character. Their clothing, though clearly their finest for the portrait, is simple and unostentatious; not for them the parlor styles of the rising middle class.

The other brothers suggest the creeping influence of middle-class style. Directly behind the two oldest brothers is Caleb, Joshua's twin and one of the siblings being groomed to take over the family farm. Far from the farming type, he looks like a nineteenth-century entrepreneur. Several of the other brothers *were* entrepreneurs: Andrew, the Boston shopkeeper; Joshua, the Milford singing-school master; Zephaniah, the Lynn grocer. Separated by a few years from their farming brothers, they seem from a different generation. Their clothing is tailored; each wears a silk vest. Each has a look of merchant bonhomie, the look of someone determined to make a good impression and sell something.

The singing Hutchinsons stand out. The manager Jesse Hutchinson Jr.'s pose seems a blend of paternal affection and artistic distraction. Standing over Joshua, he caresses his brother's forehead. His hair is uncombed. He looks away from the camera, his face evincing the far-off stare of the poet. Abby, of course, is conspicuous by her absence. The portrait was clearly meant as a testimonial to brotherly bonds. Yet from left to right, Asa, Judson, and John suggest a sensibility that is very nearly feminine. Their clothing is fine. Their hair is long. They rest their heads on their brothers' shoulders, their expressions almost precisely the same: sensitive, poetic, and soulful.[26]

The ten Hutchinson brothers suggest changes in identity commensurate with the market revolution. In the portrait are two types indicative of the period's broad changes: the old middling sort of the freehold farmer and the new middle class of the rising merchant. As well, there is something else, a third type marked by artistic yearnings, romantic sensibilities, and sensitive empathy. Looking at the image, one gets the sense that the two oldest Hutchinson brothers could butcher a pig and regard the injustice of the world without flinching. The singers look like idealists, like people trying to appear deeply

ANDREW JESSE JOSHUA   DAVID   CALEB   NOAH   JUDSON   ZEPHANIAH   JOHN
TEN OF THE HUTCHINSONS, 1844 (p. 137)

FIGURE 5.3. Two farmers, four merchants, three artists, and a manager. This photograph of the ten Hutchinson brothers suggests the changes within the family as its members made a transition to the rising middle-class standards of the 1830s and 1840s. Situated in the middle of the frame, the brothers David and Noah appear as stern New England farmers. Around them, brothers Andrew, Joshua, Caleb, and Zephaniah all have the look of a new class of professional merchants. From left to right, the singing brothers Asa (who is not named in the caption), Judson, and John strike poses that are consciously sensitive and artistic, leaning soulfully on their brothers' shoulders. Brother Jesse, the songwriter and group manager, appears to be either caressing or managing the pose of one of his siblings. "Ten of the Hutchinsons," picture from John Wallace Hutchinson, *The Story of the Hutchinsons*, vol. 1. Boston: Lee and Shepard, 1896, 137. Courtesy of American Antiquarian Society.

affected by beauty and suffering. No doubt they were sincere. Yet they also seemed determined to display alternative values and selves. As the individual members of the family suggest, there would be more to the American middle class than a bourgeois work ethic, entrepreneurial success, and etiquette-based respectability. To understand the foundations of the American middle class requires a more detailed meeting with the singing Hutchinsons.

None of the brothers was more middle class than Jesse Hutchinson Jr. And none did as much to create the message and style of the original Hutchinson Family Singers. Born in 1813, he was the third Jesse of the family. The first was the family patriarch. The second was the old man's first son and namesake, born in 1802, killed in 1809 in an accident at the family sawmill. There was a certain magic to Jesse Jr.'s place in the family. A seventh son named for a dead brother, he was not raised for the life of a farmer. Instead, in 1825, at age twelve, his parents sent him away from Milford to the nearby town of Wilton. There he was to learn the printing trade by working in the office of a Wilton newspaper, the *Farmer's Cabinet*.[27]

The paper did a lot for the farmer's son. It opened a career path away from the family homestead. It introduced him to the new commercial world of the market revolution and embroiled him in the period's social and political changes, causes, and controversies. And it provided a first outlet for what would be his most recognized talent. By the early 1830s, Jesse Hutchinson had gained a reputation as the poet of the *Farmer's Cabinet*, as a young writer who could versify on any subject. By the mid-1830s, he was dividing his time between Wilton and Milford, writing columns and poems for the paper, returning occasionally to the homestead to help out on the farm.

He was also spending time in Lynn, Massachusetts, the booming port, factory town, and center for New England's shoemaking industry. At some point in the late 1830s, he decided to settle in Lynn. He bought a shop at Number 8 Exchange Street and declared he was going into the hardware business. Father Jesse was alarmed at the news. He had lost one son to commercial trade, and worse, to Unitarianism. Learning of his son's plans, the patriarch wrote his namesake a letter. He reminded Jesse Jr. of "the rich man" who ate "sumptuously, wore the fanciest clothing, and always wanted more." Of course, he had died and gone to a hot place. "Alas he was a fool," wrote the family patriarch, for all his riches "cannot purchase him one drop of water to cool his tongue."[28] Jesse kept the letter for the rest of his life. He also opened his shop.

What did Jesse see in his father's letter? Quite likely, the value he attached to the missive involved a holdover from the traditional culture. Something of the old communal morality made its way into middle-class ideology. The moral foundation for many early etiquette guides was straightforward; it was the golden rule, the command, as one put it, to "do unto others as you would that others should do to you." With the rule in mind, guide writers addressed a host of warnings to young entrepreneurs. They inveighed against "lying, dishonesty, and connivance." They excoriated merchant efforts to "flatter appetites" and "inflame desires." They warned against the seeking of excessive profit and wealth. All, they claimed, would lead to corruption and damnation.[29] In his letter to his son, Jesse Sr. repeated a standard warning from the middle-class etiquette guide.

The admonition was complicated by the necessities of bourgeois culture. For men, middle-class respectability depended on the adoption of moral codes and standards of refined behavior. Yet there were also material requirements. Being good meant looking good; for upward-striving young men, respectability required a private and well-appointed home for the emerging standard of the nuclear family and the domestic wife, clean and fine clothing, a neat office or well-stocked store, perhaps even a decent carriage to get from home to place of business without muddying one's trousers or linens. All required a certain degree of economic success. All required money, more money than could be gained by strict honesty or by following the golden rule. For merchants, success seemed to depend on the ability to "flatter appetites." Then, as now, many would have wondered how to operate without an effort to "enflame desires."

Etiquette-guide writers struggled with these contradictions. Many found themselves slipping into an economic rationale for polite culture. "It is a man's manners that make his fortune," claimed one. Others implied that the system of middle-class codes—the table manners, the rules for politeness, the prescriptions for sincere discourse—all were forms of theater. The goal of the play was success: "an ordinary man," one claimed, "can never gain that place in life for which his talents and his merits fit him unless he is acquainted with that style of behavior which the world insists on observing."[30] Still, the same writers often inveighed against "counterfeits" of honesty, individuals who made a "show of virtue as a stock in trade."[31]

Jesse Hutchinson would spend his life trying to square the middle-class necessities of economic success and moral status. Much of his life and career, in turn, would be marked by attempts to prove that becoming a success did not come at the cost of his soul. By the early 1840s, his hardware store was doing well. One of his products was a parlor stove he credited himself for inventing, "the Hutchinson Air-Tight Stove." In marketing the invention, he displayed characteristic flair. His circulars extolled the product in poetry, in stanzas praising its "oval form," its "air-tightness" that saved wood, its "splendid base," its "symmetry and grace," and finally declaring:

> This wond'rous Stove doth well combine,
> All that's desirable; and must shine
> Throughout this region:
>
> I'm confident 'twill have a run,
> Demands already have begun
> Almost a legion![32]

Jesse's blend of mercantile sense and artistic sensibility would contribute enormously to the success of the Hutchinson Family Singers. Early in the singers' career he would write the lyrics to their signature song, "The Old Granite State." Set to an older tune called "The Old Church Yard" and published in 1843, the song established the Hutchinsons' style of self-presentation and became enormously popular. Lyrically it was simple, based on triple repe-

titions of lines giving the singers' background: "We have come from the mountains," and "We are all good Yankees." It offered audiences an introduction to
the family, presenting the singers as members of the "tribe of Jesse," with lines
listing the entire tribe from David to Abby. It also provided a moral grounding
for their efforts. According to the song's imagery, the singers were rural folk,
simple, sincere, unpretentious; they were rooted in the soil, more yeoman farmers than professional entertainers.[33]

Through the 1840s, Jesse continued as the singers' part-time manager and
sometime member of the group. He would join his siblings onstage at several
key moments in their career. He would write many of their most popular
songs, songs that nearly always had the characteristic blend of moral grounding with commercial appeal. He became one of Lynn's most successful citizens, serving as a member of several local associations, building for himself a
landmark house at "High Rock," a granite elevation just outside the city.

He remained an idealist and a man on the make. In 1844, he wrote "Get
Off the Track!" as a would-be anthem for the antislavery Liberty Party. Four
years later, he contributed several songs to the Free Soil Party's convention
in Buffalo. He then joined the gold rush to California. On his return, he con-
tracted what forty-niners called "Panama Fever." By the spring of 1853, he
lay dying in a Cincinnati sanitarium. He remained, it seems, haunted by the
question: had success come at an ethical cost? His brothers rushed to his bed-
side, and Asa Hutchinson recorded his dying words: "Look at me and see how
the gold hath become him."[34]

If Jesse Hutchinson straddled the worlds of the merchant and the poet, his
singing brothers represented an increasing immersion into artistic sensibilities. Asa Hutchinson came the closest to having what the period's merchant
types would call sense. His stolid demeanor was probably more by default than
intention. Born in 1823 and a mere eighteen years old during the singers' first
tour, Asa found the starring roles taken by his brothers. Back on the family
farm, they took up the violins; he was left with the cello. They took the leading
vocals and upper registers; he had to sing bass. Onstage they took the histrion-
ics. As Asa recalled, performing with his brothers was no exercise in fraternal
harmony. Nearly every night, he claimed, Judson and John would vie with
each other for applause, competing to see whose songs were "better received."
By concert's end, one was likely to be filled with "pride and vanity," the other
"out of sorts."[35]

Faced with this sort of thing, Asa's options were limited. He could have entered the fray. Instead, he let his brothers have center stage. Thus, even during
the high years of the family's success, critics rarely cited Asa's musical genius.
Concertgoers often failed to mention him. He was every bit as idealistic as his

brothers. "I have this morning thought," he would write during the singers' tour of 1844, "that we had better not have our concert admission fees too high for by thus doing we keep away all the poor and laboring classes." To sing "expressly for the money," he added, would place the family in thrall to "aristocratic audiences" and leave them "slaves to sordid dust." To most people who knew him, Asa was the soul of the artist: a poet "endowed with an excitable nature," a romantic whose "impulses" were "generous and noble."[36]

To his brothers, he was the responsible one. He kept the family diary. He was tasked with tracking audiences and totting up profits and expenses. The tasks took a toll. Early on he was a dead ringer for his brother John, with the same long hair and starry eyes of the young poet. By the later 1840s, he had developed the midsection spread of the bourgeois gentleman. He married young, to Worcester's Lizzie Chase, and the couple lived happily, producing three healthy children. In 1855, he traveled to the Midwest with his brothers. Together, they founded the town of Hutchinson, Minnesota. Judson and John soon tired of the prairie life and decamped for the East. Asa became a town father. For much of his life, he continued to perform, singing with his own family after the members of the original quartet went their separate ways. When he died in 1884, he would be eulogized as a "good and useful citizen," a man of "solid worth."[37]

John Hutchinson never earned such praise, or from an artistic perspective, such censure. Born in 1821, John played the role of the artist and performer all his days; and through his long life—some 87 years—he never tired of the spotlight. According to a later observer, as a young man he was "daring, ambitious, and gifted," with "an ambition that 'can't be beat.'"[38] Clearly he was ambitious. Singing in a theatrical tenor or baritone, he performed many of the solo songs of the family's programs while the others sat stiffly behind him in a row of chairs. During the group's 1842 tour, he sang nightly versions of Henry Russell's "The Maniac." As he remembered it, he out-Russelled Russell:

Judson and Asa would commence a prelude. Meanwhile, I would be in my chair behind them, with the fingers of each hand raising the hair on my head, and bringing it over in partial dishevelment. Then I would rise, with the expression of vacancy inseparable from mania, and commence:

No, by Heaven, I am not mad!
Oh, release me! Oh, release me!
No, by Heaven, I am not mad.
I loved her sincerely,
I loved her too dearly,
In sorrow and in pain.[39]

John was sure his performance impressed the critics. He was probably right. Handsome and showy, he wore his hair longer than his brothers and in the mid-1840s took to wearing a mustache and flowing beard.

He also poured a certain amount of suffering into his art, for he was example and victim of an emerging middle-class concept of romantic love. Popularized by poets, novelists, and songwriters, the concept has often been celebrated for having freed individuals from arranged marriages or pairings of economic convenience, for creating happy couples and happy endings. It did not work this way for John. At the age of twenty-two, he married Fanny Patch, a young woman he met in Lowell.[40] It was an unhappy match, and he would spend much of the rest of his life torturing himself over it. The problem was simple. John liked and respected his wife; he even shared the intimate bond of performing with her. But he did not love her.

At least, he did not love her according to the demanding standards of romantic poets and novelists. There was no brooding on the moors for Fanny Patch, no obsessive loss of appetite during their courtship, no poetry in their marriage. As John saw it, he suffered all his life from a lack of love. Asa thought the whole thing was ridiculous. Yet he had to admit that John's misery and yearning, especially when channeled into his singing, had "magnificent results." As other critics had it, to see John Hutchinson on the stage was to witness the "personification of the majestic and sublime."[41]

For depth of artistic soul, none of the brothers could match Judson Hutchinson. Almost from his birth in 1817, Judson was celebrated as a genius. He could sing before he could walk. As a child, people came from miles away to marvel at the musical prodigy. By the time the Hutchinsons took to the road, all who saw him wondered at his vocal talent, at his ability to move effortlessly from masculine tenor to soprano, as "clear and sweet as that of a woman." According to one observer, he could literally make his violin speak, bending the strings so it sang the chorus of one of his songs. He would be the group's main songwriter, early on setting well-known poems to music, later writing the music and lyrics to several original pieces.[42]

These songs revealed much about his genius. One, "The Vulture of the Alps," almost froze the audience's blood. The song's lyrics, according to John, came from an "old school reader." They told the story of a man whose infant son was carried away by a giant vulture and who, after years of mourning, climbed to the bird's nest on an alpine peak to retrieve his child's body. Judson's placement of the tale in a heavily operatic score elevated the tale to gothic horror. Audiences heard the swoop of the giant bird. They felt the father's desperation and sorrow, along with his anticipation as he climbed toward the vulture's nest. Finally, in the song's climax, they experienced the

man's shock at finding his son's bleached skeleton. Another song, "The Horticultural Wife," would have the same crowd helpless with laughter. Performed
in the character of an English gardener, the song offered the image of a man
who could envision his love only through a lens of horticultural passion:

> She's my myrtle, my geranium, / My sunflower, my sweet marjoram,
> My honeysuckle, my tulip, my violet, / My hollyhock, my dahlia, my mignonette.
> Ho! ho! she's a fickle wild rose, / A damask, a cabbage, a china rose.
> Ho ho! she's a fickle wild rose, / A damask, a cabbage, that everybody knows.[43]

Judson's genius came at a price. Though he married a distant cousin, Jeru-
sha Peabody, in 1844, he never quite settled down. He experienced wild mood
swings and suffered attacks of what he called "the horrors." During these
episodes, he became agitated with "pensiveness" and "melancholy." He had
thoughts of suicide. Onstage he could be brooding or effusive: one night singing and playing with manic zest, another night lifeless and unwilling to cast
his talent before the local swine. Tall, thin, and intense, he had an arresting
presence. No small part of his noted charisma came from his unpredictability.
In later years, stories of his erratic stage behavior abounded: his swearing off
shoes in favor of bedroom slippers; his throwing of coins into audiences in
order to return them to their vulgar sources and renounce all profits; his veg-
etarian rants against the killing of animals; his printing of concert broadsides
announcing that the rich had to buy tickets for the poor.[44]

Nowadays, Judson Hutchinson would most likely be diagnosed as a bipo-
lar personality. At the time and in the words of an observer, he was "of a ner-
vous temperament, highly susceptible to the influence of a poetic imagination." His moodiness, in other words, was in keeping with the period's artistic
aesthetics. The early nineteenth century was a time of gothic horror and romantic sensibility; and the main "influence of a poetic imagination" was the
rising middle class's favorite poet, Lord Byron. As Byron had it in poems like
the wildly popular "Child Harold's Pilgrimage," the romantic hero was melancholy and brooding, a wandering outcast who felt things—whether love, the
wrongs of the world, or the absurdity of convention—far more deeply than
the common man. The role of the masculine artist was to lose himself in his
art, immersing himself to the point of self-destruction.[45]

Judson lived and died by the standard. The family friend William Lloyd Garrison called him "dear, impulsive, noble" Judson. Another observer summed
the issue up: Judson felt things too keenly; his mind was racked by "the cruelties and wrongs he daily saw." In 1850, he would attend a séance near Rochester,
allow himself to be "mesmerized," and go into such a fit of enthusiasm that the
brothers had him committed to an insane asylum. He was soon released and

the episode would be admiringly written up in the press. Nine years later, he committed a final "rash act" that would "hardly excite surprise in those who knew him intimately." In January 1859, while staying at High Rock in Lynn, he quietly stole out of the house. A short time later, John and Fanny found his body in one of the outbuildings. He had hanged himself.[46]

Judson, John, and Asa had talent, a bit of marketing sense, and a good deal of artistic sensibility. During the years of their greatest popularity, however, the key to the singers' success would be Abby Hutchinson. Abby's joining of her brothers was initially something of a gimmick. In the fall of 1841, Jesse Hutchinson engaged Lynn's Lyceum Hall for what would be a make-or-break concert by the Aeolian Vocalists. For this performance, the brothers decided to try something different. At the time, a quintet calling itself the Ranier Family was touring the Northeast, their broadsides billing the group as having come from the Tyrolean Alps. Performing in full regalia of lederhosen, suspenders, and feathered hats, the four brothers and a sister played the romantic image for all it was worth.

It was worth quite a bit. For one thing, the fact that the group included a young woman was crucial in attracting mixed-gender audiences, audiences that were unmistakably respectable and had money to spend. For another, the Raniers' "Tyrolean melodies" caught the public fancy; the group generated an Alpine song craze that would last through the Jenny Lind–mania a decade later. Before their own concert, the Hutchinson brothers dashed to Milford and nabbed their sister Abigail. Outfitting her in a "Swiss bodice or Tyrolean costume," they had her join them onstage. The concert drew the best audience they had seen. Charged by this success, they took Abby with them as they set out for their 1842 tour, promising their worried parents they would return her in a few weeks.[47]

They never kept the promise. Only twelve years old at the outset of the singers' first tour and still in her mid-teens when they became famous, Abby left "an indelible impression." Early on a critic dubbed the singers "a nest of brothers with a sister in it." By the mid-1840s, the sister was the "chief attraction," having created "a sensation almost as great as that of Jenny Lind." She sang in a rich contralto, with a voice described as having "an indescribable liquid sweetness." Many in the audience, both men and women, wrote love poems to Abby during the family's performances. There were the standard Victorian acrostics:

> A-cross thine earthly path I pray,
> B-right sunshine e'er may beam;
> B-lessings be shower'd round thy way,
> Y-ielding a blissful stream.

There were "dumb confessions" of love and yearning:

> I caught the answer as it hung, / On Abby's roseate lip;
> And truth and candor on her tongue, / Were linked in fellowship.
> She spoke, but in the language of, / The soft expressive eye;
> She breathed—yet in the anguish of / The long imprison'd sigh.[48]

For the singers' audiences, Abby would be the embodiment of a rising middle-class ideology of female virtue: she was pious, proper, and pure. They stared adoringly at the "slender girl" with "glossy tresses" and "laughing dark eyes." Critics marveled at her "laughing lips" and "exquisite complexion." According to audience members, she was a "dear little creature" and a "vision of loveliness." And so, noted one, "everybody loves her." Another declared that she "so charmed and entranced my youthful heart that for a moment I felt it could not be a reality." Above all else, it would be her youthful innocence that attracted audiences, her "unconscious and unstudied grace," her "artless, pure, and simple nature."[49]

As the fascination with Abby suggests, individuals within a rising middle class placed an enormous emphasis on exteriors and appearances. With the market revolution, and with identity becoming increasingly subject to the theatrics of selling, the middle class too would be obsessed with an ideal of authentic selfhood. What they were looking for was sincerity, an external sign that one's internal nature or "true self" was guileless, honest, and good. Abby Hutchinson was sincerity incarnate. At the same time, her nature was largely the result of a staged persona. Her celebrated shy simplicity was part of a public performance, a product of her talent. From the age of twelve, she took to the stage with zeal. Over the years, she perfected her stage persona, playing not merely a role but a *concept* of innocent girlhood and bourgeois sincerity.

She ran a risk of becoming typecast. In 1849, at the age of nineteen, Abby married one of her versifying admirers, a wealthy New Jersey stockbroker by the name of Ludlow Patton. As the dictates of middle-class domesticity had it, she immediately retired from the stage. For a while, the brothers resorted to still listing her on their broadsides, a desperate move that generated charges of false advertising and proved her status as the star attraction. During the next two decades, she traveled the world as Abby Patton. In later years, she wrote simple poetry, artless verses that found no publisher. From time to time, she appeared in public. She even performed with her brothers on a few occasions. On these occasions, someone was almost sure to ask the question: who was that gray-haired old lady? Still a girl, always a young girl to those who remembered her, Abby Hutchinson died, after an attack of apoplexy, in 1892.[50]

The Devil's Tunes for the Temperance Cause

At the time of their 1842 tour, success lay in the Hutchinsons' future. The present looked bleak. The singers traveled from Milford to Hookset to Hanover, New Hampshire. They continued to appeal for support as native-born singers. Yet they continued to bill themselves as the "New Hampshire Raniers." They drew disappointingly small audiences. In Hanover, New Hampshire, only the men of the town came to see them, a tradition in rural areas where public spaces were segregated by gender. The tradition meant an uncomfortable evening for Abby. It also made for another small crowd.[51]

From Woodstock, Vermont, to Saratoga Springs, New York, they barely broke even. Occasionally they appeared ready to crack under the pressure of touring. In Rutland, Vermont, an argument between the brothers led to a "scuffle." Days passed brooding over hurt feelings, hours crawling by in the quiet tension of mutual silent treatments. Judson had several attacks of "the horrors." During one episode, he grabbed the family diary to record seeing "a hog as big as an elephant, 12,000 pounds." During another, he scribbled his disgust at the "skinflints" in the towns they passed.[52]

Still they carried on, always looking for an audience, continuously making changes to improve their fortunes. At the start of the 1842 tour, their concerts included up to twenty numbers. They opened with an audience-pleasing glee—usually "We Hail Thee, Mirth," or "Hail, Smiling Morn." Then they meandered through a list of instrumental pieces and melodramatic numbers, story songs like "The Ship-Wreck," the "Snow Storm," or John's flailing performance of "The Maniac." Much later, as their stage candles burned low, they closed with the rural imagery of "A Little Farm Well Tilled." There were points when the evening's energy lagged. By the end of the year, they shortened their programs to twelve or fifteen selections and dropped most of their instrumental pieces.[53] Meanwhile they worked on their original material, eventually adding two songs that thanks to Judson's music they could claim as partly their own: "The Grave of Bonaparte" and "A Trip to Cape Ann." Finally, they honed their act. They refined their harmonies and dropped their references to the Ranier Family Singers in favor of a more consciously "natural" American style.[54]

By the end of the year, critics—at least the few who saw them—commended the singers for their "fine woodland tone" along with their "clear enunciation" of lyrics and "perfect freedom from affectation or stage grimace."[55] But while their audiences grew, they remained small next to those of the Ranier Family or the popular Henry Russell. As John later recalled, the singers remained

frustrated over the tour's "indifferent results," particularly since "foreign artists were coming here and setting the public wild." There had to be some way
to overcome America's "lack of appreciation for home talent."[56] Indeed, there
was. Ultimately, the key to the Hutchinsons' first real success would be the
convergence of two seemingly disparate developments of the market revolution: commercial popular culture and moral reform.

In 1840, while staying above Andrew's dry-goods store, the Hutchinson
brothers attended a temperance rally at Boston's Marlboro Chapel. There,
they signed the "cold-water pledge," vowing total abstinence from alcohol.
Early in their 1842 tour, the Aeolian Vocalists began to include a number
of temperance songs in their programs, "Oh, That's the Drink for Me!" and
"Shun the Wine Cup."[57] By mid-tour, they announced they would stay only
in temperance hotels and inns. By tour's end, they had become full-fledged
cold-water singers. As John later put it, "there was a great temperance wave
rolling over the New England States, and we concluded to identify ourselves
with this reform movement."[58] Doubtlessly sincere as a moral statement, the
decision would come to be a career move as well. In aligning themselves with
reform, the singers found themselves on the crest of a popular and lively
phenomenon.

Popular reform emerged from the Christian revivals of the early nineteenth century. From the beginning, the phenomenon would find expression
in song. In the summer of 1801, observers in the far western states of Kentucky
and Ohio noted first thousands, then tens of thousands of people flocking to
outdoor camp meetings. There, they listened to sermons given by frontier
preachers in the earthiest of tones. They also sang camp-meeting songs, songs
that stirred the senses with tactile images. In one, meeting-goers sang of being
washed clean with a savior's blood:

> O, the blood, the precious blood,
> That Jesus shed for me
> Upon the cross, in crimson flood,
> Just now by faith I see.

In another, they sang in celebration of their own imminent death:

> Going home, going home, going home,
> We are going home to God.
> I'm glad that I was born to die,
> Going home to God.[59]

The point of the songs was to foster deep emotions, to prepare meeting-
goers for the oftentimes violent passion of a conversion experience. They

worked. According to observers, revival sermons and songs elicited "terrifying" responses, mass examples of "fainting, shouting, yelling, crying, sobbing, and grieving." In the middle of one camp-meeting song, claimed one observer, "the *power of God* came down, and pervaded the vast assembly, and it became agitated—swelling and urging like a sea in a storm." Another described meeting-goers "taken with an inward throbbing of heart; then with weeping and trembling; from that to crying-out, in apparent agony of soul; falling down and swooning away; 'till every appearance of animal life was suspended; and the person appeared in a trance." Some were "struck with terror," and tried to "make their escape." Others fell like corpses, their bodies stiff and cold to the touch. Filled with such scenes, revivals often went on for days.[60]

They also spread. Within a few years, the camp meeting crossed into western New York, and the waves of revivals that would become known as the Second Great Awakening began sweeping through the Northeast. By the 1820s and 1830s, the region of New York along the Erie Canal would be so scorched by the "heavenly fires" of frequent revivals that the area would be referred to as the "burnt over district." By this time, the meetings had become more standardized. The style of preaching and singing would remain; but it would also be picked up by ministers like the Presbyterian Charles Finney, by clergymen who could appeal to individuals on their way to middle-class status.

Still, revivals remained subject to "terrifying" scenes of emotion. As observers and critics often pointed out, a successful revival had two main requirements. The first was the dramatics of meeting-goers becoming overwhelmed by the spirit. The second focused on the theatrics of the "anxious bench" or "guilty bench," the seating area just before the pulpit to which revival preachers called individuals to come forth, sit down, and confess their sins. "Take away the *anxious bench* from camp meetings," declared one European visitor; "remove those women who fall into convulsions, shriek, and roll on the ground, [and] you will be weary of the spectacle in a hour."[61] Through the 1820s and 1830s, few Americans wearied of the spectacle: meeting-goers continued to shriek and roll; increasing numbers of guilt-ridden shopkeepers, their sins exposed and their faces wet with tears, continued to come forward to the anxious bench.

According to one historian, these revivals represented the unleashing of an "unbridled communal force." This same force would contribute to the rise of philanthropic movements and later, much larger associations of popular reform. There were several connections between revivals and philanthropy. Revivals filled the rolls of church membership. Churches, in turn, provided many of the members for philanthropic associations. Both revivals and philanthropic organizations would place an enormous stress on active

Christianity. Both would provide a public voice and place for women. In the summer of 1810, Boston's "Humane Society" met at the Chapel Church. The broadside announcing the meeting concluded with a soon-to-be-standard call: "the ladies in particular are invited to attend."[62]

Above all, both camp revival and philanthropic association would emphasize a movement beyond the boundaries of the individual, an encouragement that would come in the form of sermons, prayers, and songs. In meetings of philanthropic societies, these songs typically emphasized communion, empathy, and "brotherly love." The song "Charity," sung at an 1812 meeting of a Boston Lodge of Masons, portrayed these ideals as a "mandate" from the "Great Architect":

> When first the great Architect, master of all,
> From chaos bade rise this terrestrial ball,
> The chorus of rapture resounded above,
> As he gave the first mandate for union and love.[63]

The good mason was called to feel the pain of the "lorn widow," to hear the cry of the helpless, and to raise up and protect the "mourning orphan." An "Original Ode" sung at an 1820 meeting of Boston's "Fatherless and Widow's Society" expressed the same sentiments, appealing to the "children of affluence" to open their stores and purses:

> The brightest of gems is humanity's tear,
>   The heart's purest off'ring is brotherly love,
> And the hand that dispenses its benefits here,
>   Lays up a rich treasure in mansions above.
>
> Ye children of affluence open your stores,
>   'Tis the widow entreats, 'tis the orphan implores;
> The husband, the father lies cold in the grave,
>   But your pity may comfort, your charity save.[64]

The appeal to affluence identified both the Society's audience and its members. Through the 1820s, philanthropy would be largely dominated by small organizations, by assorted charitable institutions for widows, orphans, and the "poor and indigent." Their leadership along with most of their members came from an urban elite, from collections of "Christian Gentlemen" and "Lady Bountifuls" who developed their scope of vision and humanitarian mission. Neither went very far. Their vision tended to focus on the consequences of poverty without addressing its causes. Their mission focused on giving aid to the downtrodden, not changing their condition. Their members took pride in their benevolence. Through the 1820s, one group of Boston philanthropists organized regular soirees, during which the town's "orphan girls" and "indigent boys" had to sing their gratitude, in the one case of having been "snatch'd from the haunts of vice and care," in the other of having been taught to "hate the paths of sin."[65]

Despite their elitism, these early organizations would contribute enormously to the emergence of a middle-class ethos of humanitarianism. Judging by the frequency of its appearance, the anthem of these societies was a hymn that appeared under several names but might have been best known by its first line, "Bless'd is the Man." The hymn laid the foundations for a communal vision of humanitarianism, from the ability to feel another's pain to the caring for strangers:

> Bless'd is the Man, whose softening heart, / Feels all another's pain;
> To whom the supplicating eye, / Was never rais'd in vain.
> Whose breast expands with generous warmth, / A stranger's woes to feel,
> And bleeds in pity o'er the wounds, / He wants the power to heal.
> He spreads his kind supporting arms, / To every child of grief;
> His secret bounty largely flows, / And brings unask'd relief.[66]

By the 1830s, an American middle class was coming into focus, coalescing in large part around issues of humanitarian reform. An equally rising working class, meanwhile, had supposedly stayed loyal to vernacular tradition, drinking, carousing, and enjoying the rough music and earthy comedy of popular blackface shows. The result was the appearance, at least, of an increasing cultural divide, a split between the music of reform, rooted in the controlled traditions of Christian hymnody, and the liveliness and creative ferment that marked the secular songs of the popular stage.[67]

For a time it may have seemed that reform and the stage existed in a type of competition. In the 1830s, practically every village, town, and city ward in the Northeast had its "cold-water army." The leaders of these armies tried their best to liven up meetings. They continued to feature conversions and guilty benches; they brought in choirs and printed-up broadsides to facilitate the communal singing of hymns. Yet little suggests that early temperance meetings could be enjoyed as popular amusements. Typically held in churches and conducted by ministers, many were a lot like church services. An organ voluntary announced the start of the proceedings, as a crowd of teetotalers filed in and found seats. What followed was a standard "order of exercises": an opening prayer, a hymn, a sermon on the evils of drink, a passing of the collection plate, and a benediction.[68] The typical early temperance hymn was dry:

> Eternal God to thee we raise, / Our grateful songs this day;
> Thine is the glory, thine is the praise— / Oh! bless our cause, we pray.
> And stay, great God, that turbid tide, / Which onward rolls its wave—
> Speak, and its waters shall subside, / And close the drunkard's grave.[69]

Through much of the 1830s, the lyrical tone of temperance meetings remained ensconced in traditions of hymnody and the old jeremiad style of the Puritans. In hymn and ode, meeting-goers connected rum and Satan:

> Hark! hark! hear ye the chain,
>   That is clanking in yonder cell?
> The Demon is there, with the felon insane;
>   He is tearing a heart—he is burning a brain![70]

The imagery was not lacking in color. Yet by the end of the decade, there was a growing sense that the movement's shopworn sermons and hymns were having little effect on reducing drunkenness or increasing temperance association membership. The result was a change in the music and style of the movement.

The prime movers in this transition were the "Washingtonians." Formed in 1840, the Washingtonian Total Abstinence Society was a national temperance association composed primarily, at least in its early incarnation, of reformed drunkards. Many were self-described workingmen, exemplars of the fact that working-class individuals could adopt supposedly middle-class values. Among the association's founders was the notorious John Gough, the "poet of the delirium tremens." Gough was a former artisan laborer and a drunkard, a man with plenty of experiences to relate and translate into song. Like other favorite speakers in the movement, he occasionally fell back into his old vices. In 1845, for example, he was discovered passed-out drunk in a New York City whorehouse. The scandal added to his popularity, for it offered another riveting confession. As it turned out, much of the attraction of the Washingtonians came from the ability of men like Gough to tell tales of their own slippage, to recount, as Gough put it, many a "fiery trial . . . of the most abominable wickedness."[71]

The Washingtonians infused temperance meetings with new energy. They drew increasing numbers of young people into the teetotaler fold, along with a growing number of affiliated organizations composed of artisan workers. Within a short time, the old meeting "order of exercises" had been replaced by the sharing of experiences of temptation and a grand communal sing-along. Its older hymns were supplanted by temperance lyrics set to current and popular airs, tunes such as "Yankee Doodle," "John Anderson, My Jo," and "The Old Oaken Bucket."[72] According to one Washingtonian broadside, everything would now be done to make the "temperance jubilee . . . an occasion of innocent and profitable amusement," including the mass performance of "SONGS of a new and interesting kind." One songster preface declared it "a new era—Temperance songs will now be sung in low as well as high places. The Hymns and songs in this work are adapted to the most popular airs, . . . by which the Teetotaller can enjoy himself with delight."[73]

The Washingtonians did enjoy themselves. The "reformed inebriates," declared an observer in 1841, did an "incalculable amount of good"; and it was impossible to attend one of their meetings "without a smile." Meeting-goers gathered to sing "The Cold Water Pledge," "The Washington Appeal," and "The Tippler's Farewell to His Bottle." They listened to lectures by Gough and others, "the best . . . I ever heard," according to one listener, "much more interesting than the Lyceum lectures."[74] And they declared a joyous victory over temptation and demon drink. As the words to one song set to "Auld Lang Syne" had it, they were "high" on water:

> The sturdy oak full many a cup, / Doth hold up to the sky,
> To catch the rain—then drinks it up, / And thus the oak GETS HIGH;
> 'Tis thus the oak gets high my friends, / 'Tis thus the oak gets high,
> By having water in its cups— / Then why not you and I?[75]

The tone of these songs was ardently experiential, inviting play-acting and participatory theatrics. One, set to the tune of "All on Hobbies," called for meeting-goers to picture themselves as a real army:

> We have entered the field and are ready to fight,
> Against the rum demon from morning till night;
> The groggeries too, we're determined to crush,
> And we'll drink good cold water to nerve for the rush.[76]

Others, like "The Drunkard" or John Gough's "Inebriate's Lament," took meeting-goers on a tour of the alcoholic's degradation: the first taste of rum, the daily tippling at grog shops, the "staggering to and fro" through streets, the loss of friends, the eventual decline into debt, poverty, and imprisonment, and the death of the brokenhearted wife. The song also allowed them to experience the joy of redemption through total abstinence.[77]

Other new temperance songs offered similar joys. The "Ode to Rum," set to the tune of "The Roving Sailor," began soberly enough: "Let thy devotees extol thee / and thy wondrous virtues sum; / But the worst of names I'll call thee, / O, thou Hydra-monster RUM!" It then moved into a long string of earthy epithets describing the effects of alcohol:

> Pimple-maker—visage bloater, / Health corrupter—idler's mate;
> Mischief-breeder—vice promoter, / Credit spoiler—devil's bait.
> Utterance-boggler—stench-emitter, / Strong-man sprawler—fatal drop;
> Tumult-raiser—venom spitter, / Wrath-inspirer—coward's prop.
> Virtue-blaster—base deceiver, / Spite displayer—sot's delight;
> Noise-exciter—stomach heaver, / Falsehood-spreader—scorpion's bite.[78]

By the time the singers had reached the end of this list, which must have produced its share of hilarity, being drunk on rum may have seemed tame in comparison.

Hymns had long been set to popular folk tunes. But somehow, the temperance phenomenon seemed different to observers, perhaps because the tunes were both popular and commercial, their appeal overtly linked with the market and with mass desires. Within a few years, Washingtonians had so converged the uplift of reform with the appetites of the marketplace that it may have become difficult to tell where one began and the other ended. Published in 1844, the *Boston Temperance Songster* had what appeared to be a drunken gnome on its cover. Its songs had been set to the most lively new tunes, including several from the blackface stage. Meanwhile, its editors placed lyrics to these tunes between advertisements for patent medicines (which typically had alcohol as a key ingredient), balsam of wild cherry, and oxygenated bitters. The preface justified this interweaving of the popular with the moral:

> Some have thought, and perhaps honestly too, that many of the tunes were too lively, or the associations connected with them were such that they should be excluded from every thing that makes any pretensions to religion or morality. We recognize the truthful saying of the celebrated Whitefield, when a similar charge was brought against many of the tunes used by his denomination— that "the devil has been in possession of all the good tunes long enough." We think that Bacchus has had possession of these tunes too long altogether, and feel determined to press what we can of them into the Temperance Reform.[79]

By 1843, many New Englanders had no problem spending Christmas Day listening to John Gough lecture. Others were more than willing to devote July Fourth to a "Temperance Jubilee," to the singing of cold-water anthems set to the tune of "Yankee Doodle." Meanwhile, the movement continued to expand, from church associations through the Washingtonians to women's temperance unions, workingmen's cold-water clubs, and temperance associations for youth. "It must be admitted," claimed the editors of one of the movement's countless songsters, "that the introduction of the Song and Glee into the Temperance meetings, has been of incalculable benefit to the cause; in fact, it has created greater interest and excitement, where other means would probably have failed."[80]

The Hutchinsons announced themselves in favor of temperance in the middle of their first tour. Again, there is no reason to think their stance was anything but sincere. Yet over the next two years, the cause would go a long way toward making them famous. Near the end of 1842, Jesse gave the singers "The Old Granite State." The song provided them a chance to demonstrate their well-rehearsed harmonies while giving their audience a tour of their rural background, familial connections, and beliefs. One version also demonstrated their commitment. We are "all Washingtonians of the Old Granite State," they sang, declaring they were all "teetotalers" who had "signed the pledge."[81]

At about the same time, the brothers collaborated on "King Alcohol," a song set to the tune of "King Andrew" and inspired by the story of "Deacon Giles Distillery." A cautionary tale about making deals with demon rum, the story concerned a deacon in Salem, Massachusetts, who ran a combination Bible manufactory and distillery. He was supposed to have made a deal with Satan to hire devils to make his alcoholic concoctions on the cheap, only to have his business destroyed when his mischievous workers burned his factory. A "trio" harmonized by the brothers, the song offered a warning:

> King Alcohol has many forms, / By which he catches men,
> He is a beast of many horns. / And ever thus has been.
> For there's rum, and gin, and beer, and wine, / And brandy, of logwood hue,
> And hock, and port, and flip combine, / To make a man look blue.
> He says be merry, for here's good sherry,
> And Tom and Jerry, champaigne and perry, / And spirits of every hue.
> And are not these a fiendish crew, / As ever a mortal knew?
> And are not these a fiendish crew, / As ever a mortal knew?[82]

By the time they reached Albany, New York, in August 1842, the singers' alignment with reform had started to change their fortunes. There, they met music-store proprietor and sheet-music publisher Luke Newland. Impressed with their reform repertory, Newland arranged for a local minister to lend his church to the singers for a performance, saving them the cost of hall rental. He then convinced the editor of the *Albany Evening Journal* to write a favorable review, or "puff," for the concert, while lining up several of the city's businessmen to write complimentary endorsements. That night, the singers cleared a hundred dollars in profit.

Finally, they were on their way. From this point they adopted Newland's formula, performing whenever they could in local churches and lining up the support of clergy, press, and prominent citizens. Soon they were confident enough to enter Boston. They arranged a concert at the Melodeon, shocking members of the Handel and Haydn Society by listing on their broadsides the wildly optimistic price of fifty cents per ticket. To their critics' surprise, they drew a large crowd. As John Hutchinson put it, the tide had turned and "the press was in our favor."[83] They had a broadening reputation as singing reformers. They were fast becoming the proper choice for would-be concertgoers looking to acquire the styles, tastes, and sensibilities of a rising middle class. What they may not have foreseen was that these values would lead them to more controversial causes, or that they would make the singers targets for blackface performers.

Love Crimes

At dusk on the evening of July 9, 1834, a crowd of men gathered outside New York City's Chatham Street Chapel. Word had circulated that the chapel's new tenants, the reformers of the Five Points Mission, were planning an abolitionist meeting for the night. The crowd was there to break up the event, to let the reformers know their politics were not welcome in the working-class neighborhood. They had been trying to send the message for some time. In previous weeks one group of "Points" workingmen scattered an abolition meeting at New York's Clinton Hall; another threatened the antislavery merchants Arthur and Lewis Tappan. As the crowd grew, the chapel remained dark. Either rumors about the meeting had been wrong or the abolitionists had gotten wind of the mob and canceled the event. No one showed. For a moment it seemed the night would pass peacefully.[1]

Some of the men decided to break into the building. The next few minutes most likely had the typical elements of such occasions: the smashing of a window or two; the splintering of a few benches; the hurling of objects to the floor and the gleeful howl when something broke with particular noise and force. According to stories from the abolitionist press, the men left the chapel "very much injured."[2] Suddenly, according to other accounts, they halted the destruction for a bit of theater. One man preached a sermon in mock black dialect. Another proclaimed the opening of a "bobolition meeting." Someone proposed a resolution that all African Americans should be deported from the United States. The motion passed to roars of approval and masculine laughter. Finally, the men raised their voices in a mass sing-along:

> Wheel about an' turn about and do jis' so,
> An' ebery time I wheel about, I jump Jim Crow.[3]

Over the next several days and nights, white men in the area of the chapel went on a bender of racial violence. In what came to be known as the "Five Points Riot of 1834," they beat black people, burned black churches, and destroyed black-owned homes and businesses throughout Manhattan's Lower East Side.[4]

When it comes to events like the Five Points Riot, a simple question nearly always comes up. "What motivated this tremendous outpouring of hatred?"[5] The question contains its own answer. The motive, according to one historian who has asked it, was hatred. This "hatred"—if that is what it can be called—may have had myriad roots and causes. There was the legacy of American rationalizations about slavery; the belief that slavery, while bad for erstwhile citizens of a white republic, was perfectly acceptable for supposedly less-than-white beings of African descent. There was the market revolution, along with the white workers' increasing fear of free African Americans as potential competitors for factory work and unskilled jobs. According to common assumptions, the working-class white folks of the Five Points hated black people. Because they hated black people, they hated abolitionists. In current terminology, the riot, from the attack on the Five Points Mission to the seemingly indiscriminate attacks on black individuals, was a hate crime.

Yet there was something else to the violence, something side by side with the hatred. In the midst of vandalizing the Chatham Street Chapel, the rioters took a break to listen to a speech in black dialect. They took part in a rousing sing-along of "Jim Crow." Blackface permeated the riot. The Five Points neighborhood was in New York's Sixth Ward, and the Sixth Ward was the city's center for blackface entertainment. Before the reformers moved in to set up the Five Points Mission, the Chatham Street Chapel had been the Chatham Theatre, a venue for nightly blackface fare and a favorite site for working-class audiences.

Blackface songs and expressions appeared throughout the riot, from its first spark at the chapel, to a later episode at the Bowery Theatre, to songs summing things up once the dust cleared. The crowd of men who sparked the riot had their hatreds. Yet they loved their blackface. They seemed to hate black people. Yet they loved Jim Crow. Rather than reflecting the timelessness of a racism rooted in simple hatred and residing on the margins of American culture, the riot and its musical backdrop seem to have been something else. It may have marked the appearance of racial ideologies that could become more widespread, more generally accepted, and linked with pleasure. The riot seems to have been a manifestation of a love crime.[6]

Early Blackface and the Standardization of "Blackness"

In the years following Thomas Dartmouth Rice's performance of Jim Crow at the Bowery Theatre, blackface spread rapidly. The genre would come to dominate the Northeast, moving from the Five Points and New York City through the entertainment districts of Philadelphia, Boston, and Baltimore. Within a few years, audiences could see blackface acts at a growing number of New York theaters: the Bowery, Chatham, and Park Theaters as well as the North American Hotel, the Cornucopia, and the Olympic Circus. At theaters, saloons, and open markets, common-class audiences were able to enjoy a host of blackface characters, from Jim Crow and Zip Coon to Jim Brown, Coal Black Rose, and Dandy Jim. Their performers would become theatrical stars: James Buckley, J. P. Carter, William Whitlock, Dan Emmett, and Edwin Christy.[7]

Nearly all of these performers would make a similar claim: their songs and characters were stolen, not invented. The secret to their popularity, one writer declared later, was that they were "genuine and real." They were not "senseless and ridiculous imitations forged in the dull brain of some Northern self-styled minstrel, but the veritable tunes and words which have lightened the labor of some weary negro in the cotton fields."[8] The claim would provide later scholars of blackface with a point of departure: the genre's performers took their expressions from the South. They found them in their visits to genuine Southern plantations. They stole them from real slaves.

The fact is that blackface emerged in the American Northeast and not the South, and most early blackface performers developed their acts in Northern cities. Still, something like this could have happened. Some blackface performers did spend time in the South. Others had plenty of chances to pick up elements of black style. After all, day-to-day life in Northern cities was marked by constant interaction between white and black populations. This contact was most common in working-class neighborhoods, Boston's North End, Philadelphia's South Side, and perhaps especially, New York's Sixth Ward and the Five Points. By the 1830s, these Manhattan neighborhoods were magnets for low-paid journeymen, former artisans, and the city's common workers. The Sixth Ward's main thoroughfare was the Bowery, a broad avenue lined with hotels, bars, and cheap amusements, including the famous Bowery Theatre. Later known as the Lower East Side, the area was filled with rundown boardinghouses and low-rent tenements.

The neighborhood's low cost of housing would make it the city's destination point for poor immigrants to America and migrants to the city. At the heart of the Sixth Ward was the Five Points, an area centered on the squalid urban opening at Paradise Square. Here, several streets met: Little Water, Cross, Anthony, Orange, and Mulberry; and their meeting comprised the five points that gave the neighborhood its name. The Points had a population about twenty-five percent Irish and fifteen percent African American. The poorest of the area's black population lived in "Cow Bay," described by one observer as a "little alley" of "mephitic air," "filth," and "degradation." Yet the Five Points and parts of the Sixth Ward had numerous successful black businesses and churches; many individuals among its black population owned houses; some were landlords; and a few had a "commanding" influence in the community.[9]

Other places of routine contact included work sites and marketplaces. Outdoor city markets—such as Boston's Quincy Market or Catherine Market in Downtown Manhattan—were filled with a vibrant mix of humanity. Buyers and sellers crammed into tight squeezes between stalls of butter and cheese, buckets of oysters, and carcasses of dead hogs. White and black stall keepers sold their products in close proximity. Many followed the traditional practice of attracting buyers with song, dance, and a bit of theater. Meanwhile, down at the docks of port cities, blacks and whites worked as sailors and stevedores.[10] In neighborhoods, at marketplaces, and at various wharves and warehouses, black and white Americans lived, worked, and shopped side by side.

In the first three decades of the nineteenth century, Northern whites also had plenty of local opportunities to hear songs of African American slaves. Through much of the 1820s, after all, slavery still thrived in Connecticut, Pennsylvania, New York, and New Jersey. In these states and elsewhere, whites attended and watched African American carnivals. There were the annual Pentecost or "Pinkster" ceremonies in New York, along with "Election Day" and "Negro Training Day" festivals farther north in Connecticut and Massachusetts. According to observers, these ceremonies were characterized by songs and "Congo Dances." One account pictured a carnival "dominated by an incessant rhythm and drumming," with participants "beating lustily" on wooden containers and singing an "ever wild, though euphonic cry of *Hi-a-bomba, bomba, bomba* in full harmony with the thumping sounds." The ceremonies were filled with "the various languages of Africa," declared another white observer, "accompanied with the music of the fiddle, tambourine, the banjo, [and] drum."[11]

Given these contacts, white performers could have taken material from black sources. Even if they made no direct contact with African Americans, they could have picked up elements of black style secondhand and integrated them into blackface song. The question remains, did they? African or African

American instruments did appear in blackface, notably the banjo and the tambourine. Yet blackface song had few echoes of the style of call and response. They included few "euphonic cries" traceable to Africa. Zip Coon and Jim Crow were set to Irish folk tunes. Many blackface tunes were jigs and reels. Others would be set to English country dances and the tunes of the Anglo-American stage.[12]

The stories about blackface's origin with actual black folk, along with the constant use of the terms "authentic" and "genuine" in descriptions of its style, may have been more about context than origins. The historical context for blackface minstrelsy was the Northeast's market revolution and the emergence of a culture of the marketplace. The culture would be characterized by social relations emphasizing competition and deception for profit. It would come to be represented by a world of desire creation and illusion. Finally, the culture would be marked by an obsession with authenticity, a yearning for "the real thing" beneath the artifice of commercial promises.[13] Blackface would reflect and build on this obsession, linking authenticity to a largely invented version of black identity.

So what were the essential characteristics of genuine blackness? To begin with, there was the blackness itself. Blackface involved a constant calling of attention to its characters' physical blackness, a uniform shade produced by the application of burnt-cork paste to the white performer's face and hands. The imagery reduced race in America to a simple dichotomy: on one side was a capacious "whiteness," a non-racial category that included both the genre's audience of working-class males and its target of middle-class gentlemen; on the other side was a racialized blackness, a category always marked by earthiness and lowly self-expression.

Many blackface characters had names conveying their dark natures: with "Jim Brown," "Old Black Joe," and "Ginger Blue" suggesting a connection between character and color; with "Jim Crow," "Zip Coon," and "Old King Crow" connoting both darkness and a closer-to-nature linkage to animals or lower orders of being. Others had "white" names: "Charley White," "Cool White," and "Juliana Snow." The names denoted efforts to put on airs, to "act white." These efforts, because they went against "black nature," were always doomed to fail. In failing, they produced the genre's comedy.

Another signifier of blackness was the genre's "black style," a style expressed in song, dance, and dialect. The music of early blackface was typically a Scots-Irish jig backed with a heavy, pounding rhythm. The instrumental accompaniment was simple: usually a fiddle provided the tune; a banjo added counterpoint when plucked or rhythm when strummed; and "bones" castanets and tambourine produced a steady beat of slurred clacks and snaps, jangling cymbals, and percussive strikes. The performer's body, too, provided rhythmic accompaniment, sometimes struck with the hands in an African American style of "patting juba," more often in the form of foot-stomping on the resonant boards of the stage.

Among the elements of blackface style, perhaps the most important for creating a stage version of blackness would be dialect. Written examples suggest that blackface dialect developed over time. In songsters and broadsides from the 1820s and early 1830s, examples sometimes repeated stage versions of "Irish" or even "German" speech. Onstage the dialect would be subject to the talents of individual performers. Most gave their characters exaggerated "Southern" drawls. Some borrowed samples from the "Southwest dialect" of frontier humorists. Nearly all used malapropisms and creative word choices. As blackface grew in popularity, audiences soon expected performers to "sound black" by resorting to a standard version of dialect.[14]

Audiences also expected characteristic patterns of "black" behavior. One was a propensity toward violence. By the mid-1830s, violent imagery was a staple of blackface performance. Consider the song "Blue Tail Fly." While its most well-known chorus is the triple repetition of the line "Jimmy crack-corn and I don't care," followed by "My massa's gone away," another had performers singing "Heater, creater, nigger beater" three times, followed by "Scratch his eye wid a briar."[15] The song "Shin Bone Alley" featured the character "Clem de Weaver" taking to the streets with a cleaver in one hand, a musket in the other, shooting "a nigger," skinning him with the cleaver, then boiling his victim before selling his hide and tallow. The name of the song itself was a violent reference, pointing to the popular belief that clubbing African Americans on the head did them no harm, that in the supposed words of one police captain, "Cuffee's tender point was not the head, but the SHIN."[16]

On the surface, songs like these were little more than fantasies of racial violence. Yet they were complicated by blackface's ventriloquism effect. One of the best and thus most disturbing examples was J. W. Sweeney's "Whar Did You Cum From." The song's first verse, along with its chorus, offered white audiences a fantasy of doing violence to African Americans:

> Some folks say a nigger won't steal,
> But I cotch one in my corn field,
> So I asked him about dat corn an' he call me a liar,
> So I up wid my foot and I kick him in de fire.
>> Oh, whar did you cum from, knock a nigger down?
>> Whar did you cum from, knock a nigger down.

The second verse established the singer's "blackness," combining Sweeney's burnt-cork make-up and his mastery of blackface dialect with the symbols of the banjo, the slave dance, and the home in Virginia:

> I cum from ole Wirginny one bery fine day,
> De riber was froze and I skate all de way,
> I hab de banjo under my arm playin' did tune,
> Dat de niggas used to dance by de light ob de moon.
>   Oh, whar did you cum from, knock a nigger down?
>   Whar did you cum from, knock a nigger down.[17]

In this song, as in many others like it, the white fantasy—the urge to "knock a nigger down," as Sweeney put it—was expressed by a black character in a standardized black dialect. As perceived by the audience, the violence was black on black, a characteristic of African American nature.

The result transformed white fantasy into black nature. This same transformation can be seen in another theme of early blackface, the fight between black rivals. One example was "Coal Black Rose." Performed as an entr'act as early as 1828 and later made famous by "Buffo" Dixon, the original song told the story of a rivalry between "Sambo" and "Cuffee" for Rose's affections.[18] By the early 1830s, the song had evolved into a full skit, with fight scenes between the characters along with a transvestite performance of Rose as the "Negro Wench." In 1833, Thomas Rice developed the song into the "first Ethiopian Opera," *Oh Hush!, or, The Virginny Cupids!* Rice fleshed out the characters: Cuff became an honest bootblack; Sambo was another bootblack who, after winning a lottery, began to put on airs by pretending to read. Rose became a fickle wench who preferred Sambo's pretense to Cuff's authentic blackness. The final scene was the stuff of comedy-theater chaos: with a rousing fistfight between Sambo and Cuff, with a nice pratfall as Rose hit Cuff on the head with a frying pan, and finally with Cuff rising behind the dancing Sambo and Rose and smashing his rival's head with a fiddle.[19] The skit ended with Cuff standing over the bodies of an apparently dead Sambo and a fainted Rose, his arms raised in victory.

Here again was the genre's constantly repeated message: the triumph of the real thing over the fake, the violent vindication of Cuffee's authenticity over Sambo's pretense. As Cuff loomed over Rose, audiences may have grasped a hint of another "black" characteristic, a freely expressed and threatening sexuality. From its origins, blackface involved a bodily performance: in dances filled with pelvic thrusts, in the splayed legs of seated performers, in the positioning of banjos as phallic objects.

Some of the sexual imagery would focus on the "Negro Wench." The song "Lubly Fan Will You Cum Out To Night" offered an early version of the character. Originally developed by the blackface performer "Cool White," the song referred to "Lubly Fan" as a "pretty girl." But in a following verse, the singer revealed that the character had enormous feet, one of the period's most often-cited markers of female ugliness. In a later verse, Cool White focused on a different feature:

> Her lips are like de oyster plant,
> I try to kiss dem but I cant,
> Dey am so berry large.
>> Den lubly Fan will you cum out to night,
>> An dance by de lite ob de moon.[20]

As songs like these evolved into skits, they featured transvestite performances: one performer in the role of the black male, singing the attributes of the wench, another, in drag, performing a dance as the female character.

Yet blackface was primarily about male sexuality. The key sex symbol was the male character, the countless examples of black authenticity that followed Jim Crow. The character dominated the stage as a kind of phallus incarnate, as a jumping, dancing, and thrusting model of masculine energy. He often appeared as the libidinous black male, singing his yearnings for "Lilly White" or "Sally Snow." These were standard wench characters. At the same time, their names implied the threat of interracial sex, the supposed white nightmare of racial "amalgamation" or "miscegenation." The song "A Little More Cider" made the erotic threat explicit. While singing longingly of "Miss Snow Flake," the cider-drinking character declared, "I love de white gall and de black." Elsewhere, blackface songs contained a rich vein of phallic imagery. In the song "That Gal in Blue," the male character sang of his attraction to a "pretty yaller girl," saying that whenever his "horse" saw her, it immediately began to "rear," "jump," and "pitch."[21]

Nowhere was the phallic connection more explicit than in the song "Long Tail Blue." In an early verse, the song's title seems to refer to an article of the character's apparel:

> Some niggers they have but one coat,
> But I, you see, got two;
> I wears a jacket all the week,
> And a Sunday my long tail blue.

But as it continued, the meaning of the term changed. The character sang of meeting Jim Crow along with his wench Sue. She dropped her erstwhile

LONG TAIL BLUE.

I'VE just drop'd in to see you all,
  And ax you how you do;
I'll sing you a song, it's not very long,
  It's about my long tail blue.

CHORUS.
  Just look at my long tail blue,
    O, how do you like my blue,
  I'll sing you a song, it's not very long,
    It's about my long tail blue.

Some niggers they have but one coat,
  But I, you see, got two;
I wears a jacket all the week,
  And a Sunday my long tail blue.
      Just look, &c.

I stop'd some time at Virginia Springs,
  And at Baltimore City too;
But I guess I made the niggers squat,
  When they saw my long tail blue.
      Just look, &c.

I went to the City of Washington,
  To see what I could do;
I stop'd at one of Jackon's levees,
  And swung my long tail blue.
      Just look, &c.

Old Jackson, he came up to me,
  Said he, Sir, how do you do;
He treated me with some champagne,
  To swing my long tail blue.
      Just look, &c.

I thought it time then to be off,
  Pray stop a day or two;
So he offered me a handsome price,
  For a pattern of my long tail blue.
      Just look, &c.

So coming off soon after that,
  A thinking of my Sue;
Major Downing followed me out,
  To speak with my long tail blue.
      Just look, &c.

The Gineral's dander's up, I hear,
  Come, I will go with you,
And like all natur, stop his wrath,
  When I show my long tail blue.
      Just look, &c.

The Cabinet cried out in grief,
  O-Lord, what shall we do;
This fellow beats the Major's pen,
  With the swing of his long tail blue.
      Just look, &c.

Jim Crow was courting a brown gal,
  The white folks called her Sue;
But I guess she let the nigger drop,
  When she see my long tail blue.
      Just look, &c.

I went to a ball the other night,
  And Jim Crow was there with Sue;
I walk'd and talk'd and cut him out,
  And swung my long tail blue.
      Just look, &c.

Jim Crow got mad and swore he'd fight,
  With sword and pistol too;
But I guess I back'd the nigger out,
  When he saw my long tail blue.
      Just look, &c.

As I was going up Ridgway's lane,
  Walking home with Sue;
The watchman came and took me up,
  And he ruin'd my long tail blue.
      Just look, &c.

I took it into a tailor's shop,
  To see what he could do;
He took a needle and some thread,
  And sew'd my long tail blue.
      Just look, &c.

Now all you chaps that wants a wife,
  And don't know what to do;
Just look at me and I'll show you how
  To swing your long tail blue.
      Just look, &c.

The Boston girls are very nice,
  And very pretty too;
I guess they'd like this chap for a beau,
  And the swing of his long tail blue.
      Just look, &c.

FIGURE 6.1. Long Tail Blue, a representation of black sexuality. One of the most popular characters of early blackface, "Long Tail Blue" represented both the dandified free black of the Northeast along with the blackface characteristic of freely expressed sexual energy. The song's phallic imagery would have been hard to miss, particularly when the character informed his audience of young, working-class white men that he would "show" them how to get a wife by swinging their "long tail blue." To see this sort of thing as a simple expression of race hatred would miss the sense of it entirely. Sheet-music cover: *Long Tail Blue*. [New York]: T. Birch, n.d. Courtesy of American Antiquarian Society.

paramour, he declared, "when she see my long tail blue." At this point audiences would have expected the story of a fight between rivals. But size mattered on the blackface stage, and Crow backed down, the singer claimed, "when he saw my long tail blue." Finally, the singer made the metaphor clear in an aside to the audience:

> Now all you chaps that wants a wife,
> And don't know what to do;
> Just look at me and I'll show you how,
> To swing your long tail blue.[22]

The audience of young white men, who moments before may have been singing of their desire to "knock a nigger down," would have gone wild with feigned shock and delighted laughter. The American past is filled with examples of racist hatred. The Jacksonian era in particular was marked by racially motivated violence and dismissive stereotypes.[23] Yet this understanding of how racism works says little about the content of early blackface. To look at a theatrical act in which a black character informs an audience of young white males that he will show them how to get a wife by swinging their "long tail blue" and call it a dismissive stereotype or a hate crime fails to explain the meaning or sense of the expression.

One might call "Long Tail Blue" an example of comedy. One might call it an example of contained license, an expression allowed only the comical black of the blackface stage. In the end, the term that comes closest to fitting the expression might be love. Perhaps the strangest thing about it was that this was a type of love that could precede a beating or a lynching.

Love and Destruction

According to popular understandings, blackface minstrelsy is easy to understand, its images easy to dismiss as the hostile stereotypes of a bygone past. The genre's most well-known characters are those of contented slaves, the various "Mammies," "Aunties," and "Uncles" of literature, film, and imagined South. Early blackface performers, to the contrary, focused much of their attention on a lesser-known image: the Northern free African American. Here were figures like Jim Crow and his seemingly countless descendants. These characters were ex-slaves, if they had been slaves at all. In many ways, they were symbols of pure freedom, portrayed by their performers as free from artifice, uplift, or order itself. They could be rebellious in style and expression, free from responsibility, free of any fear of giving offense. They had a type of freedom associated with being at the rock bottom of society. From the 1830s into the early 1840s, they would dominate blackface. They would be celebrated and loved, as long as they remained models of genuine selfhood, as long as they remained lowly, at the bottom of society, and always singing and dancing.

To many in the audience, the thrill of blackface lay in its expression of rebellion and freedom. Blackface characters could say anything. They could even express criticisms of slavery. In the song "Jim Crow in London," Thomas Rice's character bragged that he jumped "aboard a big ship, An cum across de sea, And landed in ole England, Whar de nigger am free." The character "Gumbo Chaff" was more direct in his hostility to the institution. After singing of his cruel treatment and desire to escape, he cursed his master to the devil:

> Den my ole massa die on de lebenteenth ob April,
> So I put him in de troff we cotch de sugar maple;
> I dig'd a big hole, rite upon de lebel,
> An I verily believe that he gwoin to the debil.
>   For you all do know,
>   He used to lite upon me so,
>   Now he got to tote de wood and fire down below.[24]

Similar antislavery statements and subtexts appeared in a variety of blackface songs. One version of the song "Walk Jaw Bone" featured an ex-slave singing about being caught for stealing corn. As punishment, his master literally crucified him, nailing him to a cross and "putting him up as a scarecrow." Terrified when a large eagle approached, the character sang his relief when the bird winked and cried, "I'se de bird ob de free, And won't eat the meat ob slavery." Other characters sang of outwitting their masters, returning to free their loved ones, and even fighting slave traders and patrols.[25] Published in 1844, the song "Lucy Neal" contained nearly all these themes along with a clear antislavery message:

> Oh! dars de wite man comin,
> To tear you from my side;
> Stan back! You white slave dealer
> She is my betrothed bride
> De poor nigger's fate is hard,
> De white man's heart is stone,
> Dey part poor nigga from his wife,
> An brake up dare happy home.[26]

Through these expressions, white performers were able to declare a common bond between themselves and African Americans. "I used to sit with them in front of their cabins," declared Ben Cotton, a leading performer of "plantation darkies." Cotton made what would become a typical claim: he was the "first white man they had seen who sang as they did." And so, he added, "we were brothers for the time being and were perfectly happy."[27] Along with their audiences of white former artisans and common workingmen, performers like Cotton loved their black folk.

They loved them as long as they stayed true to their natures. The problem came when they did not; when, like Zip Coon, they attempted to take on elements of whiteness. Other dandies would follow Zip Coon on the stage, from "Dandy Jim" to "Deacon Snowball" to the "Dandy Broadway Swell." The characters conveyed a double message: first, they attacked the concept of uplift itself; second, they made uplift a white privilege, denying it as a possibility for African Americans. On the blackface stage, nothing corrupted a character's authenticity faster than a bit of "ejumcation." And nothing, as countless songs and acts like "Larned Nigger" demonstrated, was more foreign to the stage version of black nature. Here, the character "Professor Chalk" gave audiences a list of his "larned" subjects along with his understanding of their meanings:

> Just look, Innography de's first, / Dat's what dey rise to lay de dust;
> De study of Globes, is living on trust / And getting all you can.
> Astronomy will tell you how / To play upon de old banjo,
> And Music is de way to go / Upon de safest plan.
> Arithmetic's de way to paint, / And Drawing to study de moon;
> Chronology is what dey larns / to make de silver spoon;
> And Navigation's de way to make / De mint julep, and de old hoe cake,
> Aint I de regular wide awake / Old Larned Nigger Man?[28]

In the mid-1830s, performances of this sort began to lay the foundations for one of the genre's most popular comic features, the "stump speech." In the stump speech, performers focused on black efforts to make political commentary, recite a Shakespeare soliloquy, or give a lecture on an intellectual trend. The effort would again reveal the speaker's nature, for the speech was always composed of malapropisms and gaffes. Or it descended into nonsense. "Transcendentalism," one character proclaimed in a typical example, "is dat spiritual cognosnence ob psychological irrefragibility, connected wid conscientient ademption ob incolumbient spirituality and etherialized connection." Within a few years, the stump speech would be the genre's main vehicle for comedy. "Feller Citizens," shouted the character Jim Brown in what would become a standard introduction to the performance, "I hab de super infelicity ob undressing a few words ob millumtary tic tacs to your magnanimously insignificant and superbly extinguished corpse."[29]

These performances reveal one of the hallmarks of an emerging working-class culture: the rejection of middle-class values of uplift and polite sociability. By the 1840s, middle-class standards of respectable behavior extolled self-control and scolded violence. They placed an emphasis on controlling bodily functions or relegating them to private spaces, on chewing with the mouth closed, on modulating the voice. Middle-class values placed an enormous emphasis on education, on learning polite behavior through etiquette guides, on the acquisition of conversational ability and professional skill through institutional teaching and book-learning. They stressed moral reform, humanitarian sensibility, and a keen sense of social responsibility.

Blackface rejected all of these standards. According to the genre's messages, all covered one's true character with a layer of artifice; all blunted the individual with a culture of feminization.[30] Against this artificial character, blackface offered an identity rooted in genuine blackness, a character that was rowdy, vigorous, and masculine. While these standards placed increasing emphasis on order, education, and sensitive humanitarianism, blackface characters offered a free embrace of vernacular expression, chaos, and violence. Middle-class culture stressed respectability and repression. In blackface, the main characteristic of genuine blackness was a freedom from social convention, a limitless freedom to give in to all bodily appetites.

This included freedom from work. Though initially a working-class entertainment, blackface contained no references to artisan republicanism, nothing on the dignity of trades or the divinity of the mechanic arts. It did contain numerous references to markets and consumption. Of the many versions of Jim Crow during the 1830s and 1840s, not one referred to him as having a trade. Unfettered from work, he was free to embrace leisure, appetite, and desire; free to fully embrace the marketplace. One version made the connection explicit:

> I've been to Philadelphia, New York, and Baltimore,
> But when I got to Boston, it beat all I'd seen before.
>> Dey talk ob de Philadelphia markets, an' de New York markets
>> loud,
>> But in de market, here in Boston, will be seen among de crowd.
> No matter what is wantin', in the market you can buy,
> From a quarter of an ox, down to a punkin pie.[31]

The character Jim Brown was also at home in the marketplace. Yet he had once had a trade. He was born, he sang, "in Massachusetts, close to Nashua," where he "work'd 'pon de farm for two shillings a day." He left this employment for

Boston's Quincy Market, where he became a leader of the musical band. His task was that of the old market-stall drummer: playing music, attracting customers, and stoking their fevers of purchase.[32]

If blackface characters rarely worked, they regularly engaged in singing, dancing, and consuming. Numerous black dandies were able to collect and display fine clothing, lace sleeves, and elegant overcoats. Practically all had limitless desires: for luxuries, wenches, and food, or as one of the male characters in the song "Coal Black Rose" had it: for "possum fat, and hominy, and sometimes rice, cow heel, an sugar cane, an ebry ting nice." In one of the earliest songs, the character Sambo urged his "broders" to leave "buckra-land" for Haiti, where, as he put it, "we lib so fine, wid our coach and hors-e, / An ebry time we dine, hab one, two, tree, four cours-e." The genre would soon abound in images of grotesque orality. The blackface stage would be filled with eating contests and mouths "cramful" of food, with characters competing to see who could stuff the greatest number of objects into their mouths.[33]

Blackface performers may have meant these expressions as parodies, as satires of a supposed African American lack of self-control. They may have meant them as social criticisms of the market revolution along with the general population's growing obsession with material possession.[34] At the same time, the endless appetite of blackface characters presented a timely alternative to the virtuous artisan, a character rooted in limitless consumption as opposed to producer republicanism. There can be little doubt that an emerging working class loved the authentic blacks of the blackface stage. They loved them, that is, as long as they stayed true to their natures: poor and degraded yet happily singing, dancing, fighting, and consuming.

The best evidence for this love would be a violent defense of this version of blackness against the enemies who would destroy it. One of these enemies was a certain population of Northern African Americans: the members of black churches, the writers and readers of the period's black newspapers, the participants in black associations of self-help and benevolence. Some were like Samuel Cornish, committed to a culture of respectability, to "colored" reading rooms and temperance clubs. Others were like David Walker, more militant in their belief in uplift. In the language of blackface, these were the blacks of "nigger meetings" and "bobalition 'sieties." They were corrupted by whiteness, false to their natures. As another version of Jim Crow had it, they were foreign to the genuine black of the blackface stage, something beyond his understanding:

> In New York I went to a Nigger Meeting,
> It was on a Sunday Night,

FIGURE 6.2. A pantheon of blackface characters. Published in 1837, the sheet-music cover for the "The Crow Quadrilles" is remarkable for its gathering into one place many of the most popular characters of early blackface. Here, the iconic Jim Crow appears at the center of the page, while the lower left and right are occupied by two "dandy darkies," the uplift-corrupted Zip Coon and the phallic Long Tail Blue. The other characters include Jim Along Josey, Jim Brown, Sambo, Cuffee, Coal Black Rose, and Gumbo Chaff. Sheet-music cover: *The Crow Quadrilles*. Philadelphia: John F. Nunns, 70 South 3rd Street, 1837. Courtesy of American Antiquarian Society.

> To see ole broder Clem,
>   What dey say can read and write.
>   Wheel about and turn about an' do jis so,
>   An' ebery time I turn about I jump Jim Crow.[35]

Even as "Jim Crow" jumped and shuffled on the Bowery stage, another threat moved into the heart of the Five Points. In 1832, Thomas Hamblin leased his Chatham Street Theatre, once a site of nightly blackface fare, to a group of evangelical reformers. Nominally under the Pastorate of Charles Finney, perhaps the best-known orator of the Second Great Awakening, and funded by the merchant–abolitionist brothers Arthur and Lewis Tappan, the reformers transformed the theater into the Chatham Street Chapel. The chapel became the headquarters of the Five Points Mission. None of this generated much attention. The trouble started when the chapel became a meeting place for black and white abolitionists.[36]

Immediately, a coalition of voices expressed outrage over the radicals in their midst. One voice would come from the city's elite, the old "gentlemen of property and standing" of New York's propertied classes. Another would come from the city's rising business class, the old master artisans who still dominated the General Trades Societies but who in many cases now ran small factories. A third would come from the popular press, from newspapers such as the *New York Courier and Enquirer* and the city's most popular penny paper, the *New York Herald*. According to the abolition press, the editor of the *Courier and Enquirer*, James Watson Webb, represented the proslavery wing of the Democratic Party. He was also the "principal instigator" of violence against the city's abolitionists. The *Herald*'s editor, James Gordon Bennett, described the nation's abolitionists as "a few thousand crazy-headed blockheads." For Bennett, as for Webb, the city's abolitionists were such a threat to social harmony that "legal" means of removing them would have to be "thrown aside as too slow."[37]

A final voice in this coalition would be that of the blackface stage and its audience. Here was the blackface community that provided cover for the elite among the anti-abolition crowd. In joining the anti-abolitionist ranks, members of an emerging working class positioned themselves at the intersection of artisan republicanism, patriotism, and blackface. Many of the common workers of the Five Points still believed in a culture of artisan virtue. Most adhered to an ideal of work as connected to whiteness, dignity, and masculine independence. And so they tended to align themselves with their old masters, with the very people most responsible for their degradation. The language of patriotism, meanwhile, would associate abolition with England, which in the year before the 1834 riot banned slavery from the empire and issued several

stinging criticisms of America for maintaining the institution. Thus, abolition would be deemed a foreign or "anti-American" cause.

The imagery of blackface would further align an emerging working class
with a mercantile elite and the proslavery wing of the Democratic Party. It
would provide both a musical backdrop and a cultural cover for what one
historian calls a "strange political marriage," a coalition, that is, between the
common republicans of the North and the slaveholding elite of the South.
Finally, blackface would help identify the common enemy: Northern, free African Americans along with the other busybodies, dandies, and anti-slavery
and thus *anti-American* radicals of the rising middle class.[38]

This coalition of New York's urban elite, hostile press, and common workers would do their best to make the early years of the Five Points Mission as
miserable as possible. In the mission's first year, a mob of workingmen, spurred
by the press and led by several in the city's elite, broke up an abolitionist meeting and threatened the life of Arthur Tappan. On July 4, 1834, an "Independence
Day" mob attacked the chapel, again dispersing an antislavery lecture. Afterward, according to the *New York Sun*, the mob retired to City Hall Park, "to act
out their patriotism in knocking down the blacks."

The largest outbreak of violence came a few days later. On the evening of
July 9, a mob broke into the Chatham Street Chapel, vandalized it, engaged in
a mock "bobolition meeting," and sang a rousing version of Jim Crow. Then
the men split up. Some went across town to the fashionable address of 40 Rose
Street, the home of Lewis Tappan. They broke into the house and smashed
furniture, paintings, and whatever else they could break. Others left the chapel and made their way to the Bowery Theatre, where a benefit performance
was going on for George Farren, the theater's English stage manager.[39]

When the mob arrived at the Bowery Theatre, its leaders quickly made
their intentions known. They were outraged at Farren, for Farren was an Englishman and thus possibly an abolitionist. They were enraged at the management of the Bowery Theatre, for employing an anti-American abolitionist
and scheduling a traditional benefit to pay him. And finally, they were there to
bust up the place. In the midst of these threatening pronouncements, Thomas
Hamblin himself appeared on the stage. The Bowery's owner had been courting working-class audiences for years. He knew how to calm a mob. He came
out from the wings energetically waving two small American flags. He then
called for the house band to strike up some music for a patriotic sing-along.
The band played "Yankee Doodle" and "Zip Coon."

The twinning of patriotism and racism saved the Bowery Theatre. It also
fired up the crowd. Emerging from the theater, its members went into the night
to engage in a full-scale race riot, a riot referred to by the city papers as the

worst in the city's history. During four days and nights, crowds of Sixth Ward workingmen destroyed African American houses, businesses, and churches. In the Five Points, a mob estimated at some three thousand pulled down the "African School" on Orange Street. There too the riot saw its high point, as near midnight on July 11, a crowd numbering in "some thousands" convened on Centre Street. For the next two hours—with "fiend-like destruction," claimed the *Liberator*—the mob destroyed the neighborhood's leading black institution, the Saint Philip's African Episcopal Church.[40]

The rioters went after people as well as property. On the same night as the destruction of Saint Philip's, declared a reporter with the city paper *Journal of Commerce*, "several colored men in going home from their places of employment down town, fell into the hands of the rioters, and were shamefully beaten." The violence soon spilled into other parts of the city, to better neighborhoods around Broadway, Rose Street, and the merchants' row of Pearl Street. Here, the mob had to fight the "Coppers" as they vandalized the property of white abolitionists. In the Five Points, they were left to do all the damage they wanted. "The vengeance of the mob appeared to be directed entirely against the blacks," declared a report in the *Liberator*, adding that "whenever a colored person appeared, it was a signal of combat, fight and riot."[41]

Through the apparent chaos, the rioters chose their targets carefully. The poorest among the black population of the Five Points, those who lived in the tenements of "Cow Bay," were left almost completely untouched. Whites living in the neighborhood's many integrated blocks were directed to place candles or lanterns in their windows, marking them as off limits to the attackers. The city's newspapers picked up on the order, saying "the mob made it a rule that whenever a house was not illuminated by candles, they would dash in the windows." And so, during the riot, many houses "presented a brilliant appearance." They too were largely unscathed. The beatings, arson, and destruction centered on the bodies and the property of the area's most successful black population.[42]

If Jim Crow announced the beginning of the Five Points Riot, Dinah Crow brought it to a close, memorializing it for the neighborhood's white working-class residents. The blackface song "Dinah Crow's Abolition" summed up the event: the common white men of the Points were protecting individuals from corruption and ruination. Indeed, the song suggests that the period's rhetoric of miscegenation had two meanings. Much of this rhetoric focused on protecting the imagined "purity" of white women from the advances of a sexually potent black male. The Chatham Street abolitionists had to be expelled from the Points, declared the lyrics in characteristic dialect, for they were promoters of interracial marriage and procreation:

> Dey want to make de white gal, / Marry to de niggar,
> And dat jes' what I call, / Goin' de whole figgar.
> I heard dey gib a premium, / I tink about a guinea,
> For ebery couple what do hab, / A real brown pick-en-ninney.[43]

At the same time, the song expressed a desire to protect the earthiness of black people, to guard genuine blackness from being uplifted and ruined by middle-class reformers. As the lyrics explained, the riot was "de fault" of the "bobolitionists, de niggars, warn't to blame." In its concluding verse, the song offered a friendly warning from blackface performers and audiences, as men who understood blackness, to their black brothers:

> An now my broder darkeys, / Just please to keep your station,
> Keep clear ob de white folks, / An de devilish bobolition.
> But if we don't behave ourselves, / An mingle wid de white,
> If we got a kick on the shin, / I'm sure it sarves us right.[44]

The New York City race riot of 1834 was both permeated with blackface and a logical result of the genre's depiction of a natural and expressive black style. Both the riot and the rise of blackface reveal a major shift in the history of American racial oppression. Increasingly, this oppression would be rooted in love, articulated in a popular culture that stressed a white affinity for black song, dance, self-expression, and joyfully shameless consumption of material goods. Much like the common men who made up the audience for early blackface entertainments, generations of white Americans would come to love their black folk; provided, that is, they remained true to their authentic selves.

Blackface Triumphant

In 1843, according to some experts, blackface reached the zenith of its authentic style with one performer, one group, and one song. The performer was Dan Decatur Emmett; the group was Emmett's Virginia Minstrels; the song was Emmett's "Old Dan Tucker." Like many early blackface performers, Emmett was a Northerner with ties to artisan culture. He was born in Mount Vernon, Ohio, in 1815, the son of a village blacksmith. He was of Irish descent but not a recent immigrant, his grandfather having arrived in America before the Revolution. At age eighteen he left Mount Vernon for Cincinnati, where he apprenticed as a printer. Within a year he abandoned his trade, first to join the army where he played drum and fife in an army band, later to join the circus. He toured six years with Spalding's North American Circus, working as a clown, a banjo player, and a blackface performer.[45]

His ultimate goal was the theater district of New York's Sixth Ward. He would make it in 1842, when he began performing at Manhattan's Franklin Theatre. By January 1843, Emmett was rehearsing with three other musicians: William Whitlock, a blackface performer who regularly starred in the entr'acts at Barnum's American Museum; Dick Pelham, who was well known as part of a show called "Negro Peculiarities, Dances, and Extravaganzas"; and Frank Brower, who had gained a reputation as one of the period's best blackface dancers. Soon the quartet was playing at the Bowery's Branch Hotel, with Emmett on fiddle, Whitlock on banjo, Pelham playing tambourine, and Brower rattling the bones castanets. At some point in January, they crossed the street to the Bowery Theatre, to "charivari," as they put it, the theater's owner and convince him to put them on the bill. The strategy worked. On February 6, 1843, they went on the Bowery stage as "The Virginia Minstrels."[46]

The Virginia Minstrels would herald several changes in blackface. In their name and broadsides, they added the term "minstrels" or "minstrelsy" to the genre. From this point, blackface would be blackface minstrelsy. They also added superior musicianship, along with an increasing stress on group performance. In their songs they stuck to the genre's high-energy and masculine style. This would certainly be the case in the group's most famous song, "Old Dan Tucker." The title character of the song was a free Northern black, an urban brawler, an exemplar of unfettered self-expression.[47] In the song's verses, Tucker knocked his rivals out of line for supper, threatened the audience with a straight razor, got drunk, and made a stump speech. The tune of the song, a fast Irish jig with stomping rhythm, would be among the most raucous of the genre's history.

Within a year the song was a sheet-music best-seller. Over the next several decades, it would be picked up by a host of "blackface minstrel" groups and revised into countless versions. In one, the song's title character would be transformed into "Old Daniel Connell," the famed Irish republican and abolitionist. The song parodied Connell's antislavery stance and offered a loyalty test for Irish Americans: they would have to choose between Ireland and America, between allegiance to their homeland's most famous reformer or the Yankee style of patriotic deference to the slaveholding elite. Other versions of the song offered satires of middle-class "fashionable" music. Several pictured the black Dan Tucker as a competitor in a "fiddlin'" contest, squaring off against a "violin" virtuoso. In the 1840s, Tucker fiddled against the Norwegian and Italian violin masters Ole Bull and Niccolo Paganini. The self-taught blackface character always "took the shine off" the favorite of the parlor set.[48]

Even as blackface widened its audience in the 1840s, it continued to express a working-class style. It still embodied the working man's anger and

FIGURE 6.3. The zenith of early blackface. With the appearance of Dan Emmett's Virginia Minstrels in 1843, blackface reached what critics of the time called its most authentic expression of genuine blackness. It also became blackface minstrelsy, more respectable, with better musicianship and songwriting, and with increasing numbers of middle-class clerks in the audience. As this illustration suggests, the genre would maintain much of its energy, and the characters would continue to represent lowly desires. Yet within a few years, the songs of Stephen Foster would elevate blackface to new heights and minstrelsy would become America's gift to the world. Sheet-music cover: *Old Dan Emmitt's* [*sic*] *Original Banjo Melodies*. Boston: Keith's Music Publishing House, 67 & 69 Court Street, 1844. Courtesy of American Antiquarian Society.

class resentment, his hatred of a rising population of brain workers and pretentious dandies, his rejection of artifice, refinement, and education. Nowhere would this be more apparent than in one of the great products of blackface, the theatrical character of the "Bowery B'hoy." Pronounced "buh-hoy" and meaning something akin to a "young rowdy," the term dated to the early 1830s. In 1848, the character would become a fixture of urban popular culture with the production of Benjamin Baker's play *A Glance at New York* and the appearance of its hero, "Mose."

Mose was the representative b'hoy. He lived, of course, in the rowdy Sixth Ward, where he was a regular along the Bowery and the Five Points. He was a worker, though his work was abstract; what he actually did for a living was probably not clear to his audience. He may have been a journeyman butcher. He was definitely a volunteer fireman, for this position made him typical of the rough-and-ready young types of urban America. Finally, he was something of a dandy, duding himself up in a worker version of finery in order to pronounce his equality with the city's aristocrats. He wore his hair heavily oiled and had soaplocked sideburns. He sported a black stovepipe, a top hat, a silk vest, and a long frock coat with a flower in the lapel.[49]

Yet Mose was the stark opposite of the middle-class clerk. Opening on February 15, 1848, at the Olympic Theatre on Broadway, Baker's play featured the actor Frank Chanfrau in the lead role. A native of the Five Points, Chanfrau knew how to imbue the character with an aura of masculine authenticity. Over the years and through a variety of sequels, he added his own touches: a heavy pea-jacket, a work shirt of bright red cotton, and a "long-nine" cigar, a clear symbol of sexual potency that Mose clenched between his teeth at the fully erect angle of forty-five degrees. He gave voice to Mose's earthy phrases, from his favorite adjective "gallus," meaning good or swell, to "muss," his term for a fight, to "foo-foos," his epithet for middle-class visitors to the Points.

Sixth Ward crowds loved Chanfrau's performance. According to one approving critic, his character was marked by "boisterous roughness" and "rude manners." These attributes made him "far superior" to the city's middle-class clerks; or, as the critic put it, "the shallow-pated, milk-hearted sucklings of foppery and fashion." The character had no use for book-learning. He spent his time in the "bar-room and the engine house," where he was "always on the look-out for a fire, a fight or a frolic and seldom long without one or the other."[50] He was ardently patriotic. He believed in the superiority of native-born white Americans. He loved a good blackface entertainment.

Mose made life seem happier in the Bowery, more attuned with nature, more masculine and real. "I'm bilin' over for a rousin' good fight with someone, somewhere," he exclaimed in a typical crowing soliloquy, adding, "if I don't have a muss soon, I'll spile." The effect could be seen in *A Glance at New York in 1848*. In one of the play's scenes, Mose related the story of arriving at a burning building with his fire-gang to find a mother crying and a baby trapped in the flames. In his response, audiences would have seen and heard a white character re-masculinized with blackface style. Here was a young man with a dash of street attitude, a hint of blackface dialect, and a heart of gold. "What!" Mose declared:

> I turned my cap hindside afore, and buttoned my old fire coat, and I went in and fetched out dat baby. I never forgot dat woman's countenance wen I handed de baby to her. She fell down on her knees and blessed me. Ever since dat time I've had a great partiality for little babies. The fire-boys may be a little rough outside, but they're all right here. (Touches breast) It never shall be said dat one of de New York boys deserted a baby in distress.[51]

With these expressions, the young artisan had come out of the crisis of the early 1830s as the working-class male. The American worker, in turn, was unquestioningly white, masculine, and authentic. The result was an enormously powerful working-class culture, a style of authentic selfhood that simultaneously excluded women and African Americans from the category of worker while also making middle-class individuals, particularly young men, feel false, feminized, and weak.[52]

Things could not stay this way. The young entrepreneurs and aggressive merchants of the middle class were not about to let their working-class opposites have a monopoly on authentic masculinity. By the 1840s and 1850s, a host of middle-class individuals began frantically reaching across the class divide, looking to head off a potential conflict that an imagined bourgeois dandy, dulled by years of brain work and parlor etiquette, would certainly lose. Writers like George Lippard and Ned Buntline proclaimed themselves one with their working-class "brothers," pioneering urban novels that debunked middle-class foppery while extolling the virtues of common laborers. Walt Whitman made a career out of his rebellion against bourgeois repression, remaking his identity from sensitive poet to authentic Bowery b'hoy.

In 1841 the novelist Charles Dickens, the favorite of middle-class readers throughout the English-speaking world, visited America for a five-month tour, gathering material for a travelogue and commentary he would later publish under the title *American Notes*. During his stay in New York, Dickens crossed the American class divide, venturing from the well-lit spaces of bourgeois Broadway into the working-class haunts of the Five Points. The neighborhood, as he would portray it, was a place of dirt and earthy charm. He focused much of his attention on the antics of "Juba," the African American tap dancer who performed nightly at Almack's Saloon. Soon, growing numbers of middle-class tourists were following Dickens's lead. Many visited the Five Points accompanied by police escorts, looking for Juba, clucking at the area's scenes of poverty and vice, marveling at its colorful energy. Dickens had given birth to the middle-class pastime of slumming.[53]

Middle-class anxieties about threats from below reached their peak at the midpoint of the nineteenth century. In 1848, a series of democratic, worker-led revolutions swept Europe. Some observers, particularly in the aristocratic South, were terrified. What was to stop something similar from happening in the United States? Indeed, an upwelling from below seemed possible. For the year 1849 suffused the nation with the rowdy style of the Bowery. It was the year of the great bare-knuckle boxing match pitting "Yankee" Sullivan against Tom Hyer, a brawl that according to a New York paper caught the fancy of "the rich and the poor, the high and the low."

It was the year of the Astor Place Riot. This event, which began with a harmless dispute over acting styles, seemed to herald an all-out class war. On one side of the dispute stood the American Edwin Forrest, the muscular thespian whose over-the-top melodramatic style made him the favorite of common audiences. On the other was the Englishman Charles McCready, whose newer and more realistic style of acting made him the preference of the "fashionables" among the middle class. Forrest based his style on "showing the work," on demonstrating—with large movements and booming voice—that he was a grand thespian. McCready's style was based on convincing audiences that he was not acting, that his characters were real. Forrest's fans believed their man's style was true and honest. Those in the McCready camp saw him as vulgar and old-fashioned.

In the spring of 1849, the dispute turned serious. Forrest showed up at a McCready performance and hissed the British actor; McCready's fans responded with letters to the newspapers, admonishing the American for his loutish behavior. Then it turned violent. On the evening of May 10, some 10,000 of Forrest's supporters attacked McCready's theatrical home base, Manhattan's Astor Place Opera House. By the time the police had been overwhelmed, the militia called out, and the violence suppressed, the riot had resulted in twenty-three people killed and over one hundred wounded.[54]

It was the year of the California gold rush. Beginning in January 1849, tens of thousands of young men boarded ships, announced their hostility to foppish aristocrats and middle-class codes of repression, and sailed for the "New Eldorado." According to one account that caught the public imagination, they left singing an anthem set to a new blackface tune:

> I come from Salem City, / With my washbowl on my knee;
> I'm going to California, / The gold dust for to see.
> I'll scrape the mountains clean my boys, / I'll drain the rivers dry,
> A pocket full of rocks bring home, / So brothers, don't you cry!
> Oh, Californy! / That's the land for me,
> I'm going to Sacramento, / With my washbowl on my knee.[55]

Finally, the year marked the breakthrough for the tune's author, the young man who would become known as America's greatest songwriter: Stephen Collins Foster. Foster published "Oh Susanna!" in late 1848. In less than a year the song became the favorite of the "forty-niners." The embrace gave it instant cachet. The gold-seekers seemed the quintessential "b'hoys." Having left the women-folk behind at eastern docks, they were free of all influences that might be called feminine. Many actively compared themselves to Bowery b'hoys; they were on a manly adventure, liberated from the codes of the East.

And so they cut a swath of authentic vulgarity wherever they went. Along the way to California, they brought an "American energy" to Latin American ports of call, locking arms to roam the streets, bowling over the locals, looking for prostitutes, and leaving a trail of offenses. In California, they drank, gambled, fought, and dug for gold. They flocked to blackface shows. With Foster's "Oh Susanna!" as the event's dominant anthem, the gold rush elevated blackface into the musical theme for western expansion, "Manifest Destiny," and "Young America." The rush became in the words of more than one historian "the American 1848," an overturning of elite values heralded by a celebration of genuine working-class style.[56]

Yet it was hardly revolutionary. Northeastern gold-seekers, particularly those most likely to express themselves as genuine "b'hoys," were to a large extent middle-class types. In the early period of the rush, many were college educated; they tended to be clerks and merchants, men with solid connections and families. The costs of the adventure foreclosed it to the vast majority of urban workers. The prevailing wage of a dollar a day meant that a voyage to the gold regions required an investment of more than a year's wages. In effect, the forty-niners were slumming. At the height of the rush. a writer for the *New York Herald* caught the reality. The gold-seekers, he noted, were "educated, intelligent, civilized, and elevated men, of the best classes of society."[57]

Stephen Foster was typical of the type. Born on July 4, 1826, and raised in a well-off suburb of Pittsburgh, he lacked the junior-artisan past of Thomas Rice and Dan Emmett. His father was a merchant, a gentleman of standing who served as mayor of Allegany City, a member of the Pennsylvania Legislature, and a federal officer in the administration of James Buchanan. With the security of the well born, young Stephen could afford the time to pursue hobbies. One was an interest in acting. By age nine he was a member of a local "Thespian Society."

Another was music. As a teen, Foster wrote a string of unsuccessful ballads. By the end of these formative years, he had moved to Cincinnati, where he worked for his merchant brother as a counting-house clerk. He continued to put together a portfolio of songs. Finally, at the end of the 1840s, he found success, first with the soon-to-be blackface standard "Old Uncle Ned," then with the explosive popularity of "Oh Susanna!," then with a string of blackface hits that transformed the former clerk into the nation's premier songwriter.[58]

Foster's success established the style of blackface minstrelsy as it rose to a dominant position within American popular culture. Many of the earlier songs remained performance staples, songs like "Zip Coon," "Lubly Fan," and "De Boatman's Dance." The former clerk's songs retained their effervescence. The charm of "Camptown Races" lay in its syncopation of syllables to musical notes and percussive strikes, along with its catchy chorus of the nonsense syllables "doo dah." "Oh Susanna!" featured the genre's traditional trickster qualities, the blackface character's relentless energy along with his standard reversals of logic: according to the song, rain produced dry weather, sun caused freezing temperatures, and one could travel down the river via the telegraph.[59]

The expansion of blackface into the middle class did effect several changes. While never fully taming the genre, it added layers of meanings informed by middle-class tastes. For Foster, this seems to have been the goal. In a letter to Edwin Christy dated 1852, he wrote of being tempted to publish his blackface songs anonymously, "owing to the prejudice against them by some, which might injure my reputation as a writer of another style of music." On further thought, he decided to write the songs "without fear or shame." As he concluded: "I have done a great deal to build up a taste for Ethiopian songs among refined people by making the words suitable to their taste."[60] Christy would have agreed. By the 1850s, Christy's Minstrels would be the nation's most popular blackface group, in large part because Foster wrote songs expressly for them.

As a result of these efforts to play to the tastes of "refined people," Foster's songs offered a blending of the genre's original impulses with heavy doses of nostalgia, sentiment, and deep emotionalism. Musically the songs were slower, more pleasing in their melodies, with an emphasis on vocal harmonies. In song and performance there was a gradual backgrounding of the rebellious free black, an increasing turn to the character of the sentimental slave.

Foster's "Old Uncle Ned" reflected the shift. Here was a character that lived, worked, and died on the old plantation, a near family member whose loyalty to his "massa" earned him the patronizing endearment of "uncle" from his white folks. The ballad's mournful strains and clever juxtaposition of images undoubtedly humanized the character for some listeners. Uncle Ned was real enough to have grown old in slavery: he had lost the "wool" from his head along with his eyesight and most of his teeth. His fingers, "long like de cane in de brake," conjured images of arthritic pain won through years of hard toil. To be sure, he was only a slave, a "darkey," or even a "nigger" in some versions of the song. But he was a "good" slave, as its chorus declared, having "gone where de good darkeys go," having been tearfully missed by his beloved plantation master and mistress.

Foster's most successful blackface efforts followed the same sentimental themes. "Nelly Was a Lady" twinned middle-class conceptions of romantic love with the sentimentalization of death. The lyrics pictured a slave singing a love song to the corpse of his "dark Viginny bride." The wildly popular "Old Folks at Home" erased the difference between slave and ex-slave. Here, the character of the ex-slave sang a tuneful ballad, of his heart returning to the banks of the "Swanee River," of his continued longing for the "many happy days" and "old folks" of his former plantation.

Few images would have had more appeal to middle-class audiences. They too were experiencing the frustrating dislocations of the market revolution, the development of a world, albeit largely of their own creation, fraught with competition, deception, and fear of failure. Early blackface gave voice to working-class anger at this world, performing blackness as violent and rebellious. Foster's songs offered an outlet for middle-class anxieties. His version of blackness was noble and childlike, a deeply emotional symbol of communal yearnings. For Stephen Foster's middle-class audiences, "black song" offered a return to a simpler time; "being black" was like going home. For a time, at least, even as hostile a critic as Frederick Douglass began to see promise in the genre. In 1855, Douglass referred to Foster's songs and declared that African Americans had "allies in the Ethiopian songs."[61]

In the 1850s, blackface minstrelsy began its move from an association with vulgar working-class audiences to the center of American popular culture. Meanwhile, the number of performing groups continued to proliferate as the style became more standardized. The "minstrel show" took on its three-part format: an instrumental "Intro," followed by a kind of variety-show mixture of songs and skits called the "Olio." Here were many of the genre's staples: the slapstick fights between characters; the transvestite renditions of "negro

wenches"; the "darkey conversations" between the end-men "Tambo" and
"Bones"; and the interrogations of characters by a stiffly white "interlocutor"
that produced endless examples of "darkey wit." Finally, there was the third
part, the "Finale." Here, performers offered audiences a larger musical number, a spoof on a black ballroom dance, a "cake walk," or a "genuine plantation
scene."

There were efforts to tame the genre. In 1843, audiences at Boston's National Theatre flocked to performances of the play *Rosina Meadows*. Afterward
they could stay for the "Kentucky Minstrels," a tamed-down group of blackface performers that according to the theater's broadsides promised "pleasing
performances" of "Old Dan Tucker," "Dance de Boatman," and "Lucy Long."
In 1849, theatergoers in Worcester enjoyed a run by the "Campanologians" or
"Band of Swiss Bell Ringers." According to their broadsides, the group presented
an evening of "chaste, select & fashionable" entertainment, ringing out "The
Baden Baden Polka," "The Blue Bells of Scotland," and a "blackface medley."[62]

Echoes of the genre's earlier style continued to resound. Caricatures of free
black dandies remained popular, in countless versions of "Old Dan Tucker,"
in newer characters like "De Westchester Nigga." These characters still expressed their passion for "Negro wenches," in songs like "Miss Julia Is a Handsome Gal" and "Bress Dat Lubly Yaller Gal." They still declared their freedom
to act on any impulse, to give in to any desire. Their newfound middle-class
audiences loved them. As a writer for New York's *Daily Tribune* had it in a review of a Christy's Minstrels' show at the "Society Library," blackface offered
a "pleasing relief" from fashionable music and "high toned" opera, for "Negro
melodies are the very democracy of music."[63]

By embracing blackface, middle-class audiences valorized a version of
common-culture democracy. As a result, they were able to contain the threat
of working-class culture, consuming its style of rebellious anger, softening it
with sentiment. By 1847, blackface aficionados among the middle class could
hold that vulgarity was the genre's true style, while middle-class writers decried
its corruption by middle-class values. According to a writer for the *Spirit of
the Times*, the performances of the "Ethiopian Serenaders" at Palmo's Theatre
were a decided failure. They were "too elegant." As an aficionado with *Putnam's
Magazine* would have it a few years later, blackface had reached its zenith with
the Virginia Minstrels' "Old Dan Tucker." Since then, he declared, it had declined into "sentimental love songs" and "melancholy reminiscences of negroic
childhood," or worse, and here he certainly had Foster's "Nelly Was a Lady" in
mind, into pandering to feminized audiences with "dirges for dead wenches."[64]

The real black, according to these experts, had no use for elegance, sentiment, or melancholy. And so middle-class audiences demanded earlier ele-

ments of blackface style: its valorization of blackness as the bedrock for authentic selfhood; its anti-intellectual hostility to "big words" and "ejumcation"; its hilarious debunking of black efforts at uplift and self-improvement.

The stump speech remained a standard of the genre. By the time of the Civil War, Byron Christy of Christy's Minstrels was the recognized master of the art. "Feller citizens," began Christy in a typical example of the act, "I shall now hab de pleasure ob ondressin' ebery one of you; and I'm gwine to stick to de pints and de confluence where by I am myself annihilated." "Friends and Quadrepeds," he began in another at the outset of the Civil War, "my remarks on dis glorious 'caision . . . will be on de subjec' ob de Onion, de Constitution, and de Scar Spangled Banner!"

And so the typical stump speech would go, into political commentary and standard malapropisms: "Dey is some punkins, dem leaders ob rebellion. A man ob common intellect would naturally spose dat de green-eyed lobster, cowardice, had taken possession ob dere souls." Amid howls of laughter it would move toward a conclusion, often petering out in a lost thread, here ending with the standard image of the speaker's always-futile effort to put on airs: "I will now conclude wid a quotation from Walter Ralf Emmerson, when he says, says he, 'In de constituency ob de ancient hyperbolical belligerents, dere lies an unfathomable abyss to which only aesthetic concatenation can adequately approximate.' I agree wid him feller-stugents. Good ebenin'!"[65]

The target remained what it was during the heyday of working-class blackface: affectation, artifice, and education, ideals of middle-class uplift themselves. Yet the audience, as observers were sure to note, had expanded to include nearly everyone. Buckley's Serenaders, noted the theatrical column of the *Spirit of the Times* in 1853, were doing "flourishing business." Wood's Minstrels were "full of business, delighting every body who goes to see them." According to the columnist, the minstrel show was an expected part of a night on the town: "Strangers," he wrote, "are recommended by us to see all the Ethiopians in town, they are the most laughable entertainments we have, and a good laugh is worth something now-a-days."[66]

By attending these shows, as the foreword of one blackface songster had it in 1856, middle-class audiences would learn to laugh at the antics of "dandy darkies." They would also acquire an ability to laugh at themselves. They could thus free themselves from an ethos of respectability increasingly pictured as stiffness, from a stress on self-control recoded as humorless "Puritanism." "I cannot trust the man who never laughs," read the songster's foreword:

> I expect to find secret vices, malignant sins or horrid crimes springing up in this hot-bed of confined air and imprisoned space; and, therefore, it gives me

sincere moral gratification . . . to see innocent pleasures and popular amusements resisting the religious bigotry that frowns so unwisely upon them. Anything is better than dark, dead, unhappy social life—a prey to ennui and mor-
bid excitement, which results from unmitigated puritanism, whose second
crop is usually unbridled license and infamous folly.[67]

The minstrel show allowed middle-class audiences to remake themselves.
They too were capable of having fun. They too could release the passions and
desires welled up from the space they would one day refer to as their "dark
side."

Meanwhile, blackface would expand to other areas of the culture. The
genre's increasing focus on the slave would produce sympathy for the character and expand support for the antislavery cause. It would also cast the
nation's half million free African Americans into cultural shadow and make
invisible the members of an antebellum black middle class. For the fans of
blackface—and this would one day include nearly all Americans—the black
experience to the Civil War would be that of slavery.

Finally, blackface would clarify the race confusion fostered by promoters
of black uplift. It would re-crystallize racial boundaries. The old boundaries
had long existed, in the segregated listings of city directories, in the "Negro
pews" of Northern churches, in legislation banning free blacks from the militia and the voting booth. New ones were being created, in the exclusion of
African Americans from passenger decks of steamships and riverboats, in the
practice of including "Negro cars" on eastern railways.

By the 1840s, the system had a name. While traveling with his fellow abolitionists early in the decade, the reformer Parker Pillsbury recalled that black
speakers for the cause, including the "cultivated" and "accomplished" Charles
Lenox Remond and Frederick Douglass, were "compelled to occupy what was
called the 'Jim Crow' car." In 1848, according to an article in Douglass's *North
Star*, the black abolitionist William Nell addressed a meeting of the "Western
New York Anti-Slavery Society" on "some incidents" of "colorphobia" and race-
based persecution. The incidents included "the indignities of the Jim Crow
Car."[68] The career of Jim Crow had taken its modern turn, from a song to
America's notorious term for racial segregation. The name made sense. Blackface would give segregation lasting power, rooting it in a racism of love and
yearning as well as fear and hatred.

The Middle-Class Moment

In May 1843, the Hutchinson Family Singers made their first appearance in New York City. They spent part of their stay touring Manhattan, staring in awe at the pulsing life of America's commercial and theatrical center, their senses buzzing, their store of adjectives overtaxed. "O! *New York* is all that I have had it represented to be!" wrote Asa Hutchinson in the family diary:

> Boston does not compare with it for *life* and *business*. The Splendid Street "Broad Way" is the most Splendid Street that I ever saw, and then the Grand Park, and the Splendid *water works* where the water is thrown into the air to the height of 25 or 30 feet and then falls to the pool again in the most majestic Style. Then the Splendid "Niblos Garden" is worth a journey of 50 miles to see the fine flowers & plants.[1]

It was splendid. Meanwhile, their New York performances made their "reputation," recalled John Hutchinson. The city's music critics hailed them as the first new thing to come along in years. They drew a crowd of three thousand to Manhattan's Concert Hall. Afterward they received what would become the holy grail of American popular culture: P. T. Barnum wrote, soliciting a deal to manage their next tour.[2] While no deal with Barnum materialized, the days of performing in village churches were over. In the fall they returned to the city, where they stayed two months and gave over twenty concerts to packed houses. Their 1844 tour took them from Boston to New York, Philadelphia, Baltimore, and Washington. In each city they filled large theaters, averaging as much as five hundred dollars in nightly profits.[3]

They continued to sing for temperance. They also felt the pull of other issues. It became "practically impossible," wrote John, to avoid "being under the influence of and affected by, several other related reforms." And so they sang in favor of poor relief and the better treatment of immigrants. They announced themselves the friends of prison reform. In 1843 they published "Call the Doctor, or, Anti-Calomel." Set to the tune of "Old Hundred" from the *Bay Psalm Book*, the number offered audiences a cutting satire of modern doctors, a comic take on their practice of prescribing calomel, a poisonous compound that included mercury, as a cure-all for a variety of ailments. The medicine would be responsible for sickening or killing thousands of patients unlucky enough to seek treatment. Here was a developing Hutchinson trademark: a traditional tune—then more than two hundred years old—so well known it was irresistible; a comedic turn by Judson in his vocal characterization of the "doctor"; yet another song tying the singers to a popular reform.[4]

The trademark was evident in their performances. During the singers' rise, their concerts included the usual melodramatic pieces of the time, songs like "The Ship-Wreck" and "The Snow-Storm." They included a few patriotic numbers: "The Land of Washington" and "Yankee Doodle." They featured several songs to evoke a nostalgic past for middle-class urbanites, from "The Cot Where We Were Born" to "My Mother's Bible." To be sure, the singers were more than willing to give audiences a trifling glee like "Hark, Hark Each Spartan Hound," or a sentimental ballad such as "Near the Lake Where Drooped the Willow." But eventually they circled back to a high-minded cause, to songs like "King Alcohol" or "All Hail Washingtonians."[5]

The whole thing worked. Critics lauded the singers for their close harmonies and careful enunciation of lyrics. Nearly all cited their natural style and moral commitments as keys to their popularity, as qualities that made them representative Americans. According to a writer for the *Philadelphia Daily Observer*, their New York concerts of 1843 produced "a prodigious sensation." In the audience were two of the nation's greatest authorities on Christian ethics and moral reform, the Reverends William Patton and Lyman Beecher. The two stood, according to the reviewer, "with their arms around each other, perfectly overpowered for the time." The singers' popularity was "well merited," declared another reporter with the *Syracuse Daily Journal*. "They inculcate the most lofty and patriotic sentiments in their songs," he wrote. In music and style, he concluded, the singers were fully "American in character."[6]

They were also communists. In May 1843, shortly after their New York debut, they took a break from their tour to visit the Brook Farm commune in West Roxbury, Massachusetts. "The distinguished communists gave us a most hearty reception," recalled John Hutchinson, adding that they understood the commune to be "formed with the purpose of inaugurating a thorough reform in our civil and social society." They met the commune's members, discovering that all were "bounding with hope" and committed to the "great idea of

FIGURE 7.1. Representative Americans—popular communists. By the time of this photograph, which has been dated to 1846 and may have been a publicity photograph for the singers' tour of England and Ireland, the Hutchinsons were enormously popular and well known for their reforms. Their causes included temperance; antislavery; labor reform; the rights of women, immigrants, and Native Americans; racial integration; and communism. From left to right are the Original Hutchinson Family Singers: Asa, Abby, John, and Judson. Photograph: The Hutchinson Family, circa 1846. Courtesy of Milford Historical Society of NH.

human brotherhood." With the visit the singers became converts to another reform. "All of the principles advocated we fully endorsed," added John, "for we earnestly believed in this manner of life."[7] The cause would do nothing to hurt their popularity, their patriotic appeal, or their status as representative Americans.

The Communists Next Door

For Phineas Taylor Barnum, the social and economic exchanges of an emerging capitalist order felt right. Descended from a line of sharp traders, the showman would often regale listeners with tales of his days as a young clerk in a Connecticut country store. His customers, he recalled, were largely composed of poor people. Several were rag-pickers, women who collected bundles of discarded cloth and then brought them to the store to trade for goods. The women swore the bundles were entirely made up of good cotton and linen. So they appeared. Upon opening them, Barnum claimed he often found worthless trash, moth-eaten wool, sometimes even stones and gravel. He was comfortable with the discovery. The story offered his listeners the self-serving logic of the emerging businessman; for Barnum, the comforting point was that everyone cheated and lying for advantage was a fact of nature.[8]

The Hutchinsons had a similar connection to what they called communism. They were middle-class communists. According to some scholars, this would make them little more than dabblers in a romantic ideal, followers of a popular fad. The real issue may be that communism *was* a popular fad in the Hutchinsons' America. The most likely explanation for how and why the Hutchinsons became adherents to the cause might be that it felt right. It felt right for two reasons: first, during their young lives they were surrounded by communal influences and statements of communal values; second, there was little in their context to suggest it was wrong.

Coming of age when and where the Hutchinsons did, they could hardly avoid communal influences. Some reflected the persistence of tradition. At the center of Milford were vestiges of the ancient roland: the town square, the common, and the village green, now encircled by road, merchant shops, and meetinghouses. Milford was dominated by networks of interrelated families: Hutchinsons, Leavitts, Haywards, and Goodwins. All were connected by marriage, by church membership, or by the exchange of sons and daughters as farmhands, apprentices, or housekeepers. Dating from the earliest period of colonization, these kinship connections would serve their traditional functions into the 1830s and beyond: as networks of trade, news, and gossip; as safety nets of pooled resources during hard times.

Some influences had more recent origins. Years later the Hutchinson brothers fondly recalled the town's "Muster Day" festival, the annual day for militia training on the common. By the 1830s the day was a kind of community picnic. Townspeople also gathered on greens for the July Fourth ritual: a public reading of the Declaration of Independence, an oration by a civic father, and a mass singing of hymns to the Pilgrims or George Washington.[9]

Here again were the old communal traditions repackaged as patriotic exercises. Creating imagined communities and assumed connections between town, region, and nation, the ceremonies were no small affairs. During the 1840s, Lowell hosted a July Fourth procession, which, according to its program, included the entire town: the last marchers were the "Citizens of Lowell." Arriving at the common, the townspeople listened to a reading of the Declaration, fidgeted through an oration, and sang a new patriotic hymn that began with the line "My Country 'Tis of Thee." In the evening they gathered again for the display of fireworks or "Chinese fires." They stood awestruck beneath a "Pyramid of Candles," a "Variegated Star," and finally a "Temple of Liberty" with twin mottos "Liberty and Equality" and "July 1776" surrounded by "Stars and Rockets."[10] The display was enough for the most proudly vulgar of patriots.

The Hutchinsons grew up surrounded by a culture of revivals and philanthropy, by communal yearnings that gave rise to a spirit of humanitarian reform. They did not have to look far to find examples of communism. A short distance from Milford was a settlement of the "United Society." Americans would come to know the members of the society by the once-derisive name they embraced: they were "Shakers." The Shaker story, as a writer for a popular magazine would later put it, offered a "valuable contribution" to the "history of communism in America."[11]

Shakerism developed in America as a basis for communal settlements and as a female-centered Christian sect. The female in question was Ann Lee or, as the sect's members called her, "Mother Ann." Born the daughter of a blacksmith in Manchester, England, in or about 1736, Lee's early life was typical of the working poor of the English Midlands. It was wretched. She grew up destitute and illiterate, forced by her poverty and parents into an early marriage. By her mid-twenties she had given birth to four children. All died in infancy. At some point during these tribulations she began to receive powerful visions. The visions carried the command that she rid herself of all carnal desires and appetites.

About this time Lee fell in with a small group of "Shaking Quakers." By this time mainstream Quakers had shifted to silent services. Manchester's Shaking Quakers, who probably numbered no more than a dozen members, preferred to express the spirit when it entered them. They did so loudly, according to shocked observers, in twitches, jumps, and shouts, in "ecstatic fits." Lee, who would be remembered as stocky and athletic, may have excelled at these exercises. By the early 1770s, she had become the leader of the sect. She had also been jailed by officials and persecuted by Manchester locals, accused of heresy and making public scenes. Finally, she began receiving visions with another message: the Shaking Quakers needed to get out of England.[12]

Lee and her Shakers came to America in 1774. For several years the band scattered. In the late 1770s, its members reconvened near Albany, New York. There, they managed to buy a tract of land and establish the first Shaker settlement, a village that went under the Indian name for the area, "Niskeyuna." Over the next several years, they received a trickle of converts. They expanded their presence to enclaves in New York, Connecticut, and Massachusetts. Mother Ann often traveled between these settlements, visiting Shaker households and passing on the sect's tenets to the "elders," the society's next generation of leaders. The travel was dangerous, particularly given American attitudes toward difference and Christian approaches to rival beliefs. In 1784, Ann Lee died, most likely from a beating she took at the hands of a hostile crowd. For the next twenty years, the Shaker settlements barely survived.[13]

Then came a period of rapid growth. It began in 1801, when Shaker elders sent out emissaries to witness the camp revivals in Kentucky and Ohio and to spread the word of Shakerism. Much of the word focused on the place of Mother Ann in the sect. Shakers, the emissaries would have explained, were Christians. Yet for them, the Bible's alternative account of creation, in which the Christian God made man and woman at the same time and both in his image, meant this God had to be both male and female. The masculine side of this God had returned in the form of Christ. Mother Ann completed the return: she was a "second Christ" in female form. Thus the official name of the sect: the "United Society of Believers in Christ's Second Appearance."

Other beliefs came from testimonies of Shaker elders. The principles of Shakerism included pacifism and equality between the sexes. The spirit world was real: Shakers could receive "gifts" in the form of messages from Mother Ann and other dead occupants of this realm. These gifts would take the form of faith healings, sayings, and word of post-death conversions. Often they appeared as songs and dances. The sect's main goal was the expulsion of all carnal appetite. To convert, one had to confess all sins, not by generic category but by recounting every instance of their occurrence. The process could take weeks. Once converted, the newly minted Shaker was expected to withdraw from the world: to enter a life that was simple, honest, and humble; to join a communal society where all property belonged to the members as a whole, all labor was equal in dignity, and all were brothers and sisters. One more thing the emissaries might have added: the Shaker life would have to include sexual celibacy.[14]

The emissaries returned with a number of converts. Over the next decades, the trickle became a steady stream of new members, a gathering of thousands to the Shaker fold. What explains this increase in numbers? To begin with, the numbers were not particularly large; a few thousand converts did not indicate a mass movement. Yet for the Shakers' critics, the miracle was that the sect could attract converts at all. Their main focus, as might be expected, was on the subject of celibacy. "To enjoin celibacy" on a membership "consisting equally of either sex," declared a writer for the *North American Review* in 1823, "is, to say the least, a bold experiment in anthropology." For him, it was the sect's "most interesting" characteristic.[15]

Others found it downright titillating. And so, while the Shakers were never popular in the sense of being admired by a majority of Americans, their sexual practice—or lack of practice—did make them notorious. They certainly occupied a visible place in the period's popular culture. By the middle of the nineteenth century, Americans could read several books and stories focused on Shaker celibacy. There were confessions by supposed apostates claiming the vow placed a cork on natural desires. The desires, according to these accounts, sometimes exploded in orgies. There were stories focused on Shaker maidens made all the more lubricous by the vow, accounts of quivering virgins begging narrators to free them from the sect and liberate their passions.[16]

The celibacy-as-perversion angle did little to explain the growth in the sect's numbers. Some critics linked the converts to the unreasoning passions of revivalists, depicting both as examples of *"enthusiasm, fanaticism, and the very energy of delusion."* Others offered a more grounded explanation: Shaker converts were the losers in the upheavals of the market revolution. The Shakers, noted a writer for the *North American Review*, welcomed America's mass of "the odd, the unlucky, the unhappy":

> Their community doubtless finds recruits from the wide spread *caste* of the friendless and deserted. Many poor isolated beings exist scattered about, even in this happy land; surrounded by prosperous families but amalgamated with none, and lonely in the crowd. Single females without friends and protectors, orphan children without relations, pilgrims in the world struck with melancholy by the way, widows, and fathers who have lost their children, all those who in one way or the other seem left out of the game or the battle of life.[17]

The assessment points to a relationship: the high years of the Shaker gathering corresponded with the most disruptive years of the market revolution, the period from the opening of the Erie Canal in 1825 through the first nationwide economic depression in 1837. The attraction to Shakerism may have rested in aesthetics, in a way of life that seemed a throwback to earlier and simpler ways of being.

This aesthetic would be noted in Shaker settlements. As even critics had to admit, these offered picturesque scenery: villages that were "pleasantly situated" in the countryside, farms that were "neatly cultivated." Among the strongest tenets of the faith was that desires of the flesh could be mastered not only through prayer and reflection but through hard work and industry. As a result, the buildings at Shaker communities were always in perfect repair: the exteriors blindingly whitewashed, the interiors spotless and dust-free. Their fields and gardens were "perhaps the most productive of any in the country"; perfect exhibits of the "pleasing effects of industry and rural economy."[18] Outsiders expressed this attraction with their pocketbooks. Along with popular "Shaker seeds," which the brethren sold by mail order, Shaker-manufactured articles, particularly chairs, tables, rugs, and brooms, quickly caught on with consumers. All were "remarkable for neatness and durability." All would be celebrated for their simplicity and function, their "purity" of form and design.

In the 1820s and 1830s, Americans went in droves to visit Shaker communities. They came to see the villages, to be sure, but also to watch and listen to the "strange peculiarities" of Shaker dance and song. Dance was among the oldest of the sect's expressions of faith. In early meetings in England and America, observers described the ritual as formless, marked by the common revival behaviors of individuals taken with the spirit, "a perpetual scene," as one put it, of "trembling, quivering, shaking, sighing, crying, groaning, screaming, [and] jumping." By the nineteenth century, the dances were more controlled. One early example was the "Square Order Shuffle," a dance taught to the lyrics of a song illustrating the steps and technique:

> One, two, three step, / Foot straight at the turn.
> One, two, three, step, / Equal length, solid tap.
> Take the shuffle, little back, / Keep the body straight, erect,
> In every joint and bone.[19]

As time passed, the ritual became increasingly complex, characterized by square and ring dances done by large groups, intricate hand motions symbolizing the giving and receiving of spiritual gifts, and rhythmic foot-stomping and hand-clapping.

Shaker song provided accompaniment to the dances as well as an outlet for expressions of the sect's beliefs. Together, the songs and dances composed what Shakers called their "labors." The point was to work the body in order to drain it of desires. The opening lines to the song "Come Life, Shaker Life," stated the goal in clearest terms: "Come life, Shaker life, come life eternal, / Shake, shake out of me all that is carnal." Another song, "The Zealous Laborers," evinced the earthy physicality of the Shaker struggle against bodily desire:

> O how I long to be released, / From every feeling of the beast,
> No more to feel one poison dart, / Of his vile stuff about my heart,
> But while I'm laboring with my might, / This hateful beast will heave in sight,
> And every living step I tread / I'll try to place it on his head.
>
> I need not think of gaining much, / To give the floor an easy touch,
> Or labor in some handsome form, / That scarce will keep my ankles warm,
> For I have not so far increased, / That I can manage such a beast,
> Without my blood is nicely heat, / And my body flows with sweat.[20]

Many of the visitors who flocked to these services were touched with the sense that the whole thing was absurd, calculated only to "awaken a smile at its oddity." The Quaker poet John Greenleaf Whittier had a typical response. "I have seen the Shakers or 'Shaking Quakers' as the people sometimes call them," he wrote in a letter to a friend. "They are an unearthly set of fanatics," he added: "the men look hysterical—the women ghastly."[21] Others went to scoff only to discover expressions that were becoming recognized as among the nation's most vibrant forms of folk art. By the 1830s, Shaker membership would reach a high point of some six thousand individuals. Their settlements would come to include eighteen villages extending from New York to Ohio. One was a settlement at Canterbury, New Hampshire, a village twenty miles north of Milford.

By the early 1840s, Shaker communities had become so overrun with curious onlookers that the elders made the decision to close them off from the outside world, enacting a ban on visitors that would last several years. Barnum filled the void. In 1847, the American Museum offered several weeks of entertainments by two "Shaking Quakers." Barnum's Shakers were real enough; they were apostates from the Canterbury settlement. So were their songs and dances: according to later accounts, the two performed "The Square Order Shuffle" and "Come Life, Shaker Life," along with several songs in "unknown tongues." The showman's broadsides were another matter. These featured a Shaker maiden in ecstatic dance, twirling quickly enough to raise her skirts. Never one to avoid sensational packaging, Barnum was more than willing to cash in on the perceived erotic qualities of Shaker worship.[22]

The Hutchinsons would have most likely heard of this act. They would have heard of the Shakers' ceremonies, of their supposed orgies, of Shaker maids whose kindling desires awaited the right spark. They certainly knew of the Shaker settlement at Canterbury. In 1854, according to Shaker accounts, Joshua Hutchinson visited the village, where he gave a few lessons in modern styles of singing. If they knew all of this, they would have been aware of something else: they would have known that while the Shakers were communists, virtually no one criticized them on this account. As late as the end of the nineteenth century, observers continued to extol their orderly settlements. Some would surmise that communism might be an option for a nation still bent on avoiding the worst aspects of industrialization and capitalist profiteering.[23]

Parlor Indians

Of the songs the Hutchinsons sang and published during the 1840s, perhaps the most resonant with the communal impulses of the time was "Glide On My Light Canoe" or, as they also titled it, "The Indian's Lament." Musically, the song was a typical parlor ballad. Lyrically, it offered a criticism of Manifest

Destiny wrapped in a collection of stereotypes, a humanitarian appeal based on a picture of the Indian as a noble savage. The song focused on an unnamed Indian chief driven by "the whites" from his forest home. With nowhere to go, he paddles his canoe out to sea, where he lands at an offshore island. There, he sings a plaintive verse:

> Shall I, the bravest of the chiefs, / On this Isle make my bed;
> No! no! the white's polluted feet, / Shall ne'er tread o'er my head.
> I've buried my hatchet 'neath the turf, / But I will rest beneath the surf,
> The foaming billows shall be my grave, / For I'll not die the white man's slave.
> Glide on, my light canoe, glide on, / The Morning breeze is free;
> I'll guide thee far, far out upon / The wide and troubled sea.[24]

Though it took an Indian's voice and criticized the "white man's" ways, the song was hardly unusual. Toward the end of the 1820s, millions of Americans voted for Andrew Jackson. Millions supported Jackson's policy of forcibly removing Native Americans to a territory west of the Mississippi River. At the same time, many of these millions believed that Indians were noble and beautiful, that they were fitting subjects for poetry, paintings, novels, and songs. The result of these beliefs in popular song and elsewhere in mid-nineteenth-century culture would be the creation of a parlor Indian. The imagined character would come to symbolize broad yearnings for communal values and an existence outside the forces of the market.

From the American Revolution through much of the nineteenth century, white Americans imbued Indians with contrary meanings. They were the symbolic enemy, lurking in the darkness, threatening the margins of civilization. They were also icons of purity, innocence, and republican virtue. During the Revolution, political cartoons pictured England as an aristocratic dame, decked out in the height of fashion, America as a near-naked Indian maid, simple and uncorrupted by luxury.[25] The equation lasted for decades. Into the nineteenth century, sailors knew how to recognize an American-built ship: if the masthead carving was that of an Indian maiden, her bare breasts calming the seas before her, it was a relatively sure bet she was Yankee-made.

In culture as in politics, the character would primarily be depicted and perceived according to the "Indian problem." One element of the problem was white attraction to Indian ways. From the time of the earliest English colonies in America, authorities were shocked at the frequency with which colonists ran off to become "white Indians," assimilating into local Native American groups and cultures. For the official culture, the primary response was the captivity narrative. These popular narratives offered crucial lessons.

Indians, according to their writers, were heartless savages. White captives demonstrated their godliness by resisting their ways.[26]

The second element of the problem is better known: simply put, Indians were on land that whites wanted. The result was a practice and policy of genocide, along with a language of Indian hating that attempted to justify ethnic cleansing. Christian hymns portrayed the destruction of Indians as the will of their imagined god. One, sung at a July Fourth celebration in New London, Connecticut, in 1812, thanked the Anglo deity for removing Indians prior to colonization, for making sure the land was "Dispeopled by repeated strokes, / Of thy avenging hand."[27] Other songs spurred a more earthly hand of vengeance. Revolutionary-era ballad writers whipped up hatred against Indians by depicting them as allied with the British. In Boston, Nathaniel Coverly printed broadsides featuring English officers paying Indians for white scalps. Elsewhere, balladeers filled their songs with "tomahawks," "lurking savages," and the shrieking cries of captured patriots tortured with red-hot irons.[28]

These images would continue to proliferate in the nineteenth century and beyond. At the same time, they would be punctuated by increasing ambivalence. In 1820, the Reverend James Wallis Eastburn commenced his "poetic romance," *Yamoyden, A Tale of the Wars of King Philip*, with a shriek, a cry that rent the warm air of an American summer's eve. The poet explained: "'Tis the death wail of a departed race," a race of "brave warriors" killed by the "soulless bigotry" and "avarice" of European empire-builders.[29] Here as elsewhere, the Indian had a dramatic surge in popularity in the 1820s. This surge, interestingly, corresponded with the rise of the nation's greatest Indian-killer, Andrew Jackson. Jackson's presidency announced a more draconian policy of Indian removal. It also led to the inclusion of Indians in the rhetoric of middle-class humanitarianism.

Hard on the heels of Jackson's election, a Boston-based group calling itself the "Benevolent Ladies of the United States" issued a reaction in the form of a circular. "The present crisis in the affairs of the Indian nations," declared the circular's text, "demands the immediate and interested attention of all who make any claims to benevolence or humanity." Indians were "a cherished relic of antiquity" with "spirit of freedom and nobility." They were a "simple" and "beautiful" people who should not be left "prey of the avaricious and the unprincipled." As romantic images, they merited real salvation:

> Will the liberal and refined, those who are delighted with the charms of eloquence and poetry; those who love the legends of romance, and the records of antiquity; those who celebrate and admire the stern virtues of Roman warriors

and patriots; will these permit such a race to be swept from the earth?—a nation who have emerged from the deepest shades of antiquity; whose story, and whose wild and interesting traits are becoming the theme of the poet and novelist; who command a native eloquence unequalled for pathos and sublimity; whose stern fortitude and unbending courage, exceed the Roman renown?[30]

This blend of humanitarianism and romance would lead to the recognition of Indian removal as one of the two most shameful developments in American history. In her 1829 publication *The First Settlers of New England*, the reformer Lydia Maria Child criticized the region's settlers for "wanton cruelties" against Indians, atrocities as ugly as those of the slave trade. In its annual report for 1838, the Massachusetts Anti-Slavery Society concluded that the shameful history was ongoing. "The past year," declared the report, "has exhibited the American people covering themselves afresh with pollution and blood." The text added that if Americans were "answerable for no other crime, their treatment of the Indian tribes would suffice to justly subject them to the direct punishment that offended heaven has ever bestowed upon any nation."[31]

Another result was a growing interest in Indians. In 1826, Albert Gallatin published his "Table of Indian Tribes in the United States," noting the existence of over one hundred different tribes, nearly all with varying degrees of difference between dialects, languages, and cultures. The table would inspire generations of amateur ethnologists. By the 1840s, George Catlin's "Indian Gallery," a traveling exhibit of some 330 paintings of tribal lifeways and portraits of Indian chiefs, went from city to city, introducing Americans to the continent's "*Wildest Tribes*," all, as the gallery's broadsides had it, in their perfect "state of nature." A critic called the Gallery's Indians "the closest of all humans to God's image of mankind."[32]

The interest would move Indians to the center of popular culture. Developing equations between Indians and good health resulted in columns of penny-paper advertisements for "Indian" elixirs, tonics, and hair restorers, their bottles decorated with pictures of Indian maidens or buckskinned braves with bow, arrows, and quiver. As early as the 1820s, popular writers began reversing the plot of the captivity narrative. White male captives like Robert Montgomery Bird's "Nick of the Woods" and James Fenimore Cooper's "Leatherstocking" were allowed to give in to their captors. They thereby added a measure of Indian vibrancy to their whiteness: the knowledge of forest craft and the art of silent stalking; the skills of eagle-eyed marksmanship and bloody hatchet work.

Meanwhile, at the Park and Bowery Theaters, the grand thespian Edwin Forrest stalked the boards as King Philip in the play *Metamora*. Written expressly for the muscular actor by John Augustus Stone, the play stressed the Indian chief's nobility, eloquence, and bravery. Its effects on perceptions were powerful: a portrait of Metamora that hung for years at the National Portrait Gallery in Washington was actually a painting of Forrest, made up as he would be on the Bowery's stage.[33]

Other venues blended traditional perceptions of Indian savagery with romantic images and didactic uplift. In 1841, the Boston Museum featured a *tableau vivant* of the famous painting "The Murder of Miss Jane M'Crea." As the show's broadside promised in a bit of poetry, the tableaux would include Miss M'Crea's torn bodice and heaving "globes of snow," along with the "upraised axes" and "demon grins" of her captors:

> With eyes upturned and fleeting breath,
> In their raised axes views her instant death.
> Her hair, half lost along the shrubs she passed,
> Rolls, in loose tangles, round her lovely waist;
> Her kerchief torn, betrays the globes of snow,
> That heave responsive to her weight of woe,
> With calculating pause, and demon grin,
> They seize her hands, and through her face divine,
> Drive the descending axe.[34]

Scenes from the spectacle included a "grand council," a "corn dance," and a ritual smoking of the "calumet of peace" followed by a "dance and frolic."

Some of these performances appear to have offered employment for actual Native American people. In the 1840s, Peale's Museum in New York advertised an evening with "Five Real Indians"—along with a live boa constrictor and a display of "Animal Magnetism"—for twenty-five cents. The show featured a musical performance, promising "an interesting exhibition of INDIAN DANCES and habits," including a "Snake Dance" and a "Comic Indian Dance!" If actual Native Americans did play themselves in these spectacles, they seem to have done so with varying degrees of success in meeting white expectations. "These are not," declared the show's broadside, "the Buffalo Indians, who were hissed off the Bowery Stage."[35]

Finally, the interest in Indians would spawn a host of parlor ballads. These ballads generated an iconography of gliding canoes, sylvan forests, and sublime nature. Within them were seeds of an idea with long currency in America: Indians were children of nature, noble symbols of the uplifting sublimity

of the American landscape. One, "The Blue Juniata, or, Wild Roved the Indian Girl," featured a spritely maid running through a forest as "swift as an
Antelope," her "jetty locks" flowing in "wavy tresses." Another, "Where Are
the Poor Indians," supposedly penned by "Chief Kanenison," presented an
increasingly popular contrast between Indian purity and white corruption:

> The Indians were pure, and no evil they knew,
>   They adored the Great Spirit above,
> And delighted to keep his sweet precepts in view,
>   So enchanted were they by his love.
> But oh! dark was the cloud that the white man had spread
>   On the heart of the Indian so good,
> Till mangled with fear away they soon fled,
>   And hid themselves deep in the wood.[36]

For such songs, to take Indians out of nature was to corrupt them, to soil
them with a whiteness that, in these songs at least, was despised. Consider
the example of "The Indian Scholar." In this story ballad from the 1830s, a
Susquehannas Indian goes to Harvard, where he spends "tedious hours of
study" and listens to countless "heavy-moulded lectures." He nearly dies of
depression. Finally he returns to the forest, crying "why did I forsake my native woods for gloomy walls? / The silver brook, the limpid lake, for musty
books & college halls?" "Indian Chief," a song from 1832, offered another version of this standard imagery. Here, whites were "tormentors," Indians their
victims. Like the Hutchinsons' "Glide on My Light Canoe," the song ended in
the voice of the noble savage, the last vestige of a stoic race:

> I go to the land where my father is gone,
> His ghost will rejoice in the fame of his son;
> Death comes like a friend to relieve me from pain,
> And the son of Alknomook shall never complain.[37]

As parlor ballads, many of these songs were the stuff of middle-class social
gatherings, of comfortable evenings around the pianoforte. For critics then as
now, they were hopelessly romantic in their images, condescending, even ridiculous.[38] The producers and audiences for these images were hardly cultural
relativists. Their Indians were generic. Most were northeastern urbanites with
few, if any, contacts with Indian populations. And yet their ideals would frame
the future. White Americans would come to understand Indians as close to
nature, as stoic victims of great pain and suffering, as symbols of republican
virtue and communal values. As long as these values resonated in American
culture, so would Indians remain visible.

Visions of Utopia: From Brook Farm to Milford's Community Block

In the spring of 1843, the Hutchinsons enjoyed a stay at a communal society. Their visit was hardly unusual. Many Americans shared their curiosity in such settlements; and there were certainly many around. There were communes formed by Christian sects: the gatherings of Shakers, Rappites, Zoarites, and Moravians. There were small collectives led by visionaries: Bronson Alcott's transcendentalist farm at "Fruitlands," Adin Ballou's band of "Practical Christians" at "Hopedale." There were the experiments whose names evoked aspirations: "New Harmony," "Equity," "Modern Times." Some dated to before the Revolution. Many were products of the moment. According to Thomas Wentworth Higginson, it seemed every "reading man" of the time had "a draft of a new community in his waistcoat pocket." In the words of one historian, the decade of the 1840s was a "communitarian moment," a period in which reformers founded some fifty-nine communal settlements or utopian societies.[39]

None were more famous or colorful than Brook Farm. By the time the Hutchinsons arrived, the commune was in its second incarnation. The transcendentalist George Ripley had founded the experiment in 1840, paying $30,000 in borrowed and donated money for 200 acres of land along with an assortment of buildings. Located eight miles outside Boston, in the village of West Roxbury, the Brook Farm Association for Industry and Education opened in 1841. The Association had a colorful cast of characters. One of its original members was the novelist Nathaniel Hawthorne. Another was the young feminist and essayist Margaret Fuller. Ralph Waldo Emerson was a supporter and sometime visitor, an advisor to the commune's leaders and an influence on its early policies.[40]

Ripley stated the commune's goal in a letter to Emerson: the point was to re-establish the old connection that had existed before the market revolution, "to combine," he explained, "the thinker and the worker, as far as possible, in the same individual." To achieve the goal, the farm gathered a mix of artists, writers, and common rural laborers. The way it was supposed to work was simple: the commune's laborers would show the artists and writers how to farm; the intellectuals would imbue the artisans and farmers with high thoughts about tilling the earth. The farm's laborers, their children, and other children from the surrounding area would be able to take classes at the commune's school, from an educational program well stocked with "skillful teachers in the various branches of intellectual culture."[41] Brook Farm would be a transcendentalist experiment, an effort to re-bridge the widening gulf between man and nature, muscle and mind.

The school did well. The farm did not. Locals around West Roxbury openly mocked the agricultural efforts of the communists. Real farmers would have probably burned everything, sold the potash, run out on their creditors, and decamped for Ohio or Indiana. The transcendentalists were determined to make it work. And so they discovered something a large number of Americans already knew: farming did not pay. Still, life at the farm was pleasant. Some members, like the young Hawthorne, took the outdoor tasks seriously, cutting hay and mucking barns with romantic intensity. Others made the experiment better known for diversions: there were reveries and flirtations among the area's rolling hills; there were evening "fancy balls" attended by Boston intellectuals; there were teatime parlor games and intellectual *conversationes* at one of the central buildings, the busy place known as the "the Hive."[42]

By the spring of 1843, the transcendentalist phase of the experiment had come to an end. Hawthorne and Fuller had moved on. The farm's leaders would soon publish a new constitution, a declaration that its operations were now on a "Fourierite" or "scientific" basis. A preamble summed up the unchanged goals: one was "to substitute a system of brotherly cooperation for one of selfish competition"; another, "to diminish the desire of excessive accumulation, by making the acquisition of individual property subservient to upright and disinterested uses." The overall goal was "to impart a greater freedom, simplicity, truthfulness, refinement, and moral dignity, to our mode of life."[43]

The new constitution made an attempt to impose a few rules. All members would be guaranteed housing, board, and employment. For each member, three hundred days per year of labor would be a requirement. A regular failure to work would mean the rescinding of all benefits. Finally, the whole thing was to be done with a modicum of seriousness: "No public meeting for business or amusement," declared the bylaws, "shall be protracted beyond the hour of ten P.M."[44]

Despite the new rules, by the time the Hutchinsons arrived, the commune was still known for its social liveliness. They spent the week, John Hutchinson recalled, partaking of "pleasant musicales, picnics, conversations, and like interesting exercises." They discovered that much of the farm's spirit of reform was tied to music; and much came from its music teacher: John Sullivan Dwight. Born in Boston in 1813 and educated at Harvard, Dwight came to Brook Farm from Northampton, Massachusetts, where he had been a Unitarian minister with strong transcendentalist leanings. By the time the Hutchinsons arrived, he was teaching music and Latin. He was also leading nightly soirees in the Hive, lively evenings during which he played piano, led his fellow Brook Farmers in sing-alongs, and gave lectures on music.[45]

For Dwight, great music and communal utopia shared the same function: both provided an alternative to the marketplace. He often gave piano concerts at the Hive, playing pieces by Beethoven, Mozart, and Haydn. His goal, he declared, was to turn the farmers' minds "away from that which is but idle, sensual and vulgar," to elevate their tastes above a liking for "Swiss bell ringers and mangled psalmody." He introduced his audience to "the great violinists," Paganini, Dragonetti, and Spagnoletti, to individuals who needed but one exotic name. He informed them of proper musical terminology: terms like "adagio," "andante," and "allegro," for slow, medium, and fast rhythms; terms for striking, sustaining, and trembling notes: "staccato," "sostenuto," and "tremolo." He gave them mystery terms—"forzando," "appoggiatura," and "portamento"—that stood for something . . . something few quite remembered by the next day.[46]

As music scholars maintained and Dwight agreed, the key to the uplifting qualities of music came from its connection to nature and morality. According to one scholar, all that was pleasing in music was derived from the natural world, from the sounds of flowing rivers, chirping birds, and buzzing insects. Another scholar associated with the Boston Academy of Music explained the concept with reference to the intentions behind Beethoven's Sixth Symphony:

> The first [movement] expresses the pleasure which is felt on arriving in the country. The second movement is called "The scene by the brook," and is designed to reproduce the thoughts and feelings excited by the most agreeable of sights and sounds of rural life, the flowing brook, the clear sky, the soft air, the hum of the insect, and the song of the bird. The third movement represents "the gaiety of the country people."[47]

The ideal of nature matched the Brook Farm experiment: it was a concept of nature as harmony, as a moral force deeper and more real than the deceptions of an emerging market. "Music has been called the language of nature," declared a student of the subject, adding that good music had the ability to "calm the feelings, elevate the affections, and prepare the heart for the reception of truths." America's grand "scenery and her solitudes," predicted another expert, would promote great "national tunes," a music uncorrupted by business or politics, "love of money," or "love of party." Great music was moral, he proclaimed in a pamphlet. As proof, he cited his experience as a prosecutor in Philadelphia's courts: he had overseen some two thousand criminal cases, and "in not one of these, was a Teacher of Music concerned, as defendant or accuser." The music of nature provided a pacifying alternative to "competitors in business" and "rivals almost sanguinary in politics," declared yet another scholar on the subject, for, as he put it, "harmony of sound produces harmony of feeling." "Who will deny homage," he asked, "to an art than can make men brethren even for an hour."[48]

For these scholars as for Dwight, the point of "high" music was that it promised an antidote to the selfish spirit of the age. "Here I feel with new force the divine significance of music," Dwight wrote from Brook Farm to fellow reformer Lydia Maria Child. Great music, he added, was "spirit disembodied." It offered an escape from materialism, an aesthetic movement toward "freeing the soul." Child agreed. For her, music was a voice of reform; its key element was the way it invoked "feeling," "heart," and the "indwelling life."[49] Great music was like Brook Farm: it offered a social and communal experience, a place apart from the desires, appetites, and competitive drives of the market.

So what happened to this communal spirit at the heart of American popular culture? The Hutchinsons took quite a bit of it with them when they left Brook Farm. For one thing, the singers would extol a communal version of nature in much of their imagery. Indeed, this may partly explain their affinity for the communists at the farm, for they stressed this imagery before and after their visit. The singers, according to one of their songsters, were "ardent lovers of nature in her simple grandeur." Some of this affiliation could be seen in the alpine backdrops on their sheet-music covers; some, they expressed in their trips to natural areas such as Niagara Falls or the White Mountains of New Hampshire.

For the singers as for many of their middle-class fans, nature represented an uplifting space apart from the competitive artifice of daily life. Indeed, the idea of a mountainous landscape as a metaphor for uplift would come to dominate perceptions of nature through much of the nineteenth and twentieth centuries. Here was the middle-class antidote to the blackface concept of nature as internal, dark, and always downward in direction. For the Hutchinsons, hiking in the White Mountains was an experience of transcendent self-improvement. Climbing from the Crawford House up and over Mount Pierce, Pleasant Dome, Mount Monroe, and at last to the summit of Mount Washington symbolized an entrance to an upper world, a place of natural beauty, healthful exercise, and social communion.[50] To their audiences, the singers were nature incarnate: their songs called forth woods and mountains; their human nature allowed them to express communion with all humanity as a "brotherhood of man." "There is music in the woods," wrote a reviewer of their concerts, "where the birds hold concerts and the wild-flowers have free tickets; where the grasshoppers are worshippers, and the whole insect tribe make the temple of nature ring with song."[51]

This connection to nature allowed the singers to proudly announce themselves as American communists, for nature and human nature were communal. Returning from the Brook Farm commune, they began pooling their earnings in a "common treasury." They invested some of the treasury into the "Old Homestead," which they attempted to run as a kind of miniature Brook Farm. When a couple of the older brothers pushed to abandon the experiment, John, Judson, and Abby declared it a "matter of principle" and voted them down. That summer, John Hutchinson recalled, "we erected what is known as the 'Community Block.'" Constructed at a cost of some $5,000 and located on Milford's town square, the building was a four-story meeting hall for local reform groups. To the singers, communism resonated with tradition: it was rooted in the biblical "lives of the early apostles," the stories of early Christians and their survival through the sharing of all resources. For years, they remained convinced of "the superiority of the apostolic mode of living, as a community."[52]

Elsewhere, it might appear that communal experiments failed or drifted into unnoticed eddies in the larger culture. Not long after leaving Brook Farm in 1846, John Sullivan Dwight founded *Dwight's Journal of Music.* In the years after the Civil War, the journal became a leading voice in the promotion of "classical" music and "highbrow" taste. For at least one historian, this would make Dwight little more than an elitist. Yet Dwight's approach to music remained what it was at Brook Farm. For him, fashionable music continued to have an elevating effect on listeners, creating experiences that were disembodied, harmonious, and separate from market forces. In later years, this approach drifted into schools and colleges. For generations, it would serve as the basis for classes in "music appreciation."[53] Its utopian messages would remain; its communist roots would be forgotten.

As for the many communal societies surrounding the Hutchinsons, few lasted very long. Brook Farm disbanded after a fire ravaged the community in 1846. Other communes, such as the Northampton Association of Education and Industry in Northampton, Massachusetts, seem little more than examples of communism's failure to take root in America. Established in 1842, the commune barely managed to limp along during four years of existence. Its chosen industrial basis—silk production—required more labor and expense than anyone counted on. People took advantage of its ideals. Members drifted in and out. Outsiders treated it as a kind of work farm, demanding that it take in village lunatics and unwanted family members.[54]

The Association was a failure. Yet for those who followed its rise and fall, what mattered were the ideals. The Hutchinsons were visitors. So was Frederick Douglass. The abolitionist and later women's rights symbol Sojourner Truth was a member. Among the Association's ideals were early stances for racial and gender equality. The commune's "Articles of Association" put the issue bluntly in 1842. There were many "great evils that afflict humanity," it declared, from the "extreme ignorance" of the poor to the "self indulgence" of the rich, from the "moral pollution" promoted by new attempts to profit on desires to "war, party corruption, and selfishness." In light of these evils, what mattered was the expression of alternatives: the "vices of the present forms and practices of civilization are so gross and palpable that no apology is required for the honest attempt to escape from them," declared the commune's organizing document; "even if," its drafters added, "this attempt is neither wise nor successful."[55] For the Northampton Association as for the other communes of the time, what mattered was the yearning itself.

The Domestication of American Communism

The yearning would remain. Among the central places it remained would be middle-class gender ideology. According to the thinking, men and women occupied "separate spheres." Men occupied the world of business and exchange, a sphere of increasingly cutthroat competition. Women occupied the world of the home, a domestic sphere of communal affection. Many historians have assumed a hierarchy between the two, suggesting that ideals of domesticity reflected attempts to reduce women to subordinate positions, to imprison them in the home.[56] To middle-class individuals at the time, the two spheres were equal in importance and value. According to the ideology, without the female-run domestic sphere, the whole of American society would collapse.

It would be shattered by the forces of the marketplace. The emerging world of the market revolution and modern capitalism, as even its most vocal defenders admitted, was at best amoral. One problem was that few could put their fingers on the precise difference between amorality and immorality. For its critics, the marketplace seemed characterized by daily examples of deception and dishonesty, by the conscious stoking of base desires. Many a good Christian avoided the issue, blaming the buyer and damning the desire, all the while frantically ignoring the entrepreneurs who massaged both into being. Other sources were more honest. By the close of the 1840s, even the businessman's publication of choice, *Hunt's Merchant Magazine*, lamented the deceptions of the marketplace:

> It has become impossible to have aught to do with business transactions without encountering those who, by an air of candor and justice, succeed in duping those of their fellows not yet initiated in the mysteries of deceiving. Rarely is the man found who preserves unsullied a pure and holy integrity amidst the

game constantly played around him; and to say, there is an honest man, is to say there is a very strange man.[57]

Middle-class gender ideology provided a moral balance to the game. The key to the ideology was the home or, as the ideal's creators had it, the "haven in a heartless world." From the 1820s through the Civil War, practically every high ideal within American culture—from Christian warnings against sin to the list of republican virtues—would make its way into the imagined sphere of the middle-class home. The creators of the ideology would depict women as the rulers of this domestic sphere, the keepers of the nation's virtue. By the middle decades of the nineteenth century, only the home could provide the anchor Americans needed to define themselves as a deeply ethical people held in thrall to an amoral economic system. As the male sphere of the market was drained of moral traditions, the home became a communal utopia.

Far from restricting women to the home, the separate-spheres ideology would develop as a springboard for involvement in the public sphere. The domestic writer Lydia Maria Child would put it best in an 1833 manual for young women:

> Domestic life is a woman's sphere, and it is there that she is most usefully as well as most appropriately employed. But society too, feels her influence, and owes to her, in great measure, its balance and its tone. She may be here a corrective of what is wrong, a moderator of what is unruly, a restraint on what is undecorous. Her presence may be a pledge against impropriety and excess, a check on vice, and a protection to virtue.[58]

From the 1830s through the nineteenth century, women followed this logic into a host of reforms, from early aid societies for widows, orphans, indigents, and immigrants to temperance associations and antislavery societies.[59]

Perhaps the single greatest statement of the ideal of domesticity came at the midpoint of the nineteenth century. It all started, according to later official accounts, when P. T. Barnum—the very man *Hunt's Merchant Magazine* may have had in mind when it lamented the period's new masters of deception—got the idea of bringing the great Jenny Lind to America. Many Americans had heard of Lind. For the *cognoscenti*, she was Europe's greatest female opera singer, known for performances in the operas *La Somnambula*, *Norma*, and *Lucia de Lammermoor*. She was "purely Italian in her method," declared one. She had a "wonderfully developed 'length of breath,'" wrote another, which "enabled her to perform long and difficult passages with ease."[60]

Most of America's middle-class opera devotees were less technical. Many read a biography of the singer by her countrywoman, the actress Fredrika

Bremer. Accordingly, they knew Lind had been born a "poor little girl" in Stockholm, Sweden, in 1820. They knew she had been rescued by a mysterious Swedish nobleman, elevated from the poverty of her family, and sent to the finest singing schools. They learned she remained humble and committed to helping the poor. Above all they learned from Bremer's biography that the singer had "peculiar gifts": she was "lovely in her whole appearance" and sang in a "strong warble," as "graceful as a bird on its branch." And so, in newspapers from the political sheet the *National Era* to Frederick Douglass's *North Star*, Jenny Lind was the "Swedish Nightingale." She was an "ornament" to the "fashionable," a friend to the poor, and the "peerless vocalist of the age."[61]

By the time Barnum made his offer, press notices of the Nightingale were common and the nation was experiencing something of an opera boom. Meanwhile, Lind had decided to retire from the opera stage. Citing vocal wear, she vowed she would give only popular concerts. The timing was right, and Barnum went big: he offered $1,000 per night for 150 nights, a fee that would be split among Lind, her vocal accompanists, her musicians, and her entourage. "My agent went beyond any amount I had anticipated paying," explained the showman later. It was an astounding sum and an enormous risk. Then something happened that turned the thing into a national mania. First, Lind agreed to the contract. Then, after hearing the news while he was on a train to New York, Barnum buttonholed a conductor and declared he was bringing the great Jenny Lind to America. The man stared blankly. "Jenny Lind?" he supposedly stammered, "is she a dancer?" His words, recalled Barnum, "were ice."[62]

The showman went to work. He hired the journalist Nathaniel Parker Willis as advance man for the tour. The pair began seeding the American media with stories. They announced a contest for the best "Welcome Song" for the Nightingale, with the winner to receive $200. They leaked the terms of Lind's contract, declaring that Barnum's offer of $1,000 per night was actually less than the great diva made for her European concerts. There, Barnum averred, she typically received £600 per night. "Once," he added, "she *declined* an offer of £6,000" for twelve appearances in England. Lind was expected to land shortly in New York Harbor, they announced, but was performing to crowded houses in London. None of the city's concert halls could meet the demand for seats, and so a new theater was being built at huge cost. Tickets were selling at lottery. The honor of the first ticket had sold for $225.[63]

The American press picked up the repeated message. The whole thing was largely about money, and for that kind of money, the Nightingale had to be good. An even larger portion of the advance publicity focused on Lind's character. Newspapers everywhere printed her portrait. These depictions of a young and beautiful woman bore only passing resemblance to the older and

FIGURE 7.2. The perfect woman, and the acceptable version of domestic communism. This highly styl-
ized image of Jenny Lind was part of P. T. Barnum's publicity for the Swedish Nightingale's 1850 tour of
America. Thanks largely to Barnum's efforts, along with her adoption of the song "Home, Sweet Home" as
a concert feature, Lind came to embody a modern middle-class gender system: with one side occupied by
the lying, cheating, conniving businessman, the other by the domestic and communistic refuge provided
by the perfect woman. Publicity Portrait of Jenny Lind: C. C. Crehen [on stone], *Jenny Lind*. Printed by
Nagel & Weingartner N.Y. New York: Published by Goupil, Vibert & Co. 289 Broadway, NY, NY [1850].
Courtesy of American Antiquarian Society.

plainer singer. They did fit the parlor ideal that outward beauty reflected inner
qualities. Fredrika Bremer's wildly popular biography filled in some details.
Lind performed "without an effort of art." She contributed to countless charities. Willis and Barnum did the rest. "There is an innate grace and dignity of
manner which never leaves her," declared Willis. She gave a percentage of all
her fees to the poor. She was equally at ease with Queen Victoria and the lowest English cottager. She had a natural affinity and love for America.[64]

On September 1, 1850, Lind arrived at New York City's Canal Street Dock. A crowd estimated at some 30,000 met her ship. A smaller crowd—still in the thousands, according to observers—escorted her to her hotel. Many stayed the night outside her room, serenading her with repeated versions of "Hail Columbia" and "Yankee Doodle." Ten days later, on September 11, at the just-completed Castle Garden Theater, the Swedish Nightingale gave her first American concert. She ran through a few arias, snippets of "Norma," "Casta Diva," and "La Fille du Regiment." She performed duets with her baritone accompanist, "Signor Giovanni Belletti." She gave the crowd some popular numbers, "The Alpine Horn," "The Song of the Nightingale," and "The Bird Song," the last of which, according to an observer, she warbled in "unconscious enjoyment, as if she were indeed holding happy, careless converse with a nightingale."[65]

She sang the "National Prize Song." The winner of Barnum's $200 prize was none other than Bayard Taylor, the most popular poet in the country. Taylor wrote the lyrics, Lind's conductor supplied the tune, and the result was the Nightingale's "Welcome to America":

> I GREET, with a full heart, the Land of the West,
> Whose Banner of Stars o'er a world is unrolled;
> Whose empire o'ershadows Atlantic's wide breast
> And opes to the sunset its gateway of gold!
>
> Thou Cradle of Empire! Though wide be the foam
> That severs the land of my fathers and thee,
> I hear, from thy bosom, the welcome of home,
> For song has a home in the hearts of the Free!

The Jenny Lind–mania was on. The Castle Garden audience was "thrown into a phrenzy of excitement," claimed one reporter. "Women turned pale with intense excitement," he declared, and "men started to their feet in the most frantic manner." The audience cheered "with vehemence such as we have never witnessed." "She was all grace" and "seemed to float upon the air," declared another reporter, adding that her voice transcended description; "as she sang, our whole system vibrated responsively to her notes, as if it had been converted into a musical instrument." With Lind's performance, declared a *Herald* reporter, New Yorkers had witnessed "the perfection of musical vocalization."[66]

At the concert's end, Barnum came out from the wings and announced the proceeds for the evening at $10,000. The showman then began to work his magic. Lind, he declared, had stipulated that New York's Fire Department Fund should receive $3,000 of the night's take. She wanted the city's Musical

Fund Society to receive $2,000. She had earmarked $500 apiece for a host of city charities, starting with the "Home for the Friendless," continuing through the "Lying-in Asylum for Destitute Females, " the "Home for Colored and Aged Persons," the "New York Orphan Association," the "Roman Catholic Half-Orphan Asylum," and the "Old Ladies Asylum." With each name on the list, the Garden crowd exploded in applause. At last, Barnum announced the obvious: Lind had given away every penny of the night's profits. The Nightingale's triumph, declared one reporter, "was complete."[67]

Within a short time, some critical voices appeared. "No one can help being interested in such a sweet, womanly, pure-hearted creature as Jenny Lind," wrote a reporter nearly two months after the first concert; after all, she seemed an example of "unequaled generosity" and "unglazed simplicity." Yet, he added, actually seeing and hearing her "let my imagination down at a terrible rate!" Her singing was "showy"; her face was "well rouged" and set in an expression of "moral milk and honey." The New York triumph left many determined to debunk the mania, claimed another reporter, "led by sheer malice to attend and put her down." One critic made a predictable claim: the adulation had gone to Lind's head: she was as elegant as before but "not as simple"; her notes were as clear "but not as warm."[68]

At some point during her tour, Lind discovered the key to silencing the most jaded of American cynics. She sang—often as an encore—the single most popular ballad of the first half of the century, the middle-class favorite "Home! Sweet Home."

> 'Mid pleasures and Palaces though we may roam,
> Be it ever so humble there's no place like Home!
> A charm from the skies seems to hallow us there,
> Which seek through the world, is ne'er met with elsewhere!
> *Home! Home! Sweet, sweet Home!*
> *There's no place like Home!*
>
> An exile from Home, Splendour dazzles in vain!
> Oh! Give me my lowly thatch'd Cottage again!
> The birds singing gaily that came at my call,
> Give me them with the peace of mind dearer than all.

The song won over the holdouts. "It was not until Jenny sang 'Home, Sweet Home,'" wrote one concertgoer, that he fully understood her combination of "grace, beauty, and simple innocence." The ballad quickly became a centerpiece of her concerts. With it, the Nightingale made herself a living manifestation of a gender system balanced between competitive marketplace and communal haven, a culture whose most celebrated icons—the con artist and the redemptive woman—were simultaneously connected and at opposite ethical extremes. Barnum's man Willis summed up the effect. The Nightingale was "nature's *ne plus ultra* of the mould of woman," he wrote. "She looks," he added, "as if sin or guile were an utter impossibility of her nature, and yet as if she could love with a devotion and self-sacrifice unsurpassable on earth." Finally, he made the all-important conclusion: the "worst man's heart" would be made better "at the whisper of her name."[69]

The Hutchinson Family Singers met Jenny Lind once, during the time of her first New York concerts in 1850. The meeting was another of Barnum's publicity ploys. Lind, he announced to the press, should be introduced to "the best American singers." And so, when the Hutchinsons came through town, he set up a meeting in the diva's hotel room, an intimate get-together attended by Lind, Barnum, the Hutchinsons, and a crowd of reporters. At Barnum's urging, the Hutchinsons agreed to sing a few songs. Lind scrutinized the Americans, unable to figure out "who sang the different parts, declaring 'I never heard such perfect harmony in human voices.'" Afterward, she told the members of the press she was pleased with the "novelty." The Hutchinsons and their songs, she thought, were "particularly American."[70]

As they crossed paths, the singers seemed headed in opposite directions. The Hutchinsons' best years were behind them; Lind was about to take her New York triumph national. These appearances were deceiving. The great charm of Jenny Lind was her ethereal quality: she was "humble, simple, genial and unassuming," an "angel" who could uplift the worst man.[71] The quality was fragile. In December 1850, as she prepared for appearances in Washington and New Orleans, she suddenly faced the threat of coming into focus, of standing for something more concrete than an abstract version of womanly goodness. The threat began with an "insidious report." "It is insinuated," wrote the editor of the *Washington Union* in an open letter to Barnum, "that, besides the numerous acts of beneficence which she has conferred on our countrymen, and which do her much honor, she has presented an association of Abolitionists in the North with one thousand dollars, for the purpose of promoting their alarming and detestable projects."[72]

Lind's camp denied the charge. There was not the "slightest foundation" to the report, wrote Barnum in a published response, adding that the Nightingale's "oft-expressed admiration" for America forbade her from supporting the abolitionists' "attack upon the Union." Before the furor blew over, Lind herself was forced to make a public declaration: she had "never given any money to the abolitionists, and never meant to give any." Her denial, claimed a local paper, was given "with such charming naivité that it simply *had* to put her 'right with the Sunny South.'" For a while, it seemed this might be the case. Yet some observers were disappointed by her denial. A few hinted that she was too eager to please her critics, that she had failed to stand by her principles. Within a short time, this rebuke became a shared assessment: she was "susceptible, too susceptible, to the admiration of the multitude," wrote one critic. She became, he added, what "every ordinary artist is,—'The Slave of the public.'"[73]

Some years later, Jenny Lind passed again through New York City. This time, she sang in a music hall and her program consisted almost entirely of hymns. The price of admission ranged from three to five dollars. A few years later, after several concert tours, a couple of retirements, and a marriage, a California paper referred to "Madam Jenny Goldschmidt" as a "failure" and a "beautiful wreck." Madam Jenny Lind Goldschmidt eventually returned to England, where she died in 1887.[74] In her last years, she probably thought often of her first arrival in America, along with her brilliant triumph. She probably gave little thought to her meeting with the Hutchinsons. If she had, she might have realized that the first dimming of her career started when her name became connected to the issue of slavery. The Hutchinsons, she might have realized, had faced the same situation years earlier. In that moment, the middle-class favorites had taken their middle-class values seriously. Unlike Jenny Lind, they were willing to risk their careers. In doing so, they made their reputation.

Culture Wars

In mid-March 1845, theater agents began posting broadsides in lower Manhattan announcing another visit by the Hutchinsons. The posters included the dates of a series of concerts at Niblo's Garden, along with the planned program. Trouble started as the broadsides went up. Many Americans knew the singers were abolitionists. Yet to this point they had avoided the issue in their public concerts. Now, the Niblo's program included their notorious abolitionist anthem, the incendiary "Get Off the Track!" More than a few critics were outraged. For them, the song was the worst kind of radicalism. It was a harsh denouncement of compromise, a clear call for immediate emancipation. Most alarming, the Hutchinsons were nearing the height of their popularity and the song was extremely catchy. Their performance would make thoughts of abolition stick with audiences for weeks, perhaps months.[1]

Immediately, two of the city's anti-abolitionist newspapers, the *New York Herald* and the *New York Express*, warned the singers not to perform the song. By the day of the concert, the papers were hinting at calls for mob violence. Meanwhile, the Hutchinsons retreated to a boardinghouse near the theater. Through the day, a line of anxious friends stopped by to see them. Someone came with the rumor that "sixty young New York rowdies" had purchased tickets for the first concert. They were planning to greet the song with a hail of "brickbats and other missiles." Later, news arrived that Niblo's two thousand seats had sold out. The ruffians could be anywhere in the hall. As the time of the concert approached, the singers were unsure of what to do. Had they misread Manhattan's openness to reform? "Even our most warm and enthusiastic friends among the abolitionists took alarm," recalled Abby Hutchinson; they "begged that we might omit the song, as they did not wish to see us get killed."[2]

FIGURE 8.1. Abolition goes popular. Published in 1843, the Hutchinson Family Singers' "Get Off the Track!" would become the most popular abolition anthem of the 1840s. Part of what made the song so well known was that it was enormously controversial. Set to the tune of Dan Decatur Emmett's "Old Dan Tucker," the song would be at the center of a type of culture war between the communities who coalesced around the Hutchinsons' messages of reform and the proslavery forces gathered around blackface minstrelsy. When they listed the song on their program for an 1845 concert at Niblo's Garden Theater in New York City, the singers faced threats of a mob attack. Sheet-music cover: Jesse Hutchinson Jr., *Get Off the Track!* Boston, Jesse Hutchinson Jr., 1844. Courtesy of American Antiquarian Society.

At first glance, there may seem nothing odd about this story. As one early abolitionist put it, this was the "martyr age" of the antislavery movement, a time when mobs effected a "reign of terror" on its supporters. The 1830s and early 1840s had many days that "tried men's souls," recalled another old reformer, days when critics of slavery spoke "with their lives in their hands." In official narratives handed down through popular histories, America's early abolitionists often appear as "a small but vocal minority." The image that comes to mind is a tiny knot of men and women, usually standing in the rain outside the cell of a fugitive slave, dressed in mourning cloth and singing gloomy hymns. They are idealists, purposefully presented as ineffectual and pathetic. Seeing them, the viewer awaits the true hero of abolition, the man of action whose moderate pragmatism will get the job done.[3]

Historians have done much to support this interpretation. Some have portrayed the movement in heroic terms, focusing on abolitionist leaders as heroes ahead of their time, despised but essentially right. Others have depicted them as crackpots or hypocrites. Still others have described the movement as hopelessly split between factions. They have drawn sharp distinctions between a moderate antislavery movement, which had some support, and the more "radical" cause of abolition, which was simply too much for most Americans.[4] Recently, scholars have found that some local abolition groups were able to gain popular followings. Despite these discoveries, the overall conclusion remains unchanged. One scholar has summed it up: "Abolitionism was never a popular cause before the Civil War," for "to embrace abolitionism was to embrace radicalism."[5]

The Hutchinson Family Singers and the context of popular song may call for a questioning of this conclusion. Indeed, after further review, there *is* something odd in the story. The singers were well-known abolitionists. Yet they sold out Niblo's Garden mighty quickly. The *Herald* and the *Express* were awfully concerned with what should have been an unpopular group of singing radicals. The singers were clearly vocal in their beliefs, and they were a minority of the larger population; but the people around them do not appear to have been a small group. The abolitionism of the Hutchinson Family Singers was pervasive and entertaining. It had widespread appeal, broad support, and was impossible to ignore. As public abolitionists, the Hutchinsons would be controversial. They would also be at the very center of American popular culture. Finally, they would find themselves at the center of a culture war, a conflict that would lead to a national bloodbath, decide the fate of slavery, and define the meanings of "radical" and "mainstream" in American political culture.

"Friends of Emancipation"

By the end of 1842, the word was out: the Hutchinsons were abolitionists. The word came from Nathaniel Peabody Rogers, the editor of an abolitionist newspaper in Concord, New Hampshire, the *Herald of Freedom*. "Perhaps I am partial to the Hutchinsons," Rogers wrote following the quartet's performance in Concord, "for they are abolitionists." He admitted the information might cause them trouble. But he was unconcerned, insisting that it "need not affright them to have it announced." He encouraged the singers to take the next step along the path of reform, writing that he wished they had "a series of Anti-Slavery Melodies to sing at their Concerts." "The time is coming," he added, "when the public conscience will feel quieted at the thought of having heard music from the friends of the slave, and patronized it."[6]

The singers were not so sure. For the next two years, they confined their public performances to a "general program of glees, sentimental and harmonious pieces." They remained aware, recalled John Hutchinson, that there was an "intense, bitter spirit" against anything "that should appear tinctured with the unpopular movement towards emancipation."[7] Despite Rogers's belief that the timing was right for a wider movement, in 1842, the singers were not ready to risk their careers. Like most Americans who joined the cause, they would find the path to public abolition long and difficult.

For the Hutchinsons as for others, taking the first step along this path required seeing the problem. Growing up in rural New England in the 1830s, the future singers had practically no contact with slavery and little contact with African Americans. John Hutchinson recalled only one black person in the Milford of his youth, "a tall, well-proportioned, athletic, uneducated but witty African," who "came into the neighborhood at the abandonment of the slave system in Massachusetts." The man was a marginal figure in the town. He worked, as far as anyone could remember, as a hired hand on several local farms. His reputation for athletics came from his participation in Milford's annual "Muster Day" festival, when the menfolk treated him to drinks and encouraged him—"to the amusement of all"—to wrestle "all comers."

In later years, he became better known for being one-half of the town's only interracial couple. According to John's recollections, the couple started as a joke. At some point early in the century, one of the poorest women in the town had been jilted by a lover. In a fit of anger, she made a public vow: she would marry the first man who proposed. A group of Milford wags paid the "witty African" to make an offer. To everyone's surprise, the woman accepted. The couple married, produced several children, and "lived in comparative isolation," John recalled. The town treated them with "proper courtesy," he added, even though many "considered the match a questionable one."[8]

These recollections reveal the changing contexts of race and politics in New England. By the 1840s, Milford would be a hotbed of antislavery reform, a regular stop on the abolitionist lecture circuit. In the 1820s and 1830s, it seems, the town was a typical Northern backwater, a place where black people were practically invisible. Coming of age at this time, the sons and daughters of Jesse and Polly Hutchinson may have shared this narrowness of vision. Indeed, in his fond memory of Milford's "lone African," John Hutchinson seems to have left out some crucial information on the town's black population.

The information would come out later. In 1859, a woman named Harriet Wilson would publish a novel called *Our Nig; or, Sketches from the Life of a Free Black*. Sometimes referred to as the first novel published by an African American in the United States, the book told the story of "Frado," a teenaged servant girl to a white family in an unnamed New England town. The head of the family, "Mr. Bellmont," was one of the town's leading citizens, a reformer and a respected businessman. His wife was something else entirely, and she would be the focus of the narrative.

Mrs. Bellmont, according to Wilson's story, was a "She-Devil." The character was compelled by an inexplicable fury at all things and all people. When Mr. Bellmont was home, her anger was blunted by diffusion: to her husband, she was a "thorough scold"; to her children, she was "haughty" and "severe." Though slavery had long passed away in the novel's New England setting, she referred to Frado as the family's "nigger" or, as the book's title had it, "our nig." When her husband was away, she focused her full fury on the servant. The result was a pattern of hidden abuse that went on for years. At times the She-Devil beat Frado for trifling offenses, for "impudence" or tiny errors in daily tasks. At other times she bound, gagged, and flogged the servant out of wanton cruelty, for the perverse pleasure of the thing.

Wilson's She-Devil was clearly a psychotic. She was also, declared the novelist, an abolitionist. Poor and a single mother, Wilson's goal in writing the book was to sell copies and make money. Yet she undermined her first goal with a second, with her need to shed withering light on Northern hypocrisy, her desire to show that "slavery's shadows fall even there." By focusing her story on a young girl "maltreated by professed abolitionists, who didn't want slaves at the South, nor niggers in their own houses, North," Wilson went out of her way to offend the very group—professed abolitionists—who might have bought it. And so, while the novel was loaded with highly readable scenes of family dysfunction and physical torture, and while it found a publisher, it made barely a ripple in the period's pool of ex-slave narratives and reform-based literature.

What happened to make *Our Nig* both a readable book and a book that almost no one read? The answer, it appears, is that Wilson fell into the trap of the first-time novelist: once she started writing, she found it easiest to write about herself. The problem with *Our Nig* was that it was more memoir than novel; it had pathos and pain, but it was too true and far too bitter to be read in comfort. Wilson hinted at the book's basis, in fact, in her preface, writing, "I have purposely omitted what would provoke shame in our good anti-slavery friends at home."[9] The statement raises several questions. What was the name of Frado's New England town? Who was the She-Devil? And who were Wilson's "anti-slavery friends," the good folks at home with so much to hide?

The town was Milford, New Hampshire. Born in 1827, Harriet Wilson, or Harriet Adams, as she was then called, grew up in the southern New Hampshire village. She may have been one of the offspring of John Hutchinson's "lone African." If so, she provided a few details that John omitted. Her father died shortly after her birth. Her mother, far from being treated with courtesy, became a pariah after her interracial marriage. When she was widowed, the people of Milford ran her out of town, forcing her to abandon her children to service in white households. At some point in the 1830s, Harriet Adams became a servant in the Milford household of Nehemiah Hayward. Several years earlier, Hayward had married the woman who would become the "She-Devil" of Wilson's tortured memory. The woman's name was Rebecca Hutchinson.[10]

The "anti-slavery friends" Wilson worried about shaming were almost certainly the Hutchinson Family Singers, for Rebecca Hutchinson Hayward was their second cousin. At first glance, Wilson's *Our Nig* reveals little more than the hypocrisy of Northern abolitionists. Although they were not extremely close, the Hutchinsons and the Haywards did have a number of relationships. David Hutchinson, the "tribe's" oldest brother, was married to one of the Hayward daughters. The singing Hutchinson brothers were friends with two of the Hayward sons. Later, during their tours, they would stay with one of them in Baltimore.[11] Given the ties between the families, the future singers almost certainly visited the Hayward household in the 1830s. Did they notice the family's servant girl? Did they see bruises, scars, or tears?

Apparently, they did not. Yet more than hypocrisy, Wilson's story reveals the enormous changes of the time. In the 1830s, the town of Milford was blind to the plight of the servant girl in the Hayward household. The blindness allowed Rebecca Hutchinson Hayward to abuse young Harriet Adams for years. During the 1840s, Milford would become known as an abolition stronghold and the hometown of the Hutchinson Family Singers. Of course, this fact would not have stopped someone in the town from engaging in abusive behavior toward a black servant. But it would have changed the meaning of this behavior. By the 1850s, Wilson could assume that the singers' relationship with her abuser—even a distant relationship—would be a source of shame. What the story reveals is the tremendous growth in racial consciousness and antislavery thought between 1830 and 1859. What *Our Nig* reveals, in other words, is the emergence of a widely shared view of slavery as not merely a peculiarity of slaveholders in the South. Slavery had become the "nation's shame."

For the small band of abolitionists who founded the New England Anti-Slavery Society in 1831, the possibility that such a view would one day be widely shared seemed a long way off. Down to this time, the individuals in favor of a nationwide abolition of slavery tended to be few and far between. They tended to be Quakers, inner-light Christians, and conscience abolitionists, individuals who were sometimes ex–slave traders or slave-ship captains, people whose opposition to slavery developed out of direct and personal experience with its horrors. Or they tended to be "re-colonizationists," people like Thomas Jefferson, who favored freeing slaves and then sending "that population from among us" to "any place on the coast of Africa."[12]

At the beginning of the 1830s, two national antislavery societies appeared. One would come to be known as the New York and Ohio wing of the movement. Funded largely by the New York merchants Arthur and Lewis Tappan and centered at Charles Finney's Lane Seminary in Cincinnati, Ohio, this would be the moderate wing. Its members believed in the system, and they would work through political channels for a gradual end to slavery. The other, the New England Anti-Slavery Society, would owe its stance to William Lloyd Garrison. Garrison, who began publishing his paper, the *Liberator*, on January 1, 1831, would reject "gradualism" to push for the immediate end to slavery. The New England Society would follow suit, taking a stand that would be called "ultraism" or "immediatism." The society's "sole object," according to one of its founding documents, was "to bring about by all lawful and moral means the immediate abolition of slavery in our land."[13]

Garrison's "radicalism" would be the stance that caught on. Either a large number of Americans were fine with a radical cause or the cause was not quite as radical as some scholars have maintained. In December 1833, members of the New England Society along with abolitionists from other Northern states came together in Philadelphia to form the American Anti-Slavery Society. "We maintain," claimed the society's "Declaration of Sentiments":

> That every American citizen, who retains a human being in involuntary bondage is (according to Scripture) a MAN STEALER;

That the slaves ought instantly to be set free, and brought under the protection
of law;

That all those laws which are now in force, admitting the right of slavery, are
therefore before God utterly null and void.[14]

The point, declared the meeting-goers, was to pit abolition's "love and
truth," its "moral purity" and "spirit of repentance," against slavery's error, prejudice, and "moral corruption." Rejecting the compromises of political channels, its leaders, agents, and members focused their efforts on changing
minds about slavery. In the South, where a few societies had sprung up in
favor of gradual emancipation and recolonization, the movement's new tone
resulted in the near-disappearance of abolition from the region. In the North,
the strategies worked exceedingly well. The movement went from forty-seven
local societies in 1833 to some 1,300 by 1839. Agents from Lane Seminary and
the Garrison wing of the movement scattered throughout the country. Anti-
slavery lecturers made the rounds between Northern cities and towns. Slavery—or slavery and how to end it—became one of the most popular topics at
local lyceum halls, the public lecture buildings that constituted the period's
blending of republican uplift with entertainment.

Although often studied as a political movement, abolition owed much of its
success to popular culture. Antislavery newspapers began cropping up everywhere. National and local groups produced countless tracts. Both types of publication soon developed a standard iconography: images of lone slaves on the
auction block, looking heavenward beneath the caption "Am I not a brother?";
pictures of slave mothers or children being beaten by cruel masters. The images
went for individuals with middle-class values, people for whom motherhood
was sacred, anger was suspect, physical punishment of children was anathema,
and the release of bodily fluids (such as blood) was vulgar.[15] In many areas of
the North, local societies raised the cause's visibility by organizing antislavery
fairs. Typically run by women, these events charged between twelve and a half
cents and a quarter for admission, for which fairgoers had the pleasure of min-
gling, taking refreshments, and rummaging for donated goods.

These events were successful at spreading the word and raising money.
One fair, held in 1837 in Syracuse, New York, offered "useful and fancy articles at reasonable market prices." It invited "the patronage of the humane
and philanthropic to come and buy; remembering that it is for the poorest of
the poor—the POOR SLAVE." An organizing poster for another fair, held in
Boston in the 1840s, claimed the last year's event had raised over $2,000. "Will
not you," the broadside asked in an appeal for volunteers and donations, "be
true to your own moral nature, and gladly give time, labor, money, prayer,

sacrifice, that you may save a nation—redeem a race—ennoble an age?" The broadside for another Boston fair suggests the resultant mixture of hand-crafts and used objects. It offered "cloaks, dresses, bonnets and hoods of the Victoria pattern," along with "oil paintings, ornaments, Scottish clan tartans, rare books, Chinese toys, opera shawls, Berlin worsted, *Papier Mache* articles, [and] white gilded porcelain door handles and plates."[16]

Antislavery gatherings also offered literature, lectures, and music. Many volunteers handed out tracts and pamphlets. Others sold copies of *The Liberty Bell*, the most popular antislavery gift book of the time. Fairs and bazaars sometimes promised dances. Most formal celebrations followed the church-like "Order of Services" of the early temperance meeting, the old lineup of hymns, scripture readings, prayers, and finally an address by an abolitionist leader. One hymn sung at a July Fourth celebration repeated the imagery of the antislavery tract, the "wicked slaver," the "weeping slave and friend," and the pleadings of "mothers and children." It concluded with an appeal to the slaveholder: "Cruel Tyrant, / When will thy oppressions end?"[17]

If the movement had a radical message, the meetings packaged it in the familiar vessel of the hymn. "Think of our country's glory, / All dimmed with Afric's tears," sang a crowd at the New England Anti-Slavery Society's "Independence Day" get-together in 1832. Garrison then gave one of his typically fiery addresses. Afterward, while the collection plates went around, the crowd sang another hymn. This one had an edge to it, an admission that Christians owned slaves and countenanced slavery:

> Hears't Thou, O God, those chains,
> Clanking on Freedom's plains,
> By Christians wrought![18]

By 1838, the Female Anti-Slavery Society of Lynn, Massachusetts, attributed its "considerable accession of numbers" directly to the influence of antislavery meetings, fairs, publications, and lectures. By 1839, one of the officers of a nearby association, the Anti-Slavery Society of Greater Lynn, was none other than Jesse Hutchinson Jr. With his early apprenticeship at the *Farmer's Cabinet* and his move to Lynn, Jesse became aware of the antislavery movement sometime in advance of his siblings. As the decade turned, his involvement increased. He became acquainted with a new arrival in Lynn, a man who lived a "few rods down the street." The newcomer was Frederick Douglass.[19]

Jesse Hutchinson also became a "come outer." The position stemmed from the abolition goal of purifying the nation's church and clergy from participation in the guilt of slavery. When Milford's Baptists refused to denounce the institution, Jesse "came out" of the church, renouncing his membership. In 1842, he organized a come-outer meeting in Milford, a rally to protest the "cowardly organizations and clergy" who refused to "lift the foot from the neck of the struggling slave."[20]

When the Hutchinson Family Singers left Milford for their first tour in the winter of 1842, they were typical of young reformers with antislavery leanings. At a stop in the resort town of Saratoga Springs, New York, they saw slavery for the first time. The town represented one of the many overlapping points between the "free North" and "slave South." Just as many Northerners went south during winter months, many planters came north to escape the heat of Southern summers. They created enclaves in places like Cape May, New Jersey, and Newport, Rhode Island. They were largely responsible for making Saratoga Springs a resort destination, developing a culture of gaming there that made the town as notorious for horseracing as it was known for water and baths. Many, it seems, brought their slaves along with them. For the first time, recalled John Hutchinson, "we observed our slave-holding neighbors, clothed in their wealth, displaying the elegance of their equipages." The wealth was built on "the blood of slaves."[21]

As they widened their scope of vision, the singers deepened their interest in the abolition movement. In Concord, New Hampshire, they met Nathaniel Peabody Rogers. After their performance in the town, they spoke with the editor about their growing commitment to the cause. Rogers followed with a glowing review and an announcement: the Hutchinsons were abolitionists.

The word soon spread to the Boston offices of the American Anti-Slavery Society. At some point in the middle of 1842, Society organizer John Collins determined that the formal style of the annual meeting had grown stale. The Society, he wrote an associate, needed to "deviate from the ordinary and stereotyped plan of oratory . . . and adopt some novel method, in which all can participate." By the end of the year, he discovered his "novel method." He invited the Hutchinsons to perform at the Society's annual meeting, to be held at Boston's Faneuil Hall in January 1843. To his delight, the singers accepted. Collins then printed up a circular letter and sent it out to the association's members. The Hutchinsons' "happy influence" on an audience "must be witnessed," he wrote, "it can't be described."[22]

The Boston meeting turned out to be the Society's liveliest to date. And though Jesse Hutchinson replaced Abby for the performance, the singers were no small part of its success. Following a speech by Wendell Phillips, the brothers rushed to the stage. They burst into Jesse's "The Old Granite State," adding a new verse toward the song's end:

> Yes, we're friends of Emancipation
> And we'll sing a proclamation,
> Till it echoes through the nation,
> From the Old Granite State,
> That the tribe of Jesse,
> That the tribe of Jesse,
> That the tribe of Jesse,
> Are the friends of Equal Rights![23]

Some among the abolitionist old guard were taken aback. The Quaker Lucretia Mott found the performance overly festive and emotional, not quite in keeping with the seriousness of the cause. Nathaniel Peabody Rogers was ecstatic. "Oh, it was glorious!" he wrote a few days later, adding that the vast majority of the crowd had been receptive. "There was music in it," he declared: "I wish the whole city, and the entire country could have been there . . . Slavery would have died of that music and the response of the multitude."[24]

"We Are Going to Sing If We Have to Die for It"

Slavery was not quite ready to die. Following their triumph at the 1842 meeting of the American Anti-Slavery Society, the Hutchinsons began to include the new verses of "The Old Granite State" in a few of their public concerts. Yet they remained fearful of losing public favor. They left the verses out of their 1844 concerts in Baltimore and Washington, DC. "I feel determined to do something for the poor slave," wrote Asa in the family diary after their visits to the cities along with their slave markets. Instead, they did what entertainers did in Washington. They performed for political luminaries, giving parlor concerts attended by men like Kentucky senator Henry Clay, Virginia governor Henry Wise, and ex-President John Tyler. All three were slave owners. "These were trying times," John recalled, "and the effort to make an artistic success without doing violence to our consciences was no very easy matter."[25]

For at least one scholar, this pattern reveals "more than a suggestion of mild hypocrisy."[26] It also raises a question: given the fact that they had some evidence to the contrary, why did the singers persist in believing that any statement they made on behalf of direct abolition would destroy their popularity? Aside from simple hypocrisy—which seems a bit of a catch-all charge—the reasons seem to have centered on the cultural struggles of the time. As their popularity grew and their messages became more threatening, the Hutchinsons would be accused of "radicalism." They would be identified as middle class, affected, stiff in manners, and feminized. Finally, they would be targeted for physical violence. The charge of hypocrisy masks the possibility that the singers had real reasons to fear coming out as public abolitionists. After all, they were up against some extremely powerful forces in American society and culture.

Few ideas have had more staying power than the equation between abolition and radicalism. To be sure, there is evidence for the assertion. By the time of the formation of the American Anti-Slavery Society, slavery had existed in North America some two hundred years. Of the first seven US presidents, five were slaveholders. From at least the 1820s onward, proslavery writers did everything they could to link slavery to tradition. Many tied the institution to antiquity and biblical verse, arguing that it had doctrinal sanction, claiming its descent from the great republics of Greece and Rome.

Others tied it to the timelessness of science and the supposed universality of white America's phobia about African Americans. From the time of the Revolution, white Americans were unanimous in their knowledge that slavery was wrong, undying in their hostility to the idea of being enslaved, whether by tyrants or factory bosses. What made it right, according to many of its defenders, was ethnic difference. Blacks were like children, maintained one proslavery scholar; they were "weak, ignorant, and dependent brethren." And so they had to be enslaved and the slave owner was "the negro's friend, his only friend."[27] Still other writers stressed that while all white Americans hated slavery, they also hated black people. All one had to do to understand the radicalism of abolition, according to these writers, was to witness the treatment of free blacks in the North, where even abolitionists "shrink from them as if the touch was pollution."[28]

Constantly repeated in the 1830s, the assertion that slavery and race hatred were an American tradition worked well. In perception, at least, it marked abolition with the tinge of radicalism and seemed to marginalize the movement. Meanwhile, the rhetoric seems to have had a direct effect on early abolitionists. Early converts to the cause acquiesced in defining themselves as radical and unpopular. In its formative days, the movement was little more than "a subject for taunts," declared Harriet Martineau in her account of abolition's "martyr age." "We were right, and all the world about us was wrong," recalled John Greenleaf Whittier, admitting that "to onlookers our endeavor . . . must have seemed absurd. We could look for no response but laughs of derision or the missiles of a mob."[29]

They took quite a bit of both. In 1831, a mob in Saint Louis killed the abolitionist publisher Elijah Lovejoy. Four years later, a Boston crowd attacked William Lloyd Garrison, binding him with rope and dragging him through the city's streets. In the same year, a young man named Amos Dresser, one of the many agents sent out from Cincinnati's Lane Seminary, was arrested in

Nashville, Tennessee. When the local magistrates found no law he had broken, they simply convicted him of being a member of an antislavery society and had him whipped in the public square.

In the 1830s, anti-abolitionist violence became a hallmark of many eastern cities. The abolitionists appeared to take the violence in true martyr style. Among the most important ideals of the movement was the rejection of "carnal weapons." Using only their "earnestness of zeal" and "steadfastness of faith," their task was to confront the "Slave Power" with "moral suasion." They would marshal evidence and reason in their cause. They would talk and persuade their way to success. To many observers, this dynamic of violence on one side and meek submission on the other made it look like the world was against them.

Yet how radical and unpopular was abolition? From a world perspective, things were trending in the movement's direction. Early in the nineteenth century, a wave of independence movements swept Spanish South America. Between 1810 and 1823, some seven new nations declared independence and abolished slavery, including Chile in 1810, Columbia in 1820, and Mexico in 1821. The greatest coup came on August 28, 1833. On that day, after years of effort by individuals like William Wilberforce and Thomas Clarkson, the British Parliament abolished slavery throughout the empire. In 1848, France, under pressure from England and fired by the spirit of the Europe-wide revolutions, would declare the immediate abolition of slavery in all its possessions. By 1855, nearly the rest of Latin America followed suit. On the eve of the American Civil War, slavery, which once dominated the Western Hemisphere, had been reduced to four last bastions: Puerto Rico, Cuba, Brazil, and the US South.[30]

From the 1830s through the 1850s, abolitionist writers made sure that with every attack on an abolitionist, careful notes would be taken and the atrocity would be published. The period's reformers understood what later scholars would fail to recognize: the greater the number of anti-abolition atrocities, the greater the popularity of abolitionism. Indeed, proslavery forces seem to have recognized that the beatings played into the reformers' hands. The 1830s saw a rapid rise and fall in the number of anti-abolitionist riots. These riots reached their peak in 1835. By the end of the decade, they had all but disappeared.[31]

Meanwhile, in 1836, agents found some thirty-four thousand Americans willing to sign antislavery petitions to be sent on to the US Congress. The House of Representatives responded by passing its notorious "gag resolution," agreeing to receive the petitions only to table them and deny members any discussion of their subject or content. Immediately, abolitionist agents pinned the petition drives to the rights of redress and free speech. In 1838, with the gag renewed for a third year, agents sent petitions with three hundred thousand signatures. By 1844, when the House finally lifted the gag resolution, the number of signatures had reached some two million.[32]

By 1844, when the Hutchinson's first performed their abolitionist anthem "Get Off the Track!", it seemed to many that the forces of slavery were on the run, that abolition's time had come. The singers introduced the song at the May meeting of the American Anti-Slavery Society in Boston. According to family lore, Jesse Hutchinson wrote the lyrics to the song shortly before the meeting. The song's sheet music, which would be released later, declared that Jesse took the tune from an old slave song.

Held in Boston's Tremont Temple, the meeting was crowded. Abolitionists gathered from all over the Northeast, massing under the Society's enormous new banners proclaiming "Immediate and Unconditional Emancipation" and "No Union with Slaveholders." On the night of May 31, William Lloyd Garrison spoke. He took on the charge that abolitionists were radicals, declaring that in fact "our principles are the only ones on which a free government can stand." The Hutchinsons then took the stage. This time Abby was there along with Jesse, the extra voice giving the singers a richer sound, filling out their harmonies. "Ho! the car emancipation," they began in curiously rhythmic fashion, almost chanting:

> Rides Majestic through our nation.
> Bearing on its train the glory,
> LIBERTY! a nation's glory.
> Roll it along! Roll it along!
> Roll it along! through the nation,
> Freedom's car, Emancipation.[33]

The song moved through verses lauding Garrison and *The Liberator*, criticisms of the Northern church and clergy, and attacks on Henry Clay's politics of compromise. As they reached the song's crescendo, the singers abandoned all sense of "timing and rule," according to Nathaniel Rogers. Instead, they gave way to an increasing tempo. The rising intensity, Rogers declared, conjured forth images of abolition as a runaway train rushing toward a multitude of Americans "stupidly lingering" on the tracks, an unstoppable force heading at them with "terrible enginery and speed and danger." By the song's end, he recalled, the singers were almost shouting, crying panicked warnings of "get out of the way!" just as if they really were "about to witness a terrible railroad tragedy." They then settled back into the melody, finishing with a series of "hurrahs" as the multitude boarded "Freedom's Car."[34]

The effect was stunning. Rogers, along with some in the audience, simply stared, awestruck at the singers' theatrical power. Others stomped and clapped in time. Several, including Garrison himself, seem to have literally danced in the aisles, rhythmically punching the air with their fists.[35] Apart from the dramatics, there was something irresistible in the song, something overwhelmingly familiar. Far from being an old slave song, the tune had been taken fresh from the popular stage. It was the Virginia Minstrels' "Old Dan Tucker," the nation's most popular and ubiquitous song. Jesse Hutchinson had lifted a blackface tune for what would soon be recognized as the most blatant abolitionist anthem of the era.

Here, as elsewhere, the supposedly radical American abolition movement began to make its way into popular culture. It moved, that is, from being controversial and well known toward becoming literally popular, embraced by a large part of the population. As early as 1842, the American Anti-Slavery Society published *The Anti-Slavery Pick-Nick*, a songster "designed to interest the young in the anti-slavery cause" and a how-to guide for "public celebrations." "Public Opinion," suggested John Collins in the *Pick-Nick*'s preface, "is now so modified on the question of slavery, that common and other schools will tolerate the rehearsal of pieces which embody the principles of freedom."[36] A year later, the editors of another antislavery songster looked forward to a greater role for music in advancing the popularity of the cause:

> The influence of Temperance Songs is no longer to be questioned as a powerful means of carrying forward our cause. If the progress of *that* reform is indebted, in any degree, to the aid of *music*, will not the *Anti-Slavery cause* be advanced by the same means? Let our Anti-Slavery friends turn their attention to this subject, and organize in every town *an Anti-Slavery choir*. There are many who have not the gift of *speech-making*, but who can, by *song-singing*, make strong appeals, in behalf of the slave, to every community and to every heart.[37]

Within a short time, the choirs had been organized, and it was not uncommon to find broadsides, sheet music, and songsters with antislavery lyrics set to lively and popular tunes.[38] At the time, at least, it would be increasingly difficult to paint abolitionists as repressed sourbellies, as the enemies of all popular amusements. As one attendee of an "*Abolition* frolic" put it, these gatherings were lively social evenings as well as sites for political discussion, occasions at which the movement's supporters "tead, danced and made noisy fun until early morning."[39]

Certainly the Hutchinsons' audiences grew more noisy and numerous. Soon they began hearing shouted calls for "Get Off the Track!" while they were onstage. At a concert in Bath, Maine, they obliged. To their pleasure and surprise, they "received cheers such as we seldom heard." By the time they arrived in New York City on March 17, 1845, for a concert at Niblo's Garden, they were convinced, as John put it, "that people would take in song what they would not in any other way."[40] Despite the fact that this would be a public concert, when the broadsides with their programs went up, they included "Get Off the Track!"

Two days later, the singers were holed up in a boardinghouse near the theater, surrounded by fretting abolitionist friends, anxiously awaiting the time of their concert and the arrival of a mob of anti-abolitionist rowdies. Manhattan, they realized, perhaps even the whole country, was still "very tender" when it came to the issue of slavery. The papers had delivered their warnings, saying the family should not be allowed to sing "Get Off the Track!," adding that if they dared sing it, "they deserve to be mobbed."

As the time of the concert approached, the landlady of the house offered her services to the singers. "Boys," she said, according to Abby Hutchinson's recollections, "if any disturbance occurs in the concert you look out for yourselves. I shall rush to the stage and take Abby bodily, and carry her off in my arms." At last the singers stood and prepared to walk to the theater. "Gentlemen," said Abby Hutchinson as she gestured to the program, "we are going to sing this tonight, if we have to die for it." With their landlady marching beside them, they made their way to Niblo's Garden.[41]

In later years, the Hutchinsons would get used to criticisms and even threats of violence. At the same time, the tone of these verbal attacks, their intensity of anger and the passion of their hatred, probably made the threats seem real. Abolition may have been becoming more popular, but it still took courage to proclaim the cause in front of a crowd. From 1845 to 1850, many of the charges against the singers would be articulated in the "working class" style of masculine rowdies. One hostile reviewer, for example, summed up a typical Hutchinson concert as a crowd of "well dressed people" listening to a "selection of namby pamby ballads" performed with an "awkward stiffness of manner, and studied affectation of rusticity." The reviewer concluded with a standard attack on the presumed feminized sensibilities of both the singers and the middle class. "How much better it would be," he mused, "if they would sing good manly songs?"[42]

Others debunked the singers' popularity. One claimed they paid for their positive reviews, or "puffs," at a rate of "ten cents a line," adding that that their audiences were large only because they provided free tickets to clergy, schoolmasters and teachers, and members of "abolition, tract, temperance and moral reform societies." Another maintained that despite their "paid puffs," which depicted them as "the most wonderful artists of the age," the singers were contemptible and worthless: "The Negro melodies at southern corn shuckings are infinitely superior."[43]

Just as often, these charges came from the paternal elite, the old Whig and Democrat "gentlemen of property and standing" who continued to see themselves as the defenders of the common people against the reformist agenda of the rising urban middle class. Immediately after the sheet-music publication of "Get Off the Track!" in 1844, for example, writers for the *Boston Atlas* expressed outrage at the song's lack of good taste, particularly its criticism of Henry Clay. "When the vocalists known by the name of the 'Hutchinson Family' first made their appearance in Boston," they wrote, "we felt some interest for them, for their nativity, their simplicity of manners, and their unadorned music." Yet, they went on to say, "if audiences can be entertained with the trashy words of this song, their poetical tastes must be of a very low order."[44]

Other newspapers upbraided the singers for their "contemptible spirit of gain," along with their pretensions to the higher standards of European artists. They needed to be told, claimed one reviewer, that they were "only a company of common song-singers, whose performances sound very pleasingly to the great mass of people, ignorant of real music." Still others faulted them for their vision of middle-class inclusiveness, for allowing "Guinea Negroes" to attend their concerts, and for lowering musical standards by making "Ethiopian Serenaders" of themselves. Similarly, for writers of an editorial in the *New York Sunday Era*, the Hutchinsons were members of "Garrison's band of whitewashed nigger minstrels."[45]

This strange term reflected one of the most passionate and angry charges against the singers: the fact that once they became wildly successful they began to demand that musical hall and theater owners open their concerts to racially integrated audiences. According to their attackers, this would affect a kind of miscegenation, or "practical amalgamation," in the terminology of the time. The charge appears to have been based on a blend of beliefs: a kind of germ theory of race, in which whites in mixed-race spaces could actually "catch" blackness, along with an erotic fixation on race mixing as producing instantaneous sexual liaisons. "We have a serious charge to make against the managers of the Hutchinson Family," declared the editor of a Philadelphia paper,

> for not having announced in their handbills and advertisements, that no distinction of color would be made in admitting people to their concerts. It is well known that a distinction is made on all ordinary occasions, and that there are many persons in the community who would on no account, knowingly, place themselves and their families in promiscuous association with the colored race.[46]

The singers "need not be told," the editorial added, that the "feeling against practical amalgamation" was so strong that audience members, unless they were warned, would "feel tricked" into attending an integrated concert, forced into a "an association which they abhor." The singers needed to "learn to tell the difference between black and white," declared another critic. "Let them," he added, "make perfect 'Ethiopian Serenaders' of themselves . . . but they must not do it before 'mixed assemblies.'"[47]

Just how much did white audience members actually object to these integrated concerts? The answer probably depended on the concert hall and the crowd. At one concert in Philadelphia, one observer witnessed little more than "hardly noticeable exhibitions of displeasure . . . at the presence of a few respectable colored persons." At a concert in Rochester, New York, Frederick Douglass noted a change in feeling as the evening progressed. On entering the hall, he noted "some ill feeling towards the colored part of the audience." Yet this changed: "as the glorious harmony proceeded, caste stood abashed," and "the iron heart of prejudice" soon "melted away." In Washington, DC, on the other hand, the singers had to cancel performances at the Musical Fund Hall and the Chinese Museum, where the management refused to drop the color bar for the evening. In these cases, the abolitionist writers at the *North Star* could only chalk up the situation to "colorphobia." This condition, one declared, was marked by "fits" and "hysterics." An example, according to one writer, was "a young lady," who confessed that "the first time she saw a black man, she was well nigh thrown into convulsions"; she thought "he was the devil come to take her home."[48]

As disturbing as it was, this sort of thing was easy to turn into satire. "Oh the monstrous cruelty of these Hutchinsons," wrote one of the contributors to Douglass's paper, commenting on the "unsuspecting females" and "exquisites" who had been "subjected to the burning infamy and eternal shame of being in same concert-room" with African American men and women. "Doubtless," added the writer, the survivors of this "fiery trial" would have the reward of heaven; but what if, the editorial asked, "there should be black men and women there also, and no 'nigger pew'?"

The Hutchinsons' anti-abolitionist critics made these charges with deadly seriousness. Accordingly, their descriptions of the singers contained a heated anger. "Look at the singing tribe," declared one, "their woe-begone look of sympathy for the persecuted 'brother Nigga-man'—their perfectly characteristic 'we're all for 'mancipation' deportment, . . . their herding together with niggers, cheek by jowl!" The heat overwhelmed reason, producing the idea that this proximity literally made the singers black. At a typical concert, wrote another, the singers "tuned their harps of discord to that famous nigger air, composed and arranged expressly for this band of whitewashed niggers, called 'Clear the track' white folk, the niggers are coming." The Hutchinsons had become notorious and famous, he added, "by thrusting themselves into the society of niggers."[49]

Eventually most reviewers returned to the issue of abolition. On this subject, even Hutchinson audiences could sometimes express reservations. As John later recalled overhearing after a concert about this time: "They sing the sweetest harmony I have heard, but—their politics!" Other critics were more threatening. Hutchinson concerts offended the very "nostrils of propriety," claimed one, citing their "fiery abolitionism—their pretended love for the colored race—their rank association with the 'niggers'—their bloated philanthropy." For this writer, nothing about the Hutchinsons was above criticism, including their interests in popular trends or, as he put it, "their bepuffed, *ad nauseam*, sympathy with all the isms of the day."[50]

Their songs were not songs at all but "abolition lectures," claimed one hostile reviewer. They were the stuff of long-haired radicals, maintained another, who "have set out to make their jack by playing upon the Harp of one wooly string—abolitionism." If they "had more brains and less hair," he added, "they would, no doubt, be sent out as itinerant lecturers to retail abolition cant at half-price. But, being too shallow for orators, they 'go-a-singing' which requires nothing but wind and bellows power." The conclusions to these attacks were simple: the Hutchinsons should be "hissed tremendously"; "respectable men and women should shun them." They needed to be stopped, by violence if necessary, for they were "engaged in a singing crusade against the peace and fraternal respect of the people of the Union."[51]

On the evening of March 19, 1845, these were the hostile voices surrounding the singers. On this night, as they made their way to Niblo's stage, the threat of violence seemed real. They began the concert, most likely with "Blow On! Blow On!," a pirate's glee, according to their broadsides. They sang with a manic energy that could only have been caused by an enormous fear. At last, after some nine or ten numbers and two intermissions, they came to "Get Off the Track!" Jesse Hutchinson ran out from the wings to join his brothers and sister. Perhaps by this time they had read their audience and felt safe; perhaps, as Abby Hutchinson put it later, they felt the "stirring" of a "martyr spirit" and were "ready to die." They started in on the song "with a fervor and enthusiasm greater than was our wont."[52]

As Abby remembered it, the effect was "electric," "we were heartily cheered between all the verses, and when we sat down, the applause was tremendously overwhelming." According to John Hutchinson's recollections, the situation was more in flux: at first "the audience hissed; then some began to cheer, and there was a tug of war; finally the cheers prevailed."[53] Then, as John remembered it, something else happened that seemed to reveal a new sense of militancy within the abolitionist movement. After the performance of "Get Off the Track!," one of the singers' friends, Henry Dennison, scribbled a request for a song on a piece of paper, wrapped the paper around a penny, and threw it toward the stage. The missile struck John's violin. Immediately there were outcries from the audience: was this one of the dreaded brickbats? Had the rowdies at last made their appearance?

A near fight broke out, with Dennison frantically trying to explain himself in the middle of a knot of shouting and shoving men. The singers left the stage during the commotion, shortly returning when everyone realized what had happened. For John Hutchinson, as it likely was for many in attendance, the scene revealed something important: if there had been any "rowdies" in the hall, they would have met their physical match. John summed it up: "The blows of the abolitionists were beginning to tell."[54] Here, in the positive reception received by "Get Off the Track!" and the willingness of abolitionists to defend themselves, was a sign the movement had reached a new militancy and new popular heights.

In August 1845, the singers along with Jesse Hutchinson made a hasty decision to travel to Great Britain, joining up with Frederick Douglass for a series of concerts and abolitionist lectures in Ireland, Scotland, and England. They stayed nearly a year, finding wide success in the industrial cities of the English Midlands, adding to their popularity the cachet of having been accepted by the presumably more sophisticated European audiences.[55] They returned to the United States in July 1846, performing soon thereafter to an audience of three thousand at the Tabernacle in Manhattan. Throughout this time, they made "Get Off the Track!" a regular part of their concert program.

They remained controversial. They also remained at the center of American popular culture, attracting new audiences and supporters, encountering threats from critics, and always generating coverage in the press. In December 1846, at a series of concerts in Philadelphia, they again faced the threat of an anti-abolitionist mob. This time the threat came from the office of the mayor of Philadelphia, along with the police department, and focused on the Hutchinsons' policy of forcing theater owners to integrate their concerts. Faced with the ultimatum of closing their concert to African Americans or facing a mob supported by the local magistrates, the singers canceled the performance. Philadelphia's "Rotten Egg Volunteers," according to one paper, regretted the mayor's interference, claiming that they were ready to treat the

Hutchinsons in "such a manner as they deserve," adding the warning: "when people carry their Negro feelings beyond Massachusetts they carry their 'wool' to a market that won't pay."[56]

The conflict also evinced the growing militancy of the singers' abolitionist supporters. According to one, those who threatened violence at the concert were "bigots" and "ruffians." "All people know the Hutchinsons' positions & their principles of action," maintained another, adding that if "any Negro-hater has gone to their concerts unaware of these principles, he may thank his own ignorance or stupidity."[57] And finally, they too regretted the cancellation, for as a writer for the *Anti-Slavery Standard* put it:

> We are inclined to think that a mob, had there been one, would have found their match. There are quite a number of stout people about in this city, who don't mind a knock-down for a good cause, and would have esteemed this one; . . . though we by no means approve of violence, yet when there is no other law but mob-law, we believe in the principle of rotation in office. The pro-slavery party have been in the ascendancy quite long enough.[58]

Again, the Hutchinsons found themselves at the center of a culture war. Again, it appeared that their side had taken the threats of their enemies long enough. They were ready to move beyond "moral suasion" to a real fight.

Toward Civil War

In the mid-1840s, the Hutchinsons were at the center of the United States' popular music and the nation's most passionate political controversies. Over the next fifteen years, they would be overtaken by events and changing styles. In 1846, the original quartet toured Britain. While they were gone, Joshua Hutchinson convinced two brothers and a sister from the Milford tribe to form a "home branch" of the Hutchinson Family Singers. Soon after Abby's marriage and retirement in 1849, there were four versions of the group touring the Northeast: the home-branch Hutchinsons along with the "tribes" of Judson, John, and Asa. The result was a dilution of the family name. Some versions were better than others; some were political, while others were not. Meanwhile, styles were changing. Judson Hutchinson caught a sense of it while the original quartet was in Ireland. The popular old English singer Henry Russell, he noted in a letter home, was "going through the country singing negro songs."[59]

Russell was not alone. In the years before the Civil War, it may have seemed that blackface minstrelsy would consume everything and everyone. Stephen Foster's songs seemed everywhere, as the songwriter racked up a series of stage and sheet-music hits from "My Old Kentucky Home" (1850) to "The Old Folks

at Home" (1851) and "Massa's in the Cold Ground" (1852). In part, this was a result of the popularity of Christy's Minstrels, the group that performed so many
of Foster's blackface songs. In another part, it came from songs like "Take Me
Home." Published in 1851, "Take Me Home" was not a Stephen Foster song. Yet
it shared the same imagery and sentimental strain as his great successes:

> Take me home to the place where I first saw the light,
>   To the sweet sunny South, take me home,
> Where the mocking-bird sung me to rest every night—
> Ah! why was I tempted to roam!
>
> Take me home to the place where my little ones sleep,
> Poor massa lies buried close by,
> O'er the graves of the loved ones I long to weep,
> And among them to rest when I die.[60]

Through the 1850s, blackface would become more successful, more commercial, and more formulaic. An older style rooted in rebellious and supposedly authentic "black" expression would continue to be popular, particularly
with working-class crowds and audiences of overcompensating middle-class
clerks. Yet increasingly two characters would move to the foreground. One
was the blackface image associated with Foster, the loyal old slave or ex-slave,
the "Uncle" or "Auntie," in the patronizing terminology of the time, who sang
sentimental ballads of yearning for the Old South, the old plantation, and
the kind old "massa." The other was a character stripped down to the blackface essences of singing, dancing, and declarations of mindless happiness.
These characters, which may be summed up as the "Loyal Uncle," the "Aunt
Mammy," and the "Happy Slave," would take blackface from the stage to politics to the sphere of experiential reality.

In 1837, the onetime vice president of the United States and lifelong scowl-
ing defender of the master class, South Carolina's John C. Calhoun, delivered
a response to the flood of abolition petitions to Congress. The South's days of
apologizing for slavery were over, he declared. "Instead of an evil," he added,
slavery was "a positive good." He cited three bits of evidence. The first was that
slavery had improved the "black race of Central Africa," uprooting it from its
"degraded, and savage condition" and transporting to a place of civilization
and light. The second was the "rapid increase in numbers" of slaves in the
South. The third was suggested by the second: despite the abolitionists' "exaggerated tales to the contrary," he declared, the South's slaves were happy.[61]

Calhoun's happy slave would have been difficult to find on a Southern
plantation. The image was common in blackface minstrelsy. From its beginnings, the dancing and singing slave had been second only to the Northern

"dandy darkey" as the genre's favorite image. By the second half of the 1840s and with the commercial triumph of blackface, the happy slave became the genre's primary character. Christy's Minstrels "I'se a Happy Darkie" offered the image in all its stark simplicity:

> I'se a happy darkie, / Always blithe and gay,
> Sing and dance, and dance and sing, / All de liblong day.
> Nebber went to college, / Nebber had de chance;
> But den I play de banjo, / When de darkies dance.[62]

Examples like these would come to dominate middle-class blackface, in songs such as "Happy Are We, Darkies So Gay," "Gay Is the Life of the Colored Man," and the Buckley's Serenaders' "A Nigger's Life for Me":

> A Nigger's life for me,
>   Whereso e'er I be,
> Here among sweet scenes I roam,
>   With blooming cane growing round my home,
> And in de fields whar cotton grows,
>   At evening's fall I take my repose.
> My heart quite free from worldly woes,
>   I'm gladsome how, or where I go,
> Den sing aloud for de nigger's life,
>   Free from de care of de white man's strife.[63]

Into the 1840s and through to the Civil War, the image of the happy slave oscillated from politics to culture. Here again was evidence for the seemingly strange coalition between the working class of the North and the slaveholding elite of the South. By 1847, William Lloyd Garrison clearly saw it this way. Whatever the declarations of its performers, he averred, blackface was "in favor of slavery" and the messages of "Jim Crow" and "Zip Coon" were "derogatory to human freedom." Other abolitionists agreed. Many had long been making the argument that slavery was both wrong and a corruption of national morals. Others made the same point about blackface. As one would put it in the 1850s, "Negro Minstrels" had left "a trail of moral slime to poison not only the taste but the morals of the community."[64]

No small part of the poison came from the seductive quality of blackface imagery. Music experts were among the first seduced; and some, having partaken of blackface on the stage, imagined themselves going south for the real thing. The South's night air was thick with slave song, declared one writer with *Dwight's Journal of Music*. "Sailing down the Mississippi," he wrote, "the voyager on the deck of the steamer may often hear these strains, wild, sad, and tender, floating from the shore." He encouraged his readers to take a lesson from the songs, saying that Americans of the North were too often "taciturn and gloomy." "Let us not be ashamed," he added, "to learn the art of happiness from the poor bondman at the South." "A true southern melody is seldom sentimental and never melancholy," declared a writer for *Putnam's Magazine*. After all, he maintained, the slave's life was all "happiness and levity." Here, the memory of a slave he had known suddenly arose in his mind's eye, "the boy Quash," who was always "witty and gay" and "the very type of his race."[65]

Increasingly, the Southern defense of slavery would rest on Calhoun's happy slave. In 1847, the proslavery writer Augustus Longstreet published *A Voice from the South*, a response to abolitionist charges of the cruelties of slavery that he placed in the form of a conversation between Northern and Southern states. When a clearly feminine Massachusetts brought up the "wretched condition" of the slave, Longstreet had a very masculine Georgia provide an authoritarian and "factual" response:

> This is wider from the truth than any position yet examined. It is a common remark that there is not to be found a happier race of beings among the working classes on the face of the globe, than the slaves of the South. Most assuredly this is true. . . . They are, upon the whole, a happy people. . . . I have to do with the fact, and the fact only. At this moment I turn my eye to this class of my population; and if peace and plenty by day, and laughter and music, and dancing, and song by night, unchecked by care for the present, or thought of the future, are tokens of happiness, then there are not three millions of happier beings anywhere than my slaves.[66]

Happy slaves began cropping up everywhere. In 1848, children's story author Cornelia Tuthill published *When Are We Happiest*. The book introduced young readers to a Southern family, its dear little children, and its "funny little black babies." "Have you a dislike for negroes?" Tuthill asked her little followers. Her answer anticipated their response and countered it with a soothing image: "Ah well! you will get over it before you have been long at the South. The servants whom you will become acquainted with here are so kindly treated and so happy, that you will soon forget that they are not perfectly happy." In 1851, John Campbell's *Negro-Mania*, a widely influential "examination of the falsely assumed equality of the various races of men," would posit a love for music, along with idleness, vulgar expression, and happy laziness—all staples of the minstrel show—as proof of the racial inferiority of African Americans and their fitness for slavery. To New York City clerk and regular minstrel-show attendee George Templeton Strong, all African Americans were either "Cuff" or "Dinah." On the question of slavery, he, like many other fans of minstrelsy, believed that slaveholding was no sin and, as he put it, "the slaves of the Southern States are happier and better off than the Niggers of the North."[67]

Coming on the heels of its enormous growth during the late 1830s and early 1840s, the ubiquity of minstrel images and their use in the slavery defense threatened to overwhelm the antislavery movement. In 1848, Jesse Hutchinson wrote a series of songs for the "Free Soil Party" convention at Buffalo. There, the political wing of the movement had gathered to sing rousing versions of "The Old Free States" (set of course to the tune of "The Old Granite State"), along with an ode to the abolitionist "barn-burners." The song, alternately called "Free Soil Rally" or "The Barnburner Song," so called because abolitionists were willing to burn down the barn (or the nation) rather than share it with slavery, undoubtedly produced its share of hilarity:

> By the old burnt barns we'll plant our tree, / Hurrah! Hurrah! Hurrah!
> Its branches shall grow broad and free, / Hurrah! Hurrah! Hurrah!
>> For when the old rats to a crisp we broil,
>> *Their ashes shall enrich free soil,*
>> Hurrah! Hurrah! Hurrah! Hurrah![68]

Jesse Hutchinson could write this sort of thing in a minute. In 1851, he published "Ho! For California!," perhaps the single abolitionist anthem among the songs of the California gold rush. For a time while he was in California performing with a new group he put together called "The Alleghenians," the song was a near rival in popularity to Stephen Foster's "Oh Susanna!"[69] Few abolitionists were more attuned to the popular tastes than the old manager–songwriter of the Hutchinsons. The problem was that when Jesse died of "Chagres fever" shortly after returning from California in 1853, the movement had few songwriters of his caliber to replace him.

They tried their best. Elizabeth Chandler's "The Nation's Guilt" had plenty of lurid imagery: with mothers crying for their children as the slave driver's lash fell on their backs. Yet its tune—"the Missionary Hymn"—was more the stuff of church than the music hall. Others produced songs like "Rescue the Slave," songs of weeping and praying and the heft of a moral burden:

> Sadly the fugitive weeps in his cell,
> Listen awhile to the story we tell!
> Listen ye gentle ones! Listen ye brave!
> Lady fair, lady fair, weep for the slave!
>> Praying for liberty dearer than life;
>> Turn from his little ones, turn from his wife;
>> Flying from slavery; hear him and save!
>> Christian men, Christian men, help the poor slave!

Even William Lloyd Garrison got into the act, writing a song called "Hope for the American Slaves." Set to the tune of "America," the song's first stanza suggests its lack of spark: "Ye who in bondage pine, / Shut out from light divine, / Berift of hope."[70] None of these songs, it seems, could compete with blackface staples like "De Happy Darkie" and "Don't You Wish You Was a Nigger." None caught the public favor as much as the Buckley's Serenaders' "Laughing Chorus":

> De darkies from de South, ha ha,
>   Dey hab such a great big mouth, ha ha,
> Dat dey can't sing at all, ha ha,
>   Dey can't, can't sing at all.
>   Ha, ha, ha, ha, ha, ha, ha, ha,
>   Niggers from de South;
>   Ha, ha, ha, ha, ha, ha, ha, ha,
>   Dey cannot shut dar mouth.[71]

By the early 1850s, some of the air had gone out of the abolition movement. In 1854, at a July Fourth antislavery picnic in Framingham, Massachusetts, William Lloyd Garrison burned a copy of the Constitution. When Garrison's rivals in the New York and Ohio wing of the movement reacted with outrage, and when Frederick Douglass sided with the moderates, abolitionists like the Hutchinsons found themselves torn between factions. Following a speech in which Douglass criticized his old partner in the cause, Judson Hutchinson dashed off a letter to the *Liberator*:

> I do not endorse the sentiments uttered by Frederick Douglass at his lecture on Tuesday evening at the Music Hall. [I] supposed we were to have a hearty anti-slavery lecture . . . instead of which, we were mortified by a tirade of (to me) flimsy objections against the true reformers of our common country. . . . As far as I am concerned, I despise a slave who calls the *Constitution anti-slavery*, which admits his countrymen to be represented in Congress as cattle. Away with such trash! Give us the only motto which has any Northern grit—"NO UNION WITH SLAVEHOLDERS." I will bless a consistent man like WM. LLOYD GARRISON.[72]

Douglass found the letter, reprinted it in his own paper, and said he preferred to take the high road. He then hinted that Judson was insane and reminded his readers of the Hutchinson Family Singers' "hypocrisy" when they sang—ten years earlier—for the "arrant slaveholder" Henry Clay. Clearly, the splits within the movement would produce their share of accusations and cutting ripostes. To the defenders of slavery North and South, these splits mattered little: antislavery in whatever form remained a threat. To many in the movement, the differences between Garrisonians, Free-Soilers, Barn-Burners, Come-Outers, Loco-Focos, and antislavery Whigs and Democrats were enough to make abolition appear hopelessly divided between warring factions.

Interestingly, it would take a blackface character to heal the movement and bring its factions back together. In 1852, Harriet Beecher Stowe published *Uncle Tom's Cabin; or, Life Among the Lowly*. The novel would be a sensation. It was also a product of the expansion of blackface. For if Uncle Tom found rich soil among the middle class, it was in ground pre-furrowed by blackface images: by Stephen Foster's "Old Uncle Ned," by sentimentalized slaves deeply loyal to kind masters, by long-suffering black characters whose one superiority over whiteness was the depth of their emotion, their ability to transform sufferings into song, dance, and honest self-expression.

Stowe herself was a fan. And so, in her novel, she was unable to resist trying her pen at a few scenes of "darkey wit." A typical example would appear in the interplay between two of the novel's minor characters, the slaves Sam and Andy. "Well yer see," Stowe had Sam say,

> I'se 'quired what yet may call a habit o' *bobservation*, Andy. It's a very 'portant habit, Andy; and I 'commend yer to be cultivatin' it, now yer young. . . . Yer see, Andy, it's *bobservation* makes all de difference in niggers. Didn't I see which way the wind blew dis yer mornin? Didn't I see what Missis wanted, though she never let on? Dat ar's bobservation, Andy. I 'spects it's what you may call a faculty. Faculties is different in different peoples, but cultivation of 'em goes a long way.[73]

The style of this example, the standard blackface dialect, the comedic putting on of airs, the hilarious malapropisms, all mark it as having come directly from the minstrel show. Meanwhile, the novel's main plotline might be boiled down to a question: what would happen if Old Uncle Ned was sold away from his kindly master? What pathos would ensue if he became the property of a vicious slave driver, a man willing to take full advantage of the system's potential for cruelty, a Simon Legree, a Jew? The tragic answer would revive the abolitionist cause and turn tens of thousands of Americans against slavery.

Like many of the old guard in the abolitionist movement, Asa Hutchinson's reaction to the novel was initially dubious. "Mrs. Stowe's 'Uncle Tom's Cabin' has changed the relation of things," he wrote in his diary, adding sardonically, *"Am I not a man & an Uncle?"* By the second half of 1853, he hopped on board with the novel's imagery. Programs for his version of the Hutchinson Family featured songs like "Old Uncle Ned" and "The Ghost of Uncle

Tom." They also included "Little Topsy's Song." With lyrics by Eliza Cook and Asa's music, the song used blackface dialect to flesh out one of the novel's memorable characters:

> Topsy neber was born, Neber had a muder;
> Specks I growed a nigger brat, Just like any oder.
> Whip me 'till the blood pours down, Ole Missus used to do it;
> She said she'd cut me heart right out, But neber could get to it.
> Got no heart I don't belieb Niggers do without 'em
> Neber heard of God or Love, so can't tell much about 'em.
>   This is Topsy's savage song, Topsy cute and clever.
>   Hurrah, then for the white man's right, Slavery forever![74]

The novel produced a host of responses from the defenders of slavery. In 1853, a blackface song appeared called "Aunt Harriet Becha Stowe." The song attacked the writer according to the old charge of hypocrisy:

> I went to New York City a month or two ago,
> A hunting for dat lady, Aunt Harriet Becha Stowe;
> I see'd de Abolitions dey said she'd gone away,
> Dey told me in de city it was no use to stay.

The abolitionists, according to the song, would treat fugitive slaves badly, for aside from using them to write best-selling books for antislavery readers, they wanted nothing to do with them. At last the song turned to the imagery of the happy slave. The song's character ends up wishing he were back with his kind "ole Massa and Missus" in his "ole Southern home." As for Stowe, he ends the song with a warning:

> But don't come back Aunt Harriet, in England make a fuss,
> Go talk against your Country, put money in your puss;
> And when us happy niggers you pity in your prayer,
> Oh! don't forget de *WHITE SLAVES* dat starvin' ober dare![75]

Other responses came from proslavery propagandists. One of these, Nehemiah Adams's *A South Side View of Slavery*, purported to be by an abolitionist. At least the author claimed to have been an abolitionist until he went to the South. Upon landing in Savannah, Georgia, Adams declared he had been "surrounded" by slaves. They danced for him. They sang, producing "music of a natural order, full of genuine feeling." They charmed Adams with their genuine and earthy qualities. Above all, they demonstrated their complete happiness. "I began to like these slaves," Adams wrote. "I began to laugh with them. It was irresistible. Who could have convinced me, an hour before, that slaves could have any other effect upon me than to make me feel sad."[76]

The most direct response to Stowe's novel was William L. G. Smith's *Life at the South, Or, "Uncle Tom's Cabin" As It Is.* Smith countered Stowe's fiction with a real Southern tour, with a travelogue of well-kept plantations, kindly masters, and happy slaves. In one memorable passage, he visited the plantation of a "Mr. Erskine," where a fiddler named Jeff led his fellow slaves in a frolic:

> In a few moments, Mr. Erskine made his appearance, and the slaves appeared happier than ever. . . . So engaged, finally, did they become in the frolic, that they were not content simply with dancing, but made the grove echo with the melody of their songs. Jeff caught the contagion, and commenced singing to a familiar air—
>
> > Millwood ladies sing dis song, Du da, du da.
> >   Millwood race track five miles long, Du da, du da.
> > Go down dar wid my hat caved in, Du da, du da;
> >   Come back home wid pocket full ob tin, Du da, du da.[77]

Smith's slaves were singing a version of Stephen Foster's "Camptown Races." Here, in other words, were actual plantation slaves singing a song from the blackface stage.

There are at least three explanations for this scene. One is that Smith simply made it up, inventing it to fit the expectations of his readers. Another is that it actually happened. From its origins, Southern slaveholders were wary of blackface; its anti-aristocratic subtexts and focus on free black tricksters made it politically suspect. By the 1850s, the new focus on the loyal uncle and the happy slave allowed the genre to spread quickly into the South, so quickly that if William Smith's travelogue is to be believed, actual slaves were singing "slave songs" produced by Northern blackface songwriters. A writer with *Dwight's Journal of Music* seemed to confirm the possibility. According to his account, slaves throughout the South were hearing blackface songs by the early 1850s. They learned songs like "Old Folks at Home," integrated them into their culture, and sang them with a new "power and pathos."[78] A third possibility is that from a certain point in American history, when white people looked at black people, they saw what they wanted to see. Whatever was in front of Smith, if black people were involved he saw a minstrel show.

The Hutchinson Family Singers did not see it this way. Neither did Lydia Maria Child. One of the greatest reformers of the nineteenth century, Child seemed to know everyone and appear everywhere. Born in Massachusetts in 1802, she began her writing career with a novel she published in 1824, *Hobo-*

mok, a story that focused on what she saw as the United States' unfair treatment of Native Americans. She went on to become a celebrated writer of children's fiction and a pioneer in domestic ideology. In her instruction manuals for girls, wives, and mothers, she would express an ideal that historians have referred to as domestic feminism.

Here, she argued that women's superior moral virtue did not mean, as many writers suggested, that they needed to be placed on a pedestal or relegated to the safety of the domestic sphere.[79] Instead, it required them to redeem the world, to go into public as moral reformers. By the 1830s, she would be one of the nation's most active abolitionists. Her writings would inspire a generation to join the cause. Published in 1835, her pamphlet *Authentic Anecdotes of American Slavery* contained a host of horrors: from stories of young female slaves who were whipped to death to tales of girls sold for sexual purposes, slave families separated by greedy masters, and one tale of a slave mother who killed her children rather than see them sold on the auction block.[80]

In nearly all things, Child was a model of middle-class ideology, a living exemplar of bourgeois codes of domesticity, politeness, self-repression, and a commitment to humanitarianism. The point of nearly all her antislavery writings was simple and to the point: there was no way a middle-class individual could support slavery. Middle-class readers could not continence slavery's debasement of mothers or abuse of children; they could not stand for the slave system's internal erotics, the fact that masters were using female slaves as outlets for sexual energy, that they condoned rape, that practically every plantation slave quarters included the master's offspring; they could not sit idly by while slavery contained scenes of angry whippings, the release of bodily fluids in the form of blood, and the unleashing of lustful passions. In these writings, she seemed determined to counter every shred of propaganda from the institution's defenders. "Do you suppose," she asked in her 1836 pamphlet *The Anti-Slavery Catechism*, "they really believe what they say, when they declare that slaves are happier than freemen?" Her answer could not avoid admitting the possibility. Yet, she answered, "it would merely prove that they had fearfully brutalized immortal souls before they *could* be happy in such a situation."[81]

In the 1840s and 1850s, Child's letters to a friend, Marianne Cabot Sillsbee, reveal the power of the culture wars of the antebellum era. The friendship was characteristic of Child's ubiquity in the culture. For Silsbee was no abolitionist. Instead, she seems to have been an example of the old Northern elite, willing to put up with Child's "radical" ideas from the standpoint of the old-fashioned lady bountiful. In the late 1840s, their shared enjoyment of music held the friendship together. Indeed, the letters between the two suggest one of the most important roles of music in the culture.

It provided, that is, something to talk about for people with little or nothing in common. In an 1847 letter, Child wrote Sillsbee of a nearly teenage-type obsession with the Norwegian violinist Ole Bull. "I have written Mister Bull several times," read Sillsbee in one of these missives, "but he never returns one syllable of answer." The musician's power over her was "strange, very strange," Child wrote, adding, though at times she wished she had never heard of him, still "he claims ever the privileges of a little child, in whom one must forgive much." In 1848, Child again brought up the subject of music. This time, however, her taste might have struck Sillsbee as evidence for the growing chasm between the two friends. Here, Child reported that during a steamboat ride from Boston to New York, she joined several of her fellow passengers in a rousing version of the Hutchinsons' "Get Off The Track!" The performance, she added, received a "thundering encore" from the other passengers aboard, who were in a "merry mood, ready to be pleased with anything."[82]

By the 1850s, tensions over the slavery issue began creeping into the letters between the two friends. Child clearly knew that Silsbee did not want to hear about the issue. Yet she could not avoid it, writing in one letter of her involvement in the underground railroad, in another of her disappointment at Silsbee for supporting the fugitive slave law. "Cursed," she declared, "is that system of considering human beings as chattels!" Again she brought up music, but her reference probably did little to soothe differences. "I long," she wrote, "to get where there are no whips, or guns, and where there is *music*." Silsbee seems to have responded by suggesting the silliness of Child's cause, saying, as Child quoted her later, that she was "making a ridiculous fuss about one nigger." Here, Silsbee repeated a standard argument of the proslavery crowd. The abolitionists, that is, were silly and harmless; they were weak; they would never be able to stand up to a physical defense of slavery. The conflict would fade away.[83]

This is not what happened. In the nation at large, as in Child's letters, the cultural conflict increasingly became a real break. In May 1857, Child declared to her friend that there was a "barrier" between them, "because you have never realized the depth and strength of my feelings," and because Silsbee and her husband were "'simply amused' by the zeal of the reformers." In September, Child wrote what would be the last real letter to her old acquaintance. The "outrages" in Kansas, she declared, where abolitionists and proslavery forces were already fighting, along with the attack on the abolitionist Massachusetts Senator Charles Sumner, "struck and rung a loud tocsin through my soul."

From this point, Lydia Maria Child, one of the nation's leading lights of female domesticity and womanly virtue, an exemplary member of the Northern middle class and a promoter of its codes of polite exchange, would become one of the nation's most militant proponents of the Civil War. There was no way to go back to friendly discussions of Ole Bull. "For the first time in my life," wrote Child to her former friend Marianne Silsbee, "I felt that I might be driven to deeds of blood."[84]

9

Black America

Ralph Keeler went to his first blackface show in Toledo, Ohio, during the 1850s. He "resolved on the spot to be a negro minstrel." He bought a banjo. He practiced dancing. He soon found a place on the stage, performing with "Johnny Booker's Minstrel Troupe." At the time he thought a "negro minstrel" was "the greatest man on earth." The "life was so exciting," he remembered, "and I was so young, that I was probably as happy as an itinerant mortal can be." In the part of the act performed without make-up, he played a "Scotch girl in plaid petticoats" and danced the Highland fling. In the blackface olio, he danced as the character "Lucy Long" and was told he "looked the wench admirably." He learned the end man's tricks of the trade: how to sing and speak in understandable blackface dialect; how to toss a tambourine and spin it on his finger; how to get a laugh from the troupe's "budget of stale jokes."

Keeler would play black people onstage for years. In his account of the time, he recalled only two African Americans. One was a man named Ephraim. According to Keeler's recollections, Ephraim was an unpaid servant to the white members of Booker's Minstrel Troupe. He carried their baggage as they traveled from town to town. He spot-cleaned their suits and kept their shoes shined. In return, the musicians allowed him to tag along, feeding him and giving him a place to stay. For the most part, Ephraim's job was to provide comic relief. The members of the group treated him with contempt. When things were slow, they played practical jokes on him. He was, Keeler wrote, "one of the most comical specimens of the negro species."

The other man was dead serious. According to Keeler, the man owned a barge docked in Cairo, Illinois, a vessel he ran as a gambling saloon devoted to an African American clientele. At some point while Keeler was performing in the town, word spread that a couple of white men had entered the floating saloon and never come out. Some white locals jumped to a conclusion: the owner of the barge had killed the men. They formed a lynch mob and headed for Cairo's docks. As the mob approached, the saloonkeeper untied his vessel and took it out on the river. There may have been some history here: the formation of the lynch mob was suspiciously quick; their target seemed curiously unsurprised the mob was coming. The vigilantes followed on skiffs. The man set fire to his barge. He then took an old musket, buried its barrel in a keg of dynamite, and shouted a warning: he would die before he would be lynched.

Keeler watched the scene from the banks of the Mississippi. Determined to have their lynching, the vigilantes refused to back off. "As the flames grew thicker around him," Keeler recalled, "there the negro stood, floating down into the darkness that enveloped the majestic river, with his cocked musket still in the keg of powder, and cursing and defying his executioners. He was game to the last." Finally, the mob came too close, the man pulled the gun's trigger, and the dynamite keg disintegrated in a fiery explosion. Keeler had witnessed an event that would become something of an American pastime: a vigilante killing of a black man. Not long after this scene, Keeler began to question "whether a great negro minstrel was a more enviable man than a great senator or author." He became indifferent to the audience members; the indifference became "a positive hatred of them and myself." He quit the stage and decided to go to college.[1]

In his career as a minstrel, Ralph Keeler made several discoveries that would be widely shared in the second half of the nineteenth century. First, there were worse things than being stereotyped. Rooted in hatred and love, the minstrelsy-based perception of black people would limit and create opportunities for African Americans. As with Ephraim, actual black people could acquiesce to this minstrel perception. In doing so, they might get something out of becoming the subject of love and contempt. Or, like Keeler's black man on the Cairo barge, they could stand up, express themselves in ways that white people did not want to hear, and "be game to the last." By the close of the nineteenth century, many African Americans might have seen two choices in the dominant culture: they could play the minstrel, or they could get themselves killed.

For another, though blackface grew old and its jokes became stale, the vast majority of Americans would never tire of it. It remained popular even as the burnt cork came off, African Americans moved into the genre, and the nation moved toward an embrace of progressive ideology and consumer culture. Meanwhile, as the nation veered toward terror-based white supremacy and Jim Crow segregation, increasing numbers of white Americans discovered the pleasures of "blackness." They would find that getting in touch with one's dark or "black" side was a necessity in a culture committed to both the pleasures of consumption and the ideals of white moral superiority. In white America, vitalist racism would be the engine that made consumer capitalism go.[2]

The Civil War

The Civil War was a kind of second American Revolution, a rapid, massive, and forced transformation of the nation's society and culture. One part of this transformation has remained obvious: the United States changed from a nation with slavery to a nation without slavery. Another would be just as important: the "nation," if it could be so called in the years before the conflict, went from a loose collection of regions, states, and localities, dominated by people who were strictly local in their thinking—and in the South by many who liked it that way and wanted to keep it that way—to a nation with an increasingly national and centralized culture. This element of revolutionary change, along with the fact that it was a civil war, goes a long way toward explaining the scale and scope of its violence.[3]

The violence was astonishing. During the conflict, nearly one out of every thirty Americans would be killed, wounded, or maimed. As politicians and observers frequently pointed out, the opposing sides in the war had much in common. North or South, Union or Confederate, both shared a common language, the same religion, the same traditions.[4] The familiarity may have had tragic results. It appears to have meant there was less otherness to the enemy; slightly less fear, a bit less trepidation at the idea of killing a fellow human. Knowledge of the other side seemed to make the hatred more deeply felt, the shootings and bayonet thrusts more personal. In the Civil War, familiarity bred lasting hatred, and soldiers proved as capable of killing humanized enemies as they would the dehumanized others of later wars.

The war's music reflected the shared culture of the combatants as well as the differences exposed by the conflict. Union troops marched off singing "John Brown's Body." Later they sang the same tune with more uplifting lyrics in the form of Julia Ward Howe's "Battle Hymn of the Republic." Confederate regiments marched to "The Bonnie Blue Flag," a song that also went by the name "The Homespun Dress." Soldiers on both sides passed time in camp with a seemingly endless supply of comic songs, tearful ballads of home, and blackface tunes. One of the most popular of the blackface songs, Dan Emmett's "Dixie," or "Dixie's Land," would become the dominant Confederate anthem. Civilians expressed the war's causes and issues in racial terms. Northerners who supported the creation of black regiments sang a ditty called "Sambo's

Right to be Kilt." Southerners mocked their Northern opposites with songs such as "Abraham's the Nigger King," "All for the Nigger," and "Nigger Doodle Dandy." In the middle of the conflict, one of the most popular of the North's political songs was a satire of Republican Party war aims called "I Am Fighting for the Nigger."[5]

In music as in everything else, the conflict was a watershed. The war generated a national taste for marches, martial orchestras, and brass-band music. It transformed "Irish song" from the stuff of stereotype and stage brogue to music of mainstream taste. It made music big business, spawning publishing houses with national scope. One of these was Chicago's "Root and Cady," or later, "Root and Sons Music Company." Founded in 1858 by the songwriter George Root, the company published sheet music and songsters. Some of its best-sellers were Root's own wartime compositions: the Union anthem "The Battle Cry of Freedom"; the support-the-troops march "Tramp! Tramp! Tramp!"; the sentimental "Just Before the Battle Mother"; and finally, the paean to the war's dead "The Vacant Chair." The company would thrive in the postwar years: in part by playing on nostalgia for Civil War songs; in part by becoming a kind of vanity press for songwriters, offering to assess their songs for a fee and publish them (again for a fee) if they met the firm's musical standards.[6]

The war put music to the usual purposes. Music marked drills, marches, and military ceremonials. It offered a welcome distraction during the weeks and months spent in military encampments. It served to whip up the martial spirit of both soldiers and citizens, to drum up support for the conflict and give it direction. As the preface to one of the Union's wartime songsters explained it, the role of wartime music was simple and straightforward. First, the side with the best music was sure to win, for soldiers who marched off singing were "invincible in the terrible hour of conflict." Second, patriotic songs were sure to get folks on board with the war's causes.[7]

Yet when it came to patriotism for the Union, there was a problem. Every educated civilian, soldier, and politician knew the conflict was about slavery. At the same time, many in the North were proslavery or phobic about African Americans. Union leaders from Abraham Lincoln down to officers in the field had to be careful in their statements of the war's causes and goals: they had to worry about the press, the pockets of support for proslavery or pro-peace Democrats, and the tenuous position within the Union of several "border states." Through much of the conflict, they had to deny—even in the face of obvious reality—that slavery was the war's cause or that emancipation was its goal.[8] Thus, in the official language of the Union, at least, the war had a strange quality. It was a conflict with an absent cause; a war rooted in conscious denial. Its main cause—in terms of both what produced the conflict and the goal for which many soldiers fought—was a taboo subject. In the early days of the war, this quality would pose serious problems for its supporters.

The Hutchinsons would prove an example. By the start of the war, there were two versions of the "Hutchinson Family Singers" still standing, the "tribes" of the brothers John and Asa. Both made quick transitions from peaceful Garrisonians to ardent supporters of the conflict. Asa's family appeared at concerts and abolition conventions, singing patriotic numbers such as "The Loyal Soldier Boy to His Mother" and "The Flag of Our Union Forever," finishing with "The John Brown Army Hymn." John's tribe performed for Lincoln in the White House, singing a battle cry called "The War Drums Are Beating—Up Soldiers and Fight!" Both Asa's and John's versions of the family would find concert halls closed against them as a result of their prewar reputation. They made up the deficit by performing in black churches, where congregations also knew their reputation and invited them to perform.[9]

Predictably, it would be John Hutchinson who ran into trouble on the thorny issue of singing patriotic songs for the North. On January 14, 1862, John, along with his wife Fannie, their two children, and a military escort, showed up at a sentry post on one of the bridges out of Washington. John presented the sentry with a letter signed by Secretary of War Simon Cameron: "Permit 'the Hutchinson Family' to pass over bridge and ferry, and within the main lines of the Army of the Potomac." There, the order added, "they will be allowed to sing to the soldiers."[10]

John Hutchinson kept Cameron's order for the rest of his life. He also kept an admiring letter from Lydia Maria Child. "I was rejoiced beyond measure to hear that you and your family had gone to the camps to enliven our soldiers," Child wrote, adding that the singers had already made an "incalculable" contribution "to the cause of Freedom." As they crossed the Potomac River, the singers must have been excited; this would be their war effort. They followed their escort into Virginia. Finally, they arrived at the Union Army encampment at Fairfax Court House. The next night, on January 15, they performed the first of a planned series of evening concerts. "Everything went off gloriously," recalled John: the hall at the Fairfax Seminary was packed, and each song was greeted with "loud and prolonged" applause.[11]

Three days later, they would be expelled from the Union camp. The problem stemmed from one of their program's highlights, a poem by the "fighting Quaker" John Greenleaf Whittier. Set to John's music, the poem became a song alternately called "The Furnace Blast" or, after the Luther hymn, "Ein Feste Burg Ist Unser Gott." Still later it would be called the "Prohibited Song." Whatever its title, every one of the song's verses broke the North's wartime taboo.

What gives the wheat field blades of steel? / What points the rebel canon?
What sets the roaring rabble's heel / On the old starry pennon?
What breaks the oath / Of the men of the South?
What whets the knife / For the Union's life / Hark to the answer: "Slavery!"[12]

Whittier had an inkling the lines might cause trouble. "I am glad to know that there is any sing in my verses," he wrote John shortly before his family left for the Union camp. He wrote that while "of course" he had no objection to John's use of his poem, he was worried about what "Gen. McClellan may do with my rhymes."[13] The Union commander George McClellan, as Whittier and others knew, was among the most ardently opposed to putting the war on an antislavery footing. Later rumors would have it that "Little Mac" was unwilling to prosecute the war, that he was proslavery, pro-peace, and perhaps even pro-Confederacy.

On the night of January 17, Whittier's fears were realized. According to recollected accounts, most of the soldiers enjoyed the performance. "The men came up en masse to attend the concert," wrote one, adding that it was "very interesting to see with what zest the soldiers crowded around and within the chapel, and how wild they were with delight when some song was sung which met their approbation."[14] One member of the audience was less pleased. As John recalled it, when the family came to Whittier's poem, "a solitary hiss was heard from one corner of the room." Several men confronted the hissing soldier. The officer in charge at the Seminary, Major David Hatfield, wanted to throw him out of the room. Still the man refused to back down. He had come to hear "patriotic airs," he shouted, not "fanatics." Some soldiers came to his defense. For a moment, the situation looked like it might turn ugly. Then the crowd calmed, and John's family started in on another song. The episode seemed over.[15]

It was not. The next day, Major Hatfield received a field dispatch: "please send to the Head Quarters as soon as practicable a copy of the songs sung by the Hutchinson Family last night in the Seminary Chapel." The soldier had filed a complaint with someone near the top of command. Hatfield complied with the order, sending the headquarters the singers' program along with the lyrics to their songs. A short time later, another order came back: "By command of the Major General Commanding U.S.A., the permit given to the Hutchinson Family to sing in the Camps, and their pass to cross the Potomac, are hereby revoked, and they will not be allowed to sing to the troops."[16]

Though signed by "Brigadier General Franklin," it seems the order originated with McClellan himself, the "Major General Commanding" the Army of the Potomac. John responded with a complaint to McClellan's man in

Fairfax, General Philip Kearny. Kearny repeated the order, adding, "I reign supreme here,—you are an abolitionist,—I think as much of a rebel as I do an abolitionist." Two days later, John's tribe headed back toward Washington. Back in the Union Capital, Secretary of War Cameron overturned McClellan's order. Another Cabinet member, Treasury Secretary Salmon Chase, wrote John that President Lincoln had "expressed himself very warmly" in favor of the singers. It was too late. The war's cause had again been repressed, and the Hutchinson Family's adventure in the Union camps was over.[17]

While the Hutchinsons struggled with the complexities of singing patriotic songs for the Union, others on the Union side were discovering the human element of the war's repressed cause, the slaves of the South. In early November 1861, a flotilla of Union naval vessels and troop transports appeared off the Sea Island plantations along the coastline of South Carolina and Georgia. During the next several days, Union forces would take the islands of Port Royal, Hilton Head, and Saint Helena, along with the region's main port, Beaufort, South Carolina. The Sea Islands would become occupied territory for the duration of the war, a Union foothold in the tidewater South.

The region's planters were terrified. With Union vessels still on the horizon, many ordered their slaves to fire their cotton stores and fields. They then scampered off for Charleston or points inland, leaving behind their plantations, thousands of acres of cotton, and some ten thousand African American slaves. Union forces took control of this population. According to the logic of the time, the slaves could not be freed, since the war was officially not being fought for emancipation. Instead, they fell into a category of "contraband of war"; like the fields, the plantation buildings, and the salvaged cotton, they were property relieved of the enemy. Immediately, calls went out to reformers and humanitarians in the North: volunteers would be needed to oversee this property, to see to its upkeep while events decided its future.[18]

The situation in the Sea Islands would provide many from the North with their first opportunity to see, meet, and get to know actual African Americans from the slave South. One of the first to volunteer was Thomas Wentworth Higginson. When the war broke out, Higginson was one of the most notorious abolitionists in the North. A Harvard-educated Unitarian minister, he struck many observers as a rarity among the antislavery crowd: he was young, flashy, and apparently willing to engage in violence for his cause. In 1854, he famously led efforts to free a fugitive slave in Boston, efforts that included an assault on the city's jail. Later, he was one of the "secret six" behind John Brown's raid at Harpers Ferry, the only member of Brown's group of Northern backers who did not flee the country after the raid fell apart and the plot was revealed. Higginson remained in Boston through Brown's trial and execution, daring anyone from the outraged South to come and get him.[19]

By the summer of 1862, Higginson was a colonel in the Union Army. He had "always," as he put it, "looked for the arming of blacks." And so, in August, he agreed to take command of the first regiment of black troops formed out of the ex-slaves on the Sea Islands, a "contraband unit" called the "First South Carolina Volunteers." For the most part, since army brass followed a policy of keeping contraband units away from combat with Confederate forces, Higginson's unit performed the mundane tasks of an occupying army: running patrols, digging trenches, and maintaining roads. Still, for the dashing young colonel, it was the adventure of a lifetime.[20]

Higginson's perception of the men in his regiment, meanwhile, would do much to move blackface representations of African Americans from the stage to the "real world." He met his troops at Beaufort in November 1862. "They were," he noted in his camp diary, "as thoroughly black as the most faithful philanthropist could desire." Within days, he was "growing used to the experience" of being surrounded by five hundred black men. He enjoyed watching their "frolicking" during shooting drills. When one of them hit a target, he wrote, they engaged in "such dances of ecstasy as made the 'Ethiopian minstrelsy' of the stage appear a feeble imitation."[21]

Higginson was seeing the real thing. He spent much of his time secretly taking notes on his troops, his hand buried in his pocket, scribbling furiously with a hidden pencil and notepad. He tried to catch every detail of their nightly shouts:

> What a life is this I lead! It is a dark, mild, drizzling evening, and as the foggy air breeds sand flies, so it calls out melodies and strange antics from this mysterious race of grown-up children with whom my lot is cast. . . . [F]rom a neighboring cook-fire comes the monotonous sound of that strange festival, half pow-wow, half prayer meeting, which they know only as a "shout." . . . Then the excitement spreads . . . men begin to quiver and dance, others join, a circle forms, . . . some "heel and toe" tumultuously, others merely tremble and stagger on, others stoop and rise, others whirl, others caper sideways . . . and still the ceaseless drumming and clapping, in perfect cadence, goes steadily on. . . . And this is not rarely, . . . but night after night.[22]

Predictably, his real thing was similar to blackface minstrelsy. "Give these people their tongues, their feet, and their leisure, and they are happy," he concluded, adding that his troops seemed "the world's perpetual children, docile, gay, and loveable." The material, along with the conclusions he would draw from it, would make Higginson an authority on black song and "Negro Spirituals."[23]

Higginson was far from alone in these perceptions. As soon as the Sea Islands passed into Union hands, a host of Northern volunteers set off for Beaufort and Port Royal. The result was the "Port Royal Relief Committee." The Committee's goal was to demonstrate that the war could be fought for emancipation, that slaves could be freed without the destruction of American society, and that freedom did not mean black people would cease working, head north, or become wards of the state. The plan of action was to educate and uplift the region's ex-slave population, to teach them, as one of the experiment's leaders put it, "habits of self-respect and self support, and the lessons of morality and religion."[24]

They were a committed group. "No mortal is happier than I am in my work," declared one of the female volunteers who went south as a member of the American Missionary Association. And they were sure of the righteousness of their cause. "I give no thought of the hatred of the whites," she added, "knowing how useful it is my good fortune to be to the blacks—and how much they love me." At times some of them would slip into expressions of white supremacy. Writing home in the summer of 1862, one of the expedition's leaders, Charles Preston Ware, declared, "I will only remark at present that I find the nigs rather more agreeable, on the whole, than I expected."[25]

At other times they could be patronizing and paternalistic. In the Sea Islands African American population, the volunteers were dealing with a people who had long ago embraced the freedom-in-the-hereafter brand of Christianity foisted on them by the master class. Yet they went about their mission as if Port Royal was a heathen stronghold. They spoke of bringing Christian light to the region and dismissed local black church services as examples of "barbarism." They commandeered church buildings and ran their own services. They placed schoolmarmish monitors in the pews to patrol against spiritual excess. They festooned their altars with large cards on which they printed blurbs of piety: "Thou Shalt not Steal," "God is Love," "Fear God." They were often stumped by the Sea Islands' Gullah dialect. "We are not as yet *skilled* in negro-talk," declared one. So they did the expected: when they recorded conversations with the locals, they resorted to the dialect of *Uncle Tom's Cabin* and the minstrel show.[26]

These perceptions and struggles to understand would have a major effect on American music. At the end of 1862, the members of the Port Royal Relief Committee planned a Christmas and New Year's Day celebration. Harriet Ware, put in charge of the event, came up with the details: the volunteers and the Sea Islanders would mark January 1, 1863, with the lighting of a Christmas tree, a party, and a feast. They would also have a concert by two black choirs, one formed of children, the other of adults.

Soon a problem arose. The ex-slave population of the Sea Islands did not seem to know any slave songs. Of the songs they did know and were ready to sing, Ware found many "sad and disagreeable." Others were strange, like nothing the volunteers had heard before. Still others, which they called their "shouts," were "funny" when sung by the children's choir but disturbing and even offensive when done by the adults. "We laughed till we almost cried over the little bits of ones," wrote Ware, "but when the grown people wanted to 'shout,' I would not let them."

The solution came from points north. In the weeks before Christmas, a fresh volunteer arrived carrying a letter from one of the experiment's supporters. With the letter was a song, a number the supporter had written specifically for the Jubilee. Everyone agreed: the song, which would be called "The Negro Boatman's Song" or "The Contraband of Port Royal," was just the thing. Over the next several weeks, volunteers worked overtime teaching it to the children's choir. When the celebration came, the kids sang it with feeling:

> Oh, praise an' tanks! De Lord he come, / To set de people free;
> An massa tink it day of doom, / An' we ob jubilee,
> De Lord dat heap de Red Sea waves, / He jus' as 'trong as den;
> He say de word; we las' night slaves; / To-day de Lord's free-men.

Here was something that in theme, expression, and above all dialect was clearly a "slave song." The song's chorus and following verses would have the same comforting standards:

> De yam will grow, de cotton blow, / We'll hab de rice an' corn;
> Oh, de yam will grow, de cotton blow, / We'll hab de rice an' corn;
> Oh nebber you fear, if nebber you hear, / De driver blow his horn;
> Oh, nebber you fear, if nebber you hear, / De driver blow his horn.

> Ole massa on he trabbles gone; / He lebe de land behind;
> De Lord's breff blow him furder on, / Like corn shuck in de wind.
> We own de hoe, we own de plow, / We own de hands dat hold;
> We sell de pig, we sell de cow, / But neber chile be sold.[27]

The supporter who sent the song was John Greenleaf Whittier. The Quaker poet had been interested in writing verses based on black song for some time. During the war, he would be asked repeatedly to capture something of the exotic quality of the South. In 1864, Harriet Hawley, one of the original Port Royal volunteers, wrote the poet with just this request. She wanted him to visit the Sea Islands, to "faithfully, tho' with a loving eye, paint these strange scenes & their still stranger inhabitants—catch the strange rhythm & wild melody of the sad, barbaric songs of the negroes."[28]

She need not have bothered. Without leaving Massachusetts, the stay-at-home Whittier managed to write several "slave songs." Since he probably never got closer to Port Royal than Philadelphia, the question arises: where did he find his model and material? The answer may be found in his possessions. Here, among the scraps of material from which he took inspiration, was a cheap, eight-page, blackface songbook dated 1862. Of the songs it contained, one was a number called "A New Plantation Song." The song would have given the poet all he needed to know about "negro dialect":

> Massa, when he cut and run / *From dis ole plantation!*
> Let dese darkeys ebry one / *To work der own salbation!*
> Hallelujah! Slavery's done! / God bress Gen'ral Washington!
> Won't we hab some jam up fun / *On dis ole plantation!*
>
> Fotch de missus' pi-an-o, / *On dis ole plantation!*
> Play de hymn ob Jump Jim Crow / *'Pon dis solemn 'casion!*
> Now den, Julius, heel and toe, / Golly! boys but dis ain't slow!
> Brack folks' turn has come—dat's so! / *On dis ole plantation!*[29]

At the Port Royal Jubilee, it fell to Whittier to write a slave song that sounded authentically black. Immediately upon hearing the number, Lydia Maria Child dashed off a letter to the poet, congratulating him on his success. She also offered what would become a common phenomenon in later years: the spectacle of white people debating the authenticity of black expression:

> But that Negro Boat Song at Port Royal! . . . I keep repeating it morning, noon, and night; and, I believe, with almost as much satisfaction as the slaves themselves would do. It is a complete embodiment of African humor, and expressed as they would express it, if they were learned in the mysteries of rhyme & rhythm. I have only one criticism on the negro dialect. [It is not] "leab de land" [but] "leff de land," . . . At least, so speak all the slaves I have talked with, or whose talk I have seen reported.[30]

The Port Royal Jubilee corresponded with the return of the Civil War's repressed cause. Released about this time, Abraham Lincoln's Emancipation Proclamation would famously free no slaves. It applied only to areas under Confederate control. Still, the statement did have its effects. It went a long way toward getting rid of the category "contraband of war" for ex-slaves in Union-held territory. Clearly, there was no longer the possibility they would be returned to their former owners; and they could no more be placed in a category as property of the enemy. From 1863, slavery, which had been the cause of the war, could be spoken of as the war's cause. And so slavery would die with the Civil War. Blackface, and perceptions rooted in blackface, would survive.

The Minstrel Perception

In 1865, as the land smoldered and maimed Americans limped home from the most devastating conflict in the nation's history, "J. M. Hager's Entertainments" out of Buffalo began touring the country with a "Grand Pageant of the Great Rebellion." The pageant was certainly grand. It was backed by a brass band. It featured a legion of actors and dancers: actors playing "Truth, Justice, and the Goddess of Liberty," dancers representing "War," "Famine," and "the Army of the Potomac." It included a host of characters: a goddess, a soldier, a lady, and a "negro boy." It would have immigrants: a Hungarian, an Italian, and an Irishman. For many, its main feature would be the thirty-six dancing girls who represented the "United States."

The point of the show was to explain everything, to put the war in historical perspective. Scene one introduced the pageant's main character, the "Goddess of Liberty." In scene two, the Goddess bid welcome to the nation's immigrants. A pair of actors came out from the wings, one playing a Hungarian, the other an Italian. They took their places among the dancing states. Another actor playing an "Irishman" showed up, along with some of the old Irish minstrelsy. "A bit of land I'm wantin'—not too big," he declared in the pageant's musical couplets, "Where I can raise some praties, and a pig." To this, Liberty replied: "take it Paddy, go and pick the best, / On the free prairies of the Great Northwest."

As the dancing-girl "States" undulated and as several more dancers came onstage to join the original thirteen, it probably seemed to the audience that everything was going well. The entertainment may have seemed like a "leg show" of the early vaudeville stage, a spectacle in which the point was to ogle women's bodies.[31] But the pageant had a message. Suddenly, another figure burst onstage, a blackface actor playing "Negro Boy." The Goddess of Liberty feigned surprise. "Why in the name of patience who are you?" she declared, "Who knows where this black fellow ever grew?" Thus began scene three. "He! He! I'm little Sambo—don't you see," answered Negro Boy. He turned to the audience, saying: "Good evening white folks,—what do you think of me?" Even in the script, it is obvious: the character was baiting the crowd. Here was the cause of the Civil War. One can almost hear the audience's gasps of outrage as the scamp ran among the states, causing trouble and sparking a heated argument. "Shame, my children," declared Liberty; "think better of this mad dispute."

The states refused to listen. Suddenly, a mass of actors filled the stage, many representing War, Famine, and Pestilence, many others in the uniforms of the Union Army of the Potomac or the Confederate Army of Northern Virginia. They engaged in a swirling dance, a performance set to the band's swelling score. At last, the dance came to an exhausted end. It was time for Negro Boy to reappear. "Well, white folks, here I is again, you see," he declared, "I golly dis nigger now is clar made free." Again, he seemed to be baiting the audience, working to ramp up their hatred. Finally, the Goddess of Liberty reappeared and chased him into the wings. She returned to center stage, where she made a pronouncement: the war was fought to preserve the Union and not to free the slaves. The band played a last tune. The dancing girls came back out. The "States" hugged each other and began again to undulate happily.[32]

Here was the pageant's point: it was time for the nation to come together, bind up its wounds, and let the healing begin. In American popular culture, recovery from the Civil War would be based on creating a number of shared myths and beliefs. One was that the war was not about slavery. According to this belief, back then, "no-one" knew slavery was wrong; and so, of course, no one fought to free any slaves. Southerners fought for their rights, Northerners to "preserve the Union." The still-popular myth would serve several purposes: it would excuse slaveholders from moral responsibility; it would deny the existence of abolitionism as a popular movement; it would erase liberal idealism from the American past.

Finally, Hager's Grand Pageant suggests a more ominous belief. Slavery, as the pageant made clear, was not the cause of the Civil War. Black people were. The "Negro Boy" of the pageant was a double character: comic blackface minstrel and source of the most destructive war in American history. One of the points of the pageant was that it was acceptable to hate Negro Boy; it was understandable that some people wanted to do violence to him.

Rooted in perceptions carried over from earlier blackface minstrelsy, much of the "black" music of the postwar era would strengthen these beliefs. Much, too, would be devoted to the "healing" of the nation. In 1867, three satellite figures from the Port Royal experiment, William Francis Allen, Charles Pickard Ware, and Lucy McKim Garrison, would publish *Slave Songs of the United States*. The book, from its title to its contents, would subsume all of pre–Civil War African American history into the category of slavery. Slavery, the editors proclaimed, was marked by "crushed hopes, keen sorrow, and a dull, daily misery." But it produced a "rich vein of music." In his introduction, Allen provided a further rationale for the collection, along with the by-this-time-typical conflation of black song and blackface minstrelsy:

The musical capacity of the negro race has been recognized for so many years that it is hard to explain why no systematic effort has hitherto been made to collect and preserve their melodies. More than thirty years ago these plantation songs made their appearance which were so extraordinarily popular for a while; and if "Coal-black Rose," "Zip Coon" and "Ole Virginny nebber tire" have been succeeded by spurious imitations, manufactured to suit the somewhat sentimental taste of our community, the fact that these were called "negro melodies" was itself a tribute to the musical genius of the race.[33]

The collection included a number of songs that would become standard "Negro Spirituals," songs like "Roll, Jordan Roll," "Michael Row the Boat Ashore," and "Nobody Knows the Trouble I've Seen." It included several collected by Thomas Higginson and the members of the volunteers at Port Royal. It included a version of the song "Run, Nigger, Run!" collected in Mississippi, according to the editors, that seemed curiously blended with one of the most violent of blackface numbers, Joe Sweeney's "Knock a Nigger Down":

> O some tell me that a nigger won't steal,
> But I've seen a nigger in my cornfield;
>> O run, nigger, run, for the patrol will catch you,
>> O run, nigger run, for 'tis almost day.[34]

Finally, it contained a colorful description of an African American "shout." According to the editors, the "shout" was a phenomenon of the black church, an expression of unfettered emotion that took place at the end of the formal meeting and only when the benches had been pushed safely out of the way. Then the congregation regathered: "grotesquely half-clad field hands," women "with gay handkerchiefs twisted about their heads," younger boys and girls with "tattered" clothing. They would sing, and to their singing they would first "shuffle," then move into a stomping dance, the thud of their feet so loud it prevented sleep "within half a mile of the praise house." It was "not unlikely," concluded the editors, "that this remarkable religious ceremony is a relic of some native African dance."[35]

Within a few short years, tourists would go looking for this sort of thing. The popular *Appleton's Handbook of American Travel* published its first guide to the American South in 1866. In part, the guide was a product of a very early Civil War tourism industry. "The events of the last five years," it read, had "added materially" to the region's "historical and scenic attractions." Its readers found what would become the standard itinerary: from the tour of Virginia's battlefields to the encouragement for visitors to Charleston that they gaze across the harbor to the "ruined walls" of Fort Sumter. The guide also offered a few tips for Northern travelers. Northern bank notes, it warned,

made Southerners angry. In many places, roads and railways were so damaged that the guide could be of little help. Indeed, there was so much destruction throughout the South that the region might never recover. The guide did
offer directions for a bit of slumming. It directed travelers in New Orleans to
"Circus Place":

> Like other public grounds in the city, it is a delightful place to lounge away
> a summer evening. It was formerly known as *Congo Park*, and is the place
> where the negroes, in the "good old times before the war," were accustomed
> to congregate and go through the double shuffle to the favorite air of "Old
> Virginia never tire." Being in the colored district, it is still much frequented
> by them, but the dancing has given place to other pleasures less harmless and
> attractive.[36]

Alongside the postwar visions of national healing, many Americans had
serious hopes that the war's carnage might give way to effects beyond ending
slavery. Certainly, Northern volunteers in the South may have shared in their
culture's minstrel perception of black people. Many also held the dream of a
biracial society. Some, like Worcester's Sarah Chase, who in the earliest days
of Reconstruction was a volunteer with the American Missionary Association, saw the glimmerings of a society based on a democratic access to uplift.
Though Virginia's slave codes had forbidden slaves from learning, she found
that many freed people in Richmond could read. They were "intelligent and
thrifty," she wrote in a letter home, "and a large portion know their letters
and spell a little, having been taught by poor whites secretly and at exorbitant
rates." While she received letters from the Missionary Association's home office telling her to watch for the "evils" of freed people getting drunk, Chase
reported the formation of an African American "Educational Association" in
Savannah, Georgia, along with the founding of several black public schools.
"A very little help of the right kind," she again wrote, would be enough to advance the ex-slave population "to an independent position." "Work and justice," she added, "is all they ask."[37]

Frederick Douglass had been making this point for decades. "A great many
delusions have been swept away by this war," declared Douglass in an end-
of-the-war speech he called "What the Black Man Wants." One was that African Americans would not work. Another held that the "black man" would
not fight, "that he possessed only the most sheepish attributes of humanity;
was a perfect lamb, or an 'Uncle Tom.'" The efforts of contraband units and,
after 1863, of regular black troops like the Massachusetts 54th Regiment, had
proven otherwise. Now, "what the black man wants," Douglass explained,

were "his rights as a citizen" and to be "left alone." "Let him alone," he declared, adding that if anyone saw him "on his way to school," they should "leave him alone,—don't disturb him."[38]

African Americans would not be left alone. From the post–Civil War era through the end of the nineteenth century, they would experience the development of modern America's dominant racial ideology. This ideology would consist of roughly equal parts revulsion and attraction, hate and love. Through it, they would be forced—often violently—into positions as outsiders to the dominant, "white" American society. They would be kept in degradation and poverty. Many members of the larger, white society would expend enormous amounts of time watching them, and would be cocksure that they knew everything about "their black folk."

But they would always maintain the right to withdraw their American-ness, to relocate them to positions as outsiders and others. As the writer and folklorist George Cable would put it later, the African American "was brought to our shores a naked, brutish, unclean, captive, pagan savage." He would "accept our dress, language, religion, [and] all the fundamentals of our civilization." And "still," added Cable, "he remained to us an alien."[39]

Much of this ideology would work through patterns of violence that looked hateful. During the Reconstruction era from the late 1860s through the 1870s, whites in the South would speak of "redeeming" the region from the control of the US Congress, from radical Republicans, and above all from black people. They raged against the Freedmen's Bureau, the federal institution set up in the former Confederate states to provide aid and support for ex-slaves and poor populations. They remained angry at Yankees, for failing to understand "their negroes," for continuing to stir them up with hopes for rights in the postwar South.

Eventually, they would follow the "Mississippi Plan" for the redemption of the South. The plan, if such it could be called, was simply to use violence and terror to put an end to the experiment of Reconstruction. Groups formed to spread terror: the Knights of the White Camellia, the Ku Klux Klan. They targeted blacks who voted, who engaged in the building of any institutions of black improvement, who made a show out of going to school. They beat them and burned them out of their houses. If this did not work, they lynched them.[40]

Much of the ideology worked through love. By the mid-1870s, as Reconstruction ran up against white hatred and resistance, blackface minstrelsy and blackface-themed entertainment remained enormously popular. Indeed, by this time blackface had spread to all parts of the United States and to new corners of the world; it had become something of a "mania" in England, and was making inroads into other parts of Europe. Much would focus on the "Old South," or life on the plantation before the war. By the late nineteenth century, versions of *Uncle Tom's Cabin* appeared to be more popular than ever. Many removed the novel's antislavery message, along with its tragic ending. Instead, they turned Uncle Tom into a singing and dancing slave, and they focused on his happy relationship with his master's daughter, "Little Eva." The play grew in popularity as it became more mindlessly simple, as it became a standard minstrel show.[41]

Entertainments like these kept blackface thriving. They also kept slavery alive, at least in popular culture. A typical example was Harry Warner's "The Poor Old Slave." A hack writer with a list of derivative plays such as "Faithful Tom" and "Looking Back," Warner's 1872 production focused on Old Pete, an ancient and loyal slave to a recently dead master. The play began with a standard plantation scene: Pete sitting on his cabin porch, surrounded on both sides with potted cotton plants, singing Foster's "My Old Kentucky Home." Its middle section featured a slave conspiracy. Here, the highlight was a scene in which Pete's fellows sang "Massa's in the Cold, Cold Ground." Between verses, they conspired to kill the dead master's son for the cruelties of making them work too hard, whipping Pete, and refusing to let them sing and dance. The play ended with tragedy and a message. The freshly whipped old Pete interposes himself between his fellow slaves and his new master, receives an accidental and mortal clubbing and, just like Uncle Tom, redeems everyone with a dying speech. The play's final scene offered an old message for a new time: the old slave's friends swear they will be loyal to their new master. The plantation's new master promises to be kind.[42]

What messages did white audiences take from entertainments like these? For some, the message was that slavery still existed, in tradition if not in law. For most, the message was the old equation between slavery, authentic blackness, and expressive music. By the 1870s, according to one British music expert, this message went back some twenty years, when bands of "Negro Melodists" appeared in England, bringing with them "bones and banjos, and what professed to be negro melodies." The message continued in "Mrs. Stowe's books," in depictions that were "overdrawn" yet marked by "power and beauty." Finally, the message became real with more than twenty years of repetition. Soon enough, the "professed" qualities of blackface minstrelsy and the "overdrawn" exaggerations of *Uncle Tom's Cabin* would disappear. What remained was a "negro" made real by slavery and minstrel expressions. "The real negro," concluded the expert on the subject, "is passionately attached to music—his sorrows and joys are both accompanied by the banjo—and slave life, in which the present generation of negroes has been born and bred, is full of touching episodes and dramatic incidents."[43]

The result would be the reappearance of blackface in studies of "Negro folklore."[44] Perhaps the most well-known producer of this folklore would be Joel Chandler Harris. Harris was literally a cracker bastard: born in 1848 in the rural village of Eatonton, Georgia, he never met his father and was raised by his mother. Most likely, he had an unhappy youth. He was white and over-wrought; his fair skin, flaming red hair, and weight issues would make him pathologically shy all his life. In 1861, at the start of the Civil War, he left home, departing not to fight but to learn the printer's trade. He apprenticed at the *Countryman*, a news-sheet that claimed the distinction of being the nation's only paper published on a slave plantation. Leaving the *Countryman* at the war's end, he worked for a time at a paper in Forsyth, Georgia, where the town gardener was an African American named "Remus." By 1876, he was working for the *Atlanta Constitution* and had moved from printing to writing. He started writing a series of stories based on a character he called "Uncle Remus."[45]

In 1880, Harris published his classic *Uncle Remus: His Songs and His Sayings*. The book offered readers a collection of over thirty black songs and folktales. Many of the tales were narrated by Uncle Remus. Some were about him. Most purported to be genuine African American traditions, passed-down stories that focused on animal characters, most notably br'er (brother) rabbit, br'er bear, and br'er fox. White America loved it. Within a month of its publication, the book sold over seven thousand copies. It would eventually sell millions, becoming one of the best-loved children's books in American history.

Over the years, the focus of the book's readers would shift to the animal tales, to the trickster antics of br'er rabbit. The book's early success, however, came largely from the popularity of Uncle Remus. Harris would later swear that not one of his Uncle Remus tales was made up. Like the blackface performers of a generation before him, he freely admitted that his "black" expressions were not the product of invention. They were stolen, taken directly from an authentic source. In this case, the theft was inner-directed: Harris claimed Uncle Remus came from an inner voice. He had a black man inside him, a man who was sometimes bullying, sometimes angry, and always entertaining, a man he called "the other fellow."[46]

Uncle Remus: His Songs and His Sayings appeared in the same year Frederick Douglass published the third version of his autobiography. This would be Douglass's longest account of his life, the one that placed the most focus on his life as a dignified, educated, and successful African American, a man fully committed to the democratic promise of middle-class uplift. For white

Americans who objected to such things, Uncle Remus offered a perfect antidote. Harris's inner black man cared little for his own dignity or success. In the
tale "My Story of the War," he recounted how during the Civil War he stuck
loyally by his master. The story's plot was simple: some "Yankees" showed up
at the master's plantation, clearly looking to ransack the place. Uncle Remus
went at them with an axe. The Northern cowards ran away.[47]

Nor was the character much for education. Another story, set during Reconstruction, followed Uncle Remus into town, where he ran across a black
school child carrying a stack of books under his arm. Douglass had indicated
that Americans were likely to see this sort of thing, and when they did, they
should "leave him alone." Harris's character does no such thing. Remus glares
at the boy and his books. He tells him, menacingly, that he could beat more
sense into him with a barrel stave.

The rest of the story reads like a standard lynching narrative. The schoolboy "sasses" his tormenter. Uncle Remus responds like a Klansman. Livid
with anger, he attacks the child and begins beating him. At last, a policeman
shows up and pulls the angry old man from the beaten schoolboy. Remus offers an explanation which, though Harris does not detail it in the story, must
have included two of the key words from the Klan lexicon: "nigger" and
"sass." The cop has only one question: "Then," he asks, "you don't believe in
education?" We have reached the upshot of the story. "Hits ther ruination er
dis country," declares Uncle Remus, "I ain't larnt nuthin' in books, 'en yit I kin
count all de money I gits. No use talkin' boss. Put a spellin' book in a nigger's
han's, and right den en dar' you loozes a plow-hand." Apparently, the policeman agrees. He lets Uncle Remus go.[48]

According to Harris, Remus was a product of an inner voice and a composite character, a compendium, as he put it, of "of three or four old darkies
whom I had known." "Uncle" and "darkie," he was built on fifty years of blackface minstrelsy. Expanding from the stage, to literature, to perceived reality,
the genre had long established several keys to the character's popularity. Uncle Remus was uncorrupted by uplift. He was an example, Harris explained,
of "the old fashioned, unadulterated negro who is still dear to the heart of
the South." He was beloved by white audiences. "I trust," declared his proud
creator later, "I have been successful in presenting what must be, at least to a
large portion of American readers, a new and by no means unattractive phase
of the negro character." And finally, he would be authentic. Generations of
scholars would use Harris's stories and tales as evidence: not as evidence for
the racist ravings of a sick man, but as examples of a genuine African American oral tradition.[49]

The Highest Stage of White Supremacy

By the 1890s, the issue seemed clear: the United States was busily committing to a culture of violent white supremacy and racial segregation. "This is especially true in the Southern States," wrote Frederick Douglass in 1892. There, the African American had been "subjected to a lawless, vengeful reign of terror, more wanton, cruel and relentless, if possible, than any in the days of his bondage."[50]

The Reconstruction-era experiment in a biracial society in the South effectively came to an end by about 1875, as white "redeemers" everywhere followed the Mississippi Plan. Through threats, beatings, and lynchings, they suppressed the black vote, drove Northern carpetbaggers out of their states, and returned the old master class to power. During Reconstruction, the states in the old Confederacy had been forced to write new constitutions and reapply to the Union. The resultant "black and tan" constitutions, so called because their drafters had been a mix of whites and African Americans, included the most progressive civil rights laws in the country. By the time the army pulled out of the South in 1877, the laws were languishing on the books. They would gather dust for some eighty years.[51]

Meanwhile, the system of Jim Crow segregation was spreading to all parts of American public life. The point of the system seemed to be humiliation. The black schools, public restrooms, and railroad waiting areas were not just inferior to their white opposites; they were obviously inferior. In effect, they were designed to offer daily, even hourly humiliations, reminders to black Americans of their second-class citizenship. Their point was to demonstrate that any statement that black and white facilities were "separate but equal" was a brazen lie. They provided a message built into the landscape: that white superiority in America would be lasting and shameless.[52]

The question was: what to do? For Douglass, the answer lay in the nation's ideals of democracy. Black men, he declared, needed to vote. African Americans needed to maintain their commitment to an ideology of uplift and education. They needed, he wrote, to rise upward despite resistance:

> The resistance is not to the colored man as a slave, a servant or a menial. It is aimed at the negro as a man, a gentleman and a scholar. The negro in ignorance and in rags, meets no resistance. He is rather liked. He is thought to be in his place. It is only when he acquires education, property and influence, only when he attempts to arise and be a man and a man among men, that he invites repression.[53]

The problem, as Douglass saw it, was the individuals who pandered to the white supremacists, who sang and danced on street corners or voted for the party of white supremacy. These were "tricksters," people "of no moral or political convictions"; they were "Uncle Toms" ready "to sell their race for personal gain."[54]

The situation would get worse. Douglass died in 1895. A year later, the US Supreme Court would proclaim, in *Plessy v. Ferguson*, that the brazen lie of "separate but equal" was true. Still, the editors of the African American paper the *Cleveland Gazette* held to the ideal of dignity and uplift. In an editorial dated January 1899, the *Gazette* condemned a local group in Cleveland for attempting to raise funds for a "Home for Aged Colored People" by putting on a show for white audiences called "The Original Creole Cake Walkers." "Could they not," asked the editors, "have adopted other means more becoming to the occasion?" The editorial concluded with an attack on the genre of minstrelsy:

> The tendency of minstrelsy has no effect in elevating the race, inculcates no ennobling sentiment in the cause, inspires no feeling of emulation, no proud desire to attain results that stand as a memorial of good for coming genera-tions. No! No! The minstrelsy of to-day is but a humiliating exhibition of the weakness, imperfections and ignorant habits of the slave during the days of his bondage.[55]

By this time, the messages of Douglass and the editors of the *Gazette* may have seemed more than a little out of date. The Cleveland locals who hoped to raise money for an old folks' home with a minstrel show were following a format for black success that had been in place for at least a generation.

Among the pioneers for this kind of thing was a singing group from Fisk College, the Fisk Jubilee Singers. The singers were to a large extent the brain-child of one of the college's music teachers, George White. In nearly every way, White fit the Southern redeemer's definition of a carpetbagger. He was a white Northerner, born in 1838, the son of a village blacksmith in the upstate village of Cadiz, New York. He grew up in the village, went to public school, and developed a keen interest in music. By the 1850s, he had moved to Ohio. There, despite the fact that he never went to college and had no formal train-ing in music, he found work as a schoolteacher, teaching music, singing, and choir.

He was also an abolitionist. Banned by his public school from teaching African American children, at some point between 1857 and 1860 he started teaching interracial music classes at his own outdoor Sunday School. At the outbreak of the Civil War, he volunteered for the army and joined the 73rd Ohio Regiment. Like many Northern young men, he fought expressly to end slavery. He saw plenty of action in the bloody battles of Chancellorsville and Gettysburg.[56]

Also like many idealistic young men, White became involved in the Freedmen's Bureau. At the war's end, he was in Tennessee, working under the state's Bureau director, Clinton B. Fisk. By 1867, he had been named to the faculty of the just-established Fisk College. Located in Nashville, Tennessee, and opened in the fall of 1867 with some four hundred students, Fisk would be one of several Freedmen's Bureau Colleges established during the Civil War and Reconstruction. Others would include Kentucky's Berea College, Talladega College in Alabama, Atlanta College, Tougaloo University in Mississippi, Virginia's Hampton Institute, and Straight University in New Orleans. The goal of these schools, according to their founders at the Freedmen's Bureau, would be to import "New England ideas" to the South, to brighten and enlighten the region "like the rays of the morning sun."[57]

Within three short years, the rays were starting to dim. Even in the North, voters soon turned against their tax dollars going to black public colleges. With cuts in funding for the Freedmen's Bureau, several of the colleges began to suffer. Fisk was typically hard hit. Some of the campus's buildings fell into decay. The school struggled to house its students, and teachers went begging for classrooms. By this time, one of the favorites among these teachers was George White. Still teaching music and overseeing the choir, White was also the school's acting treasurer. He was well positioned to understand its dire economic straits. At some point during the school year 1870–1871, he came up with an idea: a group of students from the choir would go out, travel the country, and give concerts to raise money for the college.

The idea must have struck some observers as akin to a bake sale. At first, it seemed to work about as well. In October 1871, ten students, along with White and other members of the entourage, started off on their first tour. They headed north, into Ohio, then to New York State and New England. They planned concerts in Cleveland, New York City, Boston, and points between. Their first goal, it seems, was to avoid the taint of association with blackface or minstrelsy. They rejected the name "The Fisk Minstrels." They were the "The Fisk Jubilee Singers."[58]

Their second goal was to draw audiences, to compete with the many minstrel shows also touring the North. Here, they faced problems. They worried, as one of their programs later put it, whether "the large class of Christians, who would scarcely patronize negro concerts," would "deem it respectable" to attend theirs. "Was there not," the program asked, "so much odium attached to negro concerts, as represented in burnt-cork minstrels, that people of taste and character did not think it becoming to rush in crowds to a paid concert given by negroes?"

To allay such concerns, they made their programs as respectable as possible. These promised a list of hymns, songs like "Steal Away to Jesus," "That Old Time Religion," and "The Ship of Zion." They avoided any hint of the "shout" or the style of the vernacular black church. Another white music professor, Theodore Seward, did their arrangements. These established what became known as the "concert style" of gospel singing, a style formal and staid. They sang numbers already well known as "Negro Spirituals," thanks to the efforts of people like Thomas Higginson and the Port Royal volunteers, formal versions of songs like "Go Down Moses" and "Roll, Jordan, Roll."[59]

Still, for what seemed a long time, the audiences did not appear. To top it off, they faced the humiliations of Jim Crow. Even in the North, they found hotels and restaurants closed against them. On their way back to Nashville following their first tour, they traveled "first class" on the Pennsylvania Central Railroad. The journey went well until they reached Kentucky. There, at a three-hour stop to change trains, White and the singers packed into the waiting room of the Nashville Depot. Suddenly, a station worker approached with a stern declaration: Mr. White could stay; the others had to wait in the "nigger room." Initially, the members of the group refused to leave, saying they had first-class tickets. Then, another of the station's white employees arrived, this one "swinging his baton" and uttering "threats and oaths." He grabbed one of the female members of the group and began hauling her out of the room. White and the others gave in. They ended up waiting outside in the dead of winter, cold, angry, and humiliated.[60]

What ultimately saved the tour—and perhaps Fisk College—was a bit of clever marketing along with a heavy dose of the minstrel perception. At an early concert in Ohio, the Jubilee Singers performed Stephen Foster's "Old Folks at Home" as an encore. The effect was electric. Applause rose from the audience at the song's first notes; by its end, the small crowd erupted in cheers. The next day, the newspapers had the encore as the concert's high point. Though they still refused to list it on their programs, the singers made sure to add the song to their repertoire. They also began performing an abolitionist version of a slave song, "No More Auction Block for Me." Finally, someone with the tour came up with the idea of depicting the singers as slaves. Their songs, stated their programs, "are the simple and natural expressions of wrong, suffering, and slavery." They would be "sung by those who have tasted the bitterness of bondage," by singers who had "suffered all the indignities of slavery."[61]

This was a marketing ploy. Of the ten original members of the group, only four had been slaves before the Civil War, all three of the men and one of the women. Yet, as interest began to build for their concerts, it grew around a minstrel perception of the singers as slaves in the present tense. As the Reverend Theodore F. Cuyler, of Brooklyn's Lafayette Avenue Church, wrote of their performance in New York City, the singers were "the very embodiment of African heart music." He quickly explained the term: hearing their "rich, plaintive voices" had taken him back to a "veritable Uncle Tom's Cabin." Similarly, the nation's most famous clergyman, Henry Ward Beecher, described their concerts as slave music sung by slaves:

> They will charm any audience sure; they make their mark by giving the spirituals and plantation hymns as only *they* can sing them who know how to keep time to a master's whip. . . . You will hear from them the wild slave songs, some of which seem like the inarticulate wails of breaking hearts made dumb by slavery. You will hear the plantation songs—in short, the inner life of slave hearts expressed in music.[62]

The singers—or people around them—were not quite as averse to playing to blackface-framed expectations as they suggested. As their programs declared, the singing of blackface groups like Christy's Minstrels "is as false as the black on their faces." Yet the Fisk Singers too engaged in theatrics. They were college students. They worked extremely hard on their singing and the arrangements of their songs. Yet they allowed themselves to be portrayed as "child-like unfortunates." They allowed their songs to be marketed as coming from "no musical cultivation whatever," as "simple, ecstatic utterances of wholly untutored minds." They marketed a version of blackness rooted in nature and defined by slavery. Their excellent singing would never be the result of discipline and hard work. Instead, it arose from the "experience of slavery," the "heat of religious fervor," from "nature."[63]

The marketing worked. By the middle of their first tour, they began to pack in ever-larger audiences. By the end, they had raised the amazing sum of $20,000. The plan, once they returned to Nashville, was to use the money to build a new hall on the campus, a dormitory for female students to be called "Jubilee Hall." The hall would require more tours and many more concerts. But it would be built. In the spring of 1873, the Jubilee Singers began their first tour of England, where they would perform before the Queen. In 1879, they sang for John Greenleaf Whittier. The old poet supposedly "wept with joy." Everywhere they went, according to critics, their songs recalled the "magic work of Uncle Tom's Cabin." Their songs, as another critic had it, "carry us in a moment to the slave cabin, and we see and feel with the slaves."[64]

FIGURE 9.1. The reversal of minstrelsy and black empowerment. Formed in 1871, the "Jubilee Singers" of Fisk College in Nashville started a tradition of giving concerts to raise money to support the historically black Freedmen's Bureau College. The gospel group's efforts reflected the choice for African Americans during the United States' long period of white supremacy: they could resist blackface stereotypes and be ignored, or they could play the minstrel and gather some power and profit. The Jubilee Singers tried to take a middle path: they refused to call themselves minstrels. But despite their respectability and hard work, they marketed themselves as former slaves who were natural and untutored in their singing. When they had early problems attracting audiences, they added to their concerts a few of Stephen Foster's black-face favorites. This did the trick, and in their first year the Fisk Singers raised the amazing sum of $20,000 for the college. "The Fisk Jubilee Singers," from J. B. T. Marsh, ed., *The Story of the Jubilee Singers: With Their Songs*, 7th ed. London: Hodder and Stoughton, 1877, frontispiece. Courtesy of American Antiquarian Society.

The legacy of the Fisk Jubilee Singers would be one of contradictions. On one hand, the marketing of their concerts as slave songs arising from "untutored minds" would strengthen a minstrel perception of black people. So would their integration of blackface song into the category of genuine "negro spiritual." By the early years of the twentieth century, the category of genuine plantation songs included several by-then-classic spirituals: "Run to Jesus," "The Gospel Train," and "Swing Low, Sweet Chariot." It also included black-face standards: "Old Dan Tucker," "Dixie," and "Dandy Jim Ob Caroline." Plantation-song collections were sure to expand on the Fisk Singers' themes. "In the evenings," read the preface to one, "the negro gave us the gift of his child mind. That gift was simple song. It couldn't have been written if the negro did not suffer."[65] The meaning would be clear: the suffering of black people produced not degradation but nobility and art. This way of thinking was not just about putting a positive spin on black oppression; it was about denying oppression, rationalizing it, even justifying it.

On the other hand the singers provided a model of black institution-building within a context of white supremacy. W. E. B. DuBois understood what they accomplished. Whenever he visited Nashville and the Fisk College campus, he would note in his classic *The Souls of Black Folk*, "Jubilee Hall seemed ever made of the songs themselves." Following Fisk's success, other Freedmen's Bureau Colleges sent out choirs. They too would sing for white audiences, audiences that expected slave songs and pathos, audiences willing to pay if the singers took them back to Uncle Tom's Cabin and allowed them to "understand" slavery.[66] As these black choirs knew, in a culture of white supremacy there were few options: they could watch the funding for their colleges dry up and the doors close, or they could go out, speak and sing in ways that white people wanted to hear, raise money, and make sure their schools survived.

In the last two decades of the nineteenth century, interest in black expression would be more popular than ever. The writer and sometime folklorist George Cable could never quite figure it out. Throughout the country, he noted, black people were being denied "a white man's chance." They were denied civil rights, forced into a culture of poverty, and lynched. Meanwhile, "the core of the colored man's grievance," wrote Cable, was how the larger white culture perceived him. Whether "man or child," and "without regard to person, behavior, or aspirations," a majority of whites treated black people "as though the African tincture, much or little, were itself stupidity."[67]

Without realizing it, Cable would come close to identifying what made a black identity so popular in modern America, even as black people themselves remained second-class citizens, subject to abuse and oppression. Much of this came from his focus on the themes of black song. The songs, he noted, completely neglected the nature of the external world. There were no verdant valleys, sun-blessed mountains, or mossy glens in black song; there was no expression of nature as an uplifting force. Instead, black song expressed nature as internal, dark, and downward in its direction. The nature of black song, as Cable found, expressed a concept of "human nature" as a desire for thrills and good times, for gambling and quick money, for the pleasures of food, sex, and drink.[68] These themes would make sure that what passed for black song would never be respectable, that the songs would frequently be connected to vice.

Yet they would guarantee the music's overwhelming popularity. For, along with the old theme of anti-intellectual authenticity, these themes would make black song the soundtrack of modern American capitalism. What Cable missed is the possibility that degraded stupidity and a yearning to repeatedly give in to the low impulses of "human nature" would come to be increasingly celebrated in a culture devoted to consumption. The rise of an American consumer culture, in other words, would explain why black people would be forced into degradation and poverty and at the same time be extremely popular and celebrated for their low expressions.[69]

James Bland would be one of the first African Americans to really cash in on this popularity. Bland would seem like an unlikely minstrel. Born in Flushing, New York, in 1854, he was the son of one of the nation's first African Americans to complete college. Indeed, his father was most likely a daunting role model. Allan Bland had both a college degree and a white-collar position: a few years after James was born, he took an appointment as an examiner in the Federal Patent Office in Washington. Young James grew up in the nation's capital. There, he attended public school. As well, and probably as a result of his father's connections, he worked part-time as a congressional page in the US House of Representatives.

In short, James Bland was about as middle class as a young black man could get in the second half of the nineteenth century. In his late teenage years, his place in Washington's black elite became official: he was invited to join the Manhattan Club, an exclusive organization that limited its membership to young black employees of government agencies. By this time, young James appeared to be on his way. He seemed on a path his father had charted for him, headed for a life as a clerk or a state functionary.

He had other interests. At some point in his teenage years, he bought a banjo. Though clearly a busy young man, he learned to play it in his spare time, discovering both an aptitude and a passion. In the 1870s, he joined several other clerks—all members of the Manhattan Club—to form a small musical group. Together, the group of young middle-class black singers gained some local renown by playing for Washington dinners and functions. Bland had caught the stage bug. For a time, he continued along the trajectory charted by his father. He enrolled in Howard Cottage. Within a year, he had dropped out, leaving the Freedmen's Bureau College to look for work as a minstrel. Within two years, he began performing with an all-black minstrel company.[70]

There was nothing new about black blackface. All the way back in June 1849, Frederick Douglass had gone to see a performance of "Gavitt's Original Ethiopian Serenaders," going, as he put it in the North Star, "partly from a love of music, and partly from a curiosity to see persons of color exaggerating the peculiarities of their race." The group represented what was then a new phenomenon: actual African Americans performing minstrel songs. Douglass's take on the performance reflected a prescient recognition of the potential power of blackface in the hands of black performers. "It is something gained," he wrote, "when the colored man in any form can appear before a white audience."

If, that is, a large part of the white population would listen to African Americans only when they expressed themselves in blackface style, perhaps they could infiltrate the genre. Perhaps they could alter its styles and messages. Gavitt's troupe, Douglass found, had no intention of doing so. "They too had recourse to the burnt cork" to "express their characters" and "produce uniformity of complexion." Their singing "was but an imitation of white performers," their entire act little more than an effort "to exaggerate the exaggerations of our enemies." Douglass watched the spectacle with dismay and made a gloomy conclusion: "they will make themselves ridiculous wherever they go."[71]

Despite these criticisms from many middle-class blacks, increasing numbers of African Americans entered the minstrelsy business. Douglass seems to have been right: they repeated what white performers before them had done. They blackened their faces with burnt cork. They dressed in what had become the standard minstrel costume, a frock coat, striped pants, calico shirt, high silk hat, and white gloves. They performed black behaviors and spoke in the blackface version of black dialect.[72]

James Bland would become one of the most famous of these performers. By the late 1870s, he was performing with "Haverly's Genuine Colored Minstrels." The troupe had already become a huge hit with New York City audiences. He also started to write his own songs. One of the earliest, published in 1878, was "Carry Me Back to Old Virginia." With a catchy melody and moderate tempo, the song was stylistically in between the raucous tradition of old blackface and the slower strains of Stephen Foster's sentimental ballads. Yet if its style was a departure, in theme it offered the same old comforting image: the black man dreaming of being carried back to the South, the plantation, and the good old days of slavery.

The image still retained a massive audience. In the early 1880s, Bland would become known as "the Negro Stephen Foster." He would be celebrated as "the Prince of the Negro Songwriters." His income during this time may have reached $10,000 per year. In 1881, he left the United States to go on a tour of England. He ended up staying in Europe nearly twenty years. There, he found several years of success without the make-up, and without having to perform as a blackface minstrel. He clearly lived the high life. In 1901, well after his popularity had started to slip, he returned to the United States. For a time he found work as a clerk in Washington. He tried unsuccessfully to revive his career, even as others made money publishing his old songs. Dying in 1911, he would be buried in a "colored cemetery" in Philadelphia.

Bland's style was early "Tin Pan Alley." As musicologists never fail to explain, the term came from the nation's center of music publishing by the late nineteenth century, a narrow cross-street in midtown Manhattan. The street was lined with music publishing houses, all, it seems, with hack songwriters playing pianos, banging out what they hoped were sheet-music hits. The result supposedly sounded like the clattering of countless tin pans. While the name was colorful, the genre had a simple and stark *raison d'être*: the whole thing was about making money. The basis for Tin Pan Alley's style was business; and the main thrust of business at the time was toward standardization. Tin Pan Alley songwriters worked according to a four-part formula. First, the song had to be simple and the melody catchy. Second, the lyrics had to match the melody; it worked best if both were "peppy." Third, song lyrics should avoid serious topics; what worked best were lyrics focused on topics like love or sexual expression. And finally, if a song became a hit, it should be instantly copied and repeated.[73]

Bland's songs fit the bill in nearly every way. The catchy music and comforting imagery of "Carry Me Back to Old Virginia" made for a huge success. A later sheet-music version of the song would sell some two million copies; in 1940, it would be named the official state song of Virginia. In 1879, he published "Oh, Dem Golden Slippers." The song, like several Tin Pan Alley numbers, would have such a catchy melody it would reappear throughout the twentieth century as a commercial jingle. In 1880, he followed with "De Golden Wedding":

> Let's go to de golden wedding, / All the darkies will be there;
> Oh, such dancing and such treading! / And such yellow girls so fair!
> All the high-toned colored people / That reside for miles around
> Have received an invitation, / And they surely will come down.
>
> All the darkies will be there, / Don't forget to curl your hair;
> Bring along your damsels fair, / For soon we will be treading.
> Won't we have a jolly time, / Eating cake and drinking wine;
> All the high-toned darkies / Will be at the Golden Wedding.

"De Golden Wedding" was a clear effort to repeat the success of 'Oh, Dem Golden Slippers." It was also, in style and imagery, a "coon song." Coon songs have often been placed in a category of musical exotica; or they have been dismissed as examples of the type of shameless racial imagery that once existed at the nation's margins. Yet from about 1880 through the 1920s—and probably beyond—coon songs were at the very heart of the nation's popular culture. The vast majority were the stuff of Tin Pan Alley. They had a standardized rhythm, jaunty in pacing and heavily syncopated. Their melodies were peppy, perfect for commercial jingles. What gave them their special designation were their black themes. They were about black people. Many, like the songs of James Bland, were by black people.

Coon songs brought together all of blackface's themes and echoes. As their titles suggest, they tended to depict black people as "coons," a term that clearly went back to "Zip Coon" and that designated a black person who "put on airs" or tried to "act white." Others used the term "darkies." The majority, perhaps, offered the standard blackface theme of "coons" or "darkies" mimicking white culture and behavior: in black efforts to engage in highbrow dances and balls, to form their own military ranks and parade in black regiments, to attend school or college. These efforts would comprise the comedy of the songs: each effort would be exposed as the putting on of false airs, as beyond the capabilities of the "true" coon or darkey.[74]

Perhaps the most common theme in these songs was black freedom from any form of shame, morality, or ethical brake. The African American duo Bert Williams and George Walker made a career out of performing these songs, along with "coon songs" and minstrel favorites of every stripe. The two took to billing themselves as "Two Real Coons," to separate themselves from white performers in burnt cork and to stress the authentic qualities of their act. Many of these songs featured the blackface imagery of violence, with stories of razor-wielding black characters, with frequent brawls between black males. Others focused on gambling, on the characteristically "black" pastimes of cards, dice, and policy games. In these songs, money came and went quickly. The "sportin' man" would win a large amount with the roll of the dice or turn of a card. He would lose it just as quickly, spending it on women or liquor, putting it all on another long-shot wager. Often these images centered on the consumption of food. Many featured black characters as having limitless appetites. They stole chicken. They dreamed of feasts with main dishes of possum. They ate mass quantities of watermelon.[75]

By the time of the coon-song phenomenon of the late nineteenth and early twentieth centuries, the United States had reached a period that has been called "the highest stage of white supremacy." The main characteristic of this phenomenon, according to several historians, was the form of American apartheid that would be known as "Jim Crow." Perhaps the more lasting characteristic was the cultural positioning of blackness as the identity of modern consumer capitalism. From Jim Crow and Zip Coon through the Uncles Ned, Tom, and Remus, from white-invented black folklore to black-produced coon songs, generations of blackface expression constructed this identity as a body without a mind, an all-desiring self, a corridor for all the "dark" yearnings and products that the culture and the entrepreneurs who ran it could create.

This period of the highest stage of white supremacy would also be marked by the wild popularity of Black America. In 1895, Nat Salisbury, the manager of Buffalo Bill's "Wild West" and a showman in the tradition of P. T. Barnum, announced the opening of "Black America" at Ambrose Park in Brooklyn, New York. According to Salisbury, this was to be "an ethnological exhibit of unique interest." For the ticket price of twenty-five cents, the show offered a genuine "plantation village," a collection of log cabins, hen yards, hay wagons, mules, chickens, and bushes with pasted-on cotton balls. It also offered grandstand performances. According to advertisements placed in the papers, these would include black "Home Life," "Folk-lore," and "Pastimes of Dixie." Village and grandstand would be populated, according to another poster, by "Real Blacks from the Southern Plantations. NOT a lot of Northern Negroes." They would present "The Most Unique and Stupendous Entertainment Ever Put Before the Public."[76]

New Yorkers loved the spectacle. On June 13, with the show having been open for a month, the city papers announced that Black America was coming to midtown Manhattan. The performers would march along Fifth Avenue in Manhattan to the Thirty-Ninth Street Ferry, promised the New York Times, adding that "as they march along they will sing many of the old plantation melodies." Two days later, the Times reported that the parade had attracted "great attention," that it had been a major hit with the locals.

This made sense, for the whole thing was a coon song come to life. A "detachment of police" started things off. Then came, in order, "a troop of colored cavalrymen on foot"; some thirty "colored girls in white blouses and sailor suits" who did "the Golden Key drill"; and then some fifteen "colored men in evening dress suits." As observers were sure to understand, these well-dressed performers represented "dark town strutters." Here again was the minstrel character of the "dandy darkie," still with pretensions of whiteness, still "putting on airs." Finally, at the rear of the parade, came scores of "colored people wearing plantation costumes." The parade made stops at all the hotels: the Windsor, the Waldorf, the Brunswick, and the Worth. There, according to the Times, the characters sang a number of "plantation and patriotic melodies."[77]

Black America provided employment for some five hundred African Americans. All they had to do for the money was play to the expectations of white audiences. The roles included "Snowball," yet another example of the dandy darkey, along with various uncles, aunties, mammies, and plantation characters. Indeed, the spectacle offered plenty of opportunity for any black person willing to sing and dance. The singing would be done with "zest and abandon," as in the "plantation days 'befo' the wah."[78] The dancing would be a main feature at both the plantation village and the grandstand:

In their dances they go singly, in twos and in threes, and then all join in a negro revel that is beyond description. Old and young, male and female, all dance as inclined, and produce an effect that is wonderful. They dance the "heel and toe," "flim flam," "buck," "wing," and other dances to the music of their hands in rhythmic clapping and a low whistle that sounds like "a-whip, a-whip, a-whip, a-wee," in a dull monotone. Their gracefulness and light, easy motion are wonderful, and are indicative of the untrammeled out-door life that they have lived.[79]

Meanwhile, declared another writer with the *Times*, there would be the singing of "exquisite" melodies, and "choruses, in which there are hundreds of voices, that stir the listeners almost to tears." There would be continuous versions of "traditional slave songs": "My Old Kentucky Home," "Carry Me Back to Old Virginia," "Old Black Joe," and "Roll, Jordan, Roll." Finally, through the tears would be laughter and love. Every afternoon, at the show's high point, a cart filled with watermelons would be wheeled out to the center of the plantation village. The performers would play blackness, scrambling to get at its contents. The spectators would erupt in joy, cheering this scene of chaotic consumption and natural black appetite.[80] The moment would represent both the highest stage of white supremacy and the triumph of love-crime racism. Both would be lasting.

Conclusion: Musical without End

On a July 5 several years ago, I was heading from Boston to Milford, New Hampshire, to do research on one of the main subjects of this book. The route is well known, for hundreds of thousands of cars follow it every day. From Boston to Nashua is multi-lane freeway; from Nashua to Milford follows the path of an old carriage road. Back in its carriage days, the road passed through spruce groves and hillsides cleared for sheep pasture. Now it is a feeler of a megalopolis running south to Miami. There are the usual roadside sights: tangles of overhead wires; gas-station convenience stores; parking-lot deserts and wind-tumbled trash. There are passing racial stereotypes: a restaurant decorated by a neon-art gnome in a giant sombrero, napping against a cactus; an old motor court with a faded sign featuring a teepee and an Indian brave.

Musical interludes mark the traffic lights. An enormous 4x4 truck has a horn that plays "Dixie," along with two flags behind its cab, the US Stars and Stripes and the battle flag of the Confederacy. A ground-shaking, machine-like rhythm issues from another car; the driver, a young white male in backwards ball cap, jerks his head forward at each beat, like a woodpecker looking for bark grubs. There are objects suggesting a love for noise along with the blending of politics and style: gun shops, fireworks stands, thunderous motorcycles festooned with American flags and Republican Party stickers, straddled by middle-aged white men wearing what look like Nazi helmets.

On the road to Milford—and nearly everywhere else in America—there are echoes of the history of American popular song. To a large extent, popular song is about the expression of desires. Along this road are manifestations of many of modern America's deepest historical yearnings along with their current results: the fixation on buying, selling, and wanting; the need to belong to a community even if it is only formed by purchasing patterns; the expression of patriotism as vulgarity; the hate-based racism of the Confederate banner; the vitalist racism of a love for ethnic authenticity. Finally, there is the standardized rebellion against a better alternative, the militant preference for the ugly and loud over anything that might hint of uplift or social improvement, the antisocial, anti-intellectual, and anti-idealist rejection of any responsibility to a wider world.

Back in Boston, sanitation workers are cleaning up mounds of leftover trash from the city's Independence Day concert. Everyone knows about the tradition. Each July Fourth, tens of thousands of people gather in front of a giant band shell above the Charles River. By day, they mill, shout, and consume vast quantities of food and drink. Toward dusk, they settle in for an orchestral concert by the Boston Pops. The highlight of the show is the playing of the evening's patriotic centerpiece, strangely, Tchaikovsky's "1812 Overture." At the number's crescendo, there will be cannon fire. The concussions will rise above the river, killing scores of birds that no one bothers to see, ending in a massive fireworks display. The flashes and bomb bursts will produce patriotic noises from the crowd: from some, guttural bellowing; from others, sustained "woos" of shrieked appreciation.

Someone once asked me about the tradition: "What's the deal with the Tchaikovsky?" The overture, after all, is by a Russian; it includes snippets of the French anthem "La Marseillaise" and a bit of "God Save the Czar." It has nothing to do with the United States, no relation to the nation's independence, identity, or history. The choice comes from the apparent fact that Americans really do love loud noises. The key to the overture's patriotism, declares a current observer, is that it "is one of the few pieces with good musical content that has cannons exploding." The number is "undeniably non-American," admits another. He is quick to deny that the fact has any meaning: "who cares?" The crowds love the "air-splitting rounds of cannon fire along with the fireworks."[1] The implication of the Pops' playlist is clear: Americans know little and probably care less about the history of their popular music.

Ahead in Milford, there may be a reason why. Milford is like hundreds of once-small New England towns. It has become a suburb of eastern Massachusetts, a bedroom community for Boston-bound commuters. Three miles outside the town center, on old North River Road, there is a large colonial structure. According to the few brochures available to the area's few tourists, the building was formerly a tavern built by Captain Joshua Burnham in 1777. Later, it was the home of the town's most illustrious historical figures: the Hutchinson Family Singers. In 1976, to mark the bicentennial of the country

or the near-bicentennial of the house, the Milford Historical Society erected
a plaque at the location. Funding for the marker came from two sources: one
was the National Music Council; the other was the petroleum corporation
Exxon. The house was a "Landmark of American Music," claimed the monu-
ment. A brief text explained why:

> The Hutchinson Family was America's first famous singing group. For more
> than three decades after their 1839 debut, the Hutchinson sons were spokes-
> men for the Union and for Woman's Suffrage. This house was the home of the
> Hutchinson Family.[2]

The plaque raises a couple of questions. The first is obvious: why would
a corporation associated with worldwide environmental degradation be responsible for sponsoring a landmark of music? The second requires a bit of
knowledge about the Hutchinsons. Why the omissions? Apparently, whoever
wrote the marker's text felt it would be better to leave out the fact that the
"Hutchinson sons" included a daughter. They were also bent on avoiding the
singers' more controversial causes. The result is a bland image of progress.
The Hutchinsons were "for the Union" and "for Woman's Suffrage." Everything else about the singers has been erased. Far from celebrating a landmark
of American music, the marker seems an attempt to hide something.

It seems, in other words, that most of the Hutchinsons' causes, along with
the songs that expressed them, have been excised from American history. One
explanation may be the political shifts in the twentieth century; the Hutchinsons' legacy of idealistic reform could not survive two red scares, countless
lurches to the right, or the hammered message that capitalism and democracy
are not in fact complete opposites but are the same thing, and that communism has no place in the United States' past. Another may be that the singers'
causes and values do not fit a national narrative. To recognize them, after all,
would challenge the nation's ideology of progress, its official version of the
past as an inexorable march toward entrepreneurial individualism, its more
liberal belief that almost no one in America knew right from wrong until the
1960s. Seeing the songs and causes of the Hutchinsons would mean recogniz-
ing that reformers were more than colorless drudges, abolition was a popular
cause before the Civil War, conflicts over civil rights date back over a hundred
years before the countercultural sixties, and communism is a deeply rooted
American tradition.

The cultural erasure of the Hutchinsons' values would not happen over-
night. The singers remained popular during their heyday and beyond. Their
songs possessed "an eloquence beyond that of oratory," declared a writer of
a press notice some ten years after the original family performed. They sang

"plain, simple ballads and songs," added another, and made people "hear and understand every word." Their words had an effect. "Who can tell how much these simple songs have done?" asked the writer of an article in the *Saint Louis Democrat* in 1861, adding that "doubtless" they "converted thousands whom arguments less inspired could not have reached," and "perhaps" they had even put an end to slavery.[3]

For Frederick Douglass, the greatness of the singers came from the fact that they sang "for a cause first and cash afterward." William Lloyd Garrison agreed. The singers, he wrote, "had every conceivable worldly and professional inducement . . . to stand aloof from the maligned 'abolition agitation,' and give themselves exclusively to the singing of sentimental and mirth-provoking songs." They remained "proof against all temptations," declared the old abolitionist.[4]

Through much of the nineteenth century, they would be considered representative Americans, exemplars of republican virtue. Their music was wholly "American in character," declared a reviewer in 1848, and their songs were those of the "most lofty and patriotic sentiments." The key to their character was their "unaffected simplicity," claimed another, adding that as "Yankees" and "world philanthropists," they sang of "home and country," the songs of "boundless benevolence" and "fearless well-doing," the "songs of patriotism." "Americans," wrote one critic at the height of their popularity, would "rather hear Abby sing, than listen to the music of all the Donnas and Signoras in Christendom. She sings; they attitudinise and scream." In the words of another critic, they were "exactly what Americans—the children of a young, bold republic—ought to be."[5]

Long after the high point of their careers, the original singers remained committed to "fearless well-doing." In the years after the Civil War, Asa's family became known for a protest song against sweated labor, "Hannah's at the Window Binding Shoes." Even from the plains of Minnesota, Asa stayed connected to politics. In 1874, he wrote a campaign song for the Maine liberal James G. Blaine, whose presidency would mean "freedom for whites, blacks, women and all."[6] John turned to the issue of voting rights for women. In 1867, he was in Kansas, where his family "made the entire circuit of the state, singing Woman Suffrage into souls that logic could never penetrate." The result was an anthem called "Equal Rights Our Motto":

Who Votes for woman's suffrage now / Will add new laurels to his brow;
His Children's children, with holy fire, / Will chant in praise their patriot sire.
No warrior's wreath of glory shed / A brighter luster o'er his head,
Than he who battles selfish pride, / And votes with women side by side.[7]

In the summer of 1905, a widowed and recently remarried John Hutchinson would report to the press that he had finally found love. The eighty-four-year-old reformer also declared that he planned to travel the country with his new wife, singing, giving concerts, and "advocating peace, the equality of man, municipal ownership, [and] rebellion against the greedy grasp of the trusts."[8]

Testimonials to the original singers rolled in at each of their deaths. They sang "with a power and pathos never equaled by any other company of singers," declared an article in *Frederick Douglass' Paper* in response to Judson Hutchinson's suicide in 1859, adding that they "always left their hearers better than they found them." When Asa died in 1883, the staff of the local paper in Hutchinson, Minnesota, sought out fans who had seen the singers in their prime. It did not take long to find one. "I had never before been so perfectly charmed with the melody and harmony of human voices," recalled the old abolitionist. When the singers started, he added, the "white heat" of abolition "was just beginning to be fanned into a blaze, and nothing that was said or done contributed more to the final conflagration than the anti-slavery songs of the Hutchinson Family." With Abby's death in 1893, the flood of testimonials became a torrent. Abby was a "great help to our own woman's cause," wrote Susan B. Anthony. "To the present generation it will have small meaning," stated the *Boston Globe*, "but there will be grizzled men and women to whom the name Abby Hutchinson will recall a phase in the history of the country second only to the Revolution."[9]

By the dawn of the twentieth century, only John Hutchinson remained from the original singers. He lived at High Rock, the old Hutchinson estate above Lynn, Massachusetts. Phrenologists regularly appeared there in the mid-nineteenth century. Spiritualists predominated among the later visitors; and there were several séances to contact dead brothers. By the end of the century, John made the estate a magnet for "noted liberalists," "radical socialists," and "interesting talkers." To the press, he was something of a crackpot and a local institution. He was the "grand old man of Lynn" and the "bard of High Rock." He was also peculiar, a subject of interest for his radical opinions, his idealism, and after the death of his wife Fanny, his many flirtations with younger women. His music was old fashioned. By 1879, one California paper explained to its readers that "in the East," the Hutchinsons were "more widely known, and more popular than any company of singers ever heard in the United States." They were "not so well known to the younger generation."[10]

The old man sometimes left the rock. He was a regular at reunions of reformers. His singing "brought unbidden tears," declared one participant at an abolition reunion during the 1890s; his songs were those of a "past generation, to be recalled as treasured reminiscences." Hearing "The Old Granite State," wrote another, "took us back to the times of glorious conflict with oppression."[11] He continued to give concerts, hosting musical evenings filled with nostalgic songs. For these events, he had preprinted broadsides, notices that he had given "over 11,500 concerts in America and England," that for "nearly six decades" his songs had "inspired and pleased the world." A newspaper article from 1900 would refer to him as "lonely and alone." "The world is getting away from me," he declared in an interview, adding, "I don't belong here any longer." He would live another eight years, during which time "woman suffrage and socialism" would be his "most ardent themes." Finally, on October 20, 1908, John Hutchinson died, the "last of the Hutchinson Family Singers."[12]

At the time, blackface minstrelsy was also dying, at least according to several experts. "Whatever the exact cause may be," wrote the critic Brander Matthews in 1915, "there is no denying that negro-minstrelsy is on the verge of extinction." He noted several efforts to avoid the fate. One was increasing the size of minstrel groups. This trend reached its apex in the 1880s, when Jack Haverly's Mastodon Minstrels put over forty blackface performers onstage at the same time, a confusing assemblage of singers, banjos, bones, fiddles, and tambourines all stacked in vertical rows. Another involved plumbing new depths of black expression, as writers of "coon songs" continued to develop naughtier themes.

The problem, said a few experts, came from a dawning recognition: the character of the minstrel stage was a complete fabrication. One noted that the "clog dance"—though long a staple of the "olio"—had nothing at all to do with black people. Black slaves, suggested another, had never even played the banjo. The claim prompted one woman to dash off a letter to the nation's leading expert on black culture. "I should be shocked to learn that the negroes of the South know nothing of the banjo," she wrote Joel Chandler Harris, adding that it was a "great comfort to me to associate them with that instrument." Uncle Remus offered no solace: the banjo-playing slave was a myth. Indeed, added Harris, "a representation of negro life and character has never been put upon the stage, nor anything remotely resembling it."[13]

These reports of minstrelsy's imminent death were exaggerated. They do, however, reveal two important contexts for blackface as it moved into the twentieth century. One was the continued white fixation on black authenticity, the persistent search, in the terminology of the time, for the "true negro music." The other was the recognition that blackface was not only a genre of music but a way of seeing. "The stage negro," as Harris put it, was "ground into the public mind, and he cannot be ground out." The fixation would lead experts to new areas of interest: if minstrelsy expressed a fake black character, then the real thing must be in "Negro Spirituals," the blues, perhaps jazz.

Minstrel-based perceptions would structure the way white people would see these more authentic forms of black music. The wonderful thing about the spirituals, according to one expert, was the way they expressed how happily black people accepted slavery and inferior status. "These are the songs," she declared, "that made it possible for the black men to stay at home and take care of the wives and children of the entire South while the white men went to war to keep them in slavery."[14]

These songs were good for white people who worried about black anger. True "Negro Spirituals" expressed no "rebelliousness or vindictiveness," claimed one expert; instead, they expressed "only patience for this life and great hope in the next." They also offered a rationale for continued oppression. For music expert Jeannette Robinson Murphy—a woman described by her editors as a Southerner "familiar with the negro from childhood" and a dramatist at the "foremost rank of negro folklorists"—the joy and beauty of the spirituals demonstrated the benefits of slavery and the need for Jim Crow segregation. Both, she averred, allowed "the negro's race blood" to be "kept perfectly pure." The problem, she added, was that by 1903 black expressions were being ruined by proximity to "a too highly civilized white race." As a "portrayer of negro music" herself, Murphy offered a bit of advice to young people ashamed of "their old African music":

> They should be taught that slavery, with its occasional abuses, was simply a valuable training in their evolution from savagery, and not look upon their bondage and their slave music with shame. For during that period these songs could develop *because* the negro was kept in such perfect segregation, and his instincts and talents had full play.[15]

The blues and jazz, meanwhile, appeared to catch on with white audiences as antidotes to modernity. An early generation of musicologists wrote essays on "blue notes" or the "riotous rhythms" of jazz. They also provided some history. As they had it, Jazz descended from "ragtime"; ragtime contained echoes of the "bamboula," a "wild dance" of West Africa. Thus, jazz came from Africa. Or it came from slavery. All African American art, declared another jazz scholar, could be "traced to the economic institution of slavery." There was no room in this history for a black middle class. There was plenty of space for rebellion. For one expert, jazz reflected black people's "explosive attempt to be happy"; and so, he added, it was "a balm for modern ennui," a "safety valve for modern machine-ridden and convention-bound society."

The music would produce movement and dance: from black people, "perfect jazz abandon"; from white folks, movements "lame" and "wooden."[16]

Through the rest of the twentieth century, a large number of white people would do all they could to avoid being called stiff or lame, in their dancing or anything else. The effort would fuel the Harlem Renaissance. The history of black Harlem is fairly well known: in 1890, Harlem was the last stop on Manhattan's uptown subway, advertised as a bucolic refuge for wealthy whites; thirty years later, it was "the greatest Negro city in the world," a home to some 150,000 African Americans. What happened between was a story of wartime labor shortage, a "great black migration" of African Americans from the South to the North, the movement of black people into housing made cheap by a collapsed real-estate bubble, and the panicked flight of the area's whites. By 1925, according to James Weldon Johnson, a stranger driving up Seventh Avenue would be shocked by the transition at 125th Street:

> Beginning there, the population suddenly darkens and he rides through twenty-five solid blocks where the passers-by, the shoppers, those sitting in restaurants, coming out of theatres, standing in doorways and looking out of windows are practically all Negroes; and then he emerges where the population as suddenly becomes white again.[17]

For many culture leaders, these twenty-five blocks were a stage for a "pageant of contemporary Negro life." According to Harlem's newspaper, the *New York Age*, the area's rise to prominence offered black people an opportunity to show "good citizenship," to demonstrate that they could support "an adequate" number of churches, public schools, and libraries. For others, Harlem offered the nation a new black identity. The time of "aunties, uncles, and mammies" was gone, declared one writer; "Uncle Tom and Old Black Joe," wrote another, were both dead. In their place was the "New Negro." For Alain Locke, the writer who did the most to popularize the term, the image was Christian, capitalist, and respectable. Like the white go-getters of the time, Locke's "New Negro" was a firm believer in twenties bromides: he had faith in progress, self-esteem, and positive thinking; he wanted to do business and make money.[18]

For more creative writers, the character was actually new. The writer Ulysses Poston pictured the "New Negro" as not only rejecting stereotypes but getting rid of the "super-religious consciousness" foisted on him in the days of slavery. This included dumping the spirituals. Songs like "You Can Take All the World But Give Me Jesus," he noted, "had an unhealthy effect on the material progress of the negro." He claimed that while several black colleges had

made spirituals part of their mandatory Sunday exercises, increasing numbers of young students were refusing to sing them.

According to the union organizer Asa Philip Randolph, the character was a
model of dignified self-assertion. The "Old Negro," wrote the President of the
Brotherhood of Sleeping Car Porters, was ignorant, submissive, and often an
enemy to his own people. He was always "singing psalms" and repeating "the
religious nonsense" used by the "enslavers of his forefathers." Randolph's new
version was "erect, manly, bold, if necessary, defiant." He was a union man and
often a socialist. Above all, he refused to fall for "the agencies used by white
friends to sidetrack" him: the old technique of denying civil rights while "over-
stressing" black "art, spirituals, piffling poetry, jazz, [and] cabaret life."[19]

For these individuals and others, the "Harlem Renaissance" of the 1920s
was a demonstration of black culture and black respectability. White observers reveled in one and struggled with the other. The critic Carl Van Doren's
review of Locke's *The New Negro* was typical: he started on the subject of urban sociology and the color line; he quickly shifted to the "delightful barbarism" of black song and dance. According to a writer for the magazine *American Mercury*, the Renaissance represented a lost identity. Under pressure to
be respectable, he claimed, Harlem's black "strivers" were becoming embar-
rassed to be seen with a straight razor; they had taken to straightening hair
and lightening skin; they had become sensitive to terms like "nigger," "coon,"
and "darkey." The result was a corruption of authenticity:

> Thus, one by one, at the conscious and unconscious behest of the white man,
> the old traditions hooked up with the colored man's peculiar appetites are
> booted on to the bunk heap. His natural human inclinations, talents, tastes,
> preferences, prejudices and predilections, along with the bunk, are ground
> under the flat foot of American inhibition. Chicken, watermelon, spirituals,
> chitlings, pig's feet, bright colors, black faces, kinky hair, friendly congregat-
> ing, the old-fashioned razor, pork chops,—all are now in the Index Expurga-
> torius of Aframerica.[20]

By the mid-1920s, the Renaissance was in full bloom. Harlem was the nation's center for black music, art, and literature. It was home to several black
newspapers, the burgeoning black pride movement of Marcus Garvey, and
the National Association for the Advancement of Colored People. Its leaders,
individuals like W. E. B. DuBois, Walter White, and James Weldon Johnson,
were becoming nationally recognized intellectuals. Its writers, from Langston Hughes and Claude McKay to Jessie Fausset, Countee Cullen, and Zora
Neal Hurston, found eager publishers for poems, essays, and books. Yet, as
Alain Locke noted in 1925, there was "another Harlem." This was the Harlem of

"racy music and racier dancing, of cabarets famous or notorious according to their kind, of amusement in which abandon and sophistication are cheek by jowl."[21]

Much of the action was centered in Harlem's "cabarets," nightclubs that featured song, dance, and with the approval of Prohibition in 1918, illegal and often homemade alcohol. There were the old cabarets, places like "The Lybia" and "Edmond's," that had a thriving black clientele. There was "The Oriental," so named because it was in an old Chinese restaurant, and the "Garden of Joy," named for the fact that it was an open-air nightclub. Both drew black patrons and increasing numbers of whites. Then there was something new: cabarets like "Barron's" and "Immermans Place," places in which blacks served and performed, but which had an all-white clientele. This phenomenon would reach its peak with the area's most famous nightclubs: the "Cotton Club" and the "Savoy." According to the *New York Age*, such cabarets were for "white people who want to come up in Harlem to have a good time rather than for the amusement of Negroes residing in the neighborhood."[22]

The white search for a good time generated opportunities. In the twenties, "black musicals" made regular appearances along the "Great White Way" of Manhattan's Broadway theater district. There were revivals of shows like "Porgy" and "Darktown Follies," along with new spectacles straight from Harlem: "Shuffle Along," "Fidgety Feet," and "Runnin' Wild." As early as 1922, the *New York Age* declared that everything was "wide open" in Harlem, from alcohol sale to gambling to prostitution. One of the best cabarets at this moment, according to the *New York Times*, was "Little Africa." There, white observers could pleasure themselves with the smell of "stale tobacco smoke," the sound of "rich negro laughter," and the sight of erotic dancing from "Miss Lizzie from Dixieland." In other cabarets, declared the *Times* writer, "performers both sing and dance, warbling old plantation melodies."[23]

Some observers raised the question: was Harlem really this exotic? According to the social anthropologist Melville Herskovits, the answer was no: black people fit "patterns of culture typical of American life." The "most striking" example was their attitude about sex. Herskovits recounted a revealing story: while discussing "the treatment of the Negro woman in literature" with a group of black women and men, he "inadvertently" declared that "even if the sexual looseness generally attributed to her were true, it was nothing of which to be essentially ashamed." The anthropologist thought some effervescent black sexuality would be a tonic to a nation of white puritans.

He was shocked when his audience erupted in a "storm of indignation." The group "violently" asserted that black people adhered to the most rigid standards of sexual respectability. These people, Herskovits concluded, were

not nearly as exciting as he had hoped. Yet here was the dilemma: white people wanted them to be different; they *needed* them to be fascinating, dangerous, a bit naughty. The draw of the Harlem Renaissance, realized the anthropologist, was the denial that modern existence was increasingly standardized,
uniform, and dull. If black people ceased being exotic, white people would
have to face the bland banality of American life.[24]

As his inadvertent yet clearly hopeful comment about the "looseness" of
African American women suggested, Herskovits too bought the fantasies. So
did countless others. Within a short time, notices were springing up in newspapers, advertising slumming parties to Harlem. For a cost of five dollars per
head, whites on the town could hire a black host and hostess, a couple who
would assure their entry to the most authentic nightspots. They could take in
the music of Harlem's great bandleaders: Duke Ellington, Louis Armstrong,
Cab Calloway. They could hear the down-home blues of Bessie Smith and
Ma Rainey. They could dance the "Charleston." Or, if they were feeling more
"down with" their hosts, they could try the "black bottom."[25]

By 1926, the best-known Harlem slummer was the avant-garde writer Carl
Van Vechten. "The Negro," declared Van Vechten, "is in the ascendency." The
cabarets were "more popular than ever," and everyone was "trying to dance
the Charleston or to sing spirituals." The writer was an expert on both. In the
middle of the decade, he published his novel on the seamy side of Harlem life,
Nigger Heaven. If black leaders needed evidence that whites saw the Renaissance as a minstrel show, they had it now. W. E. B. DuBois called the novel
"a blow to the face." Its male characters, he noted, spent their time drinking,
gambling, and fighting; his females had catfights over their men. Both sang
and danced; both spoke in blackface dialect. For Van Vechten, according to
DuBois, all of Harlem was the cabaret; all was "surface mud" with "no depth";
all was "one damned orgy after another, with hate, hurt, gin and sadism."[26]

White people bought the book in droves. By the end of the decade, Harlem had seven major nightclubs, eighteen dance halls, and a "thousand-odd
drinking dives." Even the national press caught on to the "Negro fad." An article from *Colliers*, one of the nation's leading weekly magazines, led readers
from Iowa to Idaho on an armchair tour of Harlem's "policy players, hot-
cha and religion"; it introduced them to the area's children, the "little picka-
ninnies" who lolled on brownstone stoops; it invited them to ogle the scantily
clad "Cora LaRed," the "outstanding stepper" who danced nightly at the Cotton Club. By this time, according to the writer Rudolph Fisher, the "Caucasion" had "stormed Harlem." Whites, claimed Fisher, had taken over the cabarets and dives; black people were now the observers. "And what do we see?"
he asked:

Why, we see them actually playing Negro games. I watch them in that epidemic Negroism, the Charleston. I look on and envy them. They camel and fish-tail and turkey, they geche and black-bottom and scrunch, they skate and buzzard and mess-around—and they do them all better than I! This interest in the Negro is an active and participating interest. It is almost as if a traveler from the North stood watching an African tribe-dance, then suddenly found himself swept wildly into it, caught in its tidal rhythm.[27]

The whole thing, claimed *The New York Age*, seemed an experiment in racial reversals. "Time," it added, "can only show what the result will prove to be."[28]

The question was on a lot of minds. To Fisher, the meaning of the Renaissance was irony mixed with a touch of hope. Much of it had turned from an expression of pride to an object for white consumption. But "maybe," he added, "these Nordics" were really interested in forging a human bond; maybe they were "at last learning to speak our language." One thing the Renaissance did not mean, according to other observers, was an end to racism. Racism was thriving, they noted: in the Chicago race riot of 1919, in the revival and massive growth of the Ku Klux Klan, in the spread of "Nordicism"—political ideals of white, racial purity—"to the ends of the earth."

In the end, the meanings of the Renaissance seemed lost in ambiguities. During the twenties, two developments occurred at once: black people grew in popularity, and race oppression and hierarchy appeared to take a great leap forward. Walter White told a story illustrating the problem: on the very night a white audience showered Paul Robeson with applause for his performance in the Eugene O'Neill play *The Emperor Jones*, the owner of a midtown café refused to serve the actor. In about an hour, Robeson went from receiving a standing ovation to hearing the café owner utter the standard refrain: "she did not serve niggers."[29]

What was the explanation? Some attempts to explain seem to have been stuck in the blackface perceptions. For W. E. B. DuBois, the issue was white America's ignorance of black accomplishment. In his 1925 essay, "The Black Man Brings His Gifts," he turned to satire, creating the character "Mrs. Cadawalader Lee," a prim, white socialite on the planning committee for a "Making-of-America" pageant. Mrs. Lee wanted to include only "American" expressions in the pageant. And so she planned to include a song by Stephen Foster, an Uncle Remus tale, and a spiritual. She had no idea, according to the story, that each came from black sources. When she found out, she considered dropping them from the pageant. The story worked; yet in the end, one has to wonder if the joke was on DuBois. For Langston Hughes, the problem was the black middle class. In his 1926 essay "The Negro Artist and the Racial Mountain," Hughes claimed that most black artists came from this class, and most were marked by a "white" culture of respectability, by an "aping of things white." As a result, they turned away from the people whose expressions were the wellspring of African American art: the "low down folks," the poor-but-happy folk who nipped gin and shouted spirituals.[30]

Other explanations came closer to the issue. As some observers pointed out, the problem was not white America's ignorance of black art; it was a near-total confusion of white fantasy with black expression. The problem was not distaste for "low down" black expressions. The problem was white America's near refusal to hear anything else from black sources. According to the writer Helene Magaret, "white enthusiasm for Negroes" had a long history that traced from blackface to plantation romance to jazz. This enthusiasm, she added, was "tragically similar" to a child's for a "circus clown." To Magaret, the problem with the Renaissance was that black artists gave a white public what it wanted.

What white people wanted was the opposite of Langston Hughes's picture of repressed respectability: they wanted gin and shouted spirituals; sensual jazz and poetry in blackface dialect, plantation darkeys and sideshow cannibals. Middle-class white Americans, Magaret concluded, wanted novels like Van Vechten's *Nigger Heaven*, books they could read with vicarious pleasure and close, as she put it, with a head-shaking statement: "You can't teach morals to niggers."[31]

By the twenties, it was clear: this statement was meant as a compliment, a positive affirmation of black exoticism and white liberation. It offered an identity free from crippling ethics. Morals, after all, were both a hallmark of whiteness and the last thing people needed for the smooth running of a culture of consumption. For the writer George Schuyler, the blackface-inspired negrophilia of white America had by the twenties produced a damaging black identity. "The mere mention of the word 'Negro,'" wrote Schuyler, "conjures up in the average white American's mind a composite stereotype of Bert Williams, Aunt Jemima, Uncle Tom, Jack Johnson, Florian Slappy and the various monstrosities scrawled by the cartoonists." That black writers and entertainers played to these images also meant that black art was mostly "hokem." The mere idea of "Negro art," declared Schuyler, was "self-evident foolishness."[32]

For Schuyler, black expression was "identical in kind" to that of white culture. The problem was that white people refused to see it this way. Instead, they became experts on blackness. "White folks" from the "average peckerwood" to the "lunatic fringe of liberals," to the "mooney scions of Southern slaveholders," could all agree, he wrote: black people were "a childish, shiftless, immoral, primitive, incurably religious, incredibly odiferous, inherently musical, chronically excitable, mentally inferior people with pronounced homicidal tendencies." Whether from the North or South, whether liberal or conservative, whether Jewish, Italian, or Nordic, all appeared to "deplore the passing of Uncle Tom and Aunt Beckie." All lamented the passing of black folk who "knew how to 'act properly' and did not offend them by being self respecting or intelligent." Most important, all made sure to remind black people of one point: they were "deeply loved and thoroughly understood."[33]

The love and understanding would last. If blackface can be defined as a genre of popular music in the nineteenth century, by the middle decades of the twentieth century it may have just been American culture. It seemed to appear everywhere, from stock comedic characters in movies to product packages. The American working class, at least the *white* working class, continued to love it: from the 1920s through World War II, minstrel shows were a staple entertainment at conventions of the racially exclusive American Federation of Labor. The AFL's president, Samuel Gompers, was a fan and a strong believer in the message of the shows: the idea that African Americans would never be responsible enough for inclusion in a trade union. According to much of the mainstream labor imagery of this time, the "American worker" remained white, male, physically expressive, and authentic.[34]

It would frame and form black entertainers like Louis Armstrong, the great jazz musician who got his start at the intersection between African American music and sin, improvising on cornet with Joe "King" Oliver all night, every night, for the white clientele at the "sportin' houses" of New Orleans' famed red-light district, "Storyville." When the red-light abatement acts of the World War I era shut down Storyville—along with similar neighborhoods in cities throughout the country—Armstrong joined the "Great Black Migration" to Chicago and New York City. He became one of the favorites in Harlem, one of the very few to parlay his early fame into a career in mainstream show business. His well-known act, playing trumpet, scatting, and making bug-eyed grimaces while singing in characteristic tones that made every song unforgettable, made him a prime example of the minstrel perception.[35]

The perception would frame and form the very evidence for this book. During the Great Depression of the 1930s, one of the projects of the Works Progress Administration, the office charged with putting Americans back to work on government jobs, was to identify and interview blacks in the South who could claim a direct experience of slavery. The interviewers, many of whom were out-of-work writers, clearly saw their task as fitting their subjects to blackface expectations. They frequently invented a spurious black dialect for their subjects. Many also seemed bent on excising any anger from the interviews, on recreating the old imagery of the sunny plantation, the kind master, and the loyal slave.

One of the best qualities of the WPA slave narratives is that every so often the researcher ran across an African American interviewee who knew precisely what the questioners wanted. As one put it in a 1939 interview, "is this something about 'Gone With the Wind?'"[36] In using these documents, I have omitted the dialect and tried to keep in mind that the interviews were conducted in a context of both white supremacy and white affinity for blackface style.

This blend would last through the twentieth century and beyond, into frequent examples, including the 2001 blackface parties that began this book. Here, the patronizing affinity for a lowly black style would also contain a double rejection of an equally spurious whiteness: the stereotypical whiteness of the racist Klan member and the stiff and bland whiteness the fraternity boys associated with middle-class status. The portrayal of the Klansman would provide cover, for the image of the evil racist would throw race oppression to the margins, away from the day-to-day love crimes of these future entrepreneurs.

The second rejection of "whiteness," while it may have appeared as that of the students themselves, may have also, perhaps primarily, referred to the perceived whiteness of people like the Hutchinson Family Singers. The students, in other words, were not rejecting their own whiteness but that of prudish reformers and do-gooders; they were rejecting the paleness, in their eyes, of liberalism, social consciousness, and moral responsibility.

Since this time, the phenomenon of white students donning racially insensitive or offensive Halloween costumes has become something of a fall ritual at college campuses. The ritual produces a predictable sequence of events: a college "diversity center" issues a warning to students to avoid such costumes; someone takes it upon themselves to issue a counterstatement defending the right to engage in silly high jinks in the name of free speech; white students dress up in blackface, sombreros, Indian garb, and Muslim gear; these "incidents" produce protests and calls for someone to get fired.

Finally, a host of media figures, bloviating commentators, and writers associated with various "freedom foundations" respond by hurling vitriol on universities, charging students and professors with "political correctness," ethnic oversensitivity, or "liberal elitism." The charges are fueled by white-hot anger over the idea of "unintentional racism." White people, it seems, have become obsessed with the possibility that some racist epithet will suddenly pop out of their heads, enraged that someone will take this outburst as a sign of their internal workings. In other words, despite quite a bit of bruit about the United States having become a "post racial society," it seems that controversies centered on race continue to have a central place in the culture.[37]

The musical continues. In the winter of 1999–2000, I was at another center for research, putting hours in on the fellowship that started this book. The winter days were gloomy, and the research was sometimes fruitless. I was thrilled when the center promised the closest thing to an academic spectacle: a special evening of presentations devoted to a historical character. The character was Sojourner Truth. Truth, who lived from 1797 to 1883, exemplifies every theme in this book. She navigated a social system built on racial oppression. She was born a slave. She escaped her bondage in 1827, making the awful decision to abandon her children. In the 1830s, under the name "Isabella," she joined a bizarre, free-love, Christian cult led by Robert Matthews, a con artist who called himself the "Prophet Matthias."

When one of the cult's members died under mysterious circumstances, she had an early moment of fame. She was a co-defendant—with Matthews—in a murder trial. The trial's testimony provided plenty of material for a penny press, for it was filled with salacious details of the Prophet's sexual dalliances along with Isabella's strong-armed activities as his bodyguard.

After her acquittal, Isabella reinvented herself as Sojourner Truth, a name she took from Matthias's teachings. She resurfaced in the 1840s at a middle-class communist utopia, the Northampton Association. From about the year 1850 to her death, she became a symbol of black identity and women's rights. She was never very popular with actual blacks, particularly members of an African American middle class. But to white middle-class Americans, she was the beloved "Auntie Sojourner." She was framed and formed by blackface minstrelsy.[38]

The research center's celebration of Truth's life had two parts. The first was a presentation by the historian Nell Painter, who had recently published the excellent *Sojourner Truth: A Life, A Symbol*. The second would be a performance by a historical re-enactor, an artist who had played Truth to rave reviews. On the night of the event, the place was packed. The crowd members looked a lot like the portraits of puritans that adorned the center's walls: they were old, well educated, and white. During Painter's lecture, they seemed subdued and baffled.

The material should have been a revelation. Truth, or Isabella, as she was called, was born a slave in upstate New York. She spoke in a Dutch accent. She sang hymns but no "spirituals." She never once called a white person "honey." She most likely never made the speech for which she has long been celebrated, the famous "Ain't I Woman?" address she supposedly delivered at an Ohio women's rights convention in 1851. She did give a speech at the convention. She may have called on her white audience to accept her—along with all black women—as a sister in the cause. But as Painter explained, the "Ain't

I a Woman" speech was an imaginative invention, a reconstruction of Truth's appearance by the white reformer Frances Dana Gage. Though Painter never mentioned blackface, Gage's dialect version of Truth's speech clearly came from the minstrel stage.

So did other versions of Truth. In 1850, the reformer Olive Gilbert put together a hodge-podge of writings she titled *The Narrative of Sojourner Truth*. The book sold at a steady clip through the rest of the nineteenth century. In 1863, Harriet Beecher Stowe, the creator of *Uncle Tom's Cabin*, gave the nation "Sojourner Truth: The Lybian Sybil." Both writers provided their subject with the standard dialect of the blackface stage; Stowe's narrative placed Truth's birth in Africa, her bondage in the American South.[39]

Meanwhile, the woman once called Isabella lived and died. Only semi-literate, she allowed white reformers to put words in her mouth. She lived partly on the profits of Gilbert's book. For other expenses, she sold pictures of herself at public appearances. The most famous of these had her in respectable clothing: with layered skirts, a knit shawl, and a light-colored turban that might have been silk. According to Painter, the picture reflected Truth's adherence to ideals of Victorian respectability. She signed the pictures and taught herself to write a phrase: "I sell the shadow to support the substance." Painter finished her lecture. There was light clapping. There was a desultory question-and-answer session. The audience was not sure what to think.

Then the re-enactor appeared. She came out from the wings of the stage, or from between several bookcases, singing in a deep, rich voice, starting softly and then building in volume, eventually belting with feeling a well-known black spiritual. The crowd sat up; there was an intake of breath, an outburst of applause; this was the real Truth! The woman was dressed in the rags of a slave. She wore a bright kerchief on her head, *à la* Aunt Jemima. She spoke in a Southern accent, in a dialect descended from Gage, Gilbert, Stowe, and a host of blackface entertainers. It was comforting. She called the audience members "honey" and told them to call her "Auntie Sojourner."

Everyone in the room suddenly had a black relative. She told a couple of earthy stories and had the crowd in stitches. She told one or two emotional tales of the sufferings of slaves. Then she winked and "honeyed" the crowd. There were no grudges. She gave excerpts from her famous speech, shouting "Ain't I a Woman?" with gusto as she flexed arms made muscular by plantation slavery. Finally, she walked back to the shadows between the shelves, gently singing another spiritual.

The audience stood and applauded, grinning and shouting approval. Here was a type of history they could understand, a history that confirmed rather than challenged everything they knew. Here was a racial hierarchy built on love. Here was a way of seeing that made black respectability disappear; that made black uplift impossible; that made low-down blackness the bedrock of authenticity. This was not just a creepy embrace; it was an example of paternal affection, the attraction not to African Americans but to the right kind of black folk: the ones who sang, told colorful stories, and evinced no anger. Here was another scene in an ongoing musical.

Notes

Introduction

1. Thomas Bartlett, "An Ugly Tradition Persists at Southern Fraternity Parties," *Chronicle of Higher Education* 48, no. 14 (30 November 2001): A33–A34.

2. "Ole Miss, Auburn Fraternities Punish Members for Blackface Pictures," *Tuscaloosa News*, 9 November 2001, 5/1–3; Bartlett, "An Ugly Tradition," A33–A34.

3. Bartlett, "An Ugly Tradition," A33; Donathan Prater, "Memories of Images from Fraternity Party Still Vivid," *Opelika-Auburn News*, 31 October 2006 (online); Amy Weaver, "Five Years Later, AU Remembers Blackface Incident," *Opelika-Auburn News*, 31 October 2006 (online).

4. Scholars have noted these types of expressions of white ethnicity; see Stanley Crouch, *The Artificial White Man: Essays on Authenticity* (New York: Basic Civitas, 2005); John Strasbaugh, *Black Like You: Blackface, Whiteface, Insult and Imitation in American Popular Culture* (New York: Penguin, 2006); Tricia Rose, *Black Noise: Rap Music and Black Culture in Contemporary America* (Hanover, NH: University Press of New England, 1994); Tricia Rose, *The Hip Hop Wars: What We Talk About When We Talk About Hip Hop, and Why It Matters* (New York: Basic Civitas, 2008); Bakari Kitwana, *Why White Kids Love Hip Hop: Wankstas, Wiggers, Wannabes, and the New Reality of Race in America* (New York: Basic Civitas, 2005).

5. *Old Dan Tucker: Written and Arranged for Pianoforte by Dan Tucker, Jr.* (New York: Atwill's, 1843); a version of the song from sheet music dated 1844 may be found in *Old Dan Emmit's Original Banjo Melodies, Sung by the Virginia Minstrels* (Boston: Charles H. Keith, 1843).

6. *Get Off the Track! A Song for Emancipation, Sung by the Hutchinsons, Respectfully Dedicated to Nath'l P. Rogers* (Boston: Jesse Hutchinson Jr., 1844).

7. On the origins of "Get Off the Track!" as a campaign song for the Liberty Party, see Scott Gac, *Singing for Freedom: The Hutchinson Family Singers and the Nineteenth Century Culture of Reform* (New Haven, CT: Yale University Press, 2007); 177–179; "Get Off the Track!," from *The Granite Songster: Containing the Poetry as Sung by the Hutchinson Family, At Their Concerts* (Boston: Asa B. Hutchinson, 1847).

8. On the connections between blackface and the "common folk," see Alexander Saxton, "Blackface Minstrelsy and Jacksonian Ideology," *American Quarterly* 27, no. 1 (March 1975): 3–28; Eric Lott, "'The Seeming Counterfeit': Racial Politics and Early Blackface Minstrelsy," *American Quarterly* 43, no. 2 (June 1991): 223–254; on middle-class reform as female-centered, the feminization of culture, or prudishness, see Nancy Cott, *The Bonds of Womanhood: Women's Sphere*

in New England, 1780–1835 (New Haven, CT: Yale University Press, 1977): 151–154; William Leach, *True Love and Perfect Union: The Feminist Reform of Sex and Society* (New York: Basic Books, 1980); Ruth Bordin, *Woman and Temperance: The Quest for Power and Liberty, 1873–1900* (New Brunswick: Rutgers University Press, 1990); Ann Douglas, *The Feminization of American Culture* (New York: Avon, 1977); H. L. Mencken, *The Vintage Mencken* (New York: Vintage, 1955); C. Wright Mills, *White Collar: The American Middle Classes* (New York: Oxford University Press, 1951); David Rothman, *The Discovery of the Asylum: Social Order and Disorder in the New Republic* (Boston: Little, Brown, 1971).

9. This point about the paucity of actual reform and the seeming rarity of democratic liberalism in American history was made brilliantly by Daniel Lazare, in a *Nation* review of several books on the American Revolution; see Daniel Lazare, "Patriotic Bore," *Nation*, 12 September 2005: 31–37.

10. Perhaps the most well-known example of a book covering the whole of American popular song is Charles Hamm, *Yesterdays: Popular Song in America* (New York: Norton, 1979); see also Charles Hamm, *Music in the New World* (New York: Norton, 1983); both works reflect an analysis rooted in musicology and narrative; both have a textbook quality due to their stress on coverage; for other examples of this textbook approach, see Richard Crawford, *America's Music Life: A History* (New York: Norton, 2001); Daniel Kingman, *American Music: A Panorama* (New York: Schirmer Books, 1990); David Ewen, *History of Popular Music* (New York: Barnes and Noble, 1961); Gilbert Chase, *American Music: From the Pilgrims to the Present* (New York: McGraw-Hill, 1955); and finally, the classic John Tasker Howard, *Our American Music: Three Hundred Years of It* (New York: Thomas Y. Crowell, 1946). For a more thematic and interpretive approach stressing relationships between American popular music and social and ethnic diversity, see Adelaida Reyes, *Music in America: Experiencing Music, Expressing Culture* (New York: Oxford University Press, 2005). Musicologist Nicholas Tawa's work suggests that a coverage approach to nineteenth-century music might be done with the old two-volume technique, with the standard break at the American Civil War; see Nicholas E. Tawa, *High-Minded and Low Down: Music in the Lives of Americans, 1800–1861* (Boston: Northeastern University Press, 2000); Nicholas E. Tawa, *The Way to Tin Pan Alley: American Popular Song, 1866–1910* (New York: Macmillan, 1990); for three-volume works with a coverage approach, see Russell Sanjek, *American Popular Music and Its Business: The First Four Hundred Years* (New York: Oxford University Press, 1988); Ronald L. Davis, *A History of Music in American Life* (Huntington, NY: R. E. Krieger, 1980–1982).

11. Johan Huizinga, *Homo Ludens: A Study of the Play Element in Culture* (New York: Harper and Row, 1970), 62; Jacques Attali, *Noise: The Political Economy of Music* (Minneapolis: University of Minnesota Press, 1985), 4–9.

12. See Benedict Anderson, *Imagined Communities: Reflections on the Origin and Spread of Nationalism* (New York: Verso, 1991).

13. On Nathaniel Coverly Jr., see Arthur F. Schrader and Kate Van Winkle Keller, *Songs in Vogue with the Vulgar: The Isaiah Thomas Broadsides* (Worcester, MA: American Antiquarian Society, 2006); Daniel A. Cohen, "'The Female Marine' in an Era of Good Feelings: Cross Dressing and the 'Genius' of Nathaniel Coverly, Jr.," *Proceedings of the American Antiquarian Society* 103, part 2 (1994): 359–393.

14. On carnival as a ritual of reversal, see Mikhail Bakhtin, *Rabelais and His World* (Cambridge: Massachusetts Institute of Technology Press, 1968); Peter Stallybrass and Allon White, *The Politics and Poetics of Transgression* (Ithaca, NY: Cornell University Press, 1986).

15. This story on the background of "Yankee Doodle" comes from, among others, Joseph Muller, *The Star Spangled Banner: Words and Music* (New York: G. A. Baker and Company, 1935).

16. "The Anacreontic Song," cited in Vera Brodsky Lawrence, *Music for Patriots, Politicians, and Presidents: Harmonies and Discords of the First Hundred Years* (New York: Macmillan, 1975), 128.

17. For an example of the literature of repression and the return of the body, see Norbert Elias, *The History of Manners*, vols. 1–2 (New York: Pantheon, 1978); John F. Kasson, *Rudeness and Civility: Manners in Nineteenth-Century Urban America* (New York: Hill and Wang, 1990).

18. On tensions between middle-class ideology and the capitalist market, see Amy Dru Stanley, "Home Life and the Morality of the Market," in *The Market Revolution in America: Social, Political, and Religious Expressions, 1800–1880*, ed. Melvyn Stokes and Stephen Conway (Charlottesville: University Press of Virginia, 1996); Martin J. Wiener, "Market Culture, Reckless Passion and the Victorian Reconstruction of Punishment," in *The Culture of the Market: Historical Essays*, ed. Thomas L. Haskell and Richard F. Teichgraeber (New York: Cambridge University Press, 1993), 136–160; on caring about the suffering of strangers at a distance or, as it came to be known as, humanitarianism, see Thomas L. Haskell, "Capitalism and the Origins of the Humanitarian Sensibility," *American Historical Review* 90 (April 1995): 339–361.

19. On these developments and their place in middle-class formation, see Whitney R. Cross, *The Burned-Over District: The Social and Intellectual History of Enthusiastic Religion in Western New York, 1800–1850* (New York: Harper and Row, 1950); Nathan O. Hatch, *The Democratization of American Christianity* (New Haven, CT: Yale University Press, 1989); Stuart M. Blumin, *The Emergence of the Middle Class: Social Experience in the American City, 1760–1900* (Cambridge, MA: Harvard University Press, 1989); Paul E. Johnson, *A Shopkeeper's Millennium: Society and Revivals in Rochester, New York, 1815–1837* (New York: Hill and Wang, 1978); Mary Ryan, *Cradle of the Middle Class: The Family in Oneida County, New York, 1790–1865* (New York: Cambridge University Press, 1981); on the connections between the middle-class and vernacular etiquette, see Richard L. Bushman, *The Refinement of America: Persons, Houses, Cities* (New York: Vintage Books, 1993); John F. Kasson, *Rudeness and Civility*; on middle-class humanitarianism and reform, see Karen Halttunen, "Humanitarianism and the Pornography of Pain in Anglo-American Culture," *American Historical Review* 100, no. 2 (April 1995): 303–334; Ronald G. Walters, *American Reformers, 1815–1860* (New York: Hill and Wang, 1978).

20. Most of the literature on the Hutchinsons has been from a musicology perspective; for a recent example, see Gac, *Singing for Freedom*; earlier biographies of the singers tended toward the antiquarian and anecdotal; see for example Carol Brink, *Harps in the Wind: The Story of the Singing Hutchinsons* (New York: Macmillan, 1947), along with Philip D. Jordan, *Singin' Yankees* (Minneapolis: University of Minnesota Press, 1946); a more recent approach has been to focus on the singers as forerunners of sixties protest singers (1960s, that is); see Dale Cockrell, ed., *Excelsior: Journals of the Hutchinson Family Singers, 1842–1846* (Stuyvesant: Pendragon Press, 1989); Charles Hamm, "'If I Were a Voice': The Hutchinson Family and Popular Song as Political and Social Protest," chapter 7 of *Yesterdays: Popular Song in America* (New York: W. W. Norton, 1979), 141–161; all of these accounts portray the singers as favorites of the Northern, antebellum middle class. As for the singers' popularity, here there seems to be some question; another musicology scholar has argued that they had little popularity, that their appeal came from their use of sentimentality and nostalgia, and that their "radical" songs were not popular at all; see Caroline Mosely, "The Hutchinson Family: The Function of Their Song in Ante-Bellum America," in

American Popular Music, vol. 1, *The Nineteenth Century and Tin Pan Alley*, ed. Timothy Scheurer (Bowling Green, OH: Bowling Green State University Press, 1989), 73–74. Much of the confusion about the singers' popularity may stem from the fact that by the 1850s there were some four versions of the "Hutchinson Family Singers" touring different parts of the country. None of these later versions were anywhere near as popular as the originals of the 1840s.

21. Christopher Clark, *The Communitarian Moment: The Radical Challenge of the Northampton Association* (Amherst: University of Massachusetts Press, 1995); for the best account of the Shakers, see Stephen J. Stein, *The Shaker Experience in America: A History of the United Society of Believers* (New Haven, CT: Yale University Press, 1992); the best history of Iowa's Amana Colonies remains Bertha M. H. Shambaugh, *Amana: The Community of True Inspiration* (1908, Reprint, Iowa City: Penfield, 1988).

22. On this tendency to view middle-class reformers as fussy prudes, see John C. Burnham, *Bad Habits: Drinking, Smoking, Taking Drugs, Gambling, Sexual Misbehavior, and Swearing in American History* (New York: New York University Press, 1993); the Hutchinsons' campaign against cigarette smoking came, of course, late in the nineteenth century, and reflected one of the issues of John Hutchinson's tribe of the family; see "Bard Talks Love—Tells Post Reporter All About His Numerous Affairs of the Heart—Pets Bride and Dances to Show That He Still Defies Age," *Boston Post*, 26 August 1905. Gac's analysis does not entirely avoid this trap; as he puts it on the subject of the Hutchinsons' reforms: "Today the musicians appear noble for their antislavery, a bit prissy for their temperance"; see Gac, *Singing for Freedom*, 173.

23. For an interpretation of blackface as actual African American music, see Eileen Southern, *The Music of Black Americans: A History* (New York: Norton, 1983); for an update on this approach, see William J. Mahar, "Black English in Early Blackface Minstrelsy: A New Interpretation of the Sources of the Minstrel Show Dialect," *American Quarterly* 37 (Summer 1985): 260–285; for an example of musicology that takes the idea as given, see Christian McWhirter, *Battle Hymns: The Power and Popularity of Music in the Civil War* (Chapel Hill: University of North Carolina Press, 2012); for the best example of the interpretation that blackface reflected American patterns of racism, see Robert C. Toll, *Blacking Up: The Minstrel Show in Nineteenth-Century America* (New York: Oxford University Press, 1974); this argument is still around; for a more recent example, see Louis S. Gerteis, "Blackface Minstrelsy and the Construction of Race in Nineteenth-Century America," in *Union and Emancipation: Essays on Politics and Race in the Civil War Era*, ed. David Blight and Brooks Simpson (Kent, OH: Kent State University Press, 1997), 79–104, 203–205.

24. For the argument that blackface was, as one historian has it, "about race without being necessarily racist," see Dale Cockrell, *Demons of Disorder: Blackface Minstrels and Their World* (New York: Cambridge University Press, 1997), 59; for the most well-known example of this interpretation, see Eric Lott, *Love and Theft: Blackface Minstrelsy and the American Working Class* (New York: Oxford University Press, 1993); see also David R. Roediger, *The Wages of Whiteness: Race and the Making of the American Working Class* (New York: Verso, 1991); W. T. Lhamon Jr., *Raising Cain: Blackface Performance from Jim Crow to Hip Hop* (New York: Cambridge University Press, 1998); William J. Mahar, *Behind the Burnt Cork Mask: Early Blackface Minstrelsy and Antebellum American Popular Culture* (Urbana: University of Illinois Press, 1999); on the connections between blackface and the pre–Civil War Democratic Party, see Richard B. Stott, *Workers in the Metropolis: Class, Ethnicity, and Youth in Antebellum New York City* (Ithaca, NY: Cornell University Press, 1990); Alexander Saxton, *The Rise and Fall of the White Republic: Class Politics and Mass Culture in Nineteenth-Century America* (New York: Verso, 1990).

25. For the pioneering work connecting the presumably Anglo sea chantey to West African roots, see Roger D. Abrahams, *Deep the Water, Shallow the Shore: Three Essays on Shantying in the West Indies* (Austin; University of Texas Press, 1974); Abrahams has also pioneered the study of African traditions in slave songs; see Roger D. Abrahams, *Singing the Master: The Emergence of African-American Culture in the Plantation South* (New York: Pantheon Books, 1992).

26. For this view of the Jacksonian-era and antebellum working class as an exclusive and culturally formed solidarity, see Noel Ignatiev, *How the Irish Became White* (New York: Routledge, 1995).

27. See Barnor Hesse, "(Im)Plausible Deniability: Racism's Conceptual Double Bind," *Social Identities* 10, no. 1 (2004): 9–29, 10–14; Geraldine Heng, "The Invention of Race in the European Middle Ages I: Race Studies, Modernity, and the Middle Ages," *Literature Compass* 8, no. 5 (2011): 315–331, 323; see also Michael Mann, *The Dark Side of Democracy: Explaining Ethnic Cleansing* (New York: Cambridge University Press, 2005).

28. See especially David Theo Goldberg, *The Racial State* (Malden, MA: Blackwell, 2002), 4, 11, 27–30, 48; Reginald Horsman, *Race and Manifest Destiny: The Origins of American Anglo-Saxonism* (Cambridge, MA: Harvard University Press, 1981); Steven Hahn, *A Nation Under Our Feet: Black Political Struggles in the Rural South from Slavery to the Great Migration* (Cambridge, MA: Harvard University Press, 2003), 164–176; Allan Kulikoff, *Tobacco and Slaves: The Development of Southern Cultures in the Chesapeake, 1680–1800* (Chapel Hill: University of North Carolina Press, 1986); Sally E. Hadden, *Slave Patrols: Law and Violence in Virginia and the Carolinas* (Cambridge, MA: Harvard University Press, 2001).

29. On the rise of vitalist racism in post–Civil War America, see Matthew Frye Jacobson, *Barbarian Virtues: The United States Encounters Foreign Peoples at Home and Abroad, 1876–1917* (New York: Hill and Wang, 2000); Jackson Lears, *Rebirth of a Nation: The Making of Modern America, 1877–1920* (New York: Harper Perennial, 2009); on the history of American racism, see Winthrop D. Jordan, *White Over Black: American Attitudes Toward the Negro, 1550–1812* (Chapel Hill: University of North Carolina Press, 1968); George M. Frederickson, *The Black Image in the White Mind: The Debate on Afro-American Character and Destiny, 1817–1914* (New York: Harper and Row, 1971).

30. James Stirling, *Letters from the Slave States* (London: J. W. Parker and Son, 1857), 243–244.

31. George S. Schuyler, "Our White Folks," *American Mercury* 12, no. 48 (December 1927): 385–392.

32. Historian John Burnham argues that one of the keys to modern American consumer culture was the promotion of what he calls "lower-order parochialism," the mind-set of a character able to consume the products of a "vice-industrial complex." The problem with Burnham's analysis is that while he focuses on film outlaws and media delinquents, he misses the "black" characters of blackface minstrelsy and the "coon song." The characters fit perfectly with his lower-order type. This connection between blackface and the promotion of bad habits suggests the strength of the link between consumer culture and racism, along with why so much of consumer culture is filtered through "black" expression. See John C. Burnham, *Bad Habits*.

33. To Thomas Frank, the character of the consumer is that of the rebel, the rebel against everything except the corporate-sponsored message to "be yourself" and give in to your urges; see Thomas Frank, *The Conquest of Cool: Business Culture, Counterculture, and the Conquest of Cool* (Chicago: University of Chicago Press, 1997); for some cogent appraisals of the triumph of neo-liberal vulgarity in America, see the essays in *Boob Jubilee: The Cultural Politics of the New Economy*, ed. Thomas Frank and David Mulcahey (New York: Norton, 2003).

Chapter One

1. *Map of Boston, in the State of Massachusetts, Surveyed by J. G. Hale*, printed in Boston by George H. Walker and Company, 1814; *[Map of] Boston, 1835*, printed in Boston by Pendleton's Lithography, 1835; for the sights and smells of early Boston, see Ester Forbes, *Paul Revere and the World He Lived In* (Boston: Houghton Mifflin, 1962), 3–6, 49–51; for a treatment of nineteenth-century soundscapes, see Evan A. Kutzler, "Captive Audiences: Sound, Silence, and Listening in Civil War Prisons," *Journal of Social History* 48, no. 2 (Winter 2014): 239–263.

2. *A Record of the Streets, Alleys, Places, Etc., in the City of Boston* (Boston: City of Boston Printing Department, 1910); *The Boston Directory; Containing the Names of the Inhabitants, Their Occupations, Places of Business and Dwelling Houses. With Lists of the Streets, Lanes and Wharves; The Town Officers, Public Offices and Banks, and Other Useful Information* (Boston: E. Cotton, 47 Marlboro Street, 1816), 13, 32, 75, 188, 191, 211, 217.

3. This approach to popular culture as "the return of the repressed" is indebted to psychoanalytical theory, particularly Sigmund Freud; as well, it appears in a host of scholarship grounded in historicism and culture studies, including Herbert Marcuse, *Eros and Civilization: A Philosophical Inquiry into Freud* (New York: Vintage Books/Random House, 1955, 1962); Norbert Elias, *The Civilizing Process: The History of Manners*, vols. 1–2 (New York: Pantheon, 1978 [1939]); Raymond Williams, *Culture and Society, 1780–1950* (New York: Columbia University Press, 1958); Peter Stallybrass and Allon White, *The Politics and Poetics of Transgression* (Ithaca, NY: Cornell University Press, 1986); and of course, Michel Foucault's *Discipline and Punish: The Birth of the Prison* (New York: Vintage, 1979) and *The History of Sexuality*, vol. 1, *An Introduction* (New York: Vintage, 1980).

4. Nathaniel Hawthorne, "The Maypole of Merry Mount," from the *Works of Nathaniel Hawthorne*, vol. 1, *Twice-Told Tales*, pt. 1 (New York: Bigelow, Brown & Company, 1923), 45–59, 52.

5. See Keith Thomas, *Religion and the Decline of Magic* (New York: Scribner, 1971); John Stilgoe, *Common Landscape of America, 1580 to 1845* (New Haven, CT: Yale University Press, 1982), 8, 18–19; on traditions of Carnival in the British Isles, see Richard Suggett, "Festivals and Social Structure in Early Modern Wales, *Past and Present*, 152 (August 1996), 79–112; on the persistence of these traditions, the classic account is Robert Darnton, *The Great Cat Massacre: And Other Episodes in French Cultural History* (New York: Basic Books, 1984).

6. Stallybrass and White, *The Politics and Poetics of Transgression*, 14–16; see also Mikhail Bakhtin, *Rabelais and His World* (Cambridge: Massachusetts Institute of Technology Press, 1968).

7. Hawthorne, "The Maypole of Merry Mount," 52–59.

8. Thomas Morton, *New English Canaan, or, New Canaan*, facsimile of 1637 ed. (New York: Arno Press, 1972), 134–138.

9. William Bradford, *History of Plymouth Plantation*, ed. Charles Dean (Boston: Massachusetts Historical Society, 1856), 237–238.

10. Dempsey, ed., "introduction" to *New English Canaan*, xvii–xxi; see also Demos, "The Maypole of Merry Mount"; William Pencak, "New English Canaan by Thomas Morton of Marymount: Text, Notes, Biography and Criticism," *Ethnohistory* 52, no. 2 (Spring 2005): 437–448; Karen Ordahl Kupperman, "Thomas Morton, Historian," *New England Quarterly* 50, no. 4 (December 1977): 660–664; J. Gary Williams, "History in Hawthorne's 'The Maypole of Merry Mount,'" *Essex Institute Historical Collections* (1972): 184–185; Richard Drinnon, "The Maypole of Merry Mount," *Massachusetts Review* 21, no. 2 (Summer 1980): 382–410.

11. See Norbert Elias, *The Civilizing Process*; Herbert Marcuse, *Eros and Civilization*; John F. Kasson, *Rudeness and Civility: Manners in Nineteenth-Century Urban America* (New York: Hill and Wang, 1990).

12. Robert Oaks, "'Things Fearful to Name': Sodomy and Buggery in Seventeenth-Century New England," in Elizabeth H. Pleck and Joseph H. Pleck, *The American Man* (Englewood Cliffs, NJ: Prentice Hall, 1980), 53–76, 67.

13. "At Court," 11 June 1650 and 7 October 1662, *Ancient Town Records, New Haven Town Records, 1662–1684*, ed. Franklin Bowditch Dexter (New Haven, CT: New Haven Colony Historical Society, 1919), vol. 1, 30–32; vol. 2, 11.

14. Cornelia Hughes Dayton, *Women Before the Bar: Gender, Law, and Society in Connecticut, 1639–1789* (Chapel Hill: University of North Carolina Press, 1995), "Cases at Special Court," February 1649, 3 February 1662, and 9 January 1665, from *Ancient Town Records*, vol. 2, 26, 31, 164–165.

15. Entries for 26 and 27 May 1687 from *The Diary of Samuel Sewell*, ed. Harvey Wish (New York: G. P. Putnam's Sons, 1967), 49–50; on the persistence of mumming, see Dale Cockrell, *Demons of Disorder: Early Blackface Minstrels and their World* (New York and London: Cambridge University Press, 1997), 42–44, 57; G. A. Rowell, "Notes on Some Old-Fashioned English Customs: The Mummers; The Morris-Dancers; Whitsun-Ales; Lamb-Ales," *Folk-Lore Journal* 4, no. 2 (1886): 97–109.

16. On the popularity of dance in the sixteenth and seventeenth centuries, see Jane Garry, "The Literary History of the English Morris Dance," *Folklore* 94, no. 2 (1983): 219–228; on regional attitudes toward dance in America: Joy Van Cleef and Kate Van Winkle Keller, "Selected American Country Dances and their English Sources," in *Music in Colonial Massachusetts, 1630–1820*, vol. 1, *Music in Public Places*, ed. Barbara Lambert (Boston: Colonial Society of Massachusetts, 1980), 3–4.

17. For Puritan attitudes toward dance, see Percy Scholes, *The Puritans and Music* (London: Oxford University Press, 1934); on Stepney, see Michael G. Hall, *The Last American Puritan: The Life of Increase Mather, 1639–1723* (Middletown: Wesleyan University Press, 1988); entries for 9 November and 17 December 1685, *Diary of Samuel Sewell*, 39–40; Increase Mather, *An Arrow Against Profane and Promiscuous Dancing Drawn Out of the Quiver of the Scriptures* (Boston: 1684).

18. Van Cleef and Van Winkle Keller, "Selected American Country Dances," 3–73; *200 Country Dances* (1740); *Nancy Shepley's Book* (n.p., n.d.); *Collection of Contra Dances* (1792); *Select Collection of the Newest & Most Favorite Country Dances, Waltzes, Reels, & Cotillions* (Otsego, New York: H. E. Phinney, 1808).

19. *The Compleat Country Dancing Master* (London: J. Walsh and J. Hare, 1718).

20. John Playford, *The English Dancing Master* (1651); *A Collection of the Newest Country Dances and Cotillions* (Providence: 1788); Kate Van Winkle and Ralph Sweet, *A Choice Selection of American Country Dances of the Revolutionary Era, 1775–1795* (New York: Country Dance and Song Society of America, 1975), 11–13.

21. On the popularity of Nancy Dawson and "The Beggar's Opera," see John Richardson, "John Gay, The Beggar's Opera, and Forms of Resistance," *Eighteenth-Century Life* 24, no. 3 (2000): 19–30; Charles E. Pearce, *Polly Peachum: The Story of Lavinia Fenton and the Beggar's Opera* (Ayer Publishing, 1913), 280–292; on country dance, see Van Cleef and Van Winkle Keller, "Selected American Country Dances," 53–54; *The Dancing Master; Or, Directions for Dancing Country Dances, With the Tunes to Each Dance for the Treble Violin, The Tenth Edition, Corrected; With the Addition of Several New Dances and Tunes Never Before Printed* (London: Printed by J. Heptinstall, for H. Playford, 1698), 2.

22. *The Gentleman & Lady's Companion; Containing the Newest Cotillions and Country Dances, To Which is Added, Instances of Ill Manners, To Be Carefully Avoided by Youth of Both Sexes* (Norwich, Connecticut: J. Trumbull, 1798), 22–23.

23. Background on the Coverlys comes from "Printers File," American Antiquarian Society (AAS); Harriet Silverster Tapley, *Salem Imprints, 1768–1825: A History of the First Fifty Years of Printing in Salem Mass., With Some Account of the Bookshops, Booksellers, Bookbinders and the Private Libraries* (Salem: Essex Institute, 1927), 195–198.

24. "Printers File," AAS, Tapley, *Salem Imprints,* 197–198; Kate Van Winkle Keller, "Purveyor to the Peddlers: Nathaniel Coverly, Jr., Printer of Songs for the Streets of Boston," unpublished paper, Dublin Conference, 2005; Arthur F. Schrader and Kate Van Winkle Keller, *Songs in Vogue with the Vulgar: The Isaiah Thomas Broadsides* (Worcester: American Antiquarian Society, 2006); for Nathaniel Coverly Sr.'s address in a back building on High Street, see *Boston Directory* [1816], 24; additional background on the Coverlys from Daniel A. Cohen, "'The Female Marine' in an Era of Good Feelings: Cross Dressing and the 'Genius' of Nathaniel Coverly, Jr.," *Proceedings of the American Antiquarian Society* 103, part 2 (1994): 359–393.

25. For background on the artisan system of labor in America during this period, see Bruce Laurie, *Artisans Into Workers: Labor in Nineteenth-Century America* (Urbana: University of Illinois Press, 1989); Paul E. Johnson, *A Shopkeeper's Millennium: Society and Revivals in Rochester, New York, 1815–1837* (New York: Hill and Wang, 1978).

26. See Johnson, *A Shopkeeper's Millennium,* 43–48; on the traditional tools of the print trade, see Lawrence C. Wroth, *The Colonial Printer* (Charlottesville: Dominion Books–University Press of Virginia, 1931, reprint 1964); Tapley, *Salem Imprints,* 195.

27. On the marketplace background of the ballad, see Jean Christophe Agnew, *Worlds Apart: The Market and the Theater in Anglo-American Thought, 1550–1750* (New York: Cambridge University Press, 1986), 33–40; *The Sedition Act,* Boston, Nathaniel Coverly Jr., 1811, is one example among many with this statement: "SONGS (by the Gross, Dozen, or Single) constantly for Sale by Nathaniel Coverly, jun., corner of Theatre-alley, Milk Street, Boston."

28. *Tid Re I, Or the Marriage of Miss Kitty O'Donavan to Mr. Paddy O'Raffety,* Boston, Nathaniel Coverly Jr., 1812–1814.

29. On the ritual of the charivari, see David Hackett Fischer, *Albion's Seed: Four British Folkways in America* (New York: Oxford University Press, 1989), 82.

30. *The Female Drummer,* Boston, Nathaniel Coverly Jr., 1812–1814; *The Old Man and the Young Wife,* Boston, Nathaniel Coverly Jr., 1812–1814.

31. *The Vintner Outwitted,* Boston, Nathaniel Coverly Jr., 1812–1814.

32. On New England's tavern culture, see Allan Forbes and Ralph Eastman, *Taverns and Stagecoaches of New England,* vol. 2 (Boston: Rand Press, 1954), 16–19.

33. *Fairburn's Odd Fellows Song Book, Or Repository of Mirth, for 1806. Being an Excellent Collection of Comic, Laughable, Odd, Humorous, Characteristic, Original, Droll, Fashionable, and Favorite, SONGS, now singing and lately sung at the Theatres Royal, Nobility's Concerts, Sadler's Wells, Vauxhall, New Royal Circus, Astley's, Catamaran and Bon Vivant Club, Imperial and Independent Lodges &c.* (London: John Fairburn, 1805); the riddle's answer, of course, is this: "we all like" a "glass" (of ale); "we all love" a "lass"; and "every one dislikes being called an ass."

34. *Fairburn's Odd Fellows Song Book,* 5.

35. *The Goldfinch, Or New Modern Songster. Being a Select Collection of the Most Admired and Favourite Scots and English Songs, Cantatas &c.* (Edinburgh: A Brown, Bridge Street, 1782), 78, 158.

36. *The Goldfinch, Or New Modern Songster*, preface.

37. William Shakespeare, *The Tragedy of Hamlet, Prince of Denmark*, from *The Yale Shakespeare* (New Haven, CT: Yale University Press, 1954), 129–130.

38. George Speaight, *Bawdy Songs of the Early Music Hall* (London: David and Charles, n.d.), 5–9, 42–44.

39. *Ranordine, Together with Paddy's Seven Ages*, Boston, Nathaniel Coverly Jr., 1812–1814; *Bunch of Rushes, and a Sprig of Shillelah and Shamrock so Green*, Boston, Nathaniel Coverly Jr., 1812–1814.

40. *Corydon and Phillis*, Boston, Nathaniel Coverly Jr., 1812–1814.

41. *The Farmer's Daughter, A New Song*, Boston, Nathaniel Coverly Jr., 1812–1814.

42. See David S. Reynolds, *Beneath the American Renaissance: The Subversive Imagination in the Age of Emerson and Melville* (Cambridge, MA: Harvard University Press, 1988), 54–91.

43. *God's Judgment Upon Murder*, Boston, Nathaniel Coverly Jr., 1812; another criminal ballad in this style can be seen in *Lines Composed on the Death of Parker. Who was Hung at the Yard Arm, for Mutiny, In England*, Boston, Nathaniel Coverly Jr., 1812–1814.

44. *Captain James, Who Was Hung and Gibbeted in England, for Starving to Death His Cabin Boy*, Boston, Nathaniel Coverly Jr., n.d., 1813–1814.

45. *The American Hero. Made on the Battle of Bunker-Hill, and the Burning of Charlestown*, Boston, Nathaniel Coverly Jr., 1812–1814; *Thomas Moorhead. A Ship-Wreck'd Mariner, Who Subsisted Fifty-one Days on the Bodies of His Comrades. Taken off the Wreck by the Ship Monticello, and Arrived at New-York, The Beginning of May, 1809*, Boston, Nathaniel Coverly Jr., 1812–1814.

46. *Shocking Earthquakes*, Boston, Nathaniel Coverly Jr., 1812. The broadside is dated Charleston, 7 February 1812, and is headed with the line "Yesterday morning, about half past 3 o'clock the inhabitants of this place were very much alarmed by another tremendous shock of an Earthquake."

47. For these conceptions of hierarchy and power, see Gordon S. Wood, *The Radicalism of the American Revolution* (New York: Vintage Books, 1991), 11–56; Alfred Young, *The Shoemaker and the Tea Party: Memory and the American Revolution* (Boston: Beacon Press, 1999), 3–4, 27–29.

48. Laurel Thatcher Ulrich, *A Midwife's Tale* (New York: Vintage, 1990); *A Song for a Wedding, Or Adam and Eve*, Boston, Nathaniel Coverly Jr., 1813–1814.

49. *The Frog and the Mouse, Or, The Frog He Would A Wooing Go*, Boston, Nathaniel Coverly Jr., 1812–1814).

50. [Captain Grose], *1811 Dictionary of the Vulgar Tongue* (1811, reprint, Northfield, IL: Digest Books, 1971); Monroe Aurand, *Little Known Facts About Bundling In the New World* (Lancaster, PA: Aurand Press, 1938), 7, 10–11, 24; Henry Reed Stiles, *Bundling: Its Origins, Progress & Decline in America* (1872, reprint, Sandwich, MA: Chapman Billies, 1999), 14, 53. The original version of Stiles's book had the warning "Banned in Boston" on the cover, which suggests that bundling remained a controversial through the nineteenth century, or possibly, a good sales gimmick; for Irving's quote, see [Washington Irving], *A History of New York, From the Beginning of the World to the End of the Dutch Dynasty* (London: Thomas Tegg and Son, 1836), 141.

51. *A New Song in Favor of Courting*, no publisher or date listed; Aurand, *Little Known Facts About Bundling*, 28–29; Aurand claims the song was also known as "The Whore on the Snow Crust."

52. *A New Bundling Song*, Boston, Nathaniel Coverly Jr., 1814.

53. Stiles, *Bundling*, 81.

54. *The Farmer's Daughter; Or, Barley Maid*, Boston, Nathaniel Coverly Jr., 1812–1814.

55. *Handsome Harry, or, The Deceitful Young Man*, Boston, Nathaniel Coverly Jr., 1812–1814; *Rosanna*, Boston, Nathaniel Coverly Jr., 1812–1814.

56. Vera Brodsky Lawrence, *Music for Patriots, Politicians, and Presidents: Harmonies and Discords of the First Hundred Years* (New York: Macmillan, 1975), 52.

57. *Yankee Doodle, Or, The Farmer and his Son's Return From a Visit to the Camp*, Boston, Nathaniel Coverly, 1814. The American Antiquarian Society has what may be a version of the song from the actual Revolution, *The Farmer and his Son's Return From a Visit to the Camp; With the Jolly Miller & Jaded Pedlar*. Although the broadside has no listed publisher or date, the AAS has dated the song 1775. The lyrics are the same as the Coverly version.

58. *A Song Composed in the Year SEVENTY-FIVE, Transfer'd to 1812. Tune: The World Turn's Upside Down*, Boston, Nathaniel Coverly Jr., 1812.

Chapter Two

1. *Capture of Washington*, Boston, Nathaniel Coverly Jr., 1814.

2. A ballad commentary on the poor performance of the American infantry is *The War Hawk, Or Commercial Protector* (n.p., 1814). On the War of 1812, see Donald R. Hickey, *The War of 1812: A Forgotten Conflict* (Urbana: University of Illinois Press, 1989); Alan Taylor, *The Civil War of 1812: American Citizens, British Subjects, Irish Rebels and Indian Allies* (New York: Alfred A, Knopf, 2010); Jeremy Black, "The North American Theater of the Napoleonic Wars: Or, As it is Sometimes Called, The War of 1812," *Journal of Military History* 76, no. 4 (October 2012): 1067–1094; Nicole Eustace, *1812: War and the Passions of Patriotism* (Philadelphia: University of Pennsylvania Press, 2012); Jennifer Clark, "The War of 1812: American Nationalism and Rhetorical Images of Britain," *War and Society* 12, no. 1 (May 1994): 1–26; Walter Lord, *The Dawn's Early Light* (New York: Norton, 1972); Glenn Tucker, *Poltroons and Patriots: A Popular Account of the War of 1812* (Indianapolis: Bobbs-Merrill, 1954); C. S. Forester, *The Age of Fighting Sail: The Story of the Naval War of 1812* (Garden City, NY: Doubleday, 1956).

3. On the maritime background for the War of 1812, see Walter R. Borneman, *1812: The War That Forged a Nation* (New York: Harper Perennial, 2004), 39–40; Hickey, *The War of 1812: A Forgotten Conflict*, 5–24; Paul A. Gilje, *Free Trade and Sailor's Rights in the War of 1812* (New York: Cambridge University Press, 2013); Wade G. Dudley, *Splintering the Wooden Wall: The British Blockade of the United States, 1812–1815* (Annapolis, MD: Naval Institute Press, 2003); Jennifer Clark, "The Celebration of American Naval Victory: Popular Nationalism in the War of 1812," *Journal of the American Studies Association of Texas* 29 (November 1998): 56–79; on US designs on Canada, see Reginald Horsman, "On to Canada: Manifest Destiny and United States Strategy in the War of 1812," *Michigan Historical Review* 13, no. 2 (March 1987): 1–24.

4. This chapter is informed by a number of historical works on popular constructions of patriotism; see especially Benedict Anderson, *Imagined Communities: Reflections on the Origin and Spread of Nationalism* (London: Verso, 1983); Gordon S. Wood, *The Radicalism of the American Revolution* (New York: Vintage Books, 1993); David Waldstreicher, "Rites of Rebellion, Rites of Assent: Celebrations, Print Culture, and the Origins of American Nationalism," *Journal of American History* 82, no. 1 (June 1995): 37–61.

5. *Columbia and Independence. A New Patriotic Song Dedicated to Every Free Born American*, Boston, Nathaniel Coverly Jr., 1812–1814.

6. John Winthrop, "A Modell of Christian Charity" [1630], in *The Puritans*, vol. 1, ed. Perry Miller and Thomas Johnson (New York: Harper and Row, rev. ed., 1963), 195–199.

7. John Stilgoe, *Common Landscape of America, 1580 to 1845* (New Haven, CT: Yale University Press, 1982), 43; the centrality of community to Puritan culture would also be treated in the work of John Demos, Phillip Greven, Kenneth Lockridge, and Perry Miller.

8. Stilgoe, *Common Landscape of America*, 8–21; the term "roland" may derive from "Saint Roland" statues, "Der Roland" in German, a somewhat generic term for monuments in Germany, the Low Countries, and England that were located in village, town, and city centers; these monuments signified the community center, the marketplace, and the town or city's autonomy and self-sufficiency.

9. On the enclosures, see Ian Whyte, "Parliamentary Enclosure and Changes in Land Ownership in an Upland Environment: Westmoreland, ca. 1770–1860," *Agricultural History Review* 54, no. 2 (2006): 240–256; Tyler Anbinder, "From Famine to Five Points: Lord Landsdownes Irish Tenants Encounter North America's Most Notorious Slum," *American Historical Review* 107, no. 2 (April 2002): 351–387; Boaz Moselle, "Allotments, Enclosure, and Proletarianization in Nineteenth Century Southern England," *Economic History Review* 48, no. 3 (1995): 482.

10. Rather than the old "communal breakdown" theory of colonial development in New England, where settlements began with a communal ethos and declined into individualism, this is to say that there were communal traditions in the colonies, and that these traditions survived alongside the development of commerce; see Michael Zuckerman, *Peaceable Kingdoms: New England Towns in the Eighteenth Century* (New York, 1970); John Demos, *A Little Commonwealth: Family Life in Plymouth Colony* (New York: Oxford University Press, 1970); Richard Bushman, *From Puritan to Yankee: Character and the Social Order in Connecticut, 1690–1765* (Cambridge, MA: Harvard University Press, 1967); Christine Leigh Heyrman, *Commerce and Culture: The Maritime Communities of Colonial Massachusetts, 1690–1750* (New York: Norton, 1984).

11. On the ubiquity of village conflicts, see Richard Suggett, "Festivals and Social Structure in Early Modern Wales," *Past and Present* 152 (August 1996): 79–112; Alistair Moffat, *The Sea Kingdoms: The History of Celtic Britain & Ireland* (London: HarperCollins, 2001); on frictions caused by differences in the colonial setting, see Christine Leigh Heyrman, *Commerce and Culture*; on the witch trials, see John Putnam Demos, *Entertaining Satan: Witchcraft and the Culture of Early New England* (New York: Oxford University Press, 1982); for an example of this idea of intra-communal surveillance as the cause of witchcraft outbreaks, see Paul Boyer and Stephen Nissenbaum, *Salem Possessed: The Social Origins of Witchcraft* (Cambridge, MA: Harvard University Press, 1974).

12. *The Whole Book of Psalms Faithfully Translated into English Metre* (1640 facsimile ed., reprint, Chicago: University of Chicago Press, 1956), preface.

13. *The Whole Book of Psalms*, preface.

14. Psalm 100, or "Old Hundred" from *The Whole Book of Psalms*; the original does not have page numbers; singers were directed to the psalm by number.

15. Nathaniel Holmes, *Gospel Music. Or, The Singing of David's Psalms, &c., In the Publick Congregations, or Private Families Asserted, and Vindicated, Against a Printed Pamphlet Entitled Certain Reasons by Ways of Confutation of Singing Psalms in the Letter. Against Objections Sent In, in Writing. Against Scruples of Some Tender Consciences. By Thy Loving Brother, N.H.D.D.M.S.* (London: Henry Overton in Popes-Head Alley, 1644), 8.

16. Bruce C. Daniels, *Puritans at Play: Leisure and Recreation in Colonial New England* (New York: Saint Martin's Griffin, 1995), 53–54; Fischer, *Albion's Seed*, 122; Harriet Beecher Stowe, *Oldtown Folks* (Boston: Fields, Osgood & Co., 1869).

17. *A Pacificatory Letter About Psalmody or Singing of Psalms, Dated December 23, 1723* (Boston: Printed by J. Franklin, for Benjamin Eliot, and Sold at His Shop on Queen Street, 1724); Daniels, *Puritans at Play*, 54.

18. Watts's hymn, which is my personal favorite, is cited in E. P. Thompson, *The Making of the English Working Class* (New York: Vintage-Random House, 1966), 377.

19. Frederic Palmer, "Isaac Watts," *Harvard Theological Review* 12, no. 4 (October 1919): 371–403; *Memoires of the Lives, Characters and Writings of Those Two Eminently Pious and Useful Ministers of Jesus Christ, Dr. Isaac Watts and Dr. Philip Doddridge* (Boston: Peter Edes, 1793); *Doctor Watts' Imitation of the Psalms of David, To Which is Added a Collection of Hymns, The Whole Applied to the State of the Christian Church in General* (Hartford, CT: N. Patton, 1785); Isaac Watts, *Little Hymn Book* (Worcester, MA: S. A. Howland, 1842); *The New England Primer, Enlarged and Improved; Or, An Easy and Pleasant Guide to the Art of Reading* (Norwich, CT: Thomas Hubbard, 1795).

20. Samuel Gilman, *Memoirs of a New England Village Choir. With Occasional Reflections. By a Member* (Boston: Benjamin H. Greene, 1834), 36–38.

21. *American Taxation: A Song of Seventy-Nine*, Boston, Nathaniel Coverly Jr., 1812–1815.

22. For this focus on common people during the Revolution, along with analyses linking common agendas with the event's radical roots, see Gary B. Nash, *The Unknown American Revolution: The Unruly Birth of Democracy and the Struggle to Create America* (New York: Penguin Books, 2005), chapters 1–3, 1–149; on the messiness of the Revolution, see also Edward Countryman, *The American Revolution* (New York: Hill and Wang, 1985), prologue, 9–40.

23. William Billings, "Lamentation Over Boston," first published in *The Singing Master's Assistant* (1778), from Vera Brodsky Lawrence, *Music for Patriots, Politicians, and Presidents: Harmonies and Discords of the First Hundred Years* (New York: Macmillan, 1975), 46.

24. See for example *The Liberty Song, The Massachusetts Song of Liberty, and The New Massachusetts Liberty Song*, from Lawrence, *Music for Patriots, Politicians and Presidents*, 26, 31, 37; on the agendas of the elite and their attempts to control the rebellion, the classic study is Charles Beard, *An Economic Interpretation of the Constitution of the United States* (New York: Free Press, 2012 [1913]); see also Countryman, *The American Revolution*, 41–73.

25. For a detailed account of the "Pope's Day" processions in Boston, see Forbes, *Paul Revere and the World He Lived In*, 93–96; see also Sian Ellis, "Bonfire Night and Guy Fawkes," *British Heritage* 31, no. 5 (2010): 24; Brendan McConville, "Pope's Day Revisited, Popular Culture Reconsidered," *Explorations in American Culture* 4 (2000): 258.

26. *Massachusetts Song of Liberty*, Boston, Nathaniel Coverly, 1812–1815; *American Liberty, A New Song*, from Lawrence, *Music for Patriots, Politicians and Presidents*, 51.

27. Nash, *The Unknown American Revolution*, 25–26, 45–50.

28. *Battle of Bunker Hill. This Song was Composed by the British, After the Engagement*, Boston, Nathaniel Coverly Jr., 1812–1815; *General Burgoyne's Lamentation*, Boston, Nathaniel Coverly Jr., 1812–1815; for Burgoyne's image as a fop, see George A. Billias, *George Washington's Opponents: British Generals and Admirals in the American Revolution* (New York: William Morrow, 1969), 142–143.

29. *The British Lamentation, Together with Green on the Cape, or, The Irish Hero*, Boston, Nathaniel Coverly Jr., 1812–1815; *General Burgoyne's Lamentation*, Boston, Nathaniel Coverly Jr., 1812–1815; *A Song Made on the Taking of General Burgoyne*, Boston, Nathaniel Coverly Jr., 1812–1815; H. DeForest Hardinge, "Saratoga: Turning Point of the Revolution," *Manuscripts* 52, no. 4 (September 2001): 299–308.

30. Nash, *The Unknown American Revolution*, 76–87, 160–166.

31. Henry Blake diary, entries for 19, 20, and 21 March 1776, and [day not recorded] April 1776, AAS; on Lord Dumore's Proclamation, see Peter F. Copeland, "Lord Dunmore's Ethiopian Regiment," *Military Collector and Historian* 58, no. 4 (2006): 208; Benjamin Quarles, "Lord Dunmore as Liberator," *William and Mary Quarterly* 15, no. 4 (October 1958): 494–507.

32. *Lord Cornwallis's Surrender*, Boston, Nathaniel Coverly Jr., 1812–1815; *A Song Composed in the Year SEVENTY-FIVE, Transfer'd to 1812*, Boston, Nathaniel Coverly Jr., 1812–1815.

33. "The Negro's Lamentation, by AFRICANUS," "Repository of the Muses," *Patriotic Gazette* (Northampton, MA), 28 April 1800.

34. J. P. Kaminski, ed., *A Necessary Evil? Slavery and the Debate Over the Constitution* (Madison, WI: Madison House, 1995); Paul Finkelman, ed., *Slavery and the Law* (Madison, WI: Madison House, 1997); on the Revolution's effect on perceptions of bondage, see Noel Ignatiev, *How the Irish Became White* (New York: Routledge, 1995), 96.

35. "Ode to Washington," from the "Repository of the Muses," *Patriotic Gazette* (Northampton, MA), 2 January 1799.

36. "Ode to Washington," "George, or, The War-Torn Soldier," and "An Ode for New Year," from "Repository of the Muses," *Patriotic Gazette* (Northampton, MA), 2 January 1799; "Just Received," *Patriotic Gazette*, 24 February 1800.

37. *American Taxation: A Song of Seventy-Nine*, Boston, Nathaniel Coverly Jr., 1812–1814; Broadsides on George Washington: *The American Union and the Birth of George Washington: A Lamentation for Gen. Washington, Lines Composed on the Death of Washington, Lady Washington's Lamentation for the Death of her Husband, The Death of Washington,* and *Saw Ye My Hero George*, Boston, Nathaniel Coverly Jr., 1812–1814.

38. Mason L. Weems, *The Life of Washington* (1800, 1809, reprint, Cambridge, MA: Harvard University Press, 1962): the cherry-tree story, 12; Washington's other qualities are scattered throughout the book, but appear especially in the chapters on his character, 172–224, and in Washington's will, 225–226.

39. *An Address to the Fair Daughters of the United States, Calling on them for their Advice and Interests in the Present Important Crisis. New-York, September 17th* (New York: Southwick and Pelsue, 1811), 10.

40. On republicanism, see Joyce Appleby, "Republicanism and Ideology," and Linda Kerber, "The Republican Ideology of the Revolutionary Generation," *American Quarterly* (Special Issue on Republicanism) 37, no. 4 (Autumn 1985): 461–473, 474–495; Daniel T. Rodgers, "Republicanism: The Career of a Concept," *Journal of American History* 79, no. 1 (January 1992): 11–38.

41. See Linda Kerber, "The Republican Mother: Women and the Enlightenment—An American Perspective," *American Quarterly* 28, no. 2 (Summer 1976): 187–205; Jan Lewis, "The Republican Wife: Virtue and Seduction in the Early Republic," *William and Mary Quarterly* 44, no. 4 (October 1987): 689–721.

42. *A Series of Answers to Certain Popular Objections, Against Separating from the American Colonies, and Discarding Them Entirely, Being the Concluding Tract of the Dean of Glocester, on the Subject of American Affairs* (Gloucester, UK: R. Raikes, 1776), 22.

43. On these "radical" elements of republicanism, see Gordon Wood, *The Creation of the American Republic, 1776–1787* (Chapel Hill: University of North Carolina Press, 1969), and *The Radicalism of the American Revolution*; Steven Watts, *The Republic Reborn: War and the Making of Liberal America, 1790–1820* (Baltimore: Johns Hopkins University Press, 1987).

44. *Bonaparte. A Song, To the Tune Vicar of Bray*, Boston, Nathaniel Coverly Jr., 1812; this anti-French sentiment may also be seen in "To Arms, Columbia! A New Patriotic Song by Thomas Paine, A.M.," from "Repository of the Muses," *Patriotic Gazette*, 21 June 1799.

45. *The Sedition Act*, Boston, Nathaniel Coverly Jr., 1811.

46. *The Embargo. A Favorite New Song*, Boston, Nathaniel Coverly Jr., 1811–1814.

47. *Arise Ye Patriots*, Boston, Nathaniel Coverly Jr., 1812.

48. *The Horrors of War. A Sermon, Delivered at New Marlborough, (Mass) July 5, 1813, At the Celebration of Independence. By Jacob Catlin, A.M. Preached and Published at the Request of a Branch of the Washington Benevolent Society* (Stockbridge, MA: H. Willard, 1813), 4–7, 6.

49. Thwing, *The Crooked & Narrow Streets of the Town of Boston*, 95, 129; *A Record of the Streets, Alleys, Places, Etc., in the City of Boston*; broadside: *Articles of Agreement* (for the building of the Sloop of War *Wasp*), n.p., 1813; Marcus Rediker, *Between the Devil and the Deep Blue Sea: Merchant Seamen, Pirates, and the Anglo-American Maritime World, 1700–1750* (New York: Cambridge University Press, 1987), 62.

50. See Schrader and Keller, *Songs in Vogue with the Vulgar*; on attitudes toward sailors as among the lowliest class of workers, see Rediker, *Between the Devil and the Deep Blue Sea*; *The Sailor Boy*, Boston, Nathaniel Coverly Jr., 1812–1814; *George Reily*, New York, "Elton Printer," circa 1812; *Tom Tough*, Boston, Nathaniel Coverly Jr., 1812–1814.

51. *Naval Recruiting Song, [To the] Tune All Hands A Hoy to the Anchor*, Boston, Nathaniel Coverly Jr., 1812–1814.

52. *Hull's Victory, or, Huzza for the Constitution*, Boston, Nathaniel Coverly Jr., 1812.

53. Hull would remain a well-known hero through the nineteenth century; see, for example, Jane De Forest Shelton, "The Birthplace of Commodore Isaac Hull," *Harper's New Monthly Magazine* 85 (June 1892): 30–36.

54. For background on the engagement, see Borneman, *1812: The War That Forged a Nation*, 77–87; see also C. S. Forrester, *The Age of Fighting Sail*.

55. *The American Constitution Frigate's Engagement with the British Frigate Guerriere, Which After an Action of 25 Minutes, Surrendered, and Being Completely Shattered, Was Blown Up, It Being Impossible to Get Her into Port*, Boston, Nathaniel Coverly Jr., 1812.

56. *A New Song, Composed by James Campbell, A Boatswain's Mate on Board the Constitution*, Boston, Nathaniel Coverly Jr., 1813.

57. *The Soldier's Life*, Nathaniel Coverly Jr., 1812. For the invasion of Canada, Hull's invasion from Detroit, and his proclamation, see Borneman, *1812: The War That Forged a Nation*, 59–75; the proclamation quote is on 62.

58. *Hull's Surrender, Or Villainy Somewhere*, Boston, Nathaniel Coverly Jr., 1812.

59. The Coverly-printed broadside that best suggests this attitude is *The War Hawk! Or, Commercial Protector*, Boston, Nathaniel Coverly Jr., 1814; the song depicts American soldiers as typical "war hawks," beating drums before the conflict and whining after defeats; it portrays the New England sailor as the true protector of commerce, freedom, and national independence.

60. *NAVAL VICTORY, By the UNITED STATES Frigate CONSTITUTION and the English Frigate JAVA*, Boston, Nathaniel Coverly Jr., 1813; *Glorious Naval Victory, Obtained by Commodore Bainbridge of the United States Frigate Constitution Over His Britannic Majesty's Frigate Java*, Boston, Nathaniel Coverly Jr., 1813.

61. *Wasp Stinging Frolick, Or, Engagement Between the American Sloop of War WASP, of 18 Guns, and the British Sloop of War FROLICK, of 20 Guns*, Boston, Nathaniel Coverly Jr., 1813; *Another Glorious Victory*, Boston, Nathaniel Coverly Jr., 1813; *A Happy New Year to Commodore Rodgers, Or,*

Huzza for the President and Congress, Boston, Nathaniel Coverly Jr., 1812; *Rodgers & Victory, or, Tit for Tat, The Chesapeake Paid For in British Blood!!!,* Boston, Nathaniel Coverly Jr., 1813.

62. *Sixth Naval Victory. Free Trade and Sailor's Rights, or, We Will Box it Out,* Boston, Nathaniel Coverly Jr., 1813; on references to sailors as "noble tars," and so forth, see the previously cited broadsides as well as *The PEACOCK Stung by the HORNET, or, Engagement between the United States ship HORNET, CAPTAIN LAWRENCE, of 16 guns, and His Britannic Majesty's Brig PEACOCK, Captain PEAKE, of 19 guns, which he sank after 15 minutes close action,* Boston, Nathaniel Coverly Jr., 1813.

63. *CASH IN HAND, Occasioned by the Capture of the British Packet Swallow, by COMMODORE RODGERS, With 260,000 Dollars, in Gold and Silver on Board,* Boston, Nathaniel Coverly Jr., 1813.

64. *THE BOSTON FRIGATE'S Engagement with the French Corvette Le Berceau, and Tom Bowline's Epitaph,* Boston, Nathaniel Coverly Jr., 1812–1814; *American History,* Boston, Nathaniel Coverly Jr., 1814; *Rodgers & Victory, or, Tit for Tat, The Chesapeake Paid for in British Blood!!!,* Boston, Nathaniel Coverly Jr., 1813; *Eighth Naval Victory: Lines Composed on the Capture of His Britannic Majesty's Squadron, on LAKE ERIE, by Commodore PERRY,* Boston, Nathaniel Coverly Jr., 1813.

65. Cited in Thompson, *The Making of the English Working Class,* 58.

66. Background on the Battle of New Orleans and "The Hunters of Kentucky" comes from John William Ward, *Andrew Jackson: Symbol for an Age* (New York: Oxford University Press, 1953), 13–35; "The Hunters of Kentucky; or, The Battle of New Orleans," cited in Lawrence, *Music for Patriots,* 212.

67. *Unparalleled Victory, THE veteran and SELF-STYLED INVINCIBLES of Europe, biting the dust before the green back-woodsmen of America, and the laurels of the anticipated Governor of LOUISIANA, (PACKINGHAM) blasted by the HEAT of the climate at NEW-ORLEANS, then under the influence of OLD HICKORY,* Boston, Nathaniel Coverly Jr., 1815; Joseph G. Tregle, "Andrew Jackson and the Continuing Battle of New Orleans," *Journal of the Early Republic* 1, no. 4 (Winter 1981): 373–393.

68. *PEACE on HONORABLE terms to AMERICA. Signed by our Commissioners at Ghent, Dec. 24, 1814,—Prince Regent, Dec. 28—Ratified by the President and Senate, of the United States, Feb 17, 1815,* Boston, Nathaniel Coverly Jr., 1815.

69. *The Female Marine, or Adventures of Miss Lucy Brewer, A Native of Plymouth County, Mass.* (n.p., n.d.); for background and interpretation of the pamphlet, see Cohen, " 'The Female Marine' in an Era of Good Feelings," 359–391.

Chapter Three

1. On the existence of black artisans in the North, see Noel Ignatiev, *How the Irish Became White* (New York: Routledge, 1995), 100–102; *Ode for the Canal Celebration, Written at the Request of the Printers of New York, by Mr. Samuel Woodworth, Printer,* New York, Clayton & Van Norden, 1825.

2. Peter P. Hinks, ed., *David Walker's Appeal to the Colored Citizens of the World* (original 1830, reprint, University Park: Pennsylvania State University Press, 2000), 101, 105–106.

3. On early American worker culture, see Sean Wilentz, *Chants Democratic: New York City and the Rise of the American Working Class, 1788–1850* (New York: Cambridge University Press, 1984, 2004); on traditions of deference and their survival into the early republic, see Gordon S. Wood, *The Radicalism of the American Revolution* (New York: Vintage–Random House, 1991).

4. This chapter is an effort to build upon and add to the current scholarship on blackface; for the current interpretation of blackface as arising from an earthy working-class culture, see Richard B. Stott, *Workers in the Metropolis: Class, Ethnicity, and Youth in Antebellum New York City* (Ithaca, NY: Cornell University Press, 1990), 227, 236, 242; David R. Roediger, *The Wages of Whiteness: Race and the Making of the American Working Class* (New York: Verso, 1991), see especially 116–120; Eric Lott, *Love and Theft: Blackface Minstrelsy and the American Working Class* (New York: Oxford University Press, 1993), 3–12; Dale Cockrell, *Demons of Disorder: Early Blackface Minstrels and Their World* (New York and London: Cambridge University Press, 1997), 31–32, 56; W. T. Llamon Jr., *Raising Cain: Blackface Performance from Jim Crow to Hip Hop* (Cambridge, MA: Harvard University Press, 1998), 24–33; this chapter reverses the interpretation that blackface arose from an earthy working class to argue that blackface appeared at a specific historical moment at which working-class young men faced a loss of masculine status. Thus, blackface generated the ideal of working-class hyper-masculinity and authenticity.

5. *Ode for the Celebration of the French Revolution. In the City of New-York, November 25th, 1830. Written at the Request of the Printers of New-York,* New York, James Conner, 1830.

6. Sean Wilentz, "Artisan Festivals and the Rise of Class Conflict in New York City, 1788–1837," in *Working Class America: Essays on Labor, Community, and American Society,* ed. Michael H. Frisch and Daniel J. Walkowitz (Urbana: University of Illinois Press, 1983), 37–77, 45–46, 48.

7. *Mechanic's Song . . . by Franklin,* Boston, Leonard Deming, 1829.

8. Wilentz, "Artisan Festivals and the Rise of Class Conflict in New York City," 45; on the artisan ideal of "art," see Paul E. Johnson, *Sam Patch, The Famous Jumper* (New York: Hill and Wang, 2003), 53–55.

9. On black artisans and the phenomenon of later historians ignoring the exclusion of black workers (including slaves) from the category of the working class, see Ignatiev, *How the Irish Became White,* 105–115; as examples of this problem, Ignatiev cites the top scholars within the New Labor History, including Herbert Gutman and Sean Wilentz; see also "Records Show that Slaves Helped Build Capitol," USA TODAY.com, archives; "The Black Presence in the Era of the American Revolution," *Ebony* 28, no. 11 (1973): 44–52; Vivian Green Fryd, *Art and Empire: The Politics of Ethnicity in the United States Capitol, 1815–1860* (New Haven, CT: Yale University Press, 1992).

10. For this story and the phenomenon of white workers refusing to work alongside African American artisans, see William S. McFeely, *Frederick Douglass* (New York: W. W. Norton, 1991); Ignatiev, *How the Irish Became White,* 105–111.

11. *Advice from a Master to His Apprentice, When Leaving His Service, and Entering on Life for Himself. Tract No. 100: Publications of the American Tract Society,* vol. 5 (Andover, MA: American Tract Society, 1824).

12. *Sally in Our Alley,* Boston, Nathaniel Coverly Jr., 1810–1812.

13. "Diary of a Blacksmith," entry for 6 January 1869 manuscript collections, AAS. On trades as a source of identity and status, see *The Book of Trades* (1568); Comenius, *Orbis Pictus* (1654); these old tomes illustrating trades had their American version in *The Book of Trades, or Library of the Useful Arts* (Whitehall, Philadelphia: Jacob Johnson, 1807); reprinted as Peter Stockham, ed., *Early American Crafts and Trades* (New York: Dover, 1976).

14. On these shop traditions, see E. P. Thompson, *The Making of the English Working Class* (New York: Vintage–Random House, 1966), 217, 317; Bruce Laurie, *Artisans Into Workers: Labor in Nineteenth-Century America* (Urbana: University of Illinois Press, 1989), 36.

15. *Order of Services at the Thirteenth Triennial Festival and First Semi-Centennial Celebration of the Massachusetts Charitable Mechanic Association, At the Melodeon, On Thursday, Octo-*

ber 2nd, 1845, Boston, Dutton and Wentworth, 1845; "Political Economy," *Mechanics' and Farmers' Magazine of Useful Knowledge* [New York] 1, no. 4 (September 1830): 147.

16. On this "Market Revolution," see Charles Sellers, *The Market Revolution: Jacksonian America, 1815–1846* (New York: Oxford University Press, 1991), 70–102; George Rogers Taylor, *The Transportation Revolution*; Carol Sheriff, *The Artificial River: The Erie Canal and the Paradox of Progress, 1817–1862* (New York: Hill and Wang, 1996); Paul E. Johnson, *A Shopkeeper's Millennium: Society and Revivals in Rochester, New York, 1815–1837* (New York: Hill and Wang, 1978); Stuart Blumin, *The Emergence of the Middle Class: Social Experience in the American City, 1760–1900* (New York: Cambridge University Press, 1989), 66–106.

17. Norman Simms, "Ned Ludd's Mummers Play," *Folklore* 89, no. 2 (1978): 166–178; Cited in Thompson, *The Making of the English Working Class*, 534; the most famous modern reference to Ned Ludd may be in Edward Abbey's classic "how-to" manual in the fight against "progress," *The Monkey Wrench Gang* (1975, New York: Harper Perennial, 2000).

18. Thomas Skidmore, *The Rights of Man to Property!* (New York: "Printed for the Author by Alexander Ming, Jr.," 1829); on the cultural shift from artisanship, slavery, and bonded servitude to "free" or wage labor, see Amy Dru Stanley, *From Bondage to Contract: Wage Labor, Marriage, and the Market in the Age of Slave Emancipation* (Cambridge: Cambridge University Press, 1998); Robert J. Steinfeld, *The Invention of Free Labor: The Employment Relation in English and American Law and Culture, 1350–1870* (Chapel Hill: University of North Carolina Press, 1991).

19. *Times*, Boston, Nathaniel Coverly Jr., 1812–1815; two other Coverly examples that may be placed under the category of cheating songs are *Murder: The Death of Miss Mack Coy*, Boston, Nathaniel Coverly Jr., 1814; and *Meriden Town*, Boston, Nathaniel Coverly Jr., 1814; in the latter town, according to the song, there were "none that do good, *no not one.*"

20. *Times as They Are*, Boston, Leonard Deming, Printer, n.d. [1820s]; *Hard Times*, n.p., 1824.

21. See Sellers, *The Market Revolution*, and Blumin, *The Emergence of the Middle Class*; along with Mary P. Ryan, *Cradle of the Middle Class: The Family in Oneida County, New York, 1790–1865* (New York: Cambridge University Press, 1981).

22. See Sean Wilentz, *Chants Democratic*; Laurie, *Artisans Into Workers*.

23. *The Factory Girl's New-Year Song*, Boston, n.p., n.d., circa 1830.

24. Seth Luther, *An Address to the Working Men of New England, On the State of Education, and on the Condition of the Producing Classes in Europe and America. With Particular Reference to the Effect of Manufacturing (as now conducted) on the Health and Happiness of the Poor* (New York: George H. Evans/The Working Man's Advocate, 1833), 13; R. T. H., "White and Black Slavery," *Southern Literary Messenger* 6, no. 3 (March 1840): 193–200, 193; Reverend William Barry, *The Moral Exposure and Spiritual Wants of Manufacturing Cities* (Boston: n.p., 1850), 7.

25. On the Lowell Mills, see Thomas Dublin et al., *Handbook for the Visitor to Lowell* (Lowell: D. Bixby & Company, 1848), 8–9, 10–12; also *Lowell, The Story of an Industrial City: A Guide to Lowell National Historical Park* (Washington, DC: Government Printing Office, 2000); on the issues generated by this shift in labor, see Ava Baron, "Gender and Labor History: Learning from the Past, Looking to the Future," in Ava Baron, ed., *Work Engendered: Toward a New History of American Labor* (Ithaca, NY: Cornell University Press, 1991), 1–46.

26. Harriet H. Robinson, *Loom and Spindle, or, Life Among the Early Mill Girls, With a Sketch of "The Lowell Offering" and Some of Its Contributors* (original 1898, reprint, Kailua, HI: Press Pacifica, 1976), 4, 47, 37; Sarah Savage, *The Factory Girl* (Boston: Monroe and Francis, 1824); Lucy Larcom, *A New England Girlhood* (original 1889, reprint, Gloucester: Peter Smith, 1973), 225.

27. *Hand-book for the Visitor to Lowell*, 32; Whittier's quote cited in Robinson, *Loom and Spindle*, 45.

28. "Letters from New England. No. 4. By A Virginian," *Southern Literary Messenger* 1, no. 6 (February 1835): 273–274; Barry, *The Moral Exposure and Spiritual Wants of Manufacturing Cities*, 4.

29. *Factory Maid*, n.p., 1833.

30. Robinson, *Loom and Spindle*, 51.

31. Robinson, *Loom and Spindle*, 53.

32. *Song of the Factory Girl*, Great Falls [NH], J. G. Shorey, 1849; *A Looker On, Local Loiterings and Visits In the Vicinity of Boston* (Boston: Redding & Company, 1846), 79; Robinson, *Loom and Spindle*, 60–64, 66, 70.

33. *The Song of the Factory Girl. By Henry W. Heywood (May be Sung to the Tune of "Rory O'More")*, Claremont, NH, Young and Walker, 1848.

34. Larcom, *A New England Girlhood*, 154; "Miss Martineau and the Lowell Factory Girls," *Boston Atlas*, 26 September 1844; *A Looker On*, 76–77.

35. "Hymn," by Lewis G. Pray, from the broadside *Order of Services at the Thirteenth Triennial Festival and First Semi-Centennial Celebration of the Massachusetts Charitable Mechanic Association, At the Melodeon, On Thursday, October 2nd, 1845*, Boston, Dutton and Wentworth, 1845.

36. See Ignatiev, *How the Irish Became White*, 112–115; "Editor's Preface—Introductory," *Mechanics' and Farmers' Magazine of Useful Knowledge* [NY] 1, no. 1 (June 1830): 3.

37. "Traders' Combination," in *The Cold Water Melodies, A New Selection Designed for Social Temperance Meetings and the Family Circle, by Sam Slocum* (Providence: I. Amesbury Jr., 1851).

38. On this coalition, see Ignatiev, *How the Irish Became White*, 79.

39. Bruce A. McConachie, *Melodramatic Formations: American Theater and Society, 1820–1870* (Iowa City: University of Iowa Press, 1992), 7–8, 22; see also Cockrell, *Demons of Disorder*, 14–17; David Grimstead, *Melodrama Unveiled: American Theater and Culture, 1800–1850* (Chicago: University of Chicago Press, 1968).

40. Robert C. Allen, *Horrible Prettiness: Burlesque and American Culture* (Chapel Hill: University of North Carolina Press, 1991), 47–50, 51; see also Jonas Barish, *The Antitheatrical Prejudice* (Berkeley: University of California Press, 1981).

41. Elsewhere, scholars like Lawrence Levine, in *Highbrow/Lowbrow*, have argued that the early theater was marked primarily or only by a spirit of rough democracy; but again, the reality seems to have been a blend of patriarchal control and at least somewhat contained audience participation; see McConachie, *Melodramatic Formations*, 16–21.

42. Cockrell, *Demons of Disorder*, 30–32; McConachie, *Melodramatic Formations*, 122, 131–134; Patricia Cline Cohen, *The Murder of Helen Jewett: The Life and Death of a Prostitute in Nineteenth-Century New York* (New York: Alfred A. Knopf, 1998), 61–68.

43. *Eagle Theatre! Benefit of J. P. Addams, Sam Patch in France!*, Boston, J. H. & F. F. Farewell's Printing Office, 1843, Massachusetts Historical Society Collections.

44. George Foster, *New York by Gas-Light and Other Urban Sketches*, ed. and with an introduction by Stuart M. Blumin (originally published, New York: Dewitt and Davenport, 1850, reprint, Berkeley: University of California Press, 1990), 155–156.

45. *Jim Crow*, Boston, Leonard Deming, 1832.

46. Robert P. Nevin, "Stephen C. Foster and Negro Minstrelsy," *Atlantic Monthly* 20, no. 121 (November 1867): 608–616, 610; on the early sensation of Jim Crow as an example of popular lore, see Cockrell, *Demons of Disorder*, 65–67.

47. George C. D. Odell, *Annals of the New York Stage*, vol. 1 [of 15] (New York: Columbia University Press, 1927–1949), 103–104; Cockrell, *Demons of Disorder*, 13, 18–19, 27–28; Charles Hamm, *Yesterdays: Popular Song in America* (New York: W. W. Norton, 1979), 110–115.

48. For background on Dixon, see Cockrell, *Demons of Disorder*, 99–139; *Coal Black Rose*, Boston, Leonard Deming, 1832.

49. On Rice's background, see Cockrell, *Demons of Disorder*, 62–69.

50. "Negro Minstrelsy—Ancient and Modern," *Putnam's Monthly Magazine of American Literature, Science, and Art* 5, no. 25 (January 1855): 72; Nevin, "Stephen C. Foster and Negro Minstrelsy," 608–609.

51. Toll, *Blacking Up*, 46; for historians who have taken these claims as fact, see Eileen Southern, *The Music of Black Americans: A History* (New York: W. W. Norton, 1971), 102–104; William J. Mahar, "Black English in Early Blackface Minstrelsy: A New Interpretation of the Sources of Minstrel Show Dialect," *American Quarterly* 37, no. 2 (Summer 1985): 260–285.

52. "Dandy Pat," from the *Lager Beer Songster—Wrigley's One-Cent Songster* (New York: J. Wrigley, n.d.).

53. Roger Daniels, *Coming to America: A History of Immigration and Ethnicity in American Life* (New York: Harper and Row, 1990), 129–130; on traditional English hostility toward the Irish, see Thompson, *The Making of the English Working Class*, 429–435; on the ways these hostilities played out in America, and on connections between Irishness and blackness during the 1830s, see Ignatiev, *How the Irish Became White*.

54. *The Irish Robber*, no publisher listed but almost certainly printed by Nathaniel Coverly Jr., Boston, 1810; *O'Brian's Celebrated Irish Sermon*, Boston, Nathaniel Coverly Jr., 1810–12; others among Coverly's Irish-themed broadsides include *Erin Go Bragh*, *The Land of Sweet Erin*, *An Irishman's Observations on British Politics*, *Paddy's Land*, and *Teague's Ramble to the Camp*.

55. "The Lads Who Live in Ireland, Or, Where the Apple Praties Grow," from *Lager Beer Songster—Wrigley's One Cent Songster* (New York: J. Wrigley, n.d. [1830s–1840s]).

56. These images are taken from a variety of Irish dandy songs: *Poor Patrick O'Neal*, Boston, Leonard Deming, 1832; *Paddy Carey's Fortune*, Boston, Leonard Deming, 1832; *Roving Irishman*, Boston, Leonard Deming, 1837; "Teddy O'Gunwhale," from *Dixon's (The Celebrated Buffo Singer) Oddities. A Glorious Collection of Nerve Working, Side Cracking, Care Destroying, Mouth Tormenting Songs: As Sung by Mr. G. Dixon* (Ithaca, NY: Mack, Andrus & Woodruff, 1839); "The Raal Ould Irish Gintleman," and "Ireland, The Land of Shelalagh Law," from *Barney Brallaghan's Collection of Irish Songs. Containing all the Queer, Quizzical, Quaint, Comic and Sentimental Songs, As Sung by Powers, Collins, Hudson and Barney Williams* (New York: Murphy, Printer and Publisher, n.d.).

57. "Paddy's Dream," in *The Comic Forget-Me-Not Songster. Being the Latest, and Best, Collection of the Most Popular Comic Songs, As Sung by the Choice Spirits of the Age* (New York and Philadelphia: Turner and Fisher, 1845).

58. *Zip Coon*, Baltimore, George Willig Jr., 1834, from Lott, *Love and Theft*, 178–179.

59. *The Handsome Man, Comic Song, by John Francis Esq., Composed by J. Blewitt*, New York, James L. Hewitt, 1835.

60. *Mysteries & Miseries of New-York City, Written and Sing by J. S. Berry, at his Academy of Fun, 526 Broadway*, New York, H. De Marsan, n.d. [dated 1840s in the collections of the American Antiquarian Society]; *Dandy Song*, Boston, Leonard Deming, 1832.

61. "The Fine Ould Irish Gintleman"; *Dandy Jim From Carolina, A Popular Negro Melody, As Sung by B. Williams*, New York, Firth and Hall, 1843.

Chapter Four

1. "The Black Swan Again," *Frederick Douglass' Paper*, 18 December 1851; "From Our New-York Correspondent," *Frederick Douglass' Paper*, 9 March 1855; "Am I Not a Sister? By A. C. L.," from George W. Clark, *The Liberty Minstrel* (New-York: Leavitt & Alden, 1845), 57.

2. "The Lament of the Fugitive Slave," from *The Anti-Slavery Harp: A Collection of Songs for Anti-Slavery Meetings. By William W. Brown* (Boston: Bela Marsh, 1849); William Wells Brown, *Three Years in Europe; Or, Places I Have Seen and People I Have Met* (London: Charles Gilpin; Edinburgh: Oliver and Boyd, 1852), 137.

3. W. E. B. DuBois, *The Souls of Black Folk* (1903, reprint, New York: Dover Press, 1994), 3, 155–159; For the equation of slave songs with African American music, see Eileen Southern, *The Music of Black Americans: A History* (New York: W. W. Norton, 1971), 3–4; Eugene Genovese, *Roll, Jordan, Roll: The World the Slaves Made* (New York: Random House, 1972), 234; Lawrence Levine, *Black Culture and Black Consciousness: Afro-American Folk Thought from Slavery to Freedom* (New York: Oxford University Press, 1977), introduction, ix, 6–10; Shane White, "'It Was a Proud Day': African Americans, Festivals, and Parades in the North, 1741–1834," *Journal of American History* 81, no.1 (June 1994): 13–50, 23; John Blassingame, *The Slave Community: Plantation Life in the Antebellum South* (New York: Oxford University Press, 1972), 121–122.

4. As Eugene Genovese has it, black songs, dances, and shouts were marked by a "clearly African" display of "uninhibited frenzy." Shane White, writing about African American carnivals, claims that as "slaves were caught up in the performance their behavior became more African." According to Lawrence Levine, one of the "basic characteristics of African dance" is the "concentration upon movement outward from the pelvic region." None of these historians offer evidence for this connection between African culture and "frenzied" expression or pelvic movement. Instead, these conclusions seem taken from interpretations that have seen blackface as black or African-derived music; see Genovese, *Roll, Jordan, Roll*, 238; White, "It Was a Proud Day," 23; Levine, *Black Culture and Black Consciousness*, 16.

5. Overall, this chapter is informed by Raymond Williams's idea that the area of a culture is defined by language and understanding, and is not bounded by nation, geography, or ethnicity; it is also inspired in part by Shelly Fisher Fishkin's recognition that the "white" middle class may not have been white; see Raymond Williams, *Culture and Society, 1780–1950* (New York: Columbia University Press, 1958); Shelly Fisher Fishkin, "Interrogating 'Whiteness,' Complicating 'Blackness': Remapping American Culture," *American Quarterly* 47, no. 3 (September 1995): 434–435.

6. Frances Ann Kemble, *Journal of a Residence on a Georgia Plantation in 1838–1839* (1863, reprint, New York: Alfred A. Knopf, 1961), from the introduction by John A. Scott, ix–lxi, xxviii.

7. Kemble, *Journal of Residence on a Georgia Plantation*, 259.

8. Lambert's account cited in Levine, *Black Culture and Black Consciousness*, 13–14; the second example comes from Blassingame, *The Slave Community*, 118; George W. Cable, "Creole Slave Songs," *Century Magazine* 31, no. 6 (April 1886): 807–828, 822.

9. Harriet Ware, letter from Pine Grove, Saint Helena, 21 April 1862, in Elizabeth Ware Pearson, ed., *Letters from Port Royal, 1862–1863* (1906, reprint, New York: Arno Press–New York Times, 1969), 19; W. H. Russell description cited in William Francis Allen, Charles Pickard Ware, and Lucy McKim Garrison, *Slave Songs of the United States* (New York: Simpson and Company, 1867), introduction, 19.

10. Henry Louis McGaffrey interview, in George P. Rawick, ed., *The American Slave: A Composite Autobiography*, suppl. ser. 1, vol. 8, *Mississippi Narratives*, pt. 3 (Westport, CT: Greenwood Press, 1977), 1399.

11. The song is cited in Blassingame, *The Slave Community*, 154; *The Female Hay-Makers*, Boston, Nathaniel Coverly Jr., 1812–1815.

12. Blassingame, *The Slave Community*, 109.

13. Frederick Law Olmstead, *The Cotton Kingdom: A Traveler's Observations on Cotton and Slavery in the American Slave States* (1861, reprint, New York: Da Capo Press, 1996), 350.

14. Jesse Lemisch, "Jack Tar in the Streets: Merchant Seamen in the Politics of Revolutionary America," *William and Mary Quarterly* 25 (1968): 371–407, 375.

15. On these characteristics, see Marcus Rediker, *Between the Devil and the Deep Blue Sea: Merchant Seamen, Pirates, and the Anglo-American Maritime World, 1700–1750* (New York: Cambridge University Press, 1987).

16. See W. Jeffrey Bolster, " 'To Feel Like a Man': Black Seamen in the Northern States, 1800–1860," *Journal of American History* 76, no. 4 (1990): 1183–1185; Virginia M. Adams, ed., *On the Altar of Freedom: A Black Soldier's Civil War Letters from the Front* (New York: Warner Books–University of Massachusetts Press, 1992), introduction, xxii–xxiii.

17. Entry for 2 March 1847, "Benjamin Cushing Journal—At Sea, 1846–1848," G. W. Blunt White Library Manuscript Collections, Mystic Seaport Museum (MSM). Entry for 10 January 1841, "Log of Ship Jefferson," G. W. Blunt White Library Manuscript Collections, MSM.

18. Glenn S. Gardiner, "Aspects of Sailor Life as Depicted in Shanties and Sea Songs: An Interdisciplinary Study," unpublished paper, 1976, G. W. Blunt White Library Collections, MSM. Jared Gardiner to Harriet Gardner, "At Sea, June the __ 1841," Gardner Family Papers, Folder 3: Jared and Harriet Gardner Correspondence, Manuscript Collections, AAS.

19. See the preface and examples in William Main Doerflinger, *Songs of the Sailor and Lumberman* (Glenwood, IL: Meyerbooks, 1951), ix–xviii, 1–89.

20. " 'Round the Corner Sally," from *American Sea Chanteys: La Chasse-Maree Anthology of Sea Songs*, vols. 1–11, Mystic Seaport Museum, 1998.

21. On the expansion of the whaling industry, see Margaret S. Creighton, *Rites and Passages: The Experience of American Whaling, 1830–1870* (New York: Cambridge University Press, 1995); MS, "Journal of Whaleship Mercury, from New Bedford to Pacific Ocean, June 1837–April 1838," G. W. Blunt White Library Manuscript Collections, MSM; MS, "Log Book, Brig *William and Henry*," manuscript collections, Peabody Essex Museum, Salem, MA (PEM); MS, "Bouka Bay Paddles," Charles W. Agard Collection, Folder 1, Box 3, Manuscript Collections, AAS.

22. For this question of the origins of chanteying, see Roger D. Abrahams, *Deep the Water, Shallow the Shore* (Austin: University of Texas Press, 1975); Horace P. Beck, "West Indian Chanteys and Work Songs: The Afro-American Genre"; Tabitha Claypole Nelson, "The Triangle Trade: African Influences in the Anglo-American Sea Shanty Tradition," unpublished papers, presented at the Fourth Annual Symposium on Traditional Music of the Sea, 1980, G. W. Blunt White Library Collections, MSM.

23. "Log Book, Brig *William and Henry*, 1788–1790, On a voyage from Salem to West Coast of Africa & Bengal," manuscript collections, PEM.

24. "Journal of Voyage from New York Towards Africa in the Brig Packet, Kept by George R. Fielder, 1834," manuscript collections, PEM; "John E. Taylor, Letters of Instruction to 1st Officer, While at Gambia, 1840," G. W. Blunt White Library, manuscript collections, MSM; "Private

Journal of the United States Brig *Dolphin*, March 27, 1845, to November 1, 1847," manuscript collections, PEM.

25. Sailors' reminiscences: "Don't know too much," "Government Coal Contracts," and "Some Old Chums," Charles W. Agard Manuscript Collection, Box 3, Folder 3, AAS; for other anecdotes of illegal slaving in New England, see William W. Story, ed., *The Miscellaneous Writings of Joseph Story* (Boston: Charles Little and James Brown, 1852).

26. An example of an American ship on the Congo River patrol in the mid-nineteenth century is "Private Journal from Salem Towards Ambriz, S.W. Coast of Africa, Bark *Goldfinch*, 1857," manuscript collections, PEM; "Blow, Boys Blow," from Ewen MacColl and A. L. Lloyd, *Blow Boys Blow*, Tradition Records–Rykodisc, 1996.

27. Thomas Wentworth Higginson, *Army Life in a Black Regiment* (1870, reprint, New York: Penguin Books, 1997); "Whiskey Johnny," MacColl and Lloyd, *Blow Boys Blow*; cited in Blassingame, *The Slave Community*, 116.

28. "Tom's Gone to Hilo," from *American Sea Chanteys, La Chasse-Maree Anthology of Sea Songs*, vol. 11, Mystic Seaport Museum, 1998.

29. Frederick Douglass, *Narrative of the Life of Frederick Douglass, An American Slave, Written by Himself* (Boston: "The Anti Slavery Office," 1845), 13–14; for the classic explanation of Douglass's ambivalence to slave songs, see W. E. B. DuBois, *The Souls of Black Folk* (1903, reprint, New York: Dover Press, 1994), 3, 155–159.

30. Douglass, *Narrative of the Life of Frederick Douglass*, 113–114; on Douglass's having been directed to New Bedford, see William S. McFeely, *Frederick Douglass* (New York: W. W. Norton, 1991), 76–79.

31. For this interpretation of Douglass, see Peter F. Walker, *Moral Choices: Memory, Desire, and Imagination in Nineteenth-Century American Abolition* (Baton Rouge: Louisiana State University Press, 1978); David Leverenz, *Manhood and the American Renaissance* (Ithaca, NY: Cornell University Press, 1989).

32. Harriet Martineau, *The Martyr Age of the United States* (Boston: Weeks, Jordan, & Co., 1839), 10–11.

33. David Walker, *David Walker's Appeal to the Colored Citizens of the World* (1830, reprint, University Park: Pennsylvania State University Press, 2000), see the introduction by Peter P. Hinks, xv–xxv, 9, 30–36.

34. See Benjamin Quarles, *Black Abolitionists* (New York: Da Capo Press, 1969), 7, 18–26, 32–36, 60, 68, 90.

35. Michael Chevalier, *Society, Manners, and Politics in the United States: Letters on North America* (1836, reprint, Garden City, NY: Doubleday Books, 1961), 153, 349; David Brion Davis, "The Nonfreedom of 'Free Blacks'" in Davis, ed., *Antebellum American Culture: An Interpretive Anthology* (Lexington, MA: D. C. Heath, 1979), 274.

36. See Davis, "The Nonfreedom of 'Free Blacks,'" 274–278; for example, see *The Boston Directory; Containing Names of the Inhabitants, Their Occupations, Places of Business and Dwelling Houses. With Lists of the Streets, Lanes and Wharves; The Town Officers, Public Offices and Banks, and Other Useful Information* (Boston: E. Cotton, 1816); according to Davis, the fact that African American males could "only" vote in Massachusetts, Vermont, New Hampshire, Maine and, with property-holding requirements, New York is another example of the period's universal discrimination. Turned around, the fact that they could vote in these states in the 1840s and 1850s might be very surprising to current Americans, perhaps even evidence for an opposite conclusion.

37. On enfranchised, free blacks as a voting bloc, see Noel Ignatiev, *How the Irish Became White* (New York: Routledge, 1995), 75–76; Quarles, *Black Abolitionists*, vii–viii, 21–22; *Address to the People of the United States, by a Committee of the New England Anti-Slavery Convention, Held in Boston on the 27th, 28th, and 29th of May, 1834* (Boston: Garrison and Knapp, 1834), 14–15, 4–5.

38. Quarles, *Black Abolitionists*, 20, 35, 44, 60–61; William Lloyd Garrison, *An Address Delivered Before the Free People of Color in Philadelphia, New-York, and Other Cities, During the Month of June, 1831* (Boston: Stephen F. Foster, 1831), 3.

39. *Colored American*, 16 December 1837; "Interesting Case," *Colored American*, 23 December 1837; "Prejudice, An Anecdote," *Colored American*, 4 November 1837; "From the Boston Recorder, Read and Ponder," *Colored American*, 20 January 1838.

40. "A Victim Rescued," *Colored American*, 3 April 1841.

41. "Age of Reform," *Colored American*, 11 March 1837; Garrison, *An Address Delivered Before the Free People of Color*, 3; 1837 report cited in Quarles, *Black Abolitionists*, 91.

42. "The Cause of Hard Times," *Colored American*, 17 June 1837; "Female Education," *Colored American*, 18 March 1837; Letter to the Editor, "Female Influence," signed "Ellen," *Colored American*, 30 September 1837; "An Address. Delivered Before the Female Branch Society of Zion, by Wm. Thompson, at Zion's Church, on the 5th of April," *Colored American*, 3 June 1837; "Take Care of Number One!," *Colored American*, 27 January 1838; "Our Literary Societies," *Colored American*, 11 March 1837.

43. "Appeal to Ladies," reprinted from the *Evangelist*, *Colored American*, 7 October 1837.

44. "Agents for the Colored American," *Colored American*, 11 March 1837; "New-York Petitions to the Legislature," *Colored American*, 11 March 1837; "From the 1830 Census," *Colored American*, 18 March 1837; "Colored Population of N.Y.C.," *Colored American*, 25 March 1837.

45. "A Southerner," *Sketches of the Higher Classes of Colored Society in Philadelphia* (Philadelphia: Merrihew and Thompson, 1841), 5–6, 13–15, 22–24, 60–67.

46. H. G. Adams, ed., *God's Image in Ebony: Being a Series of Biographical Sketches, Facts, Anecdotes, Etc., Demonstrative of the Mental Powers and Intellectual Capabilities of the Negro Race* (London: Partridge and Oakey, 1854), 112–113; Wilson Armistead, *A Tribute for the Negro: Being a Vindication of the Moral, Intellectual, and Religious Capabilities of the Colored Portion of Mankind; With Particular Reference to the African Race* (London: Charles Gilpin, 1848), 456; David W. Bartlett, *Modern Agitators: or, Pen Portraits of Living American Reformers* (New York: Miller, Orton & Mulligan, 1855), 54–55.

47. On the establishment of the *North Star*, Douglass's break with Garrison, and the details of the paper, see Quarles, *Frederick Douglass* (New York: Athenaeum, 1968), 58–95; McFeely, *Frederick Douglass*.

48. "Colored School Meeting," *North Star*, 21 December 1849; "Women's State Temperance Convention, Seneca Falls, October 14, 1852," "The Delevan Temperance Union," *North Star*, 28 July 1848; *Frederick Douglass' Paper*, 29 October 1852; "First of August Celebration at Buffalo," *North Star*, 10 August 1849; "Fifth Annual Meeting of the Western N.Y. Anti-Slavery Society," *North Star*, 29 December 1848.

49. "Selected. From Our New England Correspondent, Miss Paul's Juvenile Concert," *Colored American* [NY], 4 March 1837 [reprinted from the *New York Evangelist*].

50. "A Southerner," *Sketches of the Higher Classes of Colored Society*, 59.

51. Untitled editorial comment, *Frederick Douglass' Paper*, 25 March 1859; "The Hutchinson Family—Hunkerism," *North Star*, 27 October 1848.

52. "The Late Colored Concerts, From the National Era," *Frederick Douglass' Paper*, 1 December 1854.

53. Southern, *The Music of Black Americans*, 111–112.

54. "The Black Swan Again," *Frederick Douglass' Paper*, 18 December 1851.

55. "From Our New York Correspondent," *Frederick Douglass' Paper*, 9 March 1855.

56. "Music at Home," Frederick Douglas's Paper, 29 December 1854.

57. US Census figures for 1860, cited in Philip Van Doren Stern, ed., *Prologue to Sumter: The Beginnings of the Civil War from the John Brown Raid to the Surrender of Fort Sumter* (Greenwich, CT: Fawcett Books, 1961), 19.

58. J. Miller M'Kim, *The Freedmen of South Carolina; An Address at Sansom Hall, July 9th, 1862, To the Port Royal Relief Committee* (Philadelphia: Willis P. Hazzard, 1862), 1.

59. W. R. Allen interview, in *The American Slave*, suppl. ser. 1, vol. 3, *Georgia Narratives*, pt. 1, ed. George P. Rawick (Westport, CT: Greenwood Press, 1977), 5; Simon Hare interview, Rawick, *The American Slave, Mississippi Narratives, Part 3*, 913–914; Easter Jones interview, in *The American Slave: A Composite Autobiography*, suppl. ser. 1, vol. 4, *Georgia Narratives*, pt. 2, ed. George P. Rawick (Westport, CT: Greenwood Press, 1977), 350.

60. On plantation work, see Robert Q. Mallard, *Plantation Life Before Emancipation* (Richmond, VA: Whittet and Shepperson, 1892), 31–35; T. J. Woofter Jr., *Black Yeomanry: Life on Saint Helena Island* (New York: Farrer, Straus and Giroux, 1930, 1978), 29–32; Charles Joyner, *Down by the Riverside: A South Carolina Slave Community* (Urbana: University of Illinois Press, 1984), 14–34; Orris Harris interview, Rawick, *The American Slave, Mississippi Narratives, Part 3*, 932–933.

61. Alexandre de Clouet Journal, Parish of Saint Martin, entries for 9 August through 19 September 1866, "Louisiana Papers," Box 2, Folder 2, MS, AAS.

62. Allen, Ware & Garrison, *Slave Songs of the United States*, introduction, xxii–xxiii.

63. Corn-shucking example cited in Blassingame, *The Slave Community*, 117.

64. Squire Irvin interview, Rawick, *The American Slave, Mississippi Narratives, Part 3*, 1086; Harriet Miller interview, in *The American Slave*, suppl. ser. 1, vol. 9, *Mississippi Narratives*, pt. 4, ed. George P. Rawick (Westport, CT: Greenwood Press, 1977), 1502; Jim Martin interview, Rawick, *The American Slave, Mississippi Narratives*, pt. 4, 1441–1442.

65. Olmstead, from *A Journey in the Seaboard Slave States* (1859), cited in *The Slave States*, 41; "A Virginia Girl Remembers the Christmas Eve of 1860," from *Century Illustrated Monthly Magazine* (August 1885), cited in Van Doren Stern, *Prologue to Sumter*, 186.

66. Caroline Malloy interview, Joe McCormick interview, Rawick, *The American Slave, Georgia Narratives, Part 2*, 412, 391.

67. On the Johnkannaus, see Levine, *Black Culture and Black Consciousness*, 13; Harriet Jacobs, *Incidents in the Life of a Slave Girl* [1861], 92; James Bolton interview, Carolina Ates interview, in Rawick, *The American Slave, Georgia Narratives Part 1*, 84, 25; Carrie Mason interview, in Rawick, *The American Slave, Georgia Narratives, Part 2*, 424; Malinda Mitchell interview, in Rawick, *The American Slave, Georgia Narratives, Part 2*, 441; Virginia Harris interview, Fanny Smith Hodges interview, Prince Johnson interview, in Rawick, *The American Slave, Mississippi Narratives, Part 3*, 942, 1026, 1172.

68. Robert Laird interview, in Rawick, *The American Slave, Mississippi Narratives, Part 3*, 1293; Anna Peek interview, in Rawick, *The American Slave, Georgia Narratives, Part 2*, 481.

69. Easter Reed interview, Elsie Moreland interview, in Rawick, *The American Slave, Georgia Narratives, Part 2*, 505, 455; James Lucas interview, in Rawick, *The American Slave, Mississippi Narratives, Part 3*, 1344–1345.

70. Sally E. Hadden, *Slave Patrols: Law and Violence in Virginia and the Carolinas* (Cambridge, MA: Harvard University Press, 2001), 19–22, 52–59, 114, 107–111.

71. Sally Brown interview, in Rawick, *The American Slave, Georgia Narratives, Part 1*, 96.

72. Charles Dickens, *American Notes For General Circulation* (New York: D. Appleton and Company, 1868), 94–100.

73. Easter Jones interview, in Rawick, *The American Slave, Georgia Narratives, Part 1*, 350; Henry Louis McGaffrey interview, in Rawick, *The American Slave, Mississippi Narratives, Part 3*, 1396.

74. Rev. W. B. Allen interview, in Rawick, *The American Slave, Georgia Narratives, Part 1*, 6.

75. Edward Jones interview, Jane Lewis interview, in Rawick, *The American Slave, Mississippi Narratives, Part 3*, 1205, 1324–1325; examples of patrols breaking up dances or forcing slaves to dance cited from Hadden, *Slave Patrols*, 118.

76. The classic work on the slave trade and source for the "ceremony of dancing the slaves" is Daniel P. Mannix, *Black Cargoes: A History of the Atlantic Slave Trade, 1518–1865* (New York: Penguin Books, 1962, 1976), 114.

77. Lucy Galloway interview, Orris Harris interview, in Rawick, *The American Slave, Mississippi Narratives, Part 3*, 808, 930; Harriet Miller interview, in Rawick, *The American Slave, Mississippi Narratives, Part 4*, 1503.

78. See the introduction by Paul Jefferson to William Wells Brown, *Travels of William Wells Brown, Including Narrative of William Wells Brown, a Fugitive Slave and the American Fugitive in Europe* (New York: Marcus Weiner, 1991), 1–2.

79. Brown, *Narrative of William Wells Brown*, in *Travels of William Wells Brown*, 41–42.

80. Brown, *Narrative of William Wells Brown*, in *Travels of William Wells Brown*, 42; John Little interview from Benjamin Drew, *The Refugee: A North-Side View of Slavery* (original 1856, reprint, Reading, MA: Addison-Wesley, 1969), 157.

81. Charlie Moses interview, Rawick, *The American Slave, Mississippi Narratives, Part 4*, 1603.

Chapter Five

1. Anna Quincy Thaxter Cushing diary, collection description guide, entry for 7 January 1844, manuscript collections, AAS.

2. Anna Thaxter Cushing diary, entries for 4 July, 27 July, 4 August 1844, MS, AAS.

3. Anna Thaxter Cushing diary, entries for 26 October 1846, undated entry headed "At Charlottes" [late October or early November 1846], and 3 November 1846, MS, AAS.

4. Steele, "Abby Hutchinson Patton"; John Wallace Hutchinson, *Story of the Hutchinsons*, vol. 1, (Boston: Lee and Shepard, 1896), 127, 116. Eliza E. Chase to Lucy Chase [in Philadelphia], Worcester, 28 September 1843, Chase Family Papers, AAS.

5. Harriet Farley, "Letters From Susan," *Lowell Offering*, IV [1844], cited in *The Lowell Offering: Writings by New England Women 1840–1845*, ed. Benita Eisler (New York: W. W. Norton, 1998), 58.

6. The focus here is on the original Hutchinson Family Singers of the 1840s. For full accounts of the singers, see Scott Gac, *Singing for Freedom: The Hutchinson Family Singers and the Nineteenth-Century Culture of Reform* (New Haven, CT: Yale University Press, 2007); Caroline Mosely, "The Hutchinson Family: The Function of Their Song in Ante-Bellum America," in *American Popular Music*, vol. 1, *The Nineteenth Century and Tin Pan Alley*, ed. Timothy Scheurer (Bowling Green, OH: Bowling Green State University Press, 1989), 73–74. Two older and

probably less trustworthy sources are Carol Brink, *Harps in the Wind: The Story of the Singing Hutchinsons* (New York: Macmillan, 1947); and Philip D. Jordan, *Singin' Yankees* (Minneapolis: University of Minnesota Press, 1946). Among the best accounts of the original Hutchinsons is Dale Cockrell's heavily annotated version of their touring diary from the 1840s; see Dale Cockrell, ed., *Excelsior: Journals of the Hutchinson Family Singers, 1842–1846* (Stuyvesant, NY: Pendragon Press, 1989). Finally, for a short account of the singers that pictures them as forerunners of a modern genre of "protest song," see Charles Hamm, "'If I Were a Voice': The Hutchinson Family and Popular Song as Political and Social Protest," chapter 7 of *Yesterdays: Popular Song in America* (New York: W. W. Norton, 1979), 141–161.

7. "Hutchinson Family's First Public Singing Tour," extracts from the Hutchinson Diary, hand-copied from the original, most likely by Ludlow Patton, entries for 11–30 July 1842, Hutchinson Collection, Wadleigh Library–Milford Public Library (MPL); see also Dale Cockrell, ed., *Excelsior: Journals of the Hutchinson Family Singers, 1842–1846* (New York: Pendragon Press, 1989), 30–60.

8. On the market revolution, see Charles Sellers, *The Market Revolution: Jacksonian America, 1815–1846* (New York: Oxford University Press, 1991); see also the essays in *The Market Revolution in America: Social, Political and Religious Expressions, 1800–1880*, ed. Melvyn Stokes and Stephen Conway (Charlottesville: University Press of Virginia, 1996); for the social effects of these changes, see Stuart M. Blumin, *The Emergence of the Middle Class: Social Experience in the American City, 1760–1900* (Cambridge, MA: Harvard University Press, 1989); Paul E. Johnson, *A Shopkeeper's Millennium: Society and Revivals in Rochester, New York, 1815–1837* (New York: Hill and Wang, 1978); Mary Ryan, *Cradle of the Middle Class: The Family in Oneida County, New York, 1790–1865* (New York: Cambridge University Press, 1981).

9. *The Milford Hand-Book. What Every Man, Woman and Child Ought to Know About Milford* (Milford, NH: W. W. Hemenway, 1879), 3; *New Hampshire 1840 Census Index* (Bountiful, UT: Accelerated Indexing Systems, 1976), 63.

10. *History of Milford, Family Registers* (n.p., n.d.), 783, New Hampshire Room, MPL.

11. *Milford Township Records*, New Hampshire State Archives, Concord, NH; *Report of the Selectmen for Milford, for the Year Ending March 11, 1839* (n.p., n.d.), Milford Historical Society (MHS).

12. John Wallace Hutchinson, *Story of the Hutchinsons*, vol. 1, 4, 21; Joshua Hutchinson, *A Brief Narrative of the Hutchinson Family. Sixteen Sons and Daughters of the "Tribe of Jesse"* (Boston: Lea and Shepard, 1874), 22, 27; Asa Hutchinson, *Book of Words of the Hutchinson Family; To Which is Added The Book of Brothers* (Boston: J. S. Potter, 1855), 13.

13. David Goodwin, *Historical Sketch of the Town of Milford, New Hampshire* (1846, reprint, Milford: Milford Historical Society, 1987), 10–11.

14. For names of early local musical societies, see *The Family Minstrel: A Repository of Music and Poetry* 1, no. 3 (2 March 1835) and 4 (15 April 1835).

15. George Hood, *A History of Music in New England: With Biographical Sketches of Reformers and Psalmists* (Boston: Wilkins, Carter and Company, 1846), iii–vi; *Programme. First Concert—Sixteenth Season. New-York Philharmonic Society, Academy of Music, Saturday Evening, November 21, 1857*, New York, n.p., 1857.

16. *Programme. First Concert—Sixteenth Season. New York Philharmonic*; on Barnum's taming of audiences at the American Museum Theater, see Richard Butsch, "Bowery B'hoys and Matinee Ladies: The Re-Gendering of Nineteenth-Century American Theater Audiences," *American*

Quarterly 46 (1994): 374–405; Eliza Chase to Lucy Chase, Worcester, 22 April 1851, Chase Family Papers, Box 1, Folder 5, Manuscript Collections AAS.

17. *Musical Institute*, Pittsfield, MA, n.p., n.d.; *Italian Academy of Music, 228 Washington Street, Boston*, Boston, John S. Spooner, 1860.

18. Circular, *"Mr. Lowell Mason is engaged to teach Vocal Music in Chauncy Hall School,"* Boston, n.p., 20 March 1833, MHS; Lowell Mason, *The Sacred Harp: or, Beauties of Church Music, New Edition, With Important Improvements*, vol. 1 (Boston: Shepley and Wright, 1841), 4–9.

19. For a brief background on Mason, see Gac, *Singing for Freedom*, 87–98; on Mason's version of Pestalozzianism, including the importance of singing the multiplication tables, see Lowell Mason, *A Glance at Pestalozzianism* (Boston, n.p., 1863), 4, 7–8; on Mason's success, Mason, *The Sacred Harp*, 4–9; Lowell Mason, *Address on Church Music* (Boston: J. P. Jewett, 1851), 14–16, MHS.

20. John Wallace Hutchinson, *Story of the Hutchinsons*, vol. 1, 30–31, 35; Joshua Hutchinson, *A Brief Narrative of the Hutchinson Family, Sixteen Sons and Daughters of the "Tribe of Jesse"* (Boston: Lee and Shepard, 1874), 22.

21. "An Old Time Vocalist. Reminiscences of the Famous Hutchinson Family," *Boston Herald*, 18 January 1891, Hutchinson Collection, MPL.

22. On the popularity of Fisher, see McConachie, *Melodramatic Formations*, 31–35, 48–50.

23. *Mr. H. Russell Respectfully Informs His Friends of Worcester, That He Proposes Giving a FAREWELL CONCERT, On Tuesday Evening Next, Dec. 26, at Brinley Hall*, Worcester, Mirick and Bartlett, 1837; *Programme of Mr. H. Russell's Concert, at Brinley Hall, Tuesday Evening, March 9, 1841*, Worcester, Palladium Office, 1841.

24. *The Lynn Directory and Register for the Year 1841. Containing a General Description of the Town, A list of the Town Officers, Public Institutions, The Names and Occupations of the Residents, and Other Useful Information*, vol. 1, no. 1 (Lynn: Benjamin F. Roberts, 1841): 47–48, from the collections of the Lynn Historical Society (LHS).

25. *Grand Family Concert at the Cameneum* [Portsmouth, NH]. *Positively the Last Night of the Aeolian Vocalists—The Hutchinson Family (3 brothers and sister)*, n.p., 9 February 1842, Hutchinson Collection, MPL.

26. The photograph is from John Wallace Hutchinson, *Story of the Hutchinsons*, vol. 1, 136.

27. *History of Milford, Family Registers*, 783, MPL; John Wallace Hutchinson, *Story of the Hutchinsons*, vol. 2, 235–236; Joshua Hutchinson, *A Brief Narrative of the Hutchinson Family*, 27.

28. Jesse Hutchinson Sr. to "J. J." [Jesse] Hutchinson, 6 June 1841, Hutchinson Collection, MPL.

29. L. E. Craig, *True Politeness; or, Etiquette for Ladies and Gentlemen, Containing the Rules and Usages of Polite Society, With Directions for the Toilet* (Philadelphia: L. E. Craig, 1847), 5; Lydia Maria Child, *The Girl's Own Book* (New York: Clark and Austin, 1833), 284; *The Young Man's Own Book: A Manual of Politeness, Intellectual Improvement, and Moral Deportment, Calculated to Form the Character on a Solid Basis, And to Insure Respectability and Success in Life* (Philadelphia: Key, Mielke and Biddle, 1832), 131–135; *The American Chesterfield, or, Way to wealth, honour, and distinction: being selections from the letters of Lord Chesterfield to his son, and extracts from other eminent authors, on the subject of politeness: with alterations and additions, suited to the youth of the United States* (Philadelphia: John Grigg, 1828), 228.

30. *The Young Man's Own Book*, 157, epigraph on title page; *The Canons of Good Breeding; or, The Handbook of the Man of Fashion* (Philadelphia: Lea and Blanchard, 1839), 4, 7–9;

31. Craig, *True Politeness*, 5, 38, 42.

32. Joshua Hutchinson, *A Brief Narrative of the Hutchinson Family*, 5; *Parlor Air Tight Stove* (Lynn, MA: Jesse Hutchinson Jr., 1844), from the collections of the Peabody Essex Museum Library, Salem, MA (PEM).

33. *The Old Granite State, The Celebrated Song of the Hutchinson Family*, Boston, Oliver Ditson, 1843.

34. *Free Soil Songs, Composed and Sung at the Buffalo Convention, August 9, and 10, 1848. By Messrs. Hutchinson, Jewell, Bates and Foster, of Massachusetts*, Buffalo, E. A. Maynard—Printers Republic Office, 1849; Asa Hutchinson diary, entries for 22 April 1853 through 15 May 1853, manuscript collections, AAS.

35. Journal of Asa Hutchinson, entry for 1 January 1853, in Waterville, ME, manuscript collections, AAS.

36. "Funeral of Asa B. Hutchinson," *Glencoe Register* [MN], 4 December 1884; Asa Hutchinson, diary entry for 9 January 1844, from Cockrell, *Excelsior*, 179–180.

37. Journal of Asa Hutchinson, addendum, 29 January 1867, manuscript collections, AAS; "Funeral of Asa B. Hutchinson," *Glencoe Register* [MN], 4 December 1884.

38. "The Hutchinson Family. The 'Tribe of John' now in Oakland," *Oakland* [CA] *Mirror*, 18 January 1879, MPL.

39. John Wallace Hutchinson, *Story of the Hutchinsons*, 294–295.

40. On the rise of the concept of romantic love, see Karen Lystra, *Searching the Heart: Women, Men, and Romantic Love in Nineteenth-Century America* (New York: Oxford University Press, 1989), 7–11; Ellen K. Rothman, "Sex and Self-Control: Middle-Class Courtship in America, 1770–1870," in *The American Family in Social Historical Perspective*, ed. Michael Gordon (New York: Saint Martins, 1983), 393–410; on John's marriage, "Seventy. Golden Milestone in His Path of Life. John W. Hutchinson Looks Back Upon the Journey," *Lynn Daily Bee*, 6 January 1891.

41. "Fiction Chronicles No Stranger Tales than the Love Stories of this Venerable Bard of High Rock," *Boston Sunday American*, August 1905, clipping, Hutchinson Collection, MPL; Journal of Asa Hutchinson, entry for 1 January 1853, manuscript collections, AAS; "The Hutchinson Family," *Hallowell Gazette* [ME], 16 June 1849.

42. *Book of Words of the Hutchinson Family*, 14.

43. *The Vulture of the Alps*, Boston, Oliver Ditson, 1843; Hutchinson, *Story of the Hutchinsons*, vol. 2, 297; *Horticultural Wife. Written by a Celebrated English Gardener after Disappointment in Love*, Boston, G. P. Reed, 1850.

44. On Judson's marriage, see Gac, *Singing for Freedom*, 186; for a contextual description of his stage behavior, see "The Hutchinsons," *New York Day-Book*, 13 March 1851; on Judson's throwing of concert profits into the audience, see Lewis Perry, *Radical Abolitionism: Anarchy and the Government of God in Antislavery Thought* (Ithaca, NY: Cornell University Press, 1973), 96–98; *Concert! The Original Judson J. Hutchinson and Kate H. Hutchinson! Of the Hutchinson Family!*, Boston, Forest and Farwell, n.d.

45. "Judson J. Hutchinson," undated news clipping, Hutchinson Collection, MPL; Northrop Frye, "Lord Byron," in *George Gordon, Lord Byron*, ed. Harold Bloom (New York: Chelsea House, 1986), 53–63.

46. William Lloyd Garrison to John Hutchinson, 15 March 1859, John Hutchinson Collection, LHS; "The Late Judson J. Hutchinson, *Frederick Douglass's Newspaper* [from the *New York Tribune*], 28 January 1859; "Judson Hutchinson," *Syracuse Standard*, 23 October 1850; "Obituary.

Death of Another Member of the Hutchinson Family," *New York Tribune*, 13 January 1859; "The Hutchinson Suicide," *Boston Atlas and Bee*, 13 January 1859.

47. *The Celebrated Melodies of the Ranier Family, "The Alpine Horn,"* Boston, Oliver Ditson, 1841; as stated in her advance material, Lind would also perform "The Alpine Horn," *The Life and Genius of Jenny Lind* (New York: W. F. Burgess, 1850); John Wallace Hutchinson, *Story of the Hutchinsons*, 46.

48. "Abby Hutchinson Patton," *Concord* [NH] *Monitor*, 29 November 1892; Frank B. Carpenter, "Abby Hutchinson Patton, In Memoriam," *New York Home Journal*, 7 December 1892; "The Hutchinson Family," *North Star* [from the *New Englander*], 5 December 1850; "Poetry Written to Abby J. Hutchinson," probably transcribed by Ludlow Patton, Hutchinson Collection, MPL.

49. Rowena Granice Steele, "Abby Hutchinson Patton," *San Joaquin Valley Argus* [Merced, CA], 10 March 1883; "The Hutchinson Family," *North Star*, 5 December 1850; Carpenter, "Abby Hutchinson Patton," *New York Home Journal*, 7 December 1892.

50. "Ludlow Patton. Abby Hutchinson Patton," *The Banner of Light*, 4 June 1898. Abby did self-publish her poems in a gift book that she seems to have handed out to friends, *A Handful of Pebbles*, privately printed in 1891; "Sung the People's Songs. Death at her Home of Mrs. Abby Hutchinson Patton," unidentified news clipping, Hutchinson Collection, LHS.

51. See, for example, Frances Trollope, *Domestic Manners of the Americans* (1832, reprint: New York: Knopf, 1949), 74–75, 155–157.

52. On the tour from Hookset to Saratoga Springs: Asa Hutchinson's diary entries, 12 July– 2 August 1842, on the "scuffle," 23 July 1842; Judson Hutchinson's diary entries, 25 July 1842, 10 August 1842, Manuscript, "Hutchinson Family's First Public Singing Tour," Hutchinson Collection, MPL.

53. *Aeolian Vocalists' Concert. Program*, n.p. [1841]; *Family Concert, By Aeolian Vocalists*, n.p. [1842] each include some 17–18 pieces; here, the printing is also quite primitive, without much effort at marketing; later programs are much superior for their eye appeal, have fewer songs and no listed instrumental pieces, and include credits for writers and lyricists: *Farewell Concert, By the Celebrated Aeolian Vocalists. The Hutchinson Family, (Three Brothers and Sister), Brinley Hall* [Worcester, MA], *September 6, '42*, printed by J. B. Ripley—Palladium Office, Worcester, 1842, collections of the AAS; *Second & Last Concert by the Aeolians!* [Concert in Boston at the Universalist Church], n.p., 8 November 1842, Collections of the New Hampshire Historical Society (NHHS).

54. John Wallace Hutchinson, *Story of the Hutchinsons*, 63–64.

55. The Hutchinson Singers," *Herald of Freedom*, 9 December 1842, *A Collection from the Newspapers Writings of Nathaniel Peabody Rogers* (Concord, NH: John R. French, 1847), 245.

56. "An Old Time Vocalist. Reminiscences of the Famous Hutchinson Family," *Boston Herald*, 18 January 1891, Hutchinson Collection, MPL.

57. *Book of Words of the Hutchinson Family* (1855), 17; the temperance songs appear on the following and certainly other broadside programs: *Family Concert By the Aeolian Vocalists*, n.p. [1842], Hutchinson Collection, MPL; *Sacred and Secular Concert by the Aeolian Vocalists. At the Universal Church* [Newburyport, MA], n.p., 10 February 1842, Hutchinson Collection, MPL; *Muster Night! Grand Concert of the Aeolian Vocalists. The Hutchinson Family* [Lynn, MA], n.p., 15 September 1842, LHS.

58. Diary entry by John Hutchinson, Balston, New York, 4 August 1842, Manuscript, "The Hutchinson Family's First Public Singing Tour," Hutchinson Collection, MPL; "An Old Time Vocalist. Reminiscences of the Famous Hutchinson Family," *Boston Herald*, 18 January 1891, Hutchinson Collection, MPL.

59. *The Choral Songster: A Choice Collection of Hymns and Spiritual Songs Adapted to All Occasions of Worship. Compiled and Published for the East Penn'a Camp Meeting Association by Rev's. G. W. M. Rigor & I. Baltzell* (Mountville, PA: Baltzell & Weidler Music and Job Printers, 1830), 16–17.

60. Cited in Nathan O. Hatch, *The Democratization of American Christianity* (New Haven, CT: Yale University Press, 1989), 52; Richard McNemar, *The Kentucky Revival, or, A Short History of the Late Extraordinary Out-Puring of the Spirit of God, in the Western States of America, Agreeably to Scripture Promises, and Prophesies Concerning the Latter Day, With a Brief Account of the Entrance and Progress of What the World Call Shakerism, Among the Subjects of the Late Revival in Ohio and Kentucky.* (Cincinnati: John W. Browne, 1807), 20, 23–24.

61. Michael Chevalier, *Society, Manners, and Politics in the United States, Letters on North America* (1836, reprint: Garden City, NY: Doubleday, 1961), 309.

62. The quote on the communal force of revivals comes from Hatch, *The Democratization of American Christianity*, 52; on Christian revivals as representing the uprising of communal yearnings, see also Mark Holloway, *Heavens on Earth: Utopian Communities in America, 1680–1880* (1951, reprint: Mineola, NY: Dover, 1966), 82; *Humane Society*, Boston, n.p., 1810.

63. *"Charity," An Original Song, Written for the Anniversary Meeting of St. John's Lodge, In Aid of their Charity Fund*, Boston, n.p., 1812.

64. "Original Ode," from *Order of Performances At the Boylston Hall, October 11, 1820, Being the Annual Meeting of the Fatherless and Widow's Society*, Boston, n.p., 1820.

65. *Order of Services at the Twentieth Anniversary of the Boston Female Asylum, Celebrated in the First Church, Chauncey Place, September 22, 1820*, Boston, n.p., 1820; *Order of Services at the Twenty-First Anniversary of the Boston Female Asylum, Celebrated in the First Church, Chauncey Place, September 21, 1821*, Boston, n.p., 1821; *Order of Services at the Tenth Anniversary of the Boston Asylum for Indigent Boys, Friday, April Thirteenth, 1824*, Boston, Bannister and Marvin, 1824.

66. *Humane Society*, Boston, n.p., 1810; *Boston Female Asylum. Order of Performances for the Eleventh Anniversary, September 20, 1811, At the West Church*, Boston, n.p., 1811; *Order of Services at the Twenty-First Anniversary of the Boston Female Asylum, Celebrated in the First Church, Chauncey Place, September 21, 1821*, Boston, n.p., 1821.

67. See Blumin, *Emergence of the Middle Class*; Johnson, *Shopkeeper's Millennium*; Ryan, *Cradle of the Middle Class*; on the early instability this created and the fears of unregulated youth, see Patricia Cline Cohen, *The Murder of Helen Jewett: The Life and Death of a Prostitute in Nineteenth-Century New York* (New York: A. A. Knopf, 1998); on this splitting of cultures, see Lawrence Levine, *Highbrow/Lowbrow: The Emergence of Cultural Hierarchy in America* (Cambridge, MA: Harvard University Press, 1988); Levine does not say that this process was complete by the 1840s, but implies that it was well underway. On the split between middle-class music and blackface, see Dale Cockrell, *Demons of Disorder: Early Blackface Minstrels and Their World* (New York and London: Cambridge University Press, 1997), 32–54.

68. *Anniversary Meeting of the St. Albans Temperance Society, Tuesday, February 23, 1836*, n.p., Saint Albans, VT, 1836, AAS; *Order of Exercises for the Anniversary Meeting of the Ward Four Temperance Society, In the Church on Green Street, Sabbath Evening, March 15, 1835*, n.p., Boston, 1835, AAS.

69. *Temperance Meeting, Order of Exercises*, n.p., Taunton, MA, 1833, AAS.

70. *Order of Services in St. Paul's Church, On Wednesday Evening, May 23, 1832; Being the Twentieth Anniversary of the Massachusetts Society for the Suppression of Intemperance*, Boston, n.p., 1832.

71. *The New Impulse: or, Hawkins and Reform. A Brief History of the Origin, Progress, and Effects of the Present Astonishing Temperance Movements, and of the Life and Reformation of John W. Hawkins, The Distinguished Leader, By A Teetotaler* (Boston: Samuel Dickinson, 1841); James L. Baker, *The Washingtonian Reform: An Address, Delivered Before the Hingham Total Abstinence Society, June 16, 1844* (Hingham, MA: Jedidiah Farmer, 1844); John Bartholomew Gough Diary, entry for 19 October 1846, Gough Papers, Octavo vol. 10, AAS. On the Washingtonians and Gough's New York scandal, see David S. Reynolds, *Beneath the American Renaissance: The Subversive Imagination in the Age of Emerson and Melville* (Cambridge, MA: Harvard University Press, 1988), 67–68.

72. See, for example, T. D. Bonner, *The Temperance Harp; A collection of Songs, Suitable for Washingtonian and Other Total Abstinence Societies in the United States, And Respectfully Dedicated to Them* (Northampton, MA: Printed at the Gazette Office, 1842); *Temperance Song Book of the Massachusetts Temperance Union* (Boston: Kidder and Wright, 1842).

73. *Grand Temperance Festival: Hymns for the Temperance Jubilee at the (late) Tremont Theatre, July 4, 1843* (Boston: Tuttle and Dennett, 1843); Joseph Waugh, *The Temperance Muse, A Collection of Hymns, Songs, &c. &c. For Temperance Meetings, Cold Water Celebrations, Festivals, &c.* (Providence: Printed by H. H. Brown, 1842).

74. Mary C. Todd to Lucy Chase [in Fitchburg, MA], 31 August 1841, Chase Family Papers, AAS; *Temperance Hymns. Bring this Sheet of Hymns to All Temperance Meetings*, Nashua [NH], n.p., 1840; *Hymns. Sung at the First Meeting of the Boston Washington Temperance Society of Reformed Drunkards, April 28, At the Marlborough Chapel*, Boston, n.p., 1841; Thomas Chase to Lucy Chase [Philadelphia], 1 November 1843; and Eliza Chase to Lucy Chase [Worcester, MA], 17 November 1843, Chase Family Papers, AAS.

75. *Temperance Hymns*, Nashua, n.p., 1840.

76. Waugh, *The Temperance Muse*.

77. *The Drunkard*, Epping, NH, n.p., 1843; "The Inebriate's Lament" from *Covert and Dodge's Collection of Songs, Duetts, Glees, Choruses, &c. As Sung By Them and J.B. Gough, At Their Temperance Concerts Throughout the Union.* (Boston: Keith's Music Publishing House, 67 and 69 Court Street, 1844).

78. *The Cold Water Melodies, and Washingtonian Songster* (Boston: Published by Theodore Abbot, 388 Washington Street, 1842).

79. R. K. Potter, *The Boston Temperance Songster; A Collection of Songs and Hymns for Temperance Societies, Original and Selected* (Boston: William White, 1844).

80. *Temperance Selections for Youth* (Boston: R. K. Potter, 1844); *Covert and Dodge's Collection of Songs.*

81. "The Old Granite State," from *The Granite Songster. Containing the Poetry as Sung by the Hutchinson Family, at Their Concerts* (Boston: A. B. Hutchinson–W. L. Bradbury, 1847).

82. *Deacon Giles Distillery*, copyright by Miles St. John, n.p., probably 1835, AAS; *King Alcohol, A Comic Temperance Glee*, Boston, Oliver Ditson, 1843; the song would be republished in temperance songsters; see "King Alcohol," from *The Cold Water Melodies, A New Selection Designed For Social Temperance Meetings, and the Family Circle, by Sam Slocum* (Providence: Printed by I Amesbury Jr., Agent, 9 Market Sq., 1851); the story of the song's origins comes from "Of the Tribe of Jesse. A Once Famous Family of Composers and Singers. Their Stirring Ballads of the Old Granite State. Interesting Incidents in the Life of the Hutchinsons," *Manchester Union* [NH], 6 June 1896, Hutchinson Collection, MPL.

83. John Wallace Hutchinson, *Story of the Hutchinsons*, vol. 1, 61–64, 65.

Chapter Six

1. The origins of the rumor about the meeting remain unknown; the trustees of the Chatham Street Chapel denied that a meeting of "any Anti-Slavery Society" had been planned for the night of 9 July; see "Voice of the Public Press. Causes of the Late Riots," *Liberator*, 26 July 1834; "To the Honorable Cornelius W. Lawrence, Mayor of the City of New-York," printed in the *Liberator* along with several other papers, 16 July 1834.

2. "Riots in New-York," *Liberator*, 19 July 1834.

3. Lyrics from the broadside *Jim Crow*, Boston, Leonard Deming, 1832.

4. This account of the beginning of the 1834 Five Points Riot is taken from Tyler Anbinder, *Five Points: The 19th-Century New York City Neighborhood that Invented Tap Dance, Stole Elections, and Became the World's Most Notorious Slum* (New York: Plume Books, 2002), 8–12. For a slightly different account, see Joel Tyler Headley, *The Great Riots of New York, 1712 to 1873, Including a Full and Complete Account of the Four Days' Draft Riot of 1863* (New York: E. B. Treat, 1873), 79–95.

5. Anbinder, *Five Points*, 12.

6. The idea that white racism contains elements of love as well as hate is derived in part from Eric Lott, *Love and Theft: Blackface Minstrelsy and the American Working Class* (New York: Oxford University Press, 1993); my interpretation is more than a tweaking of Lott's thesis: Lott suggests that white attraction to black style resulted in theft, and that the stealing of black style in music resulted in minstrelsy; mine is that the white attraction was toward a blackface-inspired stereotype, and that whenever actual African Americans did not adhere to white fantasies of blackness, the love could turn to violence.

7. The names of performers and characters are taken from broadsides, sheet music, songsters, and other material, most of which is cited later; for the names of theaters offering blackface entertainment in the 1830s and 1840s, see Hans Nathan, *Dan Emmett and the Rise of Early Negro Minstrelsy* (Norman: University of Oklahoma Press, 1962).

8. "Negro Minstrelsy—Ancient and Modern," *Putnam's Monthly Magazine of American Literature, Science, and Art* 5, no. 25 (January 1855): 72–79, 73.

9. Anbinder, *Five Points*, 16–19; George G. Foster, *New-York by Gaslight and Other Urban Sketches*, ed. Stuart M. Blumin (Berkeley: University of California Press, 1990), 124–125.

10. Virginia M. Adams, ed., *On the Altar of Freedom: A Black Soldier's Civil War Letters from the Front* (New York: Warner Books–University of Massachusetts Press, 1992), introduction, xix–xx; W. Jeffrey Bolster, "To Feel Like a Man: Black Seamen in the Northern States, 1800–1860," *Journal of American History* 76, no. 4 (1990): 1183–1185.

11. Shane White, "'It Was a Proud Day': African Americans, Festivals, and Parades in the North, 1741–1834," *Journal of American History* 81, no. 1 (June 1994): 13–50; Eileen Southern, *The Music of Black Americans: A History* (New York: Norton, 1983), 49–53; William Dillon Pierson, *Black Yankees: The Development of an Afro-American Subculture in Eighteenth-Century New England* (Amherst: University of Massachusetts Press, 1988), 121–122.

12. On the banjo as having originated in Africa and making its way to the United States and eventually to blackface minstrelsy, see Laurent Dubois, *The Banjo: America's African Instrument* (Cambridge, MA: Harvard University Press, 2016); Robert C. Toll, *Blacking Up: The Minstrel Show in Nineteenth-Century America* (New York: Oxford University Press, 1974), 27; it does not take much musical training at all to recognize the obvious Irish origins of blackface songs like "Jim Along Josey," "Zip Coon," "Old Dan Tucker," or many others.

13. On the obsession with authenticity, without the mention of blackface, see Miles Orvell, *The Real Thing: Imitation and Authenticity in American Culture, 1880–1940* (Chapel Hill: University of North Carolina Press, 1989), 42–49.

14. Scholarly interpretations of blackface dialect have varied: for one scholar, it was a mixture of invention and borrowing, containing authentic elements of "Black English Vernacular" or "BEV"; for another, the point was to make black speech sound "coarse, clumsy and ignorant," the stylistic opposite of the "soft tones and grace" of "cultivated speech." See William J. Mahar, "Black English in Early Blackface Minstrelsy: A New Interpretation of the Sources of the Minstrel Show Dialect," *American Quarterly* 37 (Summer 1985): 260; Nathan Huggins, *The Harlem Renaissance* (New York: Oxford University Press, 1971), 255.

15. "Blue Tail Fly," from *The Black Diamond Songster*; another version of this type of direct violence is *Manners and Customs of Ann Street, Or, A North End Frolic*, Boston, n.p., n.d., probably from the late 1820s or very early 1830s.

16. "Shin Bone Alley," from *De Kickapoo Whoop; Or Pee Dee Warbler, by Santaclaus* (New York: Elton and Harrison, n.d., early 1830s). Another version of the song offered a rare example of a blackface song with a call-and-response pattern, "De Oder Song" [to Shin Bone Alley], from *De Kickapoo Whoop*; for an example of the "shin bone" myth, see Foster, *New-York by Gaslight*, 125–126.

17. "Whar Did You Cum From!," *The Black Diamond Songster. Containing All the New Negro Songs* (New York: Turner and Fisher, 1840).

18. *Coal Black Rose*, Boston, Leonard Deming, 1832.

19. For the transformation of Coal Black Rose into "Oh Hush!" see Lott, *Love and Theft*, 133–134; and Louis S. Gerteis, "Blackface Minstrelsy and the Construction of Race in Nineteenth-Century America," in *Union and Emancipation: Essays on Politics and Race in the Civil War Era*, ed. David Blight and Brooks Simpson (Kent, OH: Kent State University Press, 1997), 79–104, 87–89.

20. "Lubly Fan Will You Cum Out To Night," Cool White–The Virginia Serenaders, 1844; the song would later be cleaned up and renamed "Buffalo Gals"; for another example of the wench character, see "Julina Johnson," from *Charles White's Black Apollo Songster* (New York: Turner and Fisher, 1844).

21. Lott, *Love and Theft*, 25; on this phenomenon in literature, see Leonard Cassuto, *The Inhuman Race: The Racial Grotesque in American Literature and Culture* (New York: Columbia University Press, 1997), 127–140; the songs "Juliana Snow," "Lilly White," "Sally Snow," and "Little More Cider" from *Buckley's Ethiopian Melodies* (Philadelphia: A Winch, 1853).

22. *Long Tail Blue*, Boston, Leonard Deming, 1832.

23. For the interpretation of the Jacksonian period as generating an upsurge of racism and hostilities toward others, see Henry L. Watson, *Liberty and Power: The Politics of Jacksonian America* (New York: Hill and Wang, 1990). For an early exploration of the possibility that mid-nineteenth-century white attitudes toward African Americans could include examples of attraction as well as dismissive stereotypes and race hatred, see George M. Frederickson, *The Black Image in the White Mind: The Debate on Afro-American Character and Destiny, 1817–1914* (Hanover, CT: Wesleyan University Press, 1971).

24. "Jim Crow in London," from *De Kickapoo Whoop*; *Gumbo Chaff*, Boston, Leonard Deming, n.d., early 1830s, probably 1832–1833.

25. "Walk Jaw Bone," from *Deacon Snowball's Negro Melodies* (New York: Turner and Fisher, 1843); "The Jolly Raftsman, words by Andrew Evans, and sung by him at his concerts WITH

GREAT SUCCESS," from the collection *Old Dan Emmit's* [sic] *Original Banjo Melodies, Never Before Published*, Boston, Keith's Music Publishing House, 1844.

26. "Lucy Neal," from *Carter's Melodies. As Sung by him and the Virginia Serenaders at Their Concerts Throughout the United States with Unbounded Applause*, Boston: Keith's Music Publishing House, 1844.

27. Toll, *Blacking Up*, 51.

28. "The Dandy Broadway Swell," from *Christy's Plantation Melodies. Published Under the Authority of E.P. Christy, Originator of Ethiopian Minstrelsy and the First to Harmonize Negro Melodies* (New York and Philadelphia: Fisher and Brother, 1851); "Larned Nigger," from *Jasper Jack's Bran New Collection of the Musicalist Nigger Melodies as Eber Whar* (New York: T. W. Strong, n.d.), most likely from the early 1840s; for this phenomenon, see Toll, *Blacking Up*, 70; and David R. Roediger, *The Wages of Whiteness: Race and the Making of the American Working Class* (New York: Verso, 1991), 125.

29. "Conundrums," from *Charley White's Black Apollo Songster* (New York: Turner and Fisher, 1844); stump speech cited in Toll, *Blacking Up*, 70; "Jim Brown's Address to his Sogers," from *Christy's Plantation Melodies* (Philadelphia and New York: Fisher and Brothers, 1851).

30. On an emerging culture of refinement, see Richard Bushman, *The Refinement of America: Persons, Houses, Cities* (New York: Alfred A. Knopf, 1992), especially 64–65, 80–81.

31. *Ole Wirginny*, Boston, Leonard Deming, n.d., 1830s; *Jim Crow*, Boston, Leonard Deming, 1832.

32. *Jim Brown*, Boston, Leonard Deming, n.d., early 1830s.

33. *Coal Black Rose*, Boston, Leonard Deming, 1832; *Sambo's 'Dress to He Bredren*, n.p., n.d., early 1830s, possibly late 1820s; *Song of the Black Shakers. Sung Nightly with Tremendous Applause, by all the Ethiopian Bands in the City*, New York, n.p., n.d., mid-1830s.

34. For example, "Brandreth's Vegatable Pills," from *De Kickapoo Whoop; Or, Pee Dee Warbler, by Santaclaus* (New York: Elton and Harrison, n.d., early 1830s).

35. On African American uplift and associationalism, see Benjamin Quarles, *Black Abolitionists* (New York: Da Capo Press, 1969); "Jim Crow's Trip to a Nigger Meeting in New York," *De Kickapoo Whoop; Or, Pee Dee Warbler* (New York: Elton and Harrison, n.d., early 1830s).

36. Ronald G. Walters, *American Reformers, 1815–1860* (New York: Hill and Wang, 1978), 22; Anbinder, *Five Points*, 8–9.

37. "Voice of the Public Press—Causes of the Late Riots," *Liberator*, 26 July 1834; "The Riots in New-York, Gotten up by the 'Courier and Enquirer,' and the 'Commercial Advertiser,'" *Liberator*, 26 July 1834; "Riots in New-York," *Liberator*, 19 July 1834.

38. On this political coalition along with the perceived ties between English abolition and American antislavery, see the fourth book of Allen Nevins history of the Civil War era, *The Emergence of Lincoln*, vol. 2, *Prologue to Civil War, 1859–1861* (New York: Charles Scribner's Sons, 1950), 140–141; Noel Ignatiev, *How the Irish Became White* (New York: Routledge, 1995), 68. On the link between blackface and the Democratic Party, see Richard B. Stott, *Workers in the Metropolis: Class, Ethnicity, and Youth in Antebellum New York City* (Ithaca, NY: Cornell University Press, 1990), 236–242; and especially Alexander Saxton, *The Rise and Fall of the White Republic: Class Politics and Mass Culture in Nineteenth-Century America* (New York: Verso, 1990), 165 and passim.

39. "Riot at Chatham Street Chapel—From the Journal of Commerce," *Liberator*, 12 July 1834.

40. "Postscript—Another Riot at New-York," *Liberator*, 12 July 1834.

41. "From the New-York Papers of Saturday Morning, Continued Riots!," *Liberator*, 19 July 1834.

42. "From the New-York Papers of Friday Evening—Riots Continued," and "From the New-York Papers of Saturday Morning—Continued Riots!," *Liberator*, 19 July 1834; Leonard L. Richards, *"Gentlemen of Property and Standing": Anti-Abolition Mobs in Jacksonian America* (New York: Oxford University Press, 1970), 10, 27–33; Anbinder, *Five Points*, 8–12; Lott, *Love and Theft*, 131–132.

43. According to Richards, anti-abolition violence received little traction until abolition "became associated with amalgamation and Negro uplift"; Richards, *Gentlemen of Property and Standing*, 41; *Dinah Crow's Abolition, Or, The Grand Rumpus at the Bowery Theatre, Chatham Chapel, 5 Points, Tappans, &c. &c.*, Boston, Leonard Deming, 1834–1835.

44. *Dinah Crow's Abolition, Or, The Grand Rumpus at the Bowery Theatre, Chatham Chapel, 5 Points, Tappans, &c. &c.*, Boston, Leonard Deming, 1834–1835.

45. Nathan, *Dan Emmett and the Rise of Early Negro Minstrelsy*, 98–116.

46. Nathan, *Dan Emmett and the Rise of Early Negro Minstrelsy*, 116–122.

47. *Old Dan Tucker. Written and Arranged for Pianoforte by Dan. Tucker, Jr.*, New York: Atwill's Music, 1843.

48. "Old Paddy Whack," from *Deacon Snowball's Negro Melodies* (New York and Philadelphia: Turner and Fisher, 1843); "Ole Bull" and "Philadelphia Ole Bull and Ole Dan Tucker," from *Charles White's Black Apollo Songster* (New York: Tuner and Fisher, 1844); on the rise of the Virginia Minstrels and their changes in blackface style, see Cockrell, *Demons of Disorder*, 145–155.

49. On the appearance of the b'hoy, see Stott, *Workers in the Metropolis*, 223–225; Stuart Blumin, *The Emergence of the Middle Class* (New York: Cambridge University Press, 1989), 111; David C. Reynolds, *Beneath the American Renaissance: The Subversive Imagination in the Age of Emerson and Melville* (Cambridge, MA: Harvard University Press, 1988); Anbinder, *Five Points*, 178–181.

50. Foster, *New-York by Gas-Light*, 170–173.

51. Richard M. Dorson, "Mose the Far-Famed and World Renowned," *American Literature* 15, no. 3 (1943): 288–300; the quote appears on page 294.

52. Reverend R. W. Bailey, "The Working Man," *Southern Literary Messenger* 14, no. 10 (October 1848): 592–596, 592; for an example of how this assumption of working-class authenticity has affected historians, see Stott, *Workers in the Metropolis*, 274. For an analysis of how workers and writers of working-class literature used the image, see Michael Denning, *Mechanic Accents: Dime Novels and Working-Class Culture in America* (New York: Verso, 1987).

53. Anbinder, *Five Points*, 2, 34.

54. On the Sullivan–Hyer match, see Elliott J. Gorn, *The Manly Art of Boxing: Bare-Knuckle Prize Fighting in America* (Ithaca, NY: Cornell University Press, 1986), 83; on the Astor Place Riot, see Peter G. Buckley, "To the Opera House: Culture and Society in New York City, 1820–1860," PhD dissertation, SUNY Stony Brook, 1984; Dennis Berthold, "Class Acts: The Astor Place Riots and Melville's 'The Two Temples,'" *American Literature* 71, no. 3 (September 1999): 429–461; David Alexander Hyde, "Acting Reality: Culture, Identity, and Politics in the American Theater, 1849–1900," PhD dissertation, Rutgers University, 2004.

55. For a contemporary recognition between the European revolutions of 1848 and the California gold rush, see "California Gold and European Revolution," *Southern Quarterly Review* 17 (July 1850): 281–283, 298; "Oh California," from *California Songster* (San Francisco: Carter's Book and Stationary Company, 1855); also cited in Lott, *Love and Theft*, 205.

56. Lott, *Love and Theft*, 171, 180, 190–201; Stott, *Workers in the Metropolis*, 253; the term "The American 1848" originated with Michael Paul Rogin, *Subversive Genealogy: The Politics and Art of Herman Melville* (New York: Alfred A. Knopf, 1983).

57. "Emigration to California," *New York Herald*, 11 January 1849.

58. Robert P. Nevin, "Stephen Foster and Negro Minstrelsy," *Atlantic Monthly* 20 (November 1867): 608–616; see also John Tasker Howard, *Stephen Foster: America's Troubadour* (New York: 1953); Ken Emerson, *Doo Dah!: Stephen Foster and the Rise of American Popular Culture* (New York: Simon and Schuster, 1997).

59. "Oh Susanna," from *Christy's Ram's Horn Nigga Songster. As Sung by White's, Christy's, Harmonist's, Sable Brothers', and Dumbleton's Bands of Nigger Minstrels* (New York: Elton Publisher, 1849).

60. Stephen Foster to E. P. Christy, 25 May 1852, cited in Deanne L. Root, "Music and Community in the Civil War Era," in *Bugle Resounding: Music and Musicians of the Civil War Era*, ed. Bruce C. Kelly and Mark A. Snell (Columbia: University of Missouri Press, 2004), 37–53, 46.

61. On Douglass's newfound respect for blackface, or at least the blackface songs of Foster, see Scott Gac, *Singing for Freedom: The Hutchinson Family Singers and the Nineteenth-Century Culture of Reform* (New Haven, CT: Yale University Press, 2007), 202, 205.

62. *National Theatre. Rosina Meadows*, Boston, n.p., 1843; *Grand Concert by the Campanologians, or Band of Swiss Bell Ringers*, Worcester, 1849.

63. *Charles White's Black Apollo Songster* [1844], and *Christy's Ram's Horn Nigga Songster* [1849]; "Christy's Minstrels," *Daily Tribune* [NY], 12 March 1847.

64. "Christy's Minstrels," *Spirit of the Times* [NY], 16 October 1847; "Negro Minstrelsy—Ancient and Modern," *Putnam's Monthly Magazine of American Literature, Science, and Art* 5, no. 25 (January 1855): 72–79.

65. "Burlesque Political—Any Other Man," "Burlesque Stump Oration," from *Christy's New Songster and Black Joker, Containing All the Most Popular and Original Songs, Choruses, Stump Speeches, Witticisms, Jokes, Conundrums, etc. etc., As Sung and Delivered by the World-Renowned Christy's Minstrels, Compiled and Arranged by E. Byron Christy and William E. Christy Successors to the Late Edwin P. Christy* (New York: Dick and Fitzgerald, Publishers, 1863), 17–20.

66. "From Things Theatrical," *Spirit of the Times* [NY], 8 October 1853, 10 September 1853, 21 January 1854.

67. "Beware the Man Who Never Laughs," preface to *Charley White's New Book of Black Wit, Illustrated. Second Series of the Kind Ever Published. And Containing a Large Collection of Laughable Anecdotes, Jokes, Stories, Witticisms, Plantation and Dandy Darkie Conversations, &c.* (New York: Dick and Fitzgerald, Publishers, No. 18 Ann Street, 1856).

68. Parker Pillsbury, *Acts of the Anti-Slavery Apostles* (Concord and Rochester, NY: Clague, Wegman, Schlicht & Co., 1883), 237–239; "Fifth Annual Meeting of the Western N.Y. Anti-Slavery Society," *North Star*, 29 December 1848.

Chapter Seven

1. Asa Hutchinson, diary entries for 10 May 1843, in *Excelsior: Journals of the Hutchinson Family Singers, 1842–1846*, ed. Dale Cockrell (Stuyvesant, NY: Pendragon Press, 1989), 112, 113–122.

2. George C. Odell, *Annals of the New York Stage*, vols. 1–15, vol. 4 (New York: Columbia University Press, 1928), 684–685; "An Old Time Vocalist. Reminiscences of the Famous Hutchinson

Family," *Boston Herald*, 18 January 1891, Hutchinson Collection, MPL; John Wallace Hutchinson, *Story of the Hutchinsons*, vol. 1 (Boston: Lee and Shepard, 1896), 87–88.

3. Scott Gac, *Singing for Freedom: The Hutchinson Family Singers and the Nineteenth-Century Culture of Reform* (New Haven, CT: Yale University Press, 2007), 64–66; Cockrell, ed., *Excelsior*, 151–238.

4. "Call the Doctor, or, Anti-Calomel" [1843], lyrics taken from *The Granite Songster. Containing the Poetry as Sung by the Hutchinson Family, at their Concerts* (Boston: Published by A. B. Hutchinson, W. L. Bradbury, Printer, 1847); Gac, *Singing for Freedom*, 155–156.

5. These programs from 1842–1843 include *Grand Family Concert at the Cameneum. Positively the Last Night of Aeolian Vocalists*, Portsmouth, NH, n.p., 1842; *Sacred and Secular Concert By the Aeolian Vocalists. At the Universal Church*, Newburyport, MA, n.p., 1842; *Aeolians' Concert, At Brinley Hall on Tuesday Evening, September 26, The "Hutchinson Family,"* Worcester, Aegis Office, 1843; *Introductory Concert! By the Aeolian Vocalists, at Concert Hall, On Saturday Evening, May 13,* New York, Tribune Office—J. A. Fraetas, 1843; "Another Concert by the Aeolians—And Positively the Last, Before Going to the Mountains," *Boston Atlas* [advertisement], 2 June 1843.

6. From the *Philadelphia Christian Observer*, cited in *Our Paper. Thirty Years of Singing! Concert in this Place! Over a Quarter Century's Career of the Hutchinson Family*, four-page broadside, n.p., 1868, Hutchinson Family Collection, LHS; "The Hutchinson Family," *Syracuse Daily Journal*, 12 October 1848.

7. John Wallace Hutchinson, *Story of the Hutchinsons*, vol. 1, 83, 84, 86; this chapter is partly informed by the question raised the German sociologist Werner Sombart at the beginning of the twentieth century: "Why is there no socialism in the United States?" For an introduction to the issue, see Eric Foner, "Why is there no Socialism in the United States," *History Workshop* 17 (Spring 1984): 57–80; Foner suggests the reason might be that historians have come at the question from the standpoint of political history along with the assumption of a type of true socialism that can only come from the working class; according to this approach, middle-class socialism or middle-class reform-based socialism is relegated to a less-than-serious category of "utopianism," "romantic socialism," or even dabbling in a fad. For one of the most powerful examples of this approach, see John L. Thomas, "Romantic Reform in America, 1815–1865," *American Quarterly* 17, no. 4 (Winter 1965): 656–681; the approach in this chapter reflects an attempt to take middle-class socialism seriously by linking it to communal traditions and by identifying communism as a once-acceptable and even popular tenet of American tradition.

8. Barnum's story cited in Jack Larkin, *The Reshaping of Everyday Life, 1790–1840* (New York: Harper and Row, 1988), 39.

9. *Psalms and Odes, For the Fourth of July—1812*, New London, n.p., 1812; *July the Fourth, 1848. Order of Exercises at the North Congregational Church, Purchase Street, New Bedford, The Seventy-Second Anniversary of the Independence of the United States of America*, New Bedford, n.p., 1848.

10. *Grand City Celebration—July 4, 1848, Orders of the Day*, Lowell, James Atkinson—Office of the *Lowell Journal*, 1848.

11. [Review of] *"A Concise History of the United Society of Believers Called Shakers*, By Charles Edson Robinson, East Canterbury, N.H., 1893," *The Manufacturer and Builder: A Practical Journal of Industrial Progress* 25, no. 8 (August 1893): 191.

12. For this background on Ann Lee and the origins of the Shakers, see Stephen J. Stein, *The Shaker Experience in America: A History of the United Society of Believers* (New Haven, CT: Yale

University Press, 1992), 2–7; Richard Francis, *Ann the Word: The Story of Ann Lee, Female Messiah, Mother of the Shakers, the Woman Clothed with the Sun* (London: Fourth Estate Limited, 2000).

13. Stein, *The Shaker Experience*, 18–25; Anna White and Leila Taylor, *Shakerism, Its Meaning and Message: Embracing An Historical Account, Statement of Belief and Spiritual Experience of the Church from Its Rise to the Present Day* (Columbus, OH: Fred J. Heer, 1905), 47–67; Priscilla J. Brewer, *Shaker Communities, Shaker Lives* (Hanover, NH: University Press of New England, 1986).

14. For these beliefs, see McNemar, *The Kentucky Revival*; McNemar himself was one of the Shaker emissaries sent to witness the frontier revivals; White and Taylor, *Shakerism*; Shaker beliefs would be codified in Benjamin S. Youngs, *The Testimony of Christ's Second Appearing Containing a General Statement of All Things Pertaining to the Faith and Practice of the Church of God in this Latter-day* (Lebanon, OH: Press of John M'Clean, 1808); see also *Testimonies of the Life, Character, Revelations and Doctrines of Mother Ann Lee, and the Elders with Her, Through whom the Word of Eternal Life was opened in this day, of Christ's Second Appearing, Collected from the Living Witnesses, in Union with the Church* (Albany, NY: Weed, Parsons & Co., 1888).

15. "The Shakers," *North American Review* 16, no. 38 (January 1823): 76–102, 93.

16. The classic apostate account is Valentine Rathbun, *An Account of the Matter, Form, and Manner of a New and Strange Religion, Taught and Propagated by a Number of Europeans, Living in a Place called Nisqueunia, in the State of New-York* (Providence, RI: Bennett Wheeler, 1781).

17. McNemar, *The Kentucky Revival*, introduction, v; "The Shakers," 95.

18. For an account of Shaker history that stresses their settlements as keys to their attraction, see Charles Edson Robinson, *The Shakers and Their Homes: A Concise History of The United Society of Believers Called Shakers* (Somersworth, NH: New Hampshire Publishing Company, 1976); "The Shakers," 87, 90.

19. Edward D. Andrews, *The Gift to be Simple: Songs, Dances and Rituals of the American Shakers* (1940, reprint, New York: Dover Books, 1967), 143, 147–152.

20. Andrews, *The Gift to be Simple*, 145.

21. "The Shakers," 93; John Greenleaf Whittier to Elizabeth Neall [in Amesbury], 26 August 1839, from *The Letters of John Greenleaf Whittier*, vol. 1, *1828–1845*, ed. John B. Pickard (Cambridge, MA: Harvard University Press, 1975), 367.

22. On this act, see Andrews, *The Gift to be Simple*, 158–159; *Third and Last Entertainment By the Shaking Quakers! From Canterbury, N.H.*, New York, n.p., 1847.

23. Charles Nordhoff, *The Communistic Societies of the United States: From Personal Visit and Observation* (1875, reprint, New York: Dover, 1966), 11–22.

24. "The Indian's Lament," from *The Granite Songster. Containing the Poetry as Sung by the Hutchinson Family, at their Concerts* (Boston: A. B. Hutchinson and W. L. Bradbury, 1847).

25. Robert F. Berkhofer Jr., *The White Man's Indian: Images of the American Indian from Columbus to the Present* (New York: Random House, 1978), 86–90; Philip J. Deloria, "Revolution, Region, and Culture in Multicultural History," *William and Mary Quarterly*, 3rd ser., 53, no. 2 (April 1996): 363–366, 365.

26. On the frequency of "white Indians," see James Axtell, "The White Indians of Colonial America," in Stanley Katz and John M. Murrin, *Colonial America: Essays in Politics and Social Development*, 3rd ed. (New York: Alfred A. Knopf, 1983), 16–47.

27. *Psalms and Odes: For the Fourth of July—1812*, New London, n.p., 1812.

28. *American Bravery: Or, Great Britain, and Her Copper-Colored Allies Defeated*, Boston, Nathaniel Coverly Jr., 1814–1815; *The American Patriot's War Song, Or, An Appeal to Freemen*,

Boston, Nathaniel Coverly Jr., 1812–1814; *A Bloody Battle. Between the United States Troops Under the Command of Governor Harrison, and Several Tribes of Indians, Near Prophet's Town, November 7th, 1811*, Boston, Nathaniel Coverly Jr., 1811; *St. Clair's Defeat: A New Song*, Boston, n.p., 1791; *A Song, Called Crawford's Defeat By the Indians, On the Fourth Day of June, 1782*, Boston, n.p., 1791.

29. Reverend James Wallis Eastburn, A. M., "and his Friend," *Yamoyden, A Tale of the Wars of King Philip: In Six Cantos* (New York: James Eastburn–Clayton & Kingsland, 1820), 3–4.

30. *Circular: Addressed to the Benevolent Ladies of the United States*, Boston, n.p., 1829.

31. Linda Kerber, "The Abolitionist Perception of the Indian," *Journal of American History* 62, no. 2 (September 1975): 271–295, 273, 278.

32. *A Table of Indian Tribes of the United States, East of the Stony Mountains, Furnished by Albert Gallatin*, n.p., 1826; *Scenes in Indian Life*, Philadelphia, n.p., 1843; *Catlin's Indian Gallery (For a Few Evenings Only), At Armory Hall, Corner of Washington and West Streets*, Boston, n.p., 1838.

33. "Original and Genuine Indian Oil and Dye," *Boston Courier*, 27 June 1839; *Park Theatre: Mr. Forrest. Last Night But One of His Engagement. Tuesday Evening, March 30th, 1847, Will be Performed (by desire) the Indian Tragedy of Metamora*, New York, Herald Job Office, 1847; Sally L. Jones, "The First but Not the Last of the 'Vanishing Indians': Edwin Forrest and Mythic Re-Creations of the Native Population," in *Dressing in Feathers: The Construction of the Indian in American Popular Culture*, ed. Elizabeth Bird (Boulder: Westview Press, 1996), 13–27, 23–24.

34. *Programme of the Exhibitions of the Indian Warriors and Squaws, Now Performing Every Evening at the Boston Museum*, Boston, S. N. Dickinson, 1841.

35. Theodore Dwight, "An Indian Dance," *Dwight's American Magazine and Family Newspaper* [NY] 3, no. 33 (3 August 1847): 520; *Last Week of the Five Real Indians! At Peale's New-York Museum! Broadway, Opposite the City Hall*, New York, n.p., early 1840s.

36. *The Blue Juniata, or, Wild Roved an Indian Girl*, Lowell, MA, I. H. Welton, printer, 1849; *Where Are the Poor Indians, Composed by the Chief Kanenison*, Boston, n.p., 1840s.

37. *Indian Chief*, Boston, Leonard Deming, 1832.

38. Among the most popular satires of the emerging middle-class romance with Indians were the comic plays of John Brougham. One, *Metamora, or, The Last of the Pollywogs*, was a takeoff on Edwin Forrest's famed character; the other, *PO-CA-HON-TAS, or, The Gentle Savage*, poked fun at the American preference for romantic fiction over history. See John Brougham, Esq., *PO-CA-HON-TAS; or, The Gentle Savage, An Original Aboriginal Erratic Operatic Semi-Civilized and Demi-Savage Extravaganza, being a Per-Version of Ye Trewe and Wonderrefulle Hystroie of Ye Rennowned Princesse* (New York: Samuel French, 1858).

39. Mark Holloway, *Utopian Communities in America, 1680–1880* (Mineola, NY: Dover, 1966); Christopher Clark, *The Communitarian Moment: The Radical Challenge of the Northampton Association* (Amherst: University of Massachusetts Press, 1995), 2–3; Richard Francis, *Transcendental Utopias: Individual and Community at Brook Farm, Fruitlands, and Walden* (Ithaca, NY: Cornell University Press, 2007).

40. For background on Brook Farm, see Carl J. Guarneri, "Brook Farm and the Fourierist Phalanxes: Immediatism, Gradualism, and American Utopian Socialism," in *America's Communal Utopias*, ed. Donald E. Pitzer (Chapel Hill: University of North Carolina Press, 1997), 159–180; Lindsay Swift, *Brook Farm: Its Members, Scholars, and Visitors* (1961, reprint, Secaucus, NJ: Citadel Press, 1973); Edith Roelker Curtis, *A Season in Utopia: The Story of Brook Farm* (Nashville: Thomas Nelson and Sons, 1961); Katherine Burton, *Paradise Planters: The Story of Brook Farm* (London: Longmans, Green and Company, 1939); Robert W. Preucel and

Steven R. Pendery, "Envisioning Utopia: Transcendentalist and Fourierist Landscapes at Brook Farm, West Roxbury, Massachusetts," *Historical Archeology* 40, no. 1 (2006): 6–19.

41. George Ripley to Ralph Waldo Emerson, 9 November 1840, in *Autobiography of Brook Farm*, ed. Henry W. Sams (Englewood Cliffs, NJ: Prentice Hall, 1958), 5–8; see Richard Francis, "The Ideology of Brook Farm," *Studies in the American Renaissance* (1977): 1–48; Joel Myerson, "James Burrill Curtis and Brook Farm," *New England Quarterly* 51, no. 3 (September 1978): 396–423.

42. On the subjects of work and diversions at the farm, see Thomas Wentworth Higginson, *Cheerful Yesterdays* (1898, reprint, New York: Arno Press, 1968), 84–85; Joel Myerson, "Rebecca Codman Butterfield's Reminiscences of Brook Farm," *New England Quarterly* 65, no. 4 (December 1992): 603–630.

43. *Constitution of the Brook Farm Association For Industry and Education, West Roxbury, Mass., With An Introductory Statement. Second Edition, With The By-Laws of the Association*, Boston, I. R. Butts, Printer, 1844, 11, AAS.

44. *Constitution of the Brook Farm Association*, 11–20, AAS.

45. John Wallace Hutchinson, *Story of the Hutchinsons*, vol. 1, 83; George Willis Cooke, *John Sullivan Dwight: Brook Farmer, Editor, and Critic of Music* (Boston: Small, Maynard, and Company, 1898), 31–49, 59, 63; Thomas J. Wesley, "John Sullivan Dwight: A Translator of German Romanticism," *American Literature* 21, no. 4 (January 1950): 427–441.

46. Cooke, *John Sullivan Dwight*, 63, 77–80; John Sullivan Dwight, "Music as a Means of Culture," *Atlantic Monthly* 26 (July 1870): 321–331. The terminology comes from William Gardiner, *The Music of Nature; or, An Attempt to Prove That What is Passionate and Pleasing in the Art of Singing, Speaking, and Performing on Musical Instruments is Derived from the Sounds of the Animated World* (Boston: J. H. Wilkins & R. B. Carter, 1837).

47. Gardiner, *The Music of Nature*, 220–232, 241–248; *Boston Academy of Music. Fifth Concert, Saturday Evening, January 3, 1846*, Boston, Press of T. R. Marvin, 1846.

48. Manuscript, "Address in Musick," Israel Kimball Papers, 1837–1839, AAS; Kimball, who went on to become a music teacher in Maine and New Hampshire, wrote the address and delivered it while a student at Bowdoin College, most likely in 1839; Samuel Rush, *A Discourse on the Moral Influence of Sounds, Delivered Before the Chester County Cabinet of Natural Science, January 18th, 1839* (Philadelphia: n.p., 1839), 29, 31–32, 23; "Music A Peacemaker," *Musical Gazette* [Boston] 1, no. 8 (11 May 1846): 60.

49. Marianne Dwight, *Letters From Brook Farm, 1844–1847* (Poughkeepsie, NY: Vassar College, 1928), 121; Lydia Maria Child to Marianne Silsbee, New York, 5 February 1847, Lydia Maria Child Collection, AAS; Child was writing in reference to the concerts of the Norwegian violinist Ole Bull; see also Aaron McClendon, "'for not in words can it be spoken': John Sullivan Dwight's Transcendental Music Theory and Herman Melville's 'Pierre; or, The Ambiguities,'" *ATQ* 19, no. 1 (March 2005): 23–36, 26–28.

50. On the Hutchinsons' relationship with the White Mountains, see Gac, *Singing for Freedom*, 117–121, 135; Asa Hutchinson, *Book of Words of the Hutchinson Family; To Which is Added the Book of Brothers* (Boston: J. S. Potter, 1855), 13.

51. "The Hutchinson Family," article reprinted from the *New Englander*, by "Crayon," *North Star*, 5 December 1850.

52. John Wallace Hutchinson, *Story of the Hutchinsons*, vol. 1, 116, 136, 80.

53. For a criticism of Dwight as a cultural elitist, see Lawrence Levine, *Highbrow-Lowbrow: The Emergence of Cultural Hierarchy in America* (Cambridge, MA: Harvard University Press, 1988), 119–122; on this connection between Dwight as communist and promoter of an ideal of

music appreciation, see Thomas J. Wesley, "John Sullivan Dwight: A Translator of German Romanticism," *American Literature* 21, no. 4 (January 1950): 427–441, 437–440.

54. *Northampton Association of Education and Industry*, Northampton, n.p., 1842; Stephen Rush to Hall Judd [Secretary of the Association], 7 July 1846, Meeting, 29 August 1846, "Record of Proceedings of the Northampton Association of Education and Industry," MS folio volume, AAS.

55. Meeting, 26 September 1846, "Record of Proceedings of the Northampton Association of Education and Industry," MS folio volume, AAS; "Articles of Association," *Northampton Association of Education and Industry*, Northampton, n.p., 1842.

56. The best-known examples of this treatment of the "cult of domesticity" may be Barbara Welter, "The Cult of True Womanhood: 1820–1835," *American Quarterly* 18, no. 2 (1966): 151–174; Nancy Cott, *The Bonds of Womanhood: "Woman's Sphere" in New England, 1780–1835* (New Haven, CT: Yale University Press, 1977).

57. "Integrity of Business Men," *[Hunt's] Merchant's Magazine and Commercial Review* 20, no. 6 (June 1849): 682–683.

58. For an assessment of the home as a repository of traditional virtue, see Christopher Lasch, *Haven in a Heartless World: The Family Besieged* (New York: Basic Books, 1977); Lydia Maria Child, *Young Lady's Own Book* (1833).

59. "Husband, Turn," from *Anniversary Meeting of the St. Albans Temperance Society, Tuesday, February 23, 1836*, Saint Albans, VT, n.p., 1836; "From Our Cincinnati Correspondent. Father Mathew and the Temperance Cause," *National Era* [Washington, DC] 4, no. 203 (November 1850): 187; "Original Ode," *Order of Exercises at the Festival of the Daughters of Temperance, Bangor, March 4, 1847*, Bangor, Maine, n.p., 1847; "Solemn Appeal," *Order of Exercises for the Anniversary Meeting of the Ward Four Temperance Society, in the Church in Green Street, Sabbath Evening, March 15, 1835*, Boston, n.p., 1835.

60. These expert assessments of Lind came after her first American tour: *Grove's Dictionary of Music and Musicians*, vol. 3, 3rd ed. (original 1876, reprint, New York: Macmillan, 1948), 201–202; C. Villiers Stanford, "Three Centenaries: Jenny Lind, Pauline Viordot-Garcia, George Grove," *Music and Letters* 2, no. 1 (January 1921): 29–34, 32; "Jenny Lind's Singing Method," *Musical Quarterly* 3, no. 4 (October 1917): 548–551.

61. Bremer's biography of Lind would reappear in installments at the time of her arrival: "Jenny Lind, by Fredrika Bremer," Part 1, *National Era* 4, no. 195 (September 1850); "Nightingale and Enchantress," *North Star*, 16 March 1849; "European Correspondence—Berlin," *National Era*, 18 February 1850; "Power of Song," *North Star*, 7 April 1849.

62. For an overview of the Jenny Lind-mania, see Neil Harris, *The Art of P. T. Barnum* (Chicago: University of Chicago Press, 1973), 113–141; the story of the train conductor's response appears on pages 118–119; W. Porter Ware and Thaddeus C. Lockhard Jr., *P. T. Barnum Presents Jenny Lind: The American Tour of the Swedish Nightingale* (Baton Rouge: Louisiana State University Press, 1980), 1–24.

63. N. Parker Willis, *Memoranda of the Life of Jenny Lind* (Philadelphia: Robert E. Peterson, 1851), 76–77; the story of the first ticket appears in Ware and Lockhard, *P. T. Barnum Presents Jenny Lind*; it was also told in the text of concert programs: *Programme of Mademoiselle Jenny Lind's Concert* (Boston: White and Potter, 1850); "Movements of the Nightingale," *National Era*, 29 August 1850.

64. "Literary Notices," *National Era*, 27 June 1850; "Jenny Lind, by Fredrika Bremer," *National Era*, 26 September 1850; Willis, *Memoranda of the Life of Jenny Lind*, 78, 45; "Jenny Lind and the Cottagers," *North Star*, 25 February 1848.

65. Ware and Lockhard, *P. T. Barnum Presents Jenny Lind*, 18–24; *The Nightingale, Or, Jenny Lind Minstrel, Containing All the New Ballads, Swedish Melodies, and Gems of the Operas, as Sung by Mad'lle Jenny Lind* (New York: G. & S. Bunce, 1850); one of the programs for the first series of concerts, *The Life and Genius of Jenny Lind* (New York: W. F. Burgess, 1850); Keith S. Hambrick, "The Swedish Nightingale in New Orleans: Jenny Lind's Visit of 1851," *Louisiana History* 22, no. 4 (Autumn 1981): 387–417, 404.

66. "Lindiana," *North Star*, 3 October 1850; "Jenny Lind in Washington," *National Era*, 19 December 1850; the *Herald* quote cited in Francis Rogers, "Jenny Lind," *Musical Quarterly* 32, no. 3 (July 1946): 437–448, 444.

67. Willis, *Memoranda of the Life of Jenny Lind*; "Lindiana," *North Star*, 3 October 1850.

68. "Letter From New York," *National Era*, 31 October 1850; "Jenny Lind at Havana," *New York Tribune*, 20 March 1851.

69. "Letter No. XII—J. G.," *Frederick Douglass' Paper*, 31 July 1851; Willis, *Memoranda of the Life of Jenny Lind*, 140–141.

70. This meeting between Jenny Lind and the Hutchinsons is recounted in "Hutchinson Day—Historical and Genealogical Tribute to Distinguished People," *Milford Cabinet* [NH], 12 May 1904, Hutchinson Collection, MPL.

71. "From Our Cincinnati Correspondent—Father Matthew and the Temperance Cause— Jenny Lind in Cincinnati," *National Era*, 21 November 1850; Willis, *Memoranda of the Life of Jenny Lind*, 141, 158.

72. Hambrick, "The Swedish Nightingale in New Orleans," 387–388; "Jenny Lind and the Union," *National Era*, 26 December 1850.

73. "Jenny Lind and the Union," *National Era*, 26 December 1850; "Jenny Lind's Concerts," *Musical Times and Singing Class Circular* 4 (1 January 1851): 114.

74. *Mademoiselle Jenny Lind Will Give Her Fifth Grand Concert Since Her Return to New-York, at the Tripler Hall, on Friday Evening, November 1*, New York, Oliver and Brother Printers, Sun Building, n.d.; "Jenny Lind," *Sacramento Daily Bee*, 11 October 1867; *Grove's Dictionary of Music and Musicians*, 201; by the end of the nineteenth century, Lind's reputation appears to have recovered, see "Jenny Lind," *Musical Times and Singing Class Circular* 32 (1 July 1891): 393–394.

Chapter Eight

1. *Get Off the Track! A Song for Emancipation, Sung by The Hutchinsons, Respectfully dedicated to Nath'l. P. Rogers*, printed by the American Anti-Slavery Society, Boston, 1844; a typical criticism of the song may be found in "New Song," *Boston Atlas*, 18 April 1844; here, as elsewhere, the paper's editors expressed outrage at the song's criticism of Henry Clay, asked the singers to avoid abolition sentiments in their public concerts, and yet admitted that the song, or at least the tune, was catchy.

2. John Wallace Hutchinson, *Story of the Hutchinsons*, vol. 1 (Boston: Lee and Shepard, 1896), 138; "Story of the Song *Get Off the Track*," as written by Mrs. Abby [Hutchinson] Patton, undated manuscript, probably written by Ludlow Patton from a recalled conversation, Hutchinson Collection, MPL; John's account differed from Abby's only in the dates.

3. Harriet Martineau, *The Martyr Age of the United States* (Boston: Weeks, Jordan & Company—Otis Broaders and Company, 1839), 20–21; Parker Pillsbury, *Acts of the Anti-Slavery Apostles* (Concord, NH: Clague, Wegman, Schlicht, and Company, 1883), 292, iii–iv; this tradition dates back to the accounts of abolitionist's themselves; for writers such as Samuel May,

abolitionism's unpopularity imbued its supporters with heroic qualities; see Samuel J. May, *Some Recollections of Our Antislavery Conflict* (Boston, 1869, Reprint: New York: Arno Press, 1968); accordingly, historians have had an easy time finding "evidence" for public hatred of the movement in the abolitionists' own writings. The gloomy and useless abolitionists singing hymns in the rain followed by the later appearance of the pragmatic man of action who gets something done for the cause are a reference to the movie *Amistad* (Dreamworks Pictures, 1999).

4. For a recent depiction of abolitionists as heroes ahead of their time, see Henry Mayer, *All On Fire: William Lloyd Garrison and the Abolition of Slavery* (New York: Saint Martin's, 1998); for a treatment of abolitionists as fanatics and zealots, see Avery Craven, *The Coming of the Civil War* (Chicago: University of Chicago Press, 1957); as zealots and nativists, see James Brewer Stewart, *Holy Warriors: The Abolitionists and American Slavery* (New York: Hill and Wang, 1976); as sexually repressed hypocrites, see Ronald Walters, "The Erotic South: Civilization and Sexuality in American Abolitionism," *American Quarterly* 25 (1973): 177–201; as hopelessly split between factions, see Eric Foner, *Free Soil, Free Labor, Free Men: The Ideology of the Republican Party Before the Civil War* (New York: Oxford University Press, 1970). According to historian William Gienapp, the distinction between "anti-slavery" and "abolition" movements made true abolitionists simply too few and far between, resulting in an estimate that they comprised no more than one percent of the nation's population, a paltry 20,000 out of a total of 20 million Americans by 1860; see William E. Gienapp, "Abolition and the Nature of Antebellum Reform," in *Courage and Conscience: Black and White Abolitionists in Boston*, ed. Donald M. Jacobs (Bloomington: University of Indiana Press, 1993), 36.

5. Edward Magdol, *The Antislavery Rank and File: A Social Profile of the Abolitionists' Constituency* (Westport, CT: Greenwood Press, 1986); Julia Roy Jeffrey, *The Great Silent Army of Abolitionism: Ordinary Women in the Antislavery Movement* (Chapel Hill: University of North Carolina Press, 1998), 3, 6, 25.

6. "The Hutchinson Singers," *Herald of Freedom*, 9 December 1842, in N. P. Rogers, *A Collection from the Newspaper Writings of Nathaniel Peabody Rogers* (Concord, NH: John R. French, 1847), 244.

7. John Wallace Hutchinson, *Story of the Hutchinsons*, vol. 1, 95–96.

8. John Wallace Hutchinson, *Story of the Hutchinsons*, vol. 1, 32–33.

9. Harriet E. Wilson, *Our Nig; or, Sketches from the Life of a Free Black, In a Two-Story White House, North, Showing that Slavery's Shadows Fall Even There* (Boston: George C. Rand & Avery, 1859, reprint, New York: Vintage–Random House, 1983), preface, 25, 34–35, 64, 66, 82, 100–101, 129.

10. Wilson, *Our Nig*, 12–15; Barbara A. White, "'Our Nig' and the She-Devil: New Information About Harriet Wilson and the 'Bellmont' Family," *American Literature* 65, no. 1 (March 1993): 19–52, 19–24, 34–37.

11. White, "'Our Nig' and the She-Devil," 35, 37.

12. Jefferson, cited in David Brion Davis, *Antebellum American Culture: An Interpretive Anthology* (Lexington, MA: D. C. Heath, 1979), 276.

13. Allan Nevins, *Ordeal of the Union*, vol. 1, *Fruits of Manifest Destiny, 1847–1852* (New York: Charles Scribner's Sons, 1947), 137–139; *Address to the People of the United States, by a Committee of the New England Anti-Slavery Convention, Held in Boston on the 27th, 28th, and 29th of May, 1834* (Boston: Garrison and Knapp, 1834), 14–15.

14. *Declaration of the National Anti-Slavery Convention*, n.p., 1833, Whittier Collection, Special Collections, Haverhill, Massachusetts Public Library (HPL).

15. Leonard L. Richards, *The Slave Power: The Free North and Southern Domination, 1780–1860* (Baton Rouge: Louisiana State University Press, 2000), 136–137, 140; Jeffrey, *The Great Silent Army of Abolitionism*, 49–66; Nevins, *Ordeal of the Union*, 86–87.

16. William A. Koelsch, "Grass Roots Garrisonians in Central Massachusetts: The Case of Hubbardston's Jonas and Susan Clark," *Historical Journal of Massachusetts* 31 (Winter 2003): 73–89; *Fair . . . Fair!!!*, Syracuse, NY, n.p.., 1837, AAS; *The Eleventh Massachusetts Anti-Slavery Fair*, Boston, n.p., 1844, AAS.

17. *Anti-Slavery Celebration, July 4, 1839. Union Meeting House, Worcester*, Worcester, Spooner and Howland, Printers, 1839.

18. *Order of Exercises, At the Celebration of the Fifty-Sixth Anniversary of American Independence, By the New England Anti-Slavery Society, at Boylston Hall, July 4th, 1832*, Boston, n.p., 1832, AAS.

19. "Second Annual Report of the Lynn Female Anti-Slavery Society—Read, June 21st, 1837, by Abbey Kelly," Lynn Female Anti-Slavery Society, Record Book 1836–1838, LHS; 13 May 1839, Anti-Slavery Society of Greater Lynn, 1832–1839, Record Book, LHS; John Wallace Hutchinson, *Story of the Hutchinsons*, vol. 1, 70.

20. George A. Ramsdell, *The History of Milford* (Concord, NH: Rumford Press, 1901), 108–110.

21. Allan Nevins, *Ordeal of the Union, The Emergence of Lincoln*, vol. 1, *Douglas, Buchanan, and Party Chaos 1857–1859* (New York: Charles Scribner's Sons, 1950), 10–17; John Wallace Hutchinson, *Story of the Hutchinsons*, vol. 1, 57.

22. John A. Collins to Isaiah C. Ray, 25 May 1842; John A. Collins to H. B. Cowing [in Weymouth, MA], 18 January 1843; AAS [American Anti-Slavery Society] Office Boston, Slavery in the United States Collection, Box 1, Folder 5, AAS.

23. *The Old Granite State, A Song, Composed, Arranged and Sung by The Hutchinson Family*, Boston, Oliver Ditson, 1843; New York, Firth, Hall, and Pond, 1843.

24. Mayer, *All on Fire*, 321; Rogers, cited in John Wallace Hutchinson, *Story of the Hutchinsons*, vol. 1, 77.

25. Asa's diary entry along with the concerts in Washington cited in Dale Cockrell, *Excelsior: Journals of the Hutchinson Family Singers* (New York: Pendragon Press, 1989), 179–180; John Wallace Hutchinson, *Story of the Hutchinsons*, vol. 1, 106.

26. Cockrell, ed., *Excelsior*, 223.

27. George Fitzhugh, *Sociology for the South; or The Failure of Free Society* (Richmond: A. Morris, 1854), reprinted in *Ante-Bellum: Writings of George Fitzhugh and Hinton Helper on Slavery*, ed. Harvey Wish (New York: Capricorn Books, 1960), 95.

28. Jeffrey, *Great Silent Army of* Abolitionism, 25; Michel Chevalier, *Society, Manners, and Politics in the United States: Letters on North America by Michel Chevalier* (originally published, 1836, New York: Anchor Books, 1961), 349; William Chambers, *Things as They Are in America* [1857], cited in Davis, *Antebellum American Culture*, 278–282.

29. Martineau, *The Martyr Age of the United States*, 45; John Greenleaf Whittier, "Read at the Semi-Centennial Celebration of the American Anti-Slavery Society at Philadelphia on the 3rd December, 1883," in *The Anti-Slavery Convention of 1833: Old South Leaflet Number 81* (n.p., n.d.), pamphlet in Whittier Collection, HPL.

30. Allan Nevins, *The Emergence of Lincoln*, vol. 2, *Prologue to Civil War, 1859–1861* (New York: Charles Scribner's Sons, 1950), 139–141.

31. On the riots, see Leonard L. Richards, *"Gentlemen of Property and Standing": Anti-Abolition Mobs in Jacksonian America* (New York: Oxford University Press, 1970), 12.

32. Leonard L. Richards, *The Slave Power: The Free North and Southern Domination, 1780–1860* (Baton Rouge: Louisiana State University Press, 2000), 136–137, 140; Jeffrey, *The Great Silent Army of Abolitionism*, 49–66.

33. *Get Off The Track! A Song for Emancipation, Sung by The Hutchinsons, Respectfully dedicated to Nath'l. P. Rogers* (Boston: American Anti-Slavery Society, 1844); *The Granite Songster. Containing the Poetry as Sung by the Hutchinson Family, at their Concerts* (Boston: Published by A. B. Hutchinson, W. L. Bradbury, Printer, 1847); in this songster, "Get off the Track" is listed as a "Railway Song" with *"Words composed and adapted to a slave melody, advocating the emancipation of the slaves, and illustrating the onward progress of the anti slavery cause in the United States."*

34. "The Hutchinsons," *Herald of Freedom* [Concord, NH], 14 June 1844, in N. P. Rogers, *A Collection from the Newspaper Writings of Nathaniel Peabody Rogers*, 272.

35. Meyer, *All on Fire*, 329.

36. John A. Collins, *The Anti-Slavery Picknick: A Collection of Speeches, Poems, Dialogues and Songs; Intended for Use In Schools and Anti-Slavery Meetings* (Boston: H. W. Williams Printer, 25 Cornhill, 1842), 3–4, 98–99, 141–142.

37. Jairus Lincoln, *Anti-Slavery Melodies: For The Friends of Freedom. Prepared by the Hingham Anti-Slavery Society* (Hingham: Elijah B. Gill, 1843).

38. See, for example, George W. Clark, *The Liberty Minstrel* (New York: Leavitt & Alden, 1845); *The Anti-Slavery Harp: A Collection of Songs for Anti-Slavery Meetings. By William W. [Wells] Brown* (Boston: Bela Marsh, 1849).

39. Eliza E. Chase to Lucy Chase [in Philadelphia], Worcester, MA, 17 November 1843, Lucy Chase to Sarah Chase [undated, mid-1840s], Salem or Lynn, MA, Chase Family Papers, AAS.

40. John Wallace Hutchinson, *Story of the Hutchinsons*, vol. 1, 128.

41. John Wallace Hutchinson, *Story of the Hutchinsons*, vol. 1, 138; manuscript, "Story of Get Off the Track, as written by Mrs. Abby Patton," Hutchinson Collection, MPL.

42. The Hutchinsons," *New York Courier and Inquirer*, undated clipping [1847].

43. "The Hutchinson Family," *New York Day Book*, 12 April 1850; "A Few More Squints. The Hutchinsons," unidentified news clipping [circa April 1850], Hutchinson Collection, MPL.

44. "New Song," *Boston Atlas*, 18 April 1844.

45. "A Word of Advice," *Philadelphia Daily Sun*, 3 April 1848; "Southern Opinion of the Hutchinson Family," unidentified newspaper clipping, Hutchinson Collection, MPL; "Garrison's Nigger Minstrels," *New York Sunday Era* [April 1850], undated clipping, Hutchinson Collection, MPL.

46. Scott Gac calls this issue of integrating their concerts the most radical aspect of the singers' career; see Scott Gac, *Singing for Freedom: The Hutchinson Family Singers and the Nineteenth-Century Culture of Reform* (New Haven, CT: Yale University Press, 2007), 213–215; "A Word of Advice," *Philadelphia Daily Sun*, 3 April 1848; on the issue of miscegenation during this period, see Elise Lemire's excellent *"Miscegenation": Making Race in America* (Philadelphia: University of Pennsylvania Press, 2002).

47. "A Word of Advice," *Philadelphia Daily Sun*, 3 April 1848; "Southern Opinion of the Hutchinson Family," undated newspaper clipping, Hutchinson collection, MPL.

48. "Most Base and Disgraceful," undated newspaper clipping, Hutchinson Collection, MPL; "The Hutchinson Family—Hunkerism," *North Star*, 27 October 1848; "The Hutchinsons," *North Star*, 31 March 1848; "The Hutchinson—Colorphobia," *North Star*, 21 April 1848.

49. "The Hutchinsons—Colorphobia," *North Star*, 21 April 1848; "The Hutchinson Family, by Joe Linchpin," undated newspaper clipping, Hutchinson Collection, MPL; "Garrison's Nigger Minstrels," *New York Sunday Era* [April 1850], undated clipping, Hutchinson Collection, MPL.

50. Hutchinson, *Story of the Hutchinsons*, vol. 1, 92; "The Hutchinson Family, by Joe Linchpin," unidentified news clipping, Hutchinson Collection, MPL.

51. "The Hutchinson Family," *New York Day Book*, 12 April 1850; "The Hutchinsons," unidentified news clipping, Hutchinson Collection, MPL.

52. "Story of the Song *Get Off the Track*," as written by Mrs. Abby [Hutchinson] Patton, undated manuscript, Hutchinson Collection, MPL.

53. "Story of the Song *Get Off the Track*," as written by Mrs. Abby [Hutchinson] Patton, undated manuscript, MPL; John Wallace Hutchinson, *Story of the Hutchinsons*, vol. 1, 138.

54. John Wallace Hutchinson, *Story of the Hutchinsons*, vol. 1, 138.

55. John Wallace Hutchinson, *Story of the Hutchinsons*, vol. 1, 142, 145–216.

56. "A Word of Advice," *Philadelphia Daily Sun*, 3 April 1848; "Most Base and Disgraceful," unidentified newspaper clipping, Hutchinson Collection; quote from an article in the *Albany Knickerbocker* in "Shame on the Craven Presses of Philadelphia," *Pennsylvania Freeman*, 11 January 1847, Hutchinson Collection, Milford Public Library (MPL).

57. "Interdict Against the Freedom of Speech," *Philadelphia Sun*, 31 December 1846; "The Daily Sun," *Pennsylvania Freeman*, April 1848, Hutchinson Collection, MPL.

58. "The Hutchinsons," *Anti-Slavery Standard*, January 1847, Hutchinson Boxes, MPL.

59. "Hutchinson Day. Historical and Genealogical Tribute to Distinguished People," *Milford Cabinet*, 12 May 1904, Hutchinson Boxes, MPL; Broadside: *Music Made Subservient to the Advancement of Peace, Freedom, and Virtue*, Leicester, England, T. Cook, Printer, 1846; Broadside: *Grand Farewell (And Positively the Last) Concert of the HUTCHINSON FAMILY, June 13th, 1846*, Manchester, England, J. Cheetham, 1846; broadsides for the different branches of the Hutchinsons include *Concert. A Branch of the Hutchinson Family Associated with the Misses Caroline and Ellen Rogers, and Ossian E. Dodge*, Boston, White and Potter, 1849; *Concert. The Hutchinson Family. Concert! John W. (Nineteen Years Before the Public), Fannie B., Henry J., and Viola G. Hutchinson of the Hutchinson Family, At Washburn Hall, February 10th and 11th*, Worcester, J. H. and F. F. Farwell Steam Job Printers, 1860; *The Hutchinson Family! Asa B., Lizzie C., Abby, and Little Freddy, New Songs and Sentiments! With a Few Standard Favorites, at Washburn Hall, On Friday Evening, November 23, 1860*, Worcester, J. H. and F. F. Farwell, 1860; Judson's letter was published as "Letter from one of the 'Hutchinson Family,' Dated Lever Street, Manchester England, October 16, 1845," *Lynn Pioneer*, 1846, Hutchinson Boxes, MPL.

60. "Christy's Minstrels," *Daily Tribune* [NY], 12 March 1847; "Take Me Home," from *Christy's Plantation Melodies. Published Under the Authority of E.P. Christy, Originator of Ethiopian Minstrelsy, And the First to Harmonize Negro Melodies* (New York: Fisher and Brothers, 1851).

61. John Calhoun, "Speech on the Reception of Abolition Petitions, 1837," in Eric L. McKitrick, *Slavery Defended: The Views of the Old South* (Englewood Cliffs, NJ: Prentice-Hall, 1963), 12–13.

62. "I'se a Happy Darkie," *Christy's Plantation Melodies* (Philadelphia–New York: Fisher and Brothers, 1851).

63. "Happy Are We, Darkies So Gay," from *Charles White's Black Apollo Songster. Being a Collection of New Negro Melodies, Not to Be Found in Any Other Work, As Sung by Charles White,*

The Black Apollo, and Other Colored Savoyards (New York: Turner & Fisher, 74 Chatham Street, 1844); "Gay Is the Life of a Color'd Man" and "A Nigger's Life for Me," from *Buckley's Ethiopian Melodies Buckley's Ethiopian Melodies* (Philadelphia: A Winch, 1853).

64. "Democracy . . . A Confession," *Liberator*, 9 April 1847; "The Late Judson J. Hutchinson, G.W.P., Peterboro, N.Y., to the Editor," *New York Tribune*, 16 January 1859.

65. "Songs of the Blacks," *Dwight's Journal of Music* [Boston], 15 November 1856; "Negro Minstrelsy—Ancient and Modern," *Putnam's Magazine* 5, no 25 (January 1855): 72–79, 74.

66. Augustus B. Longstreet, *A Voice From the South: Comprising Letters from Georgia to Massachusetts, and to the Southern States* (Baltimore: Western Continent Press, 1847), 52.

67. Cornelia Tuthill, *When Are We Happiest: Or, The Little Camerons* (Boston: Crosby and Nichols, 1848), 1–3; John Campbell, *Negro-Mania: Being An Examination of the Falsely Assumed Equality of the Various Races of Men* (Philadelphia: Campbell and Power, 1851), 161–171; George Templeton Strong, diary entry for 5 October 1850, in *Diary of George Templeton Strong*, vol. 2, *The Turbulent Fifties* (New York: Macmillan, 1952), 22.

68. Jesse Hutchinson, "Free Soil Rally," "The Old Free States," from *Official Proceedings of the National Free Soil Convention, Assembled at Buffalo, N.Y. August 9th and 10th, 1848*, Buffalo, n.p., 1848.

69. John Wallace Hutchinson, *Story of the Hutchinsons*, vol. 1, 310, 317–319; "Ho! for California!," *Hutchinson Family's Book of Words* (New York: Baker, Godwin & Co., 1851); see also "Ho! for California!," in *The Songs of the Gold Rush*, ed. Richard A. Dwyer and Richard E. Lingenfelter (Berkeley: University of California Press, 1964), 15.

70. Elizabeth Candler, "The Nation's Guilt," William Lloyd Garrison, "Hope for the American Slaves," "Jubilee Song," from Broadside: *Celebration of British West India Emancipation, At Worcester, August 1, 1850*, Worcester, MA, n.p., 1850; "Rescue the Slave," from *Anti-Slavery Tracts* (Boston: American Anti-Slavery Society, 1855), 6.

71. *Negro Melodies No. 8: Buckley's Songs* (Philadelphia: A Winch, 1857); George Swaine Buckley, "Laughing Chorus" from *Buckley's Ethiopian Melodies* (Philadelphia: A Winch, 1853).

72. Mayer, *All on Fire*, 456–457; *No Slavery! Fourth of July!*, Worcester, MA, Earle and Drew printers, 1854; "From the Liberator—A Prompt Disclaimer," *Frederick Douglass' Paper*, 23 February 1855.

73. Harriet Beecher Stowe, *Uncle Tom's Cabin; or, Life Among the Lowly* (1852, reprint: New York: Penguin Classics, 1986), 103.

74. Diary entry for 12 January 1853, Asa Hutchinson Diary, AAS; Broadside-Program: *The Hutchinson Family at the Tabernacle, Thursday Evening, December 22, 1853*, New York: J. H. and F. F. Farwell, 1853; sheet music: *Little Topsy's Song, Words by Mrs. Eliza Cook, Composed by Asa B. Hutchinson, As Sung at the Concerts of the Hutchinson Family* (Boston: Oliver Ditson, 1853).

75. *Aunt Harriet Becha Stowe, Composed by Jno. H. Hewitt* (Baltimore: H. McCaffrey, 1853).

76. Nehemiah Adams, D.D., *A South-Side View of Slavery; Or, Three Months at the South, in 1854* (Boston: T.R. Marvin, 1854), 15, 211–213.

77. William L. G. Smith, *Life at the South, or, "Uncle Tom's Cabin" As It Is. Being Narratives, Scenes, and Incidents in the Real "Life of the Lowly"* (Buffalo: George H. Derby and Co., 1852), 53–56;

78. Drew Gilpin Faust, *The Creation of Confederate Nationalism: Ideology and Identity in the Civil War South* (Baton Rouge: Louisiana State University Press, 1989), 65–67; [A Down East Music Teacher], "Letter from a Teacher at the South," *Dwight's Journal of Music*, 2 February 1853.

79. On domestic feminism along with Child's pioneering of the concept and its role in reform, see Mary Kelley, *Private Woman, Public Stage: Literary Domesticity in Nineteenth-Century*

America (New York: Oxford University Press, 1984), 15, 319–320; Jean Fagan Yellin, *Women and Sisters: The Antislavery Feminists in American Culture* (New Haven, CT: Yale University Press), 34, 53–76.

80. For an excellent survey of Child's importance to the period, see Carolyn L. Karcher, *The First Woman in the Republic: A Cultural Biography of Lydia Maria Child* (Durham, NC: Duke University Press, 1994); for examples of Child's writings, see Lydia Maria Child, *An Appeal in Favor of that Class of Americans Called Africans* (Boston: Allen and Tickner, 1833); [L. M. Child], *Authentic Anecdotes of American Slavery* (Newburyport, MA: Charles Whipple, 1835). A good example of Child as the inspiration for a young reformer at the time may be seen in Thomas Wentworth Higginson, *Cheerful Yesterdays* (Boston: Houghton Mifflin, 1898), 102, 126; Higginson cited her as his entry into both transcendentalism and antislavery.

81. Lydia Maria Child, *Anti-Slavery Catechism, By Mrs. Child* (Newburyport: Charles Whipple, 1836), 25–26.

82. Lydia Maria Child to Marianne Cabot Devereaux Sillsbee, New York, 5 February 1847; Child to Sillsbee, New York, 5 January 1848, Letters of Lydia Maria Child, Manuscript Collections, AAS.

83. Child to Sillsbee, New Rochelle, 6 February 1849; Child to Sillsbee, New Rochelle, 3 March 1849; Child to Sillsbee, 1 March 1851; Child to Sillsbee, 1 February 1857, Letters of Lydia Maria Child, Manuscript Collections, AAS.

84. Child to Sillsbee, Wayland [MA], 3 May 1857; Child to Sillsbee, Wayland, 11 September 1857, Letters of Lydia Maria Child, Manuscript Collections, AAS; this collection suggests that Child did send her friend one more communication: an invitation, dated January 1860, to the "Twenty-Sixth National Anti-Slavery Subscription Anniversary."

Chapter Nine

1. Ralph Keeler, "Three Years as a Negro Minstrel," *Atlantic Monthly* 24 (1869): 71–85.

2. This idea that the social construction of blackness was also the construction of the consumer is distilled from a variety of sources: Herbert Marcuse, *Eros and Civilization: A Philosophical Inquiry into Freud* (New York: Random House, 1962), discusses the reappearance of repressed sexual longing in consumerism, 40–49. Several historians have discussed the problem created by the disjuncture between the development of a white and middle-class culture of self-control simultaneous with the market's valorization of desire, appetite, passion, and impulse; see, for example, Thomas Richards, *The Commodity Culture of Victorian England: Advertising and Spectacle, 1851–1914* (Palo Alto, CA: Stanford University Press, 1990), 119–167; Amy Dru Stanley, "Home Life and the Morality of the Market," in *The Market Revolution in America: Social, Political, and Religious Expressions, 1800–1880*, ed. Melvyn Stokes and Stephen Conway (Charlottesville: University Press of Virginia, 1996), 74–96; Martin J. Wiener, "Market Culture, Reckless Passion and the Victorian Reconstruction of Punishment," in *The Culture of the Market: Historical Essays*, ed. Thomas Haskell and Richard F. Teichgraeber (New York: Cambridge University Press, 1993), 136–130. Finally, for two of the best works on the long history of African Americans as sources of projected white desires and corridors for the white expression of impulse and passion, see Ronald G. Walters, "The Erotic South: Civilization and Sexuality in American Abolitionism," *American Quarterly* 25, no. 2 (May 1973): 177–201; David R. Roediger, *The Wages of Whiteness: Race and the Making of the American Working Class* (New York: Verso, 1991), 118–125.

3. For this picture of the Civil War as national watershed, see James M. McPherson's three-volume history, *Ordeal By Fire: The Civil War and Reconstruction* (New York: Alfred A. Knopf, 1982); James M. McPherson, *Battle Cry of Freedom: The Civil War Era* (New York: Oxford University Press, 1988); see also Allan Nevins, *The War for the Union*, vols. 1–4 (New York: Charles Scribner's Sons, 1959).

4. For one of the most detailed accounts of the points of contact between Union and Confederate culture, see Edward L. Ayers, *In the Presence of Mine Enemies: War in the Heart of America 1859–1863* (New York: W. W. Norton, 2003).

5. For a brief survey of Civil War–era music, see Bruce C. Kelly, " 'Old Times There are not Forgotten': An Overview of Music of the Civil War Era," in *Bugle Resounding: Music and Musicians of the Civil War Era*, ed. Bruce C. Kelly and Mark A. Snell (Columbia: University of Missouri Press, 2004), 1–36; see also Christian McWhirter, *Battle Hymns: The Power and Popularity of Music in the Civil War* (Chapel Hill: University of North Carolina Press, 2012), 99–100.

6. An example of the Root and Sons manipulation of songwriters is George F. Root to Samuel Elias Staples, Chicago, 18 February 1888, Samuel Elias Staples Collection, AAS; Root sent the letter on company stationery indicating its continued marketing of the war songs "Just Before the Battle," "The Vacant Chair," and "The Battle Cry of Freedom." Staples was an amateur hymnist who in response to the lure of having his work published, appears to have sent Root and Company a number of hymns. In the end, after he sent the company a fee, apparently to review the material, his hymns were rejected.

7. *Harp of Freedom, A New and Superior Collection of Anti-Slavery, Patriotic and "Contraband" Songs, Solos, Duets and Choruses* (New York: Horace Waters, 1862), 1.

8. For one of the more recent and popular accounts of the ways Abraham Lincoln navigated these difficulties, see Doris Kearns Goodwin, *Team of Rivals: The Political Genius of Abraham Lincoln* (New York: Simon and Schuster, 2005); on the politics against putting the war on an antislavery footing, see Jennifer L. Weber, *Copperheads: The Rise and Fall of Lincoln's Opponents in the North* (New York: Oxford University Press, 2006).

9. William Wells Brown, George Downing, Charles L. Remond, "New England Anti-Slavery Convention, Thursday, May 28–Saturday, May 30, 1863," *Liberator*, 5 June 1863; [Joshua Hutchinson], *The Book of Brothers*, 2nd ser. (Boston: Franklin Printing House, 1864), 11, 22.

10. Permit signed "Simon Cameron, Secretary of War, War Department, January 14, 1862," Hutchinson Collection, LHS.

11. Lydia Maria Child to Mr. John Hutchinson, Wayland [MA], 19 January 1862, Hutchinson Scrapbook, LHS; John W. Hutchinson, *A History of the Adventures of John W. Hutchinson and his Family in the Camps of the Army of the Potomac* (Boston: Franklin Printing House, 1864), 11–12.

12. *"The Furnace Blast, or 'Prohibited Song,' As Sung by the Hutchinson Family to the Soldiers of the 'Army of the Potomac,' "* words by J. G. Whittier, Esq., music by John W. Hutchinson (New York: Firth, Pond, & Co., 1862).

13. John G. Whittier to John W. Hutchinson, Amesbury [MA], 6 March 1862, Hutchinson Collection, LHS.

14. "T.G.A." to Mary Livermore, Fairfax Court House, Virginia, 18 January 1862, in Mary Livermore, *My Story of the War* (1889, reprint, New York: Arno Press, 1972), 640–641.

15. The details of this story are taken from John Hutchinson's records, as well as McWhirter, *Battle Hymns*, 8–10.

16. Hutchinson, *A History of the Adventures of John W. Hutchinson*, 14; "Brigadier Gen. Franklin" and "Joseph C. Jackson, A.D.C.," to "Major Hatfield," Alexandria, VA, 18 January 1862; Hutchinson

Collection, LHS; "By Order of Brig. Gen'l Franklin," Head Quarters, Alexandria, VA, 18 January 1862, Hutchinson Collection, LHS.

17. McWhirter, *Battle Hymns*, 9–11; Hutchinson, *Book of Brothers*, 17; Field Communication: "Brig. Gen'l. J.T. Kearny," 19 January 1862, Hutchinson Collection, LHS.

18. See Willie Lee Rose, *Rehearsal for Reconstruction: The Port Royal Experiment* (New York: Oxford University Press, 1964); Eric Foner, *Reconstruction: America's Unfinished Revolution, 1863–1877* (New York: Harper and Row, 1988), 51–54; Laura Wood Roper, "Frederick Law Olmstead and the Port Royal Experiment," *Journal of Southern History* 31, no. 3 (August 1965): 272–284; William H. Pease, "Three Years Among the Freedmen: William C. Gannett and the Port Royal Experiment," *Journal of Negro History* 42, no. 2 (April 1957): 98–117.

19. For background on Higginson along with a romantic account of his early reform activities, see Anna Mary Wells, *Dear Preceptor: The Life and Times of Thomas Wentworth Higginson* (Boston: Houghton Mifflin, 1963); for Higginson's involvement with Brown, see Richard J. Hinton, *John Brown and His Men* (New York: Arno Press, 1968); David S. Reynolds, *John Brown, Abolitionist: The Man who Killed Slavery, Sparked the Civil War, and Seeded Civil Rights* (New York: Random House, 2006); Jeffrey Rossbach, *Ambivalent Conspirators: John Brown, the Secret Six, and a Theory of Slave Violence* (Philadelphia: University of Pennsylvania Press, 1983); for Higginson's own writings on these and other adventures, see Christopher Looby, ed., *The Complete Civil War Journal and Selected Letters of Thomas Wentworth Higginson* (Chicago: University of Chicago Press, 2000).

20. On Higginson's transition from minister to militant antislavery agitator to military officer, see Ethan J. Kytle, "From Body Reform to Reforming the Body Politic: Transcendentalism and the Militant Antislavery Career of Thomas Wentworth Higginson," *American Nineteenth Century History* 8, no. 3 (September 2007): 325–350.

21. Thomas Wentworth Higginson, *Army Life in a Black Regiment* (1870, reprint, New York: Penguin Books, 1997), 2–3.

22. Higginson, *Army Life in a Black Regiment*, 6–7, 93, 149, 13–16.

23. See Marc A. Bauch, *Extending the Canon: Thomas Wentworth Higginson and African American Spirituals* (Munich, Germany: Grin Publishing, 2013).

24. See Rose, *Rehearsal for Reconstruction*; Akiko Ochiai, "The Port Royal Experiment Revisited: Northern Visions of Reconstruction and the Land Question," *New England Quarterly* 74, no. 1 (March 2001): 94–117, 96–99; James Miller M'Kim, *The Freedmen of South Carolina: An Address to the Port Royal Relief Committee, July 9, 1862* (Philadelphia: Willis P. Hazard, 1 862), 1–3.

25. Sarah Chase to Mrs. May [in Worcester, MA], Savannah Wharf, GA, 1 December 1865, Columbus, GA, 5 February 1866, Chase Family Papers, Box 1, Folder 9, AAS; Foner, *Reconstruction*, 53; Elizabeth Ware Pearson, ed., *Letters from Port Royal, 1862–1868* (Reprint, New York: Arno Press, 1969), 75, 18.

26. Lucy Chase to "Folks at Home," Craney Island, "South Carolina," 15 January 1863 and 29 January 1863, Chase Family Papers, Box 4, Folder 1, AAS; M'Kim, *Freedmen of South Carolina*, 15.

27. "The Negro Boatman's Song, Words by J. G. Whittier, Esq., Music by L. O. Emerson," *Ethiopian and Comic Songs* (Boston: Oliver Ditson & Company, 1862), Whittier Collection, HPL; for the various names of the song, see Thomas Franklin Currier, *A Bibliography of John Greenleaf Whittier* (Cambridge, MA: Harvard University Press, 1937), 91, 582; *Song of the Negro Boatman*, words by John Greenleaf Whittier, Esq. (Boston: Russell & Talman, 1862): this version of the

song listed the music as by "E. W. Kellog"; others would list music by Ferdinand Mayer, H. T. Merrill, and S. K. Whiting.

28. Harriet W. F. Hawley to J. G. Whittier, Hartford, Connecticut, 20 March 1864, Whittier Papers, Correspondence Received, Box 3, Folder 2, PEM.

29. "A New Plantation Song," *Songs for the Times* (n.p., n.d.): the collection lists the book's date as 1862, Whittier Collection, HPL.

30. Lydia Maria Child to John G. Whittier, Wayland [MA], 21 January 1862, *Letters of Lydia Maria Child, with Biographical Introduction by John G. Whittier and an Appendix by Wendell Phillips* (Boston: Houghton Mifflin, 1883), 159–162, 160.

31. On the "Leg Show," see Robert C. Allen, *Horrible Prettiness: Burlesque and American Culture* (Chapel Hill: University of North Carolina Press, 1991), 110–114; Olive Logan, "The Leg Business," *Galaxy*, (August 1867): 40–44.

32. *Grand National Allegory and Tableaux: The Great Rebellion, Written Expressly for J. M. Hager's Grand Entertainments* (Buffalo, NY: Matthews and Warren, 1865); for an analysis of the popularity of large-scale pageants in the decades after the Civil War, see David Glassberg, *Sense of History: The Place of the Past in American Life* (Amherst: University of Massachusetts Press, 2001).

33. William Francis Allen, Charles Pickard Ware, and Lucy McKim Garrison, *Slave Songs of the United States* (New York: Simpson and Company, 1867), introduction, i–ii.

34. "Run, Nigger, Run!," in Allen, Ware, and Garrison, *Slave Songs of the United States*, 89.

35. Allen, Ware, and Garrison, *Slave Songs of the United States*, introduction, xiii–xiv.

36. *Appleton's Hand-Book of American Travel. The Southern Tour; Being a Guide through Maryland, District of Columbia, Virginia, North Carolina, South Carolina, Georgia, Florida, Alabama, Mississippi, Louisiana, Texas, Arkansas, Tennessee, and Kentucky. With Descriptive Sketches of the Cities, Towns, Waterfalls, Battle-Fields, Mountains, Rivers, Lakes*, by Edward H. Hall (New York: D. Appleton & Co., 1866), 35–36, 61, 105; for an analysis of Northern tourism in the South, see Nina Silber, *The Romance of Reunion: Northerners and the South, 1865–1900* (Chapel Hill: University of North Carolina Press, 1993).

37. Sarah Earle Chase to [family in Worcester, MA], Richmond, VA, 18 April 1865; Sarah Chase to "Mrs. May" [Worcester], Norfolk, VA, 25 May 1865, and Sarah Chase to "Mrs. May" [Worcester], "Savannah Wharf," GA, 1 December 1865, Chase Family Papers, Box 1, Folder 9, AAS; S. S. Jocelyn to Lucy Chase [in Richmond], AMA Office, New York City, 26 February 1868, Chase Family Papers, Box 2, Folder 7, AAS.

38. Frederick Douglass, "What the Black Man Wants," in *The Equality of All Men Before the Law Claimed and Defended; In Speeches By Hon. William D. Kelley, Wendell Phillips, and Frederick Douglass* (Boston: Rand & Avery, 1865), 39.

39. George Cable, "The Freedman's Case in Equity," *Century Magazine* (January 1885), in Cable, *The Negro Question: A Selection of Writings on Civil Rights in the South* (Garden City, NJ: Doubleday–Anchor, 1958), 51–54.

40. One of the best contemporary accounts of anti–civil rights violence during Reconstruction, along with how the so-called "Mississippi Plan" worked, is Albert Talmon Morgan, *Yazoo; or, On the Picket Line of Freedom in the South, A Personal Narrative* (1884, reprint, New York: Russell and Russell, 1968); on the violence of the Klan and other racist organizations, see Allen W. Trelease, *White Terror: The Ku Klux Klan Conspiracy and Southern Reconstruction* (New York: Harper and Row, 1971); David M. Chalmers, *Hooded Americanism: The First Century of*

the Ku Klux Klan, 1865–1965 (Garden City, NY: Doubleday, 1965); on the rise of lynching during Reconstruction and the Progressive era, see Paula Giddings, *Ida, a Sword Among Lions: Ida B. Wells and the Campaign Against Lynching* (New York: Amistad, 2008); Russell K. Brown, "Post Civil War Violence in Augusta, Georgia," *Georgia Historical Quarterly* 90, no. 2 (Summer 2006): 196–213.

41. On the transnational spread of blackface, see Sarah Meer, *Uncle Tom Mania: Slavery, Minstrelsy, and Transatlantic Culture in the 1850s* (Athens: University of Georgia Press, 2005); Robert Nowatski, *Representing African Americans in Transatlantic Abolitionism and Blackface Minstrelsy* (Baton Rouge: Louisiana University Press, 2010); Erik Simpson, *Literary Minstrelsy, 1770–1830: Minstrels and Improvisers in British, Irish, and American Literature* (New York: Palgrave, 2008); on changes in stage productions of "Uncle Tom's Cabin," see David Grimsted, "Uncle Tom from Page to Stage: Limitations of Nineteenth-Century Drama," *Quarterly Journal of Speech* 56, no. 3 (October 1970): 325–335; Thomas L. Riis, "The Music and Musicians in Nineteenth-Century Productions of Uncle Tom's Cabin," *American Music* 4, no. 3 (Autumn 1986): 268–286; Michele Wallace, "Uncle Tom's Cabin: Before and After the Jim Crow Era," *TDR* 44, no. 1 (Spring 2000): 136–156.

42. Harry B. Warner, *The Poor Old Slave, or Plantation Life Before the War. A Dramatic Sketch* (San Francisco: Warner and Company, 1872), 3, 6–18.

43. Rev. H. R. Hawais, M.A., *Music and Morals* (New York: Harper and Brothers, 1872), 429–430.

44. See, for example, Armistead Churchill Gordon and Thomas Nelson Page, *Befo' de War: Echos in Negro Dialect* (New York: Scribner's, 1888); Reverend John C. Williams, *De Old Plantation* (Charleston: Evans and Cogswell, 1896); Miss Howard Weeden, *Songs of the Old South* (New York: Doubleday, 1900); Archibald Rutledge, *Tom and I on the Old Plantation* (New York: Frederick A. Stokes, 1918); Dorothy Scarborough, *From a Southern Porch* (New York: Putnam's, 1919); DuBose Heyward, *Mamba's Daughters* (New York: Doubleday, 1929); Julia Mood Peterkin, *Roll, Jordan, Roll* (New York: R. O. Ballou, 1933).

45. On Harris's background, see W. J. Rorabaugh, "When was Joel Chandler Harris Born? Some New Evidence," *Southern Literary Journal* 17, no. 1 (Fall 1984): 92–95; Robert Hemenway, "Introduction: Author, Teller, and Hero," in Joel Chandler Harris, *Uncle Remus, His Songs and His Sayings* (1880, Reprint, New York: Penguin Books, 1982), 7–31.

46. Hemenway, "Introduction," *Uncle Remus*, 8, 11; Michael Price, "Back to the Briar Patch: Joel Chandler Harris and the Literary Defense of Paternalism," *Georgia Historical Quarterly* 81, no. 3 (Fall 1997): 686–712; Robert Cochran, "Black Father: The Subversive Achievement of Joel Chandler Harris," *African American Review* 38, no. 1 (Spring 2004): 21–34; Joseph M. Griska Jr., "Uncle Remus Correspondence: The Development and Reception of Joel Chandler Harris's Writing, 1880–1885," *American Literary Realism, 1870–1910* 14, no. 1 (Spring 1981): 26–37.

47. Harris, "My Story of the War," *Uncle Remus*, 177–185.

48. Harris, "As to Education," *Uncle Remus*, 215–216.

49. Hemenway, "Introduction," *Uncle Remus*, 13–14; Harris, "Introduction," *Uncle Remus*, 40; John C. Inscoe, "The Confederate Home Front Sanitized: Joel Chandler Harris' *On The Plantation* and Sectional Reconciliation," *Georgia Historical Quarterly* 76, no. 3 (Fall 1992): 652–674; Wayne Mixon, "The Ultimate Irrelevance of Race: Joel Chandler Harris and Uncle Remus in their Time," *Journal of Southern History* 56, no. 3 (August 1990): 457–480.

50. Frederick Douglass, "The Negro in the Present Political Campaign," *Lion's Herald* [Boston], vol. 70, 28 September 1892.

51. George C. Rable, *But There Was No Peace: The Role of Violence in the Politics of Reconstruction* (Athens: University of Georgia Press, 1984); Samuel Denny Smith, *The Negro in Congress, 1870–1901* (Chapel Hill: University of North Carolina Press, 1940); William Gillette, *Retreat From Reconstruction, 1869–1879* (Baton Rouge: Louisiana State University Press, 1979).

52. John Whitson Cell, *The Highest Stage of White Supremacy: The Origins of Segregation in South Africa and the American South* (New York: Cambridge University Press, 1982); on the origins of segregation, see the classic C. Vann Woodward, *The Strange Career of Jim Crow* (New York: Oxford University Press, 1974).

53. "A Common Brotherhood. Evils Chargeable to the Strife of Race and Color. The Bases of Hon. Frederick Douglass' Address as the Colored High School Commencement—He Talks About Resistance to the Rise of the Negro," *Baltimore American*, 23 June 1894.

54. Douglass, "The Negro in the Present Political Campaign."

55. Editorial: "Minstrelsy and Cake Walks," *Cleveland Gazette*, 21 January 1899.

56. Background on White from J. B. T. Marsh, *The Story of the Jubilee Singers; With their Songs*, rev. ed. (Boston: Houghton, Osgood and Company–Riverside Press, 1880), 12–13, 43–44.

57. Marsh, *The Story of the Jubilee Singers*, 6–7, 45.

58. For background on the Jubilee Singers, see Andrew Ward, *Dark Midnight When I Rise: The Story of the Jubilee Singers, Who Introduced the World to the Music of Black America* (New York: Farrar, Straus and Giroux, 2000); Tim Brooks, " 'Might Take One Disk of this Trash as a Novelty': Early Recordings by the Fisk Jubilee Singers and the Popularization of 'Negro Folk Music,' " *American Music* 18, no. 3 (Autumn 2000): 278–316; Dale Cockrell, "Of Gospel Hymns, Minstrel Shows, and Jubilee Singers: Toward Some Black South African Musics," *American Music* 5, no. 4 (Winter 1997): 417–432; Dena Epstein, "Black Spirituals: Their Emergence into Public Knowledge," *Black Music Research Journal* 10, no. 1 (Spring 1990): 58–64.

59. Gustavus D. Pike, *The Jubilee Singers, And their Campaign for Twenty Thousand Dollars* (Boston: Lea and Shepard, 1873), 107; *The Slave Songs of the Fisk Jubilee Singers, With Biographical, Illustrative, and Critical Notes* (London: W. H. Guest, 1874), 10–38.

60. Pike, *The Jubilee Singers*, 153.

61. *Slave Songs of the Fisk Jubilee Singers*, 5.

62. Cuyler's review appeared in a letter to the *New York Tribune*, 17 January 1872, in Pike, *The Jubilee Singers*, 118; Beecher's appeared in an article, "The Negro Christian Minstrels," *Christian World*, 18 April 1873, cited in *The Slave Songs of the Fisk Jubilee Singers*, 8.

63. *Slave Songs of the Fisk Jubilee Singers*, 6, 10–11; Marsh, *Story of the Jubilee Singers*, preface.

64. Marsh, *Story of the Jubilee Singers*, 37; *Slave Songs of the Fisk Jubilee Singers*, 4; Edward Wagenknecht, *John Greenleaf Whittier: A Portrait in Paradox* (New York: Oxford University Press, 1967), 34–35; Program: *Ten New and Popular American Slave Songs; Being the Additional New Songs of the Jubilee Singers, Reprinted from the American Edition Now Selling in London* (London: W. M. Symons, 1875), puffs on the back cover.

65. *The Most Popular Plantation Songs, Selected and Arranged by Gilbert Clifford Noble, AB (Harvard)* (New York: Hinds, Hayden, & Eldridge, 1911), table of contents and preface.

66. W. E. B. DuBois, *The Souls of Black Folk* (1903, reprint, New York: Dover, 1994), 155; *Jubilee and Plantation Songs, Characteristic Favorites, As Sung by the Hampton Students, Jubilee Singers, Fisk University Students, and Other Concert Companies* (Boston: Oliver Ditson, 1915), 22, 57.

67. George Cable, "The Freedman's Case in Equity," *Century Magazine* (January 1885), and "The Negro Question," *New York Tribune*, March 1888, in Cable, *The Negro Question*, 51, 126.

68. George W. Cable, "Creole Love Songs," *Century Magazine* 31, no. 6 (April 1886): 807–828, 809–810.

69. See John Burnham, *Bad Habits: Drinking, Smoking, Taking Drugs, Gambling, Sexual Misbehavior, and Swearing in American History* (New York: New York University Press, 1993); Burnham's flawed but eye-opening analysis connects the development of America's consumer culture to a rise of what he calls a "Vice-Industrial Complex," an amalgam of industry and culture leaders devoted to producing and promoting the bad habits of his title. The promotion of bad habits, he claims, involved the media extolling—in books, newspapers, magazines, and films—a form of "lower-order parochialism," a worldview based on rebellion against respectability and uplift. His analysis has two flaws. The first is his limiting of bad habits to the practices of his title; if his definition of a bad habit as antisocial, alienated from its negative effects, and lacking in responsibility for the welfare of others is taken seriously, we can see any number of additional bad habits. The second flaw is his failure to identify the racial component of the lower-order parochial. The image of the consumer as rebellious, irresponsible, and liberated from all moral or ethical considerations is a perfect fit with the blackface character, the "coon" of coon songs, and the white ideal of the black subject in the United States from the middle of the nineteenth century to nearly the present.

70. William R. Hullfish, "James A. Bland: Pioneer Black Songwriter," *Black Music Research Journal* 7 (1987): 1–33.

71. "Gavitt's Original Ethiopian Serenaders," *North Star*, 29 June 1849.

72. On black blackface, see Robert C. Toll, *Blacking Up: The Minstrel Show in Nineteenth-Century America* (New York: Oxford University Press, 1974), 262; Henry T. Sampson, *Blacks in Blackface: A Source Book on Early Black Musical Shows* (Metuchen, NJ: Scarecrow Press, 1980).

73. Nicholas E. Tawa, "The Public for Popular Song" and "The Publishers of Popular Songs," from *The Way to Tin Pan Alley: American Popular Song, 1866–1910* (New York: Macmillan, 1990), 38–53; Craig H. Roell, "The Development of Tin Pan Alley," in *America's Musical Pulse: Popular Music in Twentieth-Century Society*, ed. Kenneth J. Bindas (Westport, CT: Greenwood Press, 1992), 113–122.

74. James H. Dorman, "Shaping the Image of Post Reconstruction American Blacks: The 'Coon Song' Phenomenon of the Gilded Age," *American Quarterly* 40, no. 4 (December 1988): 450–471; on the melding of "Tin-Pan-Alley" songs with "Coon" songs, along with the increasing "black" content of popular music as commercial song integrated and contained the styles of blackface, ragtime, and jazz, see H. F. Mooney, "Popular Music Since the 1920s: The Significance of Shifting Taste," *American Quarterly* 20, no. 1 (Spring 1968): 67–85; Janet Brown, "The 'Coon-Singer' and the 'Coon Song': A Case Study of the Performer-Character Relationship," *Journal of American Culture* 7 (Spring–Summer 1984): 1–8.

75. On Bert Williams, see Ann Charters, *Nobody: The Story of Bert Williams* (New York: Macmillan, 1970); Louis Chude-Sokei, *The Last "Darky": Bert Williams, Black-on-Black Minstrelsy, and the African Diaspora* (Durham, NC: Duke University Press, 2005); Camille Forbes, *Introducing Bert Williams: Burnt Cork, Broadway, and the Story of America's First Black Star* (New York: Basic Civitas, 2008).

76. On Black America, see Toll, *Blacking Up*; Roger Allan Hall, "*Black America*: Nate Salisbury's Afro-American Exhibition," *Educational Theater Journal* 29, no. 1 (March 1977): 49–60; Advertisement: "Black America," *New York Times*, 24 May 1895; "Black America," *New York Times*, 30 June 1895; Advertisement: "Black America Opens To-day, May 25," *New York Times*, 25 May 1895.

77. "'Black America' on Parade," *New York Times*, 12 June 1895; "A 'Black America' Parade," *New York Times*, 14 June 1895.

78. "Fun for the Darkies," *New York Times*, 2 June 1895; "Black America at the Garden," *New York Times*, 17 September 1895; "Snowball at the Show—He is One of the Characters of 'Black America'—Sings, Dances, Does Some Boxing—Hardy is His Correct Name and He Comes from Washington—He is the 'Dude' Now of Ambrose Park," *New York Times*, 18 June 1895.

79. "Wild Negro Chants and Dances—In 'Black America,' Brooklyn, May Be Seen the Fun-Loving Darkey of Old Slavery Days," *New York Times*, 25 May 1895.

80. Toll, *Blacking Up*; "For 23,600 Negroes, 1000 Melons," *New York Times*, 22 June 1895; "New Cake Walk at Black America," *New York Times*, 23 June 1895; "Now For That Watermelon—Not Hanging on the Vine, But in the New-York Market," *New York Times*, 18 June 1895.

Chapter Ten

1. Carey Goldberg, "A Revolution in Fourth of July Concerts Also Started in Boston," *New York Times*, 4 July 1998; Andrew Druckenbrod, "How a Rousing Russian Tune Took Over Our July 4th," Post-Gazette.com, interactive ed. of the *Pittsburg Post-Gazette*, 4 July 2003.

2. "Hutchinson Homestead is Designated as a Landmark of American Music," *Milford Cabinet and Wilton Journal*, 19 August 1976, 22/1.

3. Press notices from *Concert. The Hutchinson Family. John W. (Nineteen Years Before the Public), Fannie B., Henry J., and Viola G. Hutchinson of the Hutchinson Family, At Washburn Hall, 1860*, Boston, J. H. and F. F. Farwell, 1860; Frank B. Carpenter to John Hutchinson, letter reprinted as a testimonial in *The Seventieth Birthday Anniversary of John W. Hutchinson (Tribe of John and Jesse), at Tower Cottage, High Rock, Lynn, Mass., January Fifth, 1891*, Lynn, Nichols Press, 1891, LHS; *Saint Louis Democrat* cited in *Our Paper. Thirty Years of Singing! Concert in this Place!* (n.p., circa 1870), LHS.

4. Frederick Douglass to John Hutchinson, Biddeford, 18 November 1874, Hutchinson Collection, LHS; Garrison's testimonial cited in [Joshua Hutchinson], *A Brief Narrative of the Hutchinson Family, Sixteen Sons and Daughters of the Tribe of Jesse* (Boston: Lea and Shepard, 1874), 6; William Lloyd Garrison to John Hutchinson, Boston, 15 March 1859, Hutchinson Collection, LHS.

5. "The Hutchinson Family," *Syracuse Daily Journal*, 12 October 1848; "Music That Is Music," *Bangor Ensign*, undated clipping, circa 1849, Hutchinson Collection, MPL; "Fashionable Music," *Saturday Evening Post*, 14 November 1846; quote from the *People's Journal*, cited in *Book of Words of the Hutchinson Family* (1855), back cover.

6. *The Hutchinson Family! Asa B., Lizzie C., Abby and Little Freddy, New Songs and Sentiments! With a Few Standard Favorites, At Washburn Hall, Worcester, On Friday Evening, November 23, 1860*, Boston: J. H. & F. F. Farwell, 1860, AAS; *Voices for Blaine, by Asa B. Hutchinson of the Hutchinson Family*, broadside printed by J. Church, 1876, AAS.

7. [John W. Hutchinson], *The Hutchinson Family's Advent ("Tribe of John") Among the Free Men and Women of Kansas* (n.p., 1867).

8. "Bard Talks Love—Tells Post Reporter All About His Numerous Affairs of the Heart—Pets Bride and Dances to Show that He Still Defies Age," *Boston Post*, 26 August 1905, Hutchinson Collection, MPL.

9. "Dispatch: The Late Judson J. Hutchinson, to the Editor of the New York Tribune," *Frederick Douglass' Paper*, 28 January 1859; "His Music is Stilled. Another Good Man Called Home."

Death of Asa Hutchinson," *Hutchinson* [Minnesota] *Leader*, 27 November 1883; Susan B. Anthony to John W. Hutchinson, Rochester, 9 December 1892, Hutchinson Collection, LHS; "Abby Hutchinson Patton," *Boston Globe*, 28 November 1892.

10. "Fiction Chronicles No Stranger Tales then the Love Stories of this Venerable Bard of High Rock," *Boston Sunday American*, August 1905, Hutchinson Collection, MPL; *Home of the Hutchinson Family, High Rock, Lynn, Mass., U.S.A.*, Lithograph, 1881, by C. A. Shaw and H. J. Hutchinson, MHS; "The Phrenological Developments and Parentage of the Hutchinson Family, Accompanied with a Likeness of Abby Hutchinson," *American Phrenological Journal* (June 1849), Hutchinson Collection, MPL; "Hutchinson Family Reunion," unidentified news clipping dated 29 August 1905, MHS.

11. "The Hutchinson Family," *San Diego Union*, 2 April 1879; *The Seventieth Birthday Anniversary of John W. Hutchinson (Tribe of John and Jesse), at Tower Cottage, High Rock, Lynn, Mass., January Fifth, 1891*, program, Lynn, Nichols Press, 1891; "John Wallace Hutchinson's Celebration of the 70th Anniversary of His Birthday," *Danvers* [MA] *Mirror*, 17 January 1891.

12. *Second Reunion of Abolitionists. Tremont Temple, Boston, September 22, 1890. Order of Exercises* (n.p., 1890), LHS; *With You Once Again. John W. Hutchinson, of the Famous Hutchinson Family* (n.p., 1897), MHS; "Gives Coins to Keep Name Green," *New York World*, 6 January 1900, Hutchinson Collection, MPL; Scott Gac, *Singing for Freedom: The Hutchinson Family Singers and the Nineteenth-Century Culture of Reform* (New Haven, CT: Yale University Press, 2007), 208.

13. Brander Matthews, "The Rise and Fall of Negro Minstrelsy," *Scribner's Magazine* 57 (June 1915): 754–759; Brander Matthews, "Banjo and Bones," *Saturday Review* [London] 67 (7 June 1884): 739–740; Joel Chandler Harris, "Plantation Music," *Critic* [NY] (15 December 1883); 505–506.

14. Frances R. Grant, "Negro Patriotism and Negro Music: How the Old 'Spirituals' Have Been Used at Penn School, Hampton, and Tuskegee to Promote Americanization," *Outlook* 121 (26 February 1919): 345–347; Gilbert Seldes, "The Negro's Songs," *Dial* 80 (March 1926): 247–251; Muna Lee, "Songs From the Heart of the American Negro," *New York Times Book Review*, 18 October 1925; Albert C. Barnes, "Negro Art and America," *Survey* 53, no. 1 (1 March 1925): 668–669.

15. Lucien H. White, "Fine Tribute to Charm and Worth of Negro Spirituals," *New York Age*, 10 March 1923; Jeannette Robinson Murphy, "The True Negro Music and Its Decline," *Independent* [NY] (23 July 1903): 1723–1730, quote from 1730.

16. "Blue Notes," *New Republic* 45 (3 February 1926): 292–293; V. F. Calverton, "The Negro's New Belligerent Attitude," *Current History* 30 (September 1929): 1081–1088; J. A. Rogers, "Jazz at Home," *Survey* 53, no. 11 (1 March 1925): 665–667, 712.

17. James Weldon Johnson, "The Making of Harlem," *Survey* 53, no. 1 (1 March 1925): 635–639, 635; on labor in Harlem, see Charles S. Johnson, "Black Workers and the City," *Survey* 53, no. 11 (1 March 1925): 718–720.

18. "Harlem an Opportunity," *New York Age*, 9 September 1922; Alain Locke, "Harlem," *Survey* 53, no. 11 (1 March 1925): 625–626; E. Franklin Frazier, "The American Negro's New Leaders," *Current History* 28 (April 1928): 56–59; Alain Locke, "Youth Speaks," and "Enter the New Negro," *Survey* 53, no. 11 (1 March 1925): 659–660, 631–634.

19. For this more radical conception of the "New Negro," see Ulysses S. Poston, "The Negro Awakening," *Current History* 19 (December 1923): 473–480; Asa Philip Randolph, "New Negro

and Old?," *The Messenger* (21 October 1927); V. F. Calverton, "The New Negro," *Current History* (February 1926): 694–698.

20. Carl Van Doren, "The Roving Critic—The Negro Renaissance," *Century Magazine* 3 (March 1926): 635–639, 635–36; Eugene Gordon, "The Negro's Inhibitions," *American Mercury* 13 (February 1928): 159–165, 165; "Literary Buffoonery," *New York Age*, 4 February 1928.

21. Alain Locke, "Harlem," *Survey* 53, no. 11 (1 March 1925): 625–626.

22. On these cabarets, see Rudolph Fisher, "The Caucasian Storms Harlem," *American Mercury* 11 (May 1927): 393–398; on Immerman's Place, see "Is Harlem to be a 'Chinatown'?," *New York Age* (27 October 1923).

23. "A Wide Open Harlem," *New York Age*, 2 September 1922; "In the Negro Cabarets—Nightly Attractions in Harlem's 'Little Africa,'" *New York Times*, 5 September 1922.

24. Melville Herskovits, "The Dilemma of Social Pattern," *Survey* 53, no. 11 (1 March 1925): 676–678, 677.

25. Konrad Bercovici, "The Rhythm of Harlem," *Survey* 53, no. 11 (1 March 1925): 679; "The Slumming Hostess," *New York Age*, 6 November 1926; Langston Hughes, "The Big Sea," in *Voices From the Harlem Renaissance*, ed. Nathan Irving Huggins (New York: Oxford University Press, 1995), 373.

26. "Giving Harlem a Bad Name," *New York Age*, 23 July 1927; Van Vechten quote from "The Negro City," *American Review of Reviews* 73 (1926): 323–324; W. E. B. DuBois, "Books" [review of Carl Van Vechten's *Nigger Heaven*], *Crisis* 33–34 (December 1926): 81–82.

27. John B. Kennedy, "So this is Harlem!," *Colliers* 92 (28 October 1933): 22, 50; Rudolph Fisher, "The Caucasion Storms Harlem," *American Mercury* 11 (May 1927): 393–398.

28. "Nordic Invasion of Harlem," *New York Age*, 6 August 1927.

29. Fisher, "The Caucasian Storms Harlem," 398; Kelly Miller, "The Harvest of Race Prejudice," *Survey* 53, no. 11 (1 March 1925): 682–683, 711–712; Walter F. White, "Color Lines," *Survey* 53, no. 11 (1 March 1925): 680–682.

30. W. E. Burghardt DuBois, "The Black Man Brings His Gifts," *Survey* 53, no. 11 (1 March 1925): 655–657, 710; Langston Hughes, "The Negro Artist and the Racial Mountain," *Nation* 122 (23 June 1926): 692–694.

31. Helene Magaret, "The Negro Fad," *Forum* 87 (January 1932): 39–43.

32. George S. Schuyler, "The Negro-Art Hokum," *Nation* 122 (16 June 1926): 662–663.

33. George S. Schuyler, "Our White Folks," *American Mercury* 12, no. 48 (December 1927): 385–392.

34. See Paul Buhle, *Taking Care of Business: Samuel Gompers, George Meany, Lane Kirkland, and the Tragedy of American Labor* (New York: Monthly Review Press, 1999), 22–23.

35. On Storyville and jazz, see Herbert Asbury, *The French Quarter: An Informal History of the New Orleans Underground* (New York: Knopf, 1936); "Cleaning Up New Orleans," *Literary Digest* 54 (24 March 1917): 821–822; Stephen Longstreet, *Sportin' House* (Los Angeles: Sherbourne House, 1965); LeRoy Ostransky, *Jazz City* (Englewood Cliffs, NJ: Prentice Hall, 1978).

36. See John W. Blassingame, "Using the Testimony of Ex-Slaves: Approaches and Problems," *Journal of Southern History* 4, no. 4 (November 1975): 473–492; the subversive quote is from George Rawick, ed., *The American Slave: A Composite Autobiography*, vol. 4, *Georgia Narratives*, pt. 2 (Westport, CT: Greenwood Press, 1977), 372.

37. Thomas Bartlett, "An Ugly Tradition Persists at Southern Fraternity Parties, *The Chronicle of Higher Education* 48, no. 14 (30 November 2001): A33–A34; for a recent example of this

sort of thing, see Greg Lukianoff and Jonathan Haidt, "The Coddling of the American Mind," *Atlantic* online, September 2015.

38. For this background on Truth, see Nell Irvin Painter, *Sojourner Truth: A Life, A Symbol* (New York: W. W. Norton, 1996); Paul E. Johnson and Sean Wilentz, *The Kingdom of Matthias: A Story of Sex and Salvation in 19th Century America* (New York: Oxford University Press, 1994); also Nell Irvin Painter, "Representing Truth: Sojourner Truth's Knowing and Becoming Known," *Journal of American History* 81, no. 2 (September 1994): 461–492.

39. Harriet Beecher Stowe, "Sojourner Truth: The Libyan Sibyl," *Atlantic Monthly* 11 (April 1863): 473–481.

Index

Page numbers in italics refer to figures.

abolition, 5–6, 12, 75, 89, 112, 157, *215*, 330n38; antislavery groups and, 220, 221, 222, 300n22, 339n4; emancipation, 5, 59, 217–24, 227, 254, 256; England and, 172, 226, 233; Five Points (*see* Five Points Riot); Hutchinsons and, 214–17, 222–24, 229, 232, 300n22, 338n1 (*see also* Hutchinson Family Singers); Jenny Lind and, 212–13; masculinity and (*see* masculinity); middle class and, 221–34 (*see also* middle class); music and, 103, 228; patriotism and, 172; popular culture and, 216, 221–34, 339n4; proslavery forces and, 16, 18, 112, 172, *215*, 225, 235–37, 241, 244, 249; radicalism and, 214, 216, 220, 224–25; violence and, 225–26, 244, 331n43; women and, 218, 243; working class and, 157; world perspective, 226. *See also* slavery

African Americans, 15, 16, 21, 267; artisan tradition and, 78, 311n1; blackface and, 16, 21, 170, 247, 272–73, 275, 276, 300n23, 350n72 (*see also* blackface); carnival and, 121, 160, 320n67 (*see also* carnival traditions); churches and, 115, 254 (*see also* religion); civic associations, 115; emancipation, 5, 59, 217–24, 227, 254, 256; free, 4, 18, 20, 59, 94, 114, 158, *165*, 166, 173, 186, 267, 270; identity and, 17, 187, 248, 256, 262–63, 271, 279, 283–86, 290–93, 344n2; Johnkannaus festival, 121, 320n67; newspapers and, 113–15, 116, 170, 286, 350n69; performers, 273, 275, 276; population statistics, 115; racism and, 112–13 (*see also* racism); segregation and, 112–13, 186, 265, 275, 349n52 (*see also* Jim Crow); shouts and, 253, 255, 259, 268; slavery (*see* slavery); vigilantes and, 246–47; voting and, 113; whites

and, 160–61, 167–68, 225, 231, 329n23, 344n2 (*see also* whites); working class and, 75, 179

alcohol, 10, 36, 304n32, 350n69. *See also* temperance
American Anti-Slavery Society, 220, 223–28
American Revolution, 46, 54–64, 196, 248
Anderson, Benedict, 7
antislavery movement, 220, 222, 300n22, 339n4. *See also* abolition
apartheid. *See* segregation
Armstrong, Louis, 291
artisan tradition, 33, 304n25; blacks and, 78, 311n1; factory system and, 82, 88; festivals and, 88–89; hierarchy and, 79; industrialism and, 81; republicanism and, 76–83; white-collar workers and, 81–82; working class and, 77–78
Astor Place Riot, 180
Attali, Jacques, 7
audiences, 80–92, 314n41
authenticity: blackface and, 16, 21, 93–99, *100*, 161–64, 168, 175, *177*, 179, 184, 329n13; blackness and, 17, 161, 185, 187, 235, 256, 262, 263, 271, 279, 283–86, 290–93, 295, 344n2; identity and, 102, 146; masculinity and, 18, 20, 22, 178 (*see also* masculinity); working class and, 170, 179, 291, 312n4, 331n52

Baker, Benjamin, 178
banjo, 272, 283, 328n12
Barnum, Phineas Taylor, 132, 189–90, 195, 207–13, 322n16
Beethoven, Ludwig von, 203
"Beggar's Opera, The," 303n21
b'hoy (character), 178, 179, 181, 322n16
Black America (show), 276

CPSIA information can be obtained
at www.ICGtesting.com
Printed in the USA
LVHW080133270219
608877LV00011B/42/P

MAR 3 0 2019

9 780226 451640